S0-AIY-724

Amadeus W. Grabau (1905), then Professor of Paleontology at Columbia University. Courtesy of Columbia University, Columbiana Collection.

GEOLOGY AND PALAEONTOLOGY

OF

EIGHTEEN MILE CREEK

AND THE

LAKE SHORE SECTIONS OF ERIE COUNTY, NEW YORK

By
Amadeus W. Grabau

New, facsimile edition
with Foreword by
Jerold C. Bastedo

Published for the Hamburg Natural History Society, Inc.
By Data Reproductions Corporation, Auburn Hills, MI.
Originally published by the Buffalo Society of Natural Sciences.

Reprinting of this classic paleontology text was made possible by the generous support of the Buffalo Geological Society, Inc.

Dedicated to amateur scientists and natural historians everywhere.

Library of Congress Cataloguing-in-Publication Data

Grabau, Amadeus W. (Amadeus William), 1870-1946.
Geology and palaeontology of Eighteen Mile Creek and the lake shore sections of Erie County, New York. — New, facsim. ed. / with foreword by Jerold C. Bastedo.
p. cm.
Originally publised in 2 v.: Buffalo, N.Y : Buffalo Society of Natural Sciences, 1898-1899.
Includes bibliographical references and index.
ISBN 1-882903-01-3: $34.95
1. Geology—New York (State)—Erie County. 2. Geology, Stratigraphic—Devonian. 3. Paleontology—Devonian. 4. Paleontology—New York (State)—Erie County. I. Hamburg Natural History Society (Hamburg, N.Y.) II. Title.
QE 146.E75G74 1994 94-13701
557.47'96—dc20 CIP

Printed by
Data Reproductions Corporation
4545 Glenmeade Lane, Auburn Hills, Michigan 48326

FOREWORD TO FACSIMILE EDITION

The *Geology and Palaeontology of Eighteen Mile Creek and the Lake Shore Sections of Erie County, New York* by Amadeus W. Grabau is a classic publication that has been unavailable for decades. The Buffalo Society of Natural Sciences published this "Handbook for the Use of Students and Amateurs" as a two-part bulletin in 1898 and 1899.

Part I contained an introduction; discussion of the structural geology of the area; and a description of the eight sections of most importance in the Eighteen Mile Creek gorge and those along the Lake Erie Shore. Many photographs of these sections in Eighteen Mile Creek and areas along the Lake Erie shoreline, east and west of the mouth of the creek, were included.

Part II focused on the paleontology of the area discussing the methods of fossilization, collection of fossils, and discussions of the various fossils preserved in the rock strata within Eighteen Mile Creek and surrounding lake shore areas of Erie County. This part of the publication contained excellent illustrations and descriptions of the invertebrate fossils, a glossary of paleontological terms, and a list of references.

The Hamburg Natural History Society, Inc. recognizes the desire and need to have the *Geology and Palaeontology of Eighteen Mile Creek* reprinted. For the past few decades, this publication could only be obtained through book dealers, estate sales, *etc.* Here, it is reprinted as one volume with no alterations made to either the text or illustrations.

Eighteen Mile Creek is an internationally renowned geological and paleontological site. The classic exposure of 375 million year-old Middle and Upper Devonian shales and limestones, which contain diverse and abundant varieties of marine invertebrate and vertebrate fossils excellently preserved, has made this site an exceptional outdoor classroom in which to study geology and paleontology. Amateur and professional geologists, students, and hobbyists from all over the world have been visiting this area since the early 1800s to collect fossils and study the local stratigraphy. College and university classes from New York, Pennsylvania, Ohio, Canada, and many other areas regularly bring students to study the geology and paleontology exposed in Eighteen Mile Creek. Today, access to the areas described in this publication may be limited by private landowners, and permission should be secured before visiting them.

The Hamburg Natural History Society, Inc. was formed as a non-profit organization in 1993 to acquire, develop, administrate and maintain the former Penn Dixie Quarry in Hamburg, New York, thus providing a regional fossil park to foster and encourage a medium for the public to study and collect fossils. The Society promotes the study of the natural sciences, with an emphasis on the field activities associated with the geological and biological sciences in Western New York, encourages the development of "green space" and recreation in the Town of Hamburg, and promotes the training of inservice and pre-service teachers. The Society anticipates and welcomes future opportunities to publish reprinted or new scientific publications that are commensurate with the goals of the Hamburg Natural History Society, Inc. Purchase of this publication will aid in supporting the goals and objectives of the Society, including its initial goal of purchasing and preserving the former Penn Dixie Quarry from future industrial park development.

Jerold C. Bastedo
President
Hamburg Natural History Society, Inc.
Box 772
Hamburg, New York 14075

February 1994

GEOLOGY AND PALÆONTOLOGY

. . OF . .

EIGHTEEN MILE CREEK

AND THE

LAKE SHORE SECTIONS

. . OF . .

ERIE COUNTY, NEW YORK.

A HAND-BOOK FOR THE USE OF STUDENTS AND AMATEURS.

. . BY . .

AMADEUS W. GRABAU,

Fellow in Palæontology, Harvard University; Late Instructor in Palæontology in the Massachusetts Institute of Technology.

BUFFALO, N. Y.
PUBLISHED BY THE BUFFALO SOCIETY OF NATURAL SCIENCES.

BUFFALO SOCIETY OF NATURAL SCIENCES.
"VERE SCIRE EST PER CAUSAS SCIRE."
ORG'D DEC. 5, 1861.

Dedication.

To

WILLIAM OTIS CROSBY,

Teacher, Investigator and Author,

the friend who first offered me encouragement

in my studies, and whose kindly interest

and criticism have been a constant

help, this work is grate-

fully dedicated.

PREFACE.

This book is intended as the first of a series of hand-books of local geology, which treat the subject with special reference to the needs of the student. The advantage of beginning the study of geology with the special consideration of a selected field, instead of the general text-book study, must be apparent, even though it seems like a complete inversion of the normal order of procedure.

In order that the student who comes to the field without a preliminary training in geology may take up the subject intelligently, the first portion of the introductory chapter of Part I. is devoted to a brief consideration of the elementary geological principles involved in the structure of the region under consideration. Hence no apology is needed for the introduction of such matters here. In chapters one and two the eight sections of the most important portion of the gorge of Eighteen Mile Creek and those of the Lake Shore, are considered in detail. Lists of fossils found in the various beds are not given, but such lists will be found in the author's paper on the "Faunas of the Hamilton Group of Eighteen Mile Creek and Vicinity."* As far as this guide treats of the Hamilton group, it is based directly on that paper, and constant references are made to it in the text.

In chapter three of Part I., an attempt is made to present in popular form the succession of geological events in this region, as revealed in the sections described in the earlier chapters.

---

*16th Ann. Rept. N. Y. State Geologist for 1896, Albany 1898 (in press). This paper has precedence over the present one in date of communication.

Part II. may be considered an elementary text book of the Palæontology of this region, as described in Part I. The introductory chapter treats of the general principles of Palæontology, and discusses the methods of fossilization. Chapter I. is devoted to the methods of collecting fossils from the beds of this region, and preparing them for study. Chapter II. treats of the fossils themselves. A brief description of the structural characters of each class precedes the discussion of the genera and species in that class. The generic descriptions are given with some detail, but under the species, only the leading features are mentioned, these, together with the illustrations, being intended chiefly as aids in the identification of the species. References to the most important works are given, and these should be consulted as much as possible. The magnificent volumes of the Palæontology of New York, contained in all the larger libraries, are of special importance to the advanced student, and the descriptions and illustrations there given, deserve the most careful study. The species considered are those which have been collected by the author, and those which have been previously described as coming from the Eighteen Mile Creek or Lake Shore region. A few descriptions have been introduced, of species recorded from Erie County only, but the association of which led to the inference that they belonged somewhere in the beds described in Part I. While all the species, which have so far come under the author's notice as found in the beds discussed, have been included, no pretension of completeness is made. It remains for the local student to discover new forms for this region, and to find new associations for those here described.

The plant remains from this region are not described, as the material obtained is very unsatisfactory, with the exception of the spores, which are discussed on pages 15 and 16, of Part I.

The etymology of the generic names is, in almost all cases, taken directly from S. A. Miller's admirable reference book: "North American Geology and Palæontology."

A number of species included in Chapter II. have never been described in print, but have simply been illustrated in the "Illustrations of Devonian Fossils," published in the Palæontology of New York series. In the case of these species, the descriptions here given were made up from the illustrations and explanations of the plates of the above book.

The localities given for the fossils are those described in Part I. Fossils quoted from West Hamburgh and Hamburgh-on-the-Lake probably come from Avery's Creek.

Chapter III. deals with the problems of the distribution and migration of marine invertebrates, and in Chapter IV. a glossary of Palæontological terms is given. The list of reference works of both general and special character is added in the hope, that it may meet the demand of many who wish to extend their study beyond what is given in the succeeding pages.

I wish in this place to acknowledge my indebtedness to numerous friends for aid received in the preparation of this guide. In the field-work, I have had the constant and able assistance of my brother, Mr. P. L. Grabau. For special courtesies received in the field I am under obligation, among others, to Mr. A. J. Hutchinson and family of North Evans, to Dr. F. W. Hinckel of Athol Springs, and to Mr. Truman G. Avery of Hamburgh-on-the-Lake. In the preparation of the drawings for Part II., I have received the very able assistance of Mr. John A. Hutchinson, who made pen and ink copies of all the gastropods and cephalopods, besides numerous other forms. Acknowledgements for assistance in this part of the work are also due Mr. I. C. Hanscom, Miss A. D. Savage and Miss K. B. Wentworth. Unless otherwise stated, the figures of Part II. are reproduced, either directly or by drawings from the volumes of the Palæontology of New York, through the courtesy of the officers of that survey. The use of the plates for the figures in the introduction of Part I. was courteously granted by the Massachusetts Institute of Technology.

For criticisms, while the work was passing through the press, my thanks are due to Professor W. O. Crosby and to Dr. R. T. Jackson. To Professor Irving P. Bishop of Buffalo, special acknowledgements are due for the care and labor he has gratuitously given to the preparation of the photographs from which the full page plates of Part I. are made. Finally, to Dr. Lee H. Smith and the other members of the publication committee, my thanks are due for the liberality which they have shown in the number and character of the illustrations.

In conclusion it should be mentioned that a portion of this paper was prepared during the author's connection with the Massachusetts Institute of Technology, and that a series of the fossils described in Part II., is contained in the collection of that institution. Another series is to be found in the collections of the Buffalo Society of Natural Sciences. Other specimens, from which illustrations and descriptions were prepared, are contained in the Student Palæontological collection at Harvard University. The types of the new species, unless otherwise noted, are in the author's collection.

Harvard University,
CAMBRIDGE, Mass., Feb. 12, 1898.

CONTENTS OF PART I.

LIST OF PLATES.

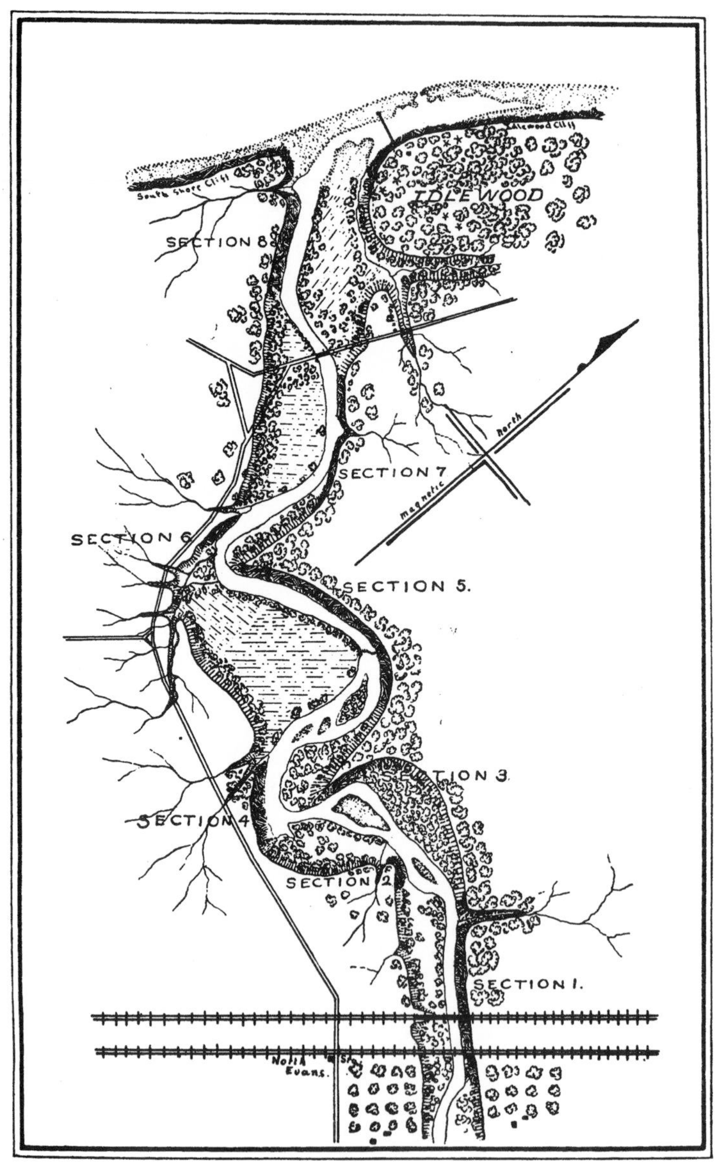

PLATE II.

Topographical Map of Eighteen Mile Creek below the railroad bridges. The sections are indicated by cross-hachures. Scale, 1 inch=1,600 feet.

From a compass survey made in 1895 by P. L. Grabau.

Part I.

GEOLOGY.

There rolls the deep where grew the tree;
O earth, what changes hast thou seen!
There, where the long street roars hath been
The stillness of the central sea.

—*Tennyson.*

INTRODUCTION.

Ever since the publication of the New York State Geological Reports, Eighteen Mile Creek and the shore of Lake Erie has been classic ground for the stratigraphist and palæontologist. Probably no other locality is so frequently referred to in the literature of the Middle Devonian of this country, as is this, under one of the following names: "Eighteen Mile Creek," "Shore of Lake Erie," "Hamburgh, Erie County," "West Hamburgh," or "Hamburgh-on-the-Lake."

The exposures in this area represent a continuous section, from near the base of the Middle Devonian to near the top of the Upper Devonian, and the total thickness of these beds is only a few hundred feet. Furthermore, the beds exposed represent deposits made at a considerable distance from the land, which was the source of the mechanical sediment. The conditions of the water in this area were consequently more uniform, and the deposits less complex than was the case in regions nearer to the old shore line. For these reasons the study of the Middle and Upper Devonian beds is profitably commenced in this locality. The sections furthermore, on account of the limited thickness of the formations, enable the student to take a more comprehensive view of the whole series than is possible farther east, in which direction the old shore-line is to be sought.

Structure.—It should be borne in mind, that the gorge of Eighteen Mile Creek is simply a deep, broad trench, cut into the strata, which before the cutting of the gorge, continued without interruption. In the walls of the gorge, where not obscured by vegetation, the cut edges of the strata appear on opposite sides, the portion of the beds cut out between, having been removed by the stream. This process of gorge cutting by natural agencies may be compared to artificial trench cutting for laying water pipes, where the sides of the trench commonly show the cut edges of the layers of sand, gravel or rock, which before cutting, were continuous. The tools with which nature cuts are: rock fragments, broken off by frost action, and carried by the stream over the bed-rock; loose stones and sand which the current sweeps along, and cakes of ice, which in early spring, float down stream. The mode of cutting the natural trench differs from that employed in cutting the artificial trench, in that it consists of a scraping, graving and pounding action, instead of a digging and blasting action. The results are similar in both cases, but the time occupied by nature in doing the work is vastly longer than that occupied by man in cutting a trench of similar magnitude by his more improved methods. But as nature has all eternity at her disposal, it matters not how slow she works.

While the trench is slowly deepened and widened, the atmosphere attacks the cut sides and breaks up the exposed portions of the strata. This is accomplished by the mechanical activity of freezing water in the fissures and between the layers, which are pried apart by the growing ice crystals, as well as by the chemical activity of the atmospheric gases and moisture, which cause the decomposition or decay of the rock. Thus the sides are degraded from perpendicular naked precipices to gently descending soil-covered slopes. The bed of Lake Erie may be regarded as such a natural trench of excessive width as compared with its depth. The opposite side of this trench is formed by the cliffs of the Canadian shore, though these, from the direction of the trench and the dip of the strata, consist of a different kind of rock. The New York bank of this trench is kept more or less fresh by the continual cutting of the waves, which has gone on ever since the waters of Lake Erie filled the trench and converted it into a lake.

V.

The rocks of this region are shales and limestones, with sandy layers in the upper portion of the exposed series. The shales predominate, and commonly split into thin laminæ or lenticular pieces, which lie essentially parallel to the bedding plane. These shales weather into clayey soil by the solution of the carbonate of lime, which here commonly forms an important cementing constituent. In this clayey soil we find a return to the more primitive condition of the material, for these slates were beds of clay before they assumed their present consolidated character. This clay, which was spread out over what was formerly the ocean floor, was derived from the disintegration of the rocks which formed the land at that period of the earth's history, rocks which were constantly attacked by the waves on the shore, the rivers and streams along certain lines on the surface of the land, and the atmosphere, wherever they were exposed. When the streams had brought their load of debris into the sea, where the waves and shore currents could distribute it, an assortment took place, the coarsest material being deposited near shore and the finer farther out to sea, in direct proportion to the degree of its fineness, and the strength of the current. It was only the clay—the result of the chemical decomposition of the rocks, and the finest rock flour—the result of the most effective comminution of the rocks, which were carried out into the comparatively quiet water at a distance from shore, and there deposited to form beds of mud. The empty shells of dead animals, which were strewn over the bottom of the sea in this region, as well as many still occupied by the animals, were buried in this accumulating mud, just as empty shells are buried on the modern beach, and as living mussels are buried more or less deeply in the fine material deposited off shore. The fine mud gradually found its way between the valves and filled the space once occupied by the soft parts, a condition characteristic of the occurrence of most bivalve shells on modern mud-flats. When in the course of time the mud became a shale, the shells became incorporated

Fig. i.—Anticlinal fold near St. Abb's Head, Scotland. (Geikie).

Fig. ii.—Synclinal fold near Banff, Scotland. (Geikie).

in the rock as fossils. The solid condition of most of the shells now found fossil in these rocks is due to the great induration which the filling of mud between the valves has undergone.

By the time that the mud-beds had completely hardened they had been raised above the surface of the ocean. This is indicated by the crowded condition of the strata about the enclosed concretionary masses, a condition which points to settling or shrinking of the strata, after the loss of the contained water, which could only occur after elevation. The elevation was probably due to those crust-movements which are termed "epeirogenic," and which produce extensive changes of level without involving the formation of mountains. The mountain-building or "orogenic" movements, which occurred towards the close of Palæozoic time, and to which the Appalachian ranges owe their existence, unquestionably affected this region. The initial inclination or "dip" which the strata had at the time of their deposition was accentuated, and the very slight undulations of the strata, which are observable in several places in Western New York, and of which slight indications occur in the Eighteen Mile Creek region, were probably produced at that time. Other structural features, common in mountainous regions were produced, the most pronounced of which are the folds and faults, which occur in a number of places as noted beyond. A *fold*, as the name implies, is a bend in the strata. A simple arch is called an *anticlinal fold* (fig. i.). When it is inverted, *i.e.* when it bends downward, it is called a *synclinal fold* (fig. ii.). When the strata are bent upwards, or downwards, and then continue as before, in other words, when the fold represents only half of an anticline or half of a syncline, it is called a *monoclinal fold* or *flexure* (fig. iii. and Plate XVI.).

A *fault* in stratified rocks, consists of a displacement of the beds along a plane of fracture, which is called the *fault plane*. Occasionally the fracture or fault plane is vertical (fig. iv.),

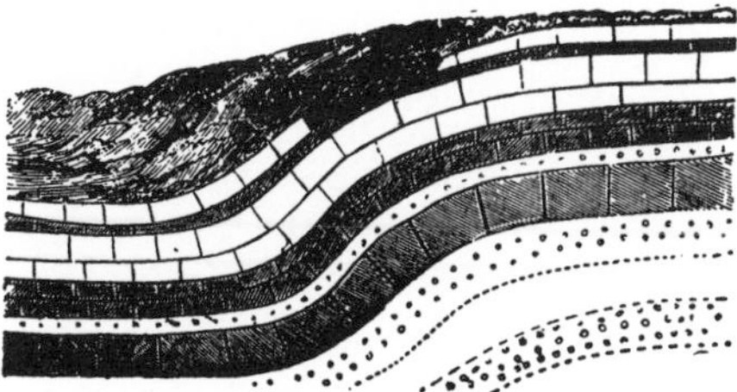

Fig. iii.—A monoclinal fold or flexure. (Powell).

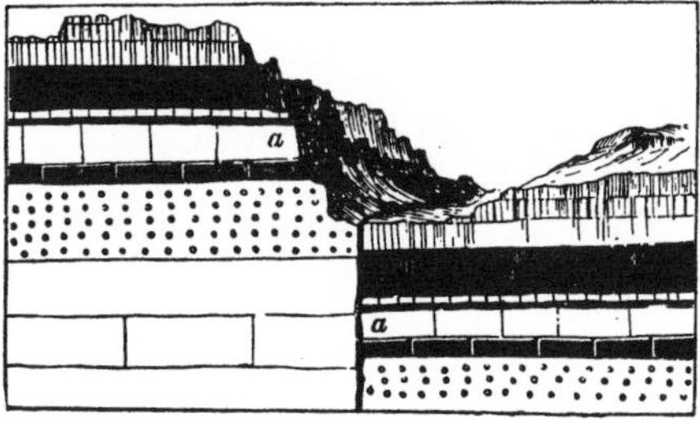

Fig. iv.—Section across a simple fault. (Powell).

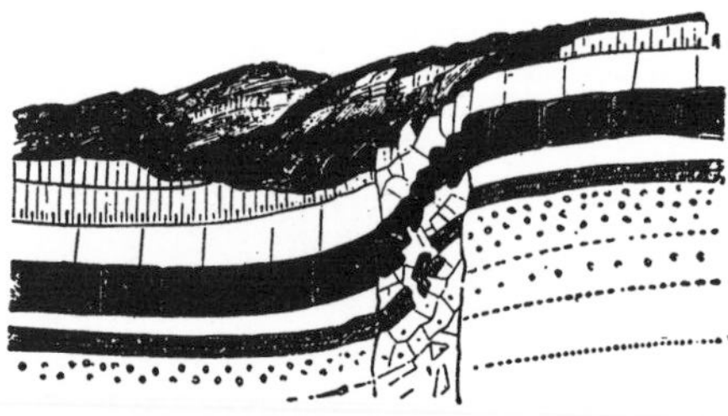

Fig. v.—Section across a monocline which is passing, by crushing of the strata, into a fault. (Powell). Compare Plate XVI.

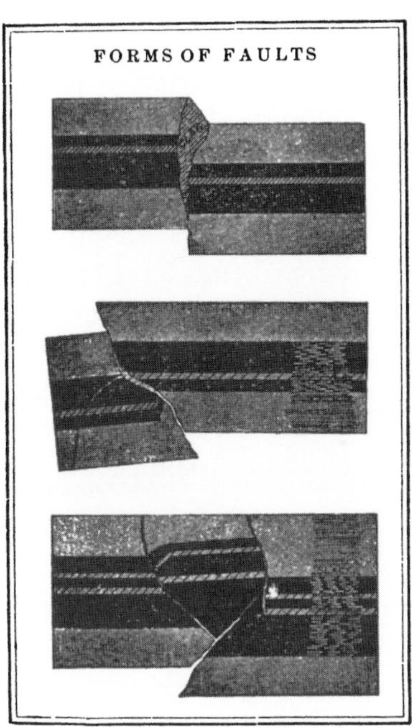

Fig. vi.—Gravity, and simple and compound thrust faults.

but more frequently it is inclined. The angle which the fault plane makes with the vertical in this latter case, is the angle of *hade*. The overlying portion of the strata, along an oblique fault plane, constitutes the *hanging wall* of the fault. The underlying portion constitutes the *foot wall*. If the hanging wall of the fault has slipped down, tension is indicated, for the strata now occupy more horizontal space than before, as can be easily tested by an experiment, with blocks to represent the strata. In such a case, the faulting was caused by the action of gravity, which pulled down the hanging wall. Therefore such a fault is called a "*gravity fault*," and in as much as most faults are gravity faults, they are commonly called "*normal faults*" (fig. vi., 1). If however, the hanging wall slips up, a compression is indicated, which shortens the beds, so that they occupy less horizontal space than before. A thrust force is required for the production of such faults, and they are therefore called "*thrust faults*." Being of less frequent occurrence than the other class, they are also called "*reversed faults*" (fig. vi., 2, 3). It is the latter kind which occurs in this vicinity.

Related to the disturbances which produced faults and folds, are those which produced *joint cracks*, *i. e.* those prominent fissures which traverse all the rocks of this region (see Plates III., XXVI. and XXVII.). One explanation of these is, that they originated through the action of earthquake shocks, which traversed the rocks, and produced a series of earth-waves, which in unconsolidated material would produce little effect, but in solid rock would produce these fissures at regular intervals (Crosby). The other well accepted explanation which accounts for these joints is, that by unequal elevation, the beds have become twisted and have been subjected to a torsion strain, and that this has produced the parallel and intersecting joints (Daubrée). Both causes undoubtedly co-öperate in the formation of these joints, as is well illustrated, when a sheet of glass is twisted and then a shock sent through it by a

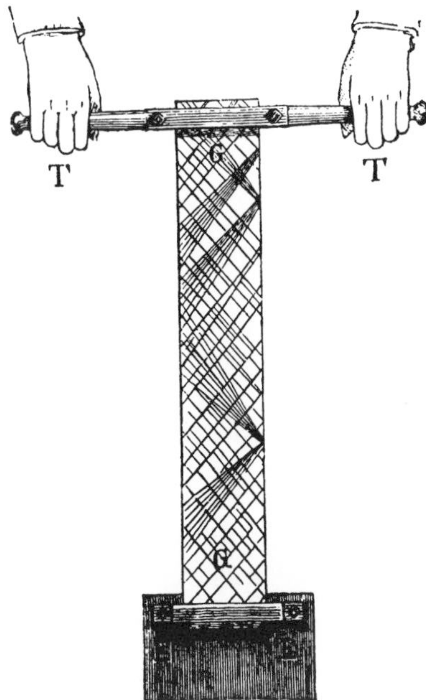

Fig. vii.—Apparatus for breaking plates of glass by torsion, with an example of the results produced. (Daubrée).

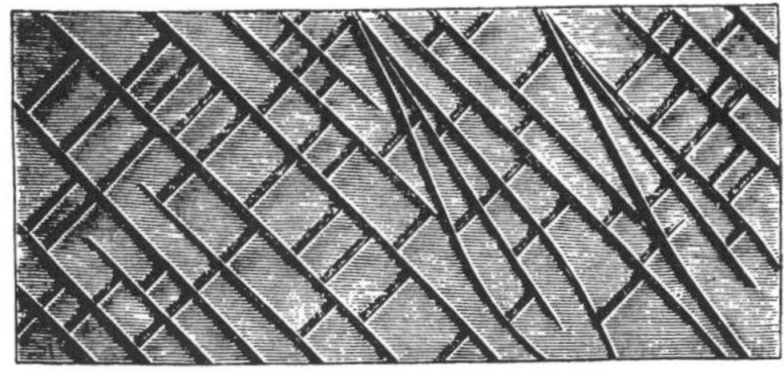

Fig. viii.—Arrangement of fractures in a large plate of glass which was broken by torsion. (Daubrée).

blow given in its vicinity. The glass will break, with the formation of two sets of parallel fractures, which intersect each other at a constant angle in a given piece (figs. vii. and viii.).

Nomenclature.—In the study of the geological formations of any region, it becomes necessary that a classification of the various beds should be made, and that a proper nomenclature should exist, so that each division and subdivision may be properly designated. Professor H. S. Williams has discussed the various systems of nomenclature which have been used for stratified rocks, and for a full account the reader is referred to his book.* A brief synopsis, and definitions of the various terms employed, are given here.

In the first place it must be remembered that we are dealing both with the rocks, and with the time occupied in their deposition. Consequently, a dual nomenclature and classification is necessary, and two kinds of scales must be adopted, namely: the "formation scale" and the "time scale."† The formation scale of classification takes account of the rock formations only, while the time scale is only concerned with geologic time and its subdivision. The time scale will be considered first.

The whole of geologic time is divided as follows:

CENOZOIC TIME—Time of "modern life."
MESOZOIC TIME—Time of "mediæval life."
PALÆOZOIC TIME—Time of "ancient life."
PROTEROZOIC TIME—Time of "first life."
AZOIC TIME—Time of "no life."

Each of these great "Time" divisions is characterized by the progress of life during its continuance, such progress being indicated by the names.

---

*Geological Biology, 1895.

†See H. S. Williams, Dual Nomenclature in Geological Classification. Journal of Geology, Vol. II., pp. 145–160.

The times are divided into eras, which have received locality names, as Devonic era from Devonshire, England, old historic names, as Siluric era, from the old tribe of Silures, or names derived from the lithological character of beds deposited during the era, as Carbonic era, from the coal beds deposited at that time. The division is chiefly based on biological changes.

The subdivision of eras is not a uniform one. The best is that proposed by H. S. Williams,* who would recognize in general an early, a middle and a later period in each era. The terms *Eo*, *Meso* and *Neo*, proposed by him, form suitable prefixes to which can be added the distinctive era name. Thus *Eodevonian*, *Mesodevonian* and *Neodevonian* are proper names to apply to the early, middle and later periods of the Devonic era.

Periods are divided into epochs, these latter marking the continuance of a characteristic species and its associates. The name applied to the epoch should be the specific name of the important species, a rule which as yet is not very generally followed. From the nature of the division it follows that it can not hold over very wide areas, and that its length may vary in different regions. The epoch during which the Hamilton shales of New York were deposited—here called the Spiriferoides epoch, from *Athyris spiriferoides* —can perhaps not be recognized outside of north-eastern United States and portions of Canada. The Stringocephalus epoch of Europe is, in part at least, its foreign equivalent. On the other hand, the Disjunctus and Intumescens epochs (Table B) are recognized in Europe, where they are marked by the same species. So too, the Acuminatus epoch, during which the Corniferous limestone of eastern North America was deposited, may be recognized in European geological history as the time during which *Spirifer cultrijugatus*, the European equivalent of *S. acuminatus*, existed.

---

*Loc. cit.

The term "age" is frequently used in the succeeding pages. It is to be understood as capable of a general application in speaking of divisions of the time scale, whether large or small. The term age, is also used in designating the time occupied in the formation of a particular stratum, or sub-stage, thus: Encrinal age, Moscow age and Styliolina age, or age of the Styliolina limestone.

The unit of classification in the formation scale is the *stratum*. Each *stratum* comprises a section of the formation, which consists throughout its thickness of the same rock material. Thus the Encrinal limestone is a stratum. Similarly the eight or nine feet of black uniform carbonaceous Genesee shales form one stratum. The stratum may be subdivided into *beds*, of which, in a thick stratum, there may be many. The bed may again be divided into *layers*, of which there may be several in one bed. A *rock formation* or *terrane* may consist of a single stratum, or of a number of strata, according to the magnitude of the division under consideration, but all the related strata of that particular division are included in the term *formation*. Thus the *Devonian formation* includes all the strata of the Devonian division, and the *Genesee formation* includes all the strata of the Genesee division.

The smallest division of the formation scale is the *stage*. This may comprise a number of strata, as in the case of the Hamilton stage. It may be subdivided into smaller formations, as is the case in the example here cited. The names applied to the stages are commonly locality names, but as in the Corniferous stage, the lithological character may furnish the name. The strata comprised within a stage are usually restricted in distribution, seldom covering more than a few hundred square miles of area, and they were all deposited during the continuance of the corresponding epoch. The stages are united into *groups*, the groups into *series*, and the series into *systems*. Groups are local in distribution, their formation depending on the physical conditions which existed during the corresponding period of time at the place where they occur. On this account rock groups commonly receive local names, such names being taken from the locality where the group is best developed, or where it was first studied. A number of local rock groups, known by various names, were deposited during each geological period, each group characterizing a different locality, and indicating different physical conditions during the time and at the place of its deposition. For purposes of correlation it is desirable to have one name to which the local groups can be referred, and such a name must be of general applicability. None of the local group names can be selected, no matter how much priority any one of them may have. For example: the Huamampampa sandstone of Bolivia was probably deposited while the Hamilton sediments were accumulating over New York, but the Huamampampa sandstones are not Hamilton. They are Middle Devonian just as the Hamilton sediments are Middle Devonian. It is therefore proposed to use the terms Lower, Middle and Upper to designate a threefold division of each rock *series* deposited during the corresponding geologic era. Thus the *Devonic series*, built up during the *Devonic era*, is divisible into three groups, the Lower, Middle and Upper Devonian groups, which were deposited respectively during the Eo, Meso and Neodevonian periods. This division may seem somewhat artificial, especially as some rock series are divisible into more or less than three groups in different localities. Thus in Tennessee the whole of the Devonic series is represented by the Chattanooga black shale, which in places is only twelve feet thick and shows no subdivisions. But in those twelve feet of shale are probably included the Lower, Middle and Upper Devonian groups. One division may be unrepresented, as is probably the case in the Devonic or Old Red Sandstones of Scotland, where only a Lower and an Upper group are recognized, the place of the Middle group being represented by an unconformity. Where a rock series is locally divisible into more or fewer than three groups, one of these local groups may correspond to a portion of a group in the general division, or to more than one of those groups. It remains for the student of the local group to adjust them to the general scheme, which is to serve as a basis for correlation and comparison.

The rock systems include those rocks which were formed during the corresponding great time division. Both series and system take the names of the corresponding eras and times.

In Table A, the subdivisions of the Palæozoic time and system are given, with the New York and other equivalents in common use. In Table B, the detailed subdivision of the New York Devonic is given.

NOTE.—*Tropidoleptus carinatus* is a much more widely distributed Hamilton species than *Athyris spiriferoides*. The former occurs in Middle Devonian beds throughout New York, at the Falls of the Ohio, and at various localities in Ohio, Pennsylvania and Illinois. It is also abundant in the Middle Devonian sandstones of the Rio Maecurú in the Amazonian district, S. A., and in the Erere, Province of Para, Brazil. It furthermore occurs in Devonian beds at Lake Titicaca; on the Rio Sicasica, Bolivia; in South Africa; in France, Germany and England. In many of these localities it is associated with *Vitulina pustulosa*. In some of the last mentioned localities however, the beds characterized by these species are regarded as of Eodevonian age. The wide distribution of *Tropidoleptus carinatus* would make the adoption of the name *Carinatus epoch* for a single epoch of the Mesodevonian period desirable (the Marcellus to be included in this epoch), were it not for the discrepancy in the ages of the beds characterized by this species at the various localities.

TABLE A.—PALÆOZOIC SUBDIVISIONS.

TIME SCALE.	FORMATION SCALE.	PROMINENT NORTH AMERICAN EQUIVALENTS. (CHIEFLY NEW YORK STATE EQUIVALENTS).
PALÆOZOIC TIME.	**PALÆOZOIC SYSTEM.**	
5. CARBONIC ERA.	5. CARBONIC SERIES.	
c. Neocarbonian period	*c.* Upper Carbonian group	UPPER BARREN MEASURE GROUP. (Pennsylvania). (Permian).
b. Mesocarbonian period	*b.* Middle Carbonian group	PENNSYLVANIAN* GROUP. (Pennsylvania). (Carboniferous—Equivalent to: Coal measures and Millstone grit of Mississippi Valley).
a. Eocarbonian period	*a.* Lower Carbonian group	MISSISSIPPIAN* GROUP. (Mississippi Valley). (Sub-carboniferous—Equivalent to: Mauch Chunk and Pocono of Pennsylvania).
4. DEVONIC ERA.	4. DEVONIC SERIES.	
c. Neodevonian period	*c.* Upper Devonian group	CHEMUNG GROUP.
b. Mesodevonian period	*b.* Middle Devonian group	HAMILTON GROUP.
a. Eodevonian period	*a.* Lower Devonian group	UPPER HELDERBERG GROUP.
3. SILURIC ERA.	3. SILURIC SERIES.	
c. Neosilurian period	*c.* Upper Silurian group	LOWER HELDERBERG GROUP.
b. Mesosilurian period	*b.* Middle Silurian group	ONONDAGA GROUP.
a. Eosilurian period	*a.* Lower Silurian group	NIAGARA GROUP.
2. ORDOVICIC ERA.	2. ORDOVICIC† SERIES.	
c. Neoördovician period	*c.* Upper Ordovician group	TRENTON GROUP.
b. Mesoördovician period	*b.* Middle Ordovician group	
a. Eoördovician period	*a.* Lower Ordovician group	CANADIAN GROUP.
1. CAMBRIC ERA.	1. CAMBRIC SERIES.	
c. Neocambrian period	*c.* Upper Cambrian group	POTSDAM GROUP.
b. Mesocambrian period	*b.* Middle Cambrian group	ACADIAN GROUP. (Eastern Provinces).
a. Eocambrian period	*a.* Lower Cambrian group	GEORGIAN GROUP. (New England).

*H. S. Williams, Bull. 80, U. S. Geol. Survey, 1891.

†Lapworth's name is here used in place of the old "Lower Silurian." Only two groups are recognized in New York State, the Canadian and Trenton, but in the typical British locality, three groups are recognized: 1–Arenig, 2–Llandeilo, and 3–Bala and Caradoc Groups.

TABLE B.

SUB-DIVISIONS OF THE NEW YORK DEVONIC.

TIME SCALE.	FORMATION SCALE.
DEVONIC ERA.	DEVONIC SERIES.
c. Neodevonian period..........	...*c.* Chemung group.
2. *Disjunctus* epoch......	........2. Chemung stage. (2). Chemung sandstones and shales. (1). Portage sandstone.
1. *Intumescens* epoch......	........1. Genesee stage. (3). Naples shales. (2). Genesee shales, including Styliolina limestone. (1). Tully limestone.
b. Mesodevonian period......	...*b.* Hamilton group.
2. *Spiriferoides* epoch......	........2. Hamilton stage. (3). Upper or Moscow shales. (2). Encrinal limestone. (1). Lower or Hamilton shales.
1. *Minuta* epoch........	........1. Marcellus stage. (1). Marcellus shales.
a. Eodevonian period........	...*a.* Upper Helderberg group.
3. *Acuminatus* epoch......	........3. Corniferous stage. (2). Corniferous limestone. (1). Onondaga limestone.
2. *Caudagalli* epoch......	........2. Schoharie stage. (1). Schoharie grit and Esopus shales.
1. *Hipparionyx* epoch......	........1. Oriskany stage. (1). Oriskany sandstone.

The name "*Disjunctus* epoch" (H. S. Williams) is derived from the characteristic fossil *Spirifer disjunctus*, while the name "*Intumescens* epoch" is derived from the characteristic fossil *Goniatites intumescens*.* "*Spiriferoides* epoch" and "*Minuta* epoch" are derived from the fossils *Athyris spiriferoides* and *Orbiculoidea minuta*, which are practically confined to their respective epochs. The names are of limited applicability.† In the Eodevonian period, the name "*Acuminatus* epoch" is used for the last epoch, it being derived from the characteristic fossil *Spirifer acuminatus* Conrad. This species is represented by *S. cultrijugatus* F. Roemer, in the upper (Coblenzian) part of the Rhenan or Lower Devonian

*See J. M. Clarke, Intumescens fauna, Am. Geol., Vol. VIII., p. 86 et seq.
†See note page xvi.

of the Eifel in western Germany, and in the Ardennes on the borders of France and Belgium. The same species is found in the Lower Devonian rocks of South Devonshire. If, as is held by many authors, the two species are identical, Roemer's name must give way to the earlier one of Conrad. The "*Caudagalli* epoch" is named from the peculiar sea-weed, the *Spirophyton* (*Taonurus*) *caudagalli*, which abounds in the rocks formed during that epoch, while the "*Hipparionyx* epoch" is so called after the brachiopod *Orthis hipparionyx* (*Hipparionyx proximus*).

The rock formations have, with few exceptions, received their names from typical localities in New York State. Thus Chemung is derived from Chemung Narrows; Portage from Portage on the Genesee River; Naples from Naples, Ontario County, (the two shales comprised under this name, *i. e.* the Gardeau and Casbaqua, having received their names from the Gardeau flats on the Genesee, and from Cashaqua Creek, respectively); Genesee from the Genesee River at Mt. Morris; Tully from Tully, Onondaga County, (this rock is absent in the Eighteen Mile Creek region); Moscow from Moscow, Livingston County; Hamilton from Hamilton, Madison County; Marcellus from Marcellus, Onondaga County; Helderberg (both upper and lower) from the Helderberg mountains; Onondaga from Onondaga County; Schoharie from Schoharie County, and Oriskany from Oriskany Falls, Oneida County. All of these localities exhibit typical exposures. The other names, viz, Encrinal (crinoid bearing) and Corniferous (chert or hornstone bearing), are names derived from the character of the rock.

When we study the rocks in greater detail, we find in them associations of fossils which do not occur above or below a certain level. This association is called a *fauna*. The Century Dictionary definition for fauna is: "the total of the animal life of a given region or period; the sum of the animals living in a given area or time." Thus the Lake Erie fauna includes the present animal life of that region. Similarly the Hamilton fauna is the sum of the animal life which existed during that period. We may speak of the fauna of a stratum, as for instance the "Encrinal limestone fauna," or the "Spirifer sculptilis fauna," or the fauna of a bed viz: the "Demissa fauna."

Methods of Study.—In beginning the study of the stratified rocks of this region, it is highly desirable that a stratum be selected which may be used as a datum plane, with reference to which the position of all the beds may be ascertained. There are two such reference strata in this region, both of which, on account of their great areal extent over Western New York, will also serve in the correlation of the strata of the Eighteen Mile Creek region with those of more eastern localities. These strata are the Styliolina limestone, which here forms the base of the Upper Devonian, and the Encrinal limestone, which separates the Moscow and Hamilton shales. The first of these is seen in seven of the eight sections in Eighteen Mile Creek, and again in the first of the South Shore Cliffs. The Encrinal limestone is first exposed in Section 5 in Eighteen Mile Creek, and appears in all the sections below that one, as well as in the cliffs on both sides of the mouth of Eighteen Mile Creek. While therefore, the Styliolina limestone forms a reference plane for the upper strata of this region, the Encrinal limestone becomes a convenient datum plane for the lower beds.

A third stratum which may be used as a reference plane in this region, is the Strophalosia bed, which lies fifty feet below the Encrinal limestone, and is considered the top bed of the Marcellus stage. This bed is exposed in Avery's Creek, and in Erie and Athol Springs Cliffs.

The study of the several cliffs is best undertaken in the order in which they are described in chapters one and two. The following itinary is suggested: Leave the train at North Evans station, and descend into the gorge by the steps of the abutment of the stone railroad bridge (see Plate IV.). The stream can usually be crossed near the bridge, where the Styliolina limestone forms the bed of the stream. Taking this stratum as the first datum plane, the overlying beds, exposed in the section can be studied with reference to it. The loose blocks in the bed of the stream will well repay attention, and the shale outcrops between Sections 1 and 2 should not be overlooked.

By following the map, the various sections can be examined, and the rocks studied in descending order. The Styliolina bed will always serve as a guide for the determination of the position of the various beds. Below Section 4, are numerous exposures of the Moscow shale in the bed of the stream, and these deserve attention. In Sections 5 to 7, the Styliolina limestone occurs only at a considerable elevation above the base of the section, but the Encrinal limestone can here be selected as the reference plane.

The first of the South Shore Cliffs is conveniently examined after the Eighteen Mile Creek sections, as it will afford a review, in ascending order, of the strata studied in the gorge, in descending order.

After reaching Pike Creek, leave the shore and return by the Lake-shore road or along the top of the cliffs, to the left or southern bank of Eighteen Mile Creek, and follow the road, which in many places skirts the bank, and affords good general views of the sections, all the way to North Evans village, and beyond.

The Lake Shore Cliffs south of Pike Creek are best approached from Derby or stations further south. A bicycle will be found convenient, as the cliffs are all approachable from the Lake-Shore road. A full day should be devoted to the examination of these cliffs, while weeks may be advantageously spent on them in detailed study.

The North Shore Cliffs can be approached from Lake View station or the Lake-shore road. The study of the Idlewood and Wanakah Cliffs will occupy the time of one excursion, the Erie and Athol Springs Cliffs, together with the ravine of Avery's Creek affording sufficient material for a second, and Bay View Cliff for a third, rather shorter excursion. All these can be approached from the Lake-Shore road. Erie and Athol Springs Cliffs are best approached from Hamburgh-on-the-Lake station (p. 60), while the Bay View Cliff may be easily approached from Woodlawn Beach.

After the sections have been studied in a general way, the details of the various beds will demand the attention of the student, and the longer the time occupied in their study, the more satisfactory will be the results. Attention should be given to the proper succession of the beds, and collections from the talus should not be made while engaged in the study of stratigraphy, unless it be from fragments of beds whose position is definitely known.

In Table C, the beds of this region, with the sub-divisions shown in the sections, are given.

TABLE C.

STRATIGRAPHY OF EIGHTEEN MILE CREEK AND THE LAKE SHORE SECTIONS IN ERIE COUNTY, NEW YORK.

THICKNESS OF BEDS.	RELATION OF BASE OF BEDS TO: TOP OF STYLIOLINA LIMESTONE.	TOP OF ENCRINAL LIMESTONE.	BASE OF ENCRINAL LIM'STN'E.	NAME OR DESCRIPTION OF BEDS.	CLASSIFICATION OF BEDS.		
	+48 to 50′	+66 to 68′	....	Gardeau shales (base)..............................		Upper	Naples Shales.
8 inches.	+ 32′	+ 50′	....	Goniatite bed..		Lower	Naples Shales.
30 ft.	+ 18′	+ 36′	....	Cashaqua shales (base)...........................		Lower	Naples Shales.
9.5 "	+ 8.5′	+ 26.5′	....	Upper, black Genesee shales....................	Genesee Shales.		
8.5 "	+ 0′	+ 18′	....	Lower, gray Genesee shales.....................	Genesee Shales.		
.5 "	— .5′	+ 17.5′	....	**Styliolina limestone**............................	Genesee Shales.		
.25 "	— .75′	+ 17.25′	....	Conodont limestone................................	Genesee Shales.		
.25 "	— 1′	+ 17′	....	Spore-bearing shales..............................	Genesee Shales.		
12-14 inches.	— 2′	+ 16′	....	Transition beds with Schizobolus fauna, (*Schizobolus truncatus*, *Liorhynchus multicostus*, *Ambocoelia præumbona*).	*Spirifer tullius* fauna.	Upper	Upper Hamilton or Moscow Shales.
3 ft.	— 5′	+ 13′	....	Shales and concretionary beds................	*Spirifer tullius* fauna.	Upper	Upper Hamilton or Moscow Shales.
8 "	— 13′	+ 5′	....	Barren shales, containing near the middle a thin band, with *Orbiculoidea media*, *Schizobolus truncatus*, and a few other species, all rare....................................		Middle	Upper Hamilton or Moscow Shales.
3.25 "	— 16.25′	+ 1.75′	....	Shale with *Spirifer consobrinus*, etc.........	*Spirifer consobrinus* fauna.	Lower	Upper Hamilton or Moscow Shales.
.25 "	— 16.5′	+ 1.5′	....	Coral layer, with *Heliophyllum halli*, *Cystiphyllum*, *Atrypa aspera*, etc.........	*Spirifer consobrinus* fauna.	Lower	Upper Hamilton or Moscow Shales.
1.5 "	— 18′	+ 0′	....	Shale with *Chonetes* and *Ambocoelia umbonata*..	*Spirifer consobrinus* fauna.	Lower	Upper Hamilton or Moscow Shales.

TABLE C.—CONTINUED.

THICKNESS OF BEDS.	RELATION OF BASE OF BEDS TO: TOP OF STYLIOLINA LIMESTONE.	TOP OF ENCRINAL LIMESTONE.	BASE OF ENCRINAL LIM'ST'NE.	NAME OR DESCRIPTION OF BEDS.	CLASSIFICATION OF BEDS.
1.5 ft.	— 19.5′	— 1.5′	0	**ENCRINAL LIMESTONE**..............	Spirifer sculptilis fauna.
1 inch.	— 20′	— 2′	— .5′	Stictopora bed, (*Stictopora incisurata*, *Nucleospira concinna*, crinoid joints)...	Spirifer mucronatus fauna. Lower Shales or Hamilton Shales proper.
4 inches.	— 20.5′	— 2.5′	— 1′	Demissa bed, (*Stropheodonta demissa*, *Spirifer mucronatus*, and more than 70 other species)................................	
.5 ft.	— 23.5′	— 5.5′	— 4′	Tentaculite bed, with *T. gracilistriatus* and *Styliolina fissurella*.....................	
.75 "	— 28.5′	— 10.5′	— 9′	Athyris spiriferoides bed.........................	
.5 "	— 39.5′	— 21.5′	— 20′	Lower Athyris spiriferoides bed..............	
1 to 2 inches.	— 44.5′	— 26.5′	— 25′	Modiomorpha subalata bed..................	
1 ft.	— 53.1′	— 35′	— 33.5′	Calcareo argillaceous bed......................	
2.5 "	— 61.5′	— 43.5′	— 42′	Trilobite beds, with intercalated shales (base of Eighteen Mile Creek sections).	
2.25 "	— 63.75′	— 45.75′	— 44.25′	Fossiliferous shale, with Bryozoa bed at base (1 inch)......................................	
1 inch.	— 66′	— 48′	— 46.5′	Hard bed, with *Spirifer granulosus*, etc...	
1.5 ft.	— 68.5′	— 50.5′	— 49′	Upper and Middle Pleurodictyum beds, with shales..	
4 inches.	— 69.5′	— 51.5′	— 50′	Nautilus bed, base of Hamilton shales.....	
5 ft.	....	— 52′	— 50.5′	Strophalosia truncata bed, (*Strophalosia truncata* and Mollusca).....................	Transition beds. (Upper Marcellus Shales.)
29.5 "	....	— 81.5′	— 80′	Transition shales..................................	
3 inches.	....	— 82′	— 80.5′	Pteropod bed...	Upper Marcellus beds.
2 inches.	....	— 88′	— 86.5′	Ambocoelia bed......................................	

PLATE III. (*a*).—View of the cliffs in the gorge of Eighteen Mile Creek, above North Evans.

(*b*).—View of the joint structure in the Gardeau black shales, above North Evans.
—Photographed by A. W. GRABAU.

CHAPTER I.

THE GEOLOGY OF EIGHTEEN MILE CREEK.

General Description.—Eighteen Mile Creek belongs to the St. Lawrence drainage system, its waters being tributary to the basin of Lake Erie. The course of the stream lies wholly within the southern portion of Erie County, N. Y., its most important sections, from a stratigraphical point of view, lying within, or on the borders of the township of Hamburgh.

Taking its origin in the southern uplands of the county, it flows northward and westward, receiving numerous tributaries, until its united waters are poured into Lake Erie at a point just eighteen miles south-west, along the lake shore, from the former village of Black Rock, at the head of the Niagara River, a site now included within the limits of the city of Buffalo.

The general direction of the stream in the last two miles of its course is north-westerly, and for this distance it forms the boundary line between the townships of Evans and Hamburgh. For the greater part of its course the stream flows through a rocky gorge, the walls of which, in many places, rise to a perpendicular height of a hundred feet or more.

The strata exposed in the gorge of the main stream and its tributaries all belong to either the middle or upper part of the Devonian series. The lowest beds found in the gorge are exposed at the mouth of the main stream and belong near the base of the Hamilton stage. The highest beds exposed in the upper portions of the gorge probably belong to the lower Chemung, *i. e.* the Portage sandstone, but this is simply a matter of inference as the upper gorge and branches have not been examined.

The lower portion of the gorge is wider than other parts. This is to be accounted for by the presence of the softer Hamilton shales, which first become prominently exposed about a mile from the lake shore. The stream also makes a greater number of turns in this part of its course, thus furnishing sections which extend in different directions. The widening of the gorge in this portion is due to lateral planation or undercutting in the soft shales, which causes the upper shales and calcareous beds to fall down. This destruction of the banks is materially advanced by the very perfect development of joint fissures which traverse all these rocks and which allow the separation of the shale and limestone masses after they have been undermined by the stream. Such of the fallen material as comes within the transporting power of the current, is carried away, and only the larger rocks remain. (See Plate XI.). These may accumulate in such numbers at the foot of the cliff as to form an effectual protection against the current when the amount of undercutting will be reduced to a minimum. The foundations for a talus thus laid, rock fragments broken from the cliffs by frost and heat will slide down and accumulate, and finally the sloping bank is produced, which from the decomposition of the rock becomes soil covered and overgrown with vegetation. In this manner a talus may form even though the stream keeps close to the base of the cliff as in Section 7. (Plate XII.). In Section 6 a talus would probably be formed were it not for the fact that the blocks of Encrinal limestone are carried away for building purposes. Ordinarily, however, the cliff is kept free from such accumulations as long as the stream keeps close to its base. But if the deflection of the current transfers the cutting zone to another portion of the stream bed, the cliff will rapidly be degraded by atmospheric action, a heavy talus will accumulate, and vegetation growing upon this talus will completely hide the underlying rock.

As will be noted by reference to the map (Plate II.) the talus is best developed upon the inside of the bends, where deposition, rather than erosion takes place, while the banks on the outside of the bends are usually kept perpendicular by the current which continually undermines them.

Fronting the degraded banks, we usually find level terraces built up during seasons of high water from the material derived by the stream in the upper part of its course. These terraces rise from three to five or six feet—rarely more—above the stream bed and they are very level on top. The more extensive ones are utilized as farm and garden lands. Such is the case with the terrace below the Idlewood Camp Grounds opposite Section 8, with the Glen Flora terrace opposite Section 7, and with the extensive terrace opposite Section 5. The other terraces indicated upon the map are uncultivated. A few cultivated terraces of small extent exist in the gorge opposite North Evans village, but above this the terraces and flats along the river side are largely in a state of nature.

At the North Evans station, about a mile and a half above the mouth of the creek, the gorge is spanned by two railroad bridges—that of the Lake Shore and Michigan Southern Railroad, a stone bridge, and that of the Western New York and Pennsylvania and the Nickel Plate Railroads, an iron structure. At the stone bridge the gorge has a depth of eighty-eight feet, and it is between this point and the lake shore that the most interesting sections are exposed, these alone being considered in the following pages.

Age of the Gorge.—The gorge is wholly post-glacial in origin; there is, however, a pre-glacial valley which mouths about a mile to the north of the present gorge. This valley which is over a thousand feet wide, and a section of which is seen in the bank on the lake shore, is deeply filled with drift material, containing many Corniferous Limestone boulders. The valley of this old river, which may be called the pre-glacial Idlewood river, underlies the estate of Mr. Albert Myer, but it has not been traced inland beyond this. Mr.

P. L. Grabau, however, reports its existence near Water Valley and near North Boston.

Detailed Description of the Sections.—There are eight sections between the railroad bridges and the lake shore. These will be considered in descending order, beginning with the one at the stone railroad bridge on the right side of the stream, which will here be designated Section 1.* (Plate IV.).

Section 1 (H).

Plate IV.

This section has a total height of ninety and one-half feet, although at the bridge the height is only eighty-eight feet. The length of the section is about eight hundred feet, and it extends north 50 degrees west, by south 50 degrees east. The strata dip one degree to the south-east. Near the lower end of the section is a small lateral ravine ("Philip's ravine") which extends back three hundred feet or more, where a vertical wall of shale terminates it. This ravine affords a good opportunity for the examination of the upper beds of this section, especially the "Cashaqua" shales.

The following is the thickness of the various beds exposed in this section, taking them in descending order:

Black Naples or Gardeau	40	feet.
†Grey Naples or Cashaqua	30	"
‡Black Genesee	9.5	"
Gray Genesee	8.5	"
Styliolina bed	.5	"
Conodont Limestone	.25	"
Shale	.25	"
Moscow Limestone and Shale	1.50	"
Total	90.50	feet.

*This is the way in which these sections were designated in the field notes, but in my paper on the "Faunas of the Hamilton Group of Eighteen Mile Creek and Vicinity" they are lettered from the lake shore upwards, the present one being Section H.

†Prof. Hall assigns a thickness of thirty-three feet to this rock on the shore of Lake Erie.—Geol. Rept., 4th Dist., 1843, p. 227.

‡The whole thickness of the Genesee on the shore of Lake Erie is made by Hall twenty-three feet and seven inches.—Ibid, p. 221.

PLATE IV.—View of Section 1 at the stone railroad bridge. The rock in the foreground is the Styliolina limestone. The black Genesee shales project from the bank, and above them the gray Naples (Cashaqua) shales form a sloping bank. —Photographed by I. P. Bishop.

The Black Naples Shales (Gardeau shales).—These are highly bituminous, dark brown or black shales, with a chocolate colored streak. They split into thin layers, which often have iridescent surfaces. When struck with a hammer they emit a strong petroleum odor. The joint fissures are well developed, two sets usually being recognizable. These, together with the fissility of the shales, often give the cliff the appearance of having been cut up artificially, smooth walls, projecting prisms and parallelepipeds resulting, while deep fissures frequently penetrate into the rock. Fossils are rare and consist mainly of plant remains, commonly in an unidentifiable condition.

This rock forms the walls of the gorge for many miles above the bridges, the lower strata having entirely disappeared beneath the bed of the stream. The black shale is succeeded by olive shales, some of which are more sandy than others, but all are quite destitute of fossils as far as known at present. Without doubt, however, diligent search will reveal an interesting, though limited fauna, probably containing a number of fish remains.

Although the rock is generally deficient in calcareous material on account of the scarcity of fossils, such material does occur at intervals in the form of calcareous concretions. These are often of great size—sometimes eight or ten feet in diameter, but usually much smaller. They are commonly lense shaped, though gobular or loaf shaped forms are not uncommon. Imitative forms of grotesque appearance are frequent. The stratification is sometimes continuous through them, at other times the strata bend over and under them exhibiting a crowded appearance, as if the growing concretion had forced them apart. It is probable, however, that the concretion was fully formed before the lithification of the adjoining strata had taken place, and that on the contraction of the rock consequent upon lithification, the strata settled down, and produced this crowded and bent appearance. The source of the calcareous material is to be looked for in the scattered shells and other calcareous remains, which were dissolved by the percolating waters. The exterior of the concretion seldom shows any veining, but when broken, a series of calcite veins, usually branching and intercrossing, is seen. These veins are often beautifully banded, exhibiting white crystalline calcite in the center, and successive bands of darker impure calcite towards the margin. The veins are largest in the center and thin out towards the periphery of the concretion. When exposed to the mechanical wear of the stream, and to the solvent action of the water, the outer crust is removed, and as more and more of the claystone is worn away the veins begin to stand out in relief, because the pure crystalline calcite is much less soluble than the amorphous particles which cement the clay. The septate or divided appearance thus produced has given rise to the name "septaria," commonly applied to this class of concretions. Where a considerable portion of the concretion has been worn away, the calcite veins—usually stained yellow or brown by hydrous oxide of iron—appear very prominent, and by their intercrossing cause a resemblance of the concretion to the back of a turtle, on which, account these rocks are often called "turtle stones," "turtle backs" or "petrified turtles."

Large numbers of these concretions, derived from the shale banks above the bridge, are carried down every spring by the floating ice, and strewn over the flats and the river bed in the lower portion of the gorge, where they form one of the curious attractions, exciting commonly more interest than the large numbers of finely preserved fossils occuring with them.

Regarding the mode of formation of these concretions little is known. They undoubtedly bear a genetic relation to the clay stones common in unconsolidated deposits in various portions of this and other countries. When lithification of the concretion begins, chiefly through the loss of the combined water, a radial contraction takes place, which must be towards the periphery of the concretion, since the weight of the superincumbent strata prevents the formation of cracks in the outer shell. Consequently the cracks are widest towards the center and disappear towards the periphery of the concretion. Whether the calcite and other mineral matter filling these cracks, is derived from without, by infiltration, or from the concretion itself by segregation, is still an open question. If the latter occurs, the processes of widening of the fissures by radial contraction of the rock mass, and of segregation of the mineral matter are probably simultaneous, so that at no stage are there any open fissures.

The Gray Naples Shales (Cashaqua shales).—These shales are greenish gray in color, much less fissile than the preceding, and prone to weather into a tenacious clay. They embrace numerous layers of concretions, but in general these do not exhibit the septarium structure. This is probably due to the fact that the calcareous matter is more abundant in these shales than in the black shales above, and hence the concretions partake more of the nature of concretionary limestone masses.

The upper fifteen feet of these shales, while rich in concretions, seem to be very poor in organic remains, no fossils having been noted in them. They form the lower part of the vertical wall which terminates Philip's ravine, but in the main section they face the stream in a sloping, more or less weathered and talus covered bank, supporting vegetation in some places. Below this, at the base of the terminal wall of Philip's ravine, and forming a prominent band in the main section, is a layer of calcareous concretions, or better a concretionary bed of impure limestone, eight inches in thickness. This probably corresponds to J. M. Clarke's "Goniatite concretionary layer,"* in as much as specimens of *Goniatites* are of common occurrence in it, usually forming the nucleus of the concretion. Several species of *Goniatites* occur, but they are seldom found in a good state of preservation. They are commonly found in a very much compressed condition, frequently perfectly flattened, and from having been replaced by iron pyrites which subsequently oxidized, much, if not all of the structure is obliterated. The external form and amount of involution therefore become the only characters

---

*J. M. Clarke: On the higher Devonian faunas of Ontario County, N. Y. Bull. 16, U. S. Geol. Survey, 1885, p. 38 et seq.

by which to identify the species, and this, at best, can be but an unsatisfactory identification. In a few cases, in the specimens collected, the septal sutures are shown, allowing a more precise determination. The most abundant and characteristic species of *Goniatites* in these concretions are *Goniatites intumescens* (Beyr.) and *G. lutheri* (Clarke). The non-umbilicated species are rare, a single doubtful specimen having been noted. Besides the *Goniatites* a few other fossils occur in this rock. Those found are:

Coleolus aciculum (Hall).
Styliolina fissurella (Hall).
Cardiola retrostriata (von Buch).
Lingula spatulata (Vanux.).
Chonetes lepida (Hall).

Cardiola retrostriata (von Buch) is the only other common fossil, and although most of the specimens are small, they show all the characteristic features. *Lingula spatulata* (Vanux.) is represented by small specimens only. This and the other species are rare.

In the shale below the Goniatite bearing layer, fossils are rare. Occasionally in the immediate neighborhood of the layer, Goniatites occur, but these are usually so poorly preserved that specific determination is out of the question. *Cardiola retrostriata* (von Buch) also occurs, though much less commonly than in the concretionary layer. *Lunulicardium fragile* (Hall) is sparingly represented, and with it occurs usually the minute pteropod *Styliolina fissurella* (Hall). *Coleolus aciculum* (Hall) is another sparingly represented species, and a few Orthoceratites occasionally occur. One well-preserved specimen of *Orthoceras* allied to *O. mephisto* (Clarke) was found.

On the whole, the fauna of these beds is a very meagre one, and were it not for the *Goniatites*, which are frequently found, lying at the foot of the cliff, it might be entirely overlooked.

In Ontario County and the Genesee Valley, this shale has a much greater thickness, amounting, according to Hall* to about 150 feet in Ontario County. Correspondingly we find a richer fauna, sixty-six species having been recorded by Clarke in 1885.† The fauna is rich in *Goniatites*, and as Clarke has shown, recalls the characteristic association of fossils found in the "Intumescens" beds of the lower Upper Devonian of the continent of Europe. It is therefore regarded as representing the transatlantic development of the European "Intumescens fauna." (See J. M. Clarke—"The fauna with *Goniatites intumescens* (Beyr.) in Western New York." Am. Geol., Vol. VIII, p. 86.)

The Black Genesee Shales.—These shales recall the bituminous Naples shales, the latter representing a recurrence of the conditions under which the bituminous Genesee shales were deposited. These shales are fissile when weathered, but appear heavy bedded in the fresh mass. Pyrite in minute disseminated grains, and in larger concretionary masses is very common, and from its oxidation, the surfaces of the weathered shale laminae are covered with a coating of red and brown iron rust. There are, however, no large calcareous concretions, such as are common in the black shales above. The jointing is very perfect, and frequently blocks produced by the intersection of the joints, project from the wall, ready to fall. The joint faces are often thickly covered with an efflorescence of alumn.

The oxidation of the pyrite furnishes free sulphuric acid, which, if in excess, will attack the shale and form aluminium sulphate and silica. The reactions may be written:

a. $2\,Fe\,S_2 + 7\,O_2 + 2\,H_2O = 2\,Fe\,SO_4 + 2H_2\,SO_4$.

b. $6\,H_2SO_4 + Al_2(Si\,O_3)_3\,Al_2O_5H_4$‡$= 2\,Al_2(Si\,O_4)_3 + 3\,Si\,O_2 + 8\,H_2O$.

The aluminium sulphate will crystallize in dry places.

Fossils are rare in these beds and consist mainly of the characteristic Genesee species, viz: *Lunulicardium fragile* (Hall) and *Styliolina fissurella* (Hall).

The Gray Genesee Shales.—These consist in descending order of:

---

*Geol. N. Y. Rep't, 4th Geol. Dist., 1843, p. 221.

†Bull, 16 U. S. Geol. Survey. The number of species has been added to since then,

‡The approximate formula for clay slate,

a. Seven feet of grayish and purplish shales with bands of bituminous shales. Towards the top these shales weather considerably, but farther down they are more resistant, and large thin slabs may be obtained.

b. Eighteen inches of bituminous black shales, with two bands of limestone, each an inch in thickness, and made up of the exuviae of the minute pteropod *Styliolina fissurella* (Hall).

This latter mass contains an interesting association of fossils, representing a commingling of Hamilton and Genesee species, but with a preponderance of the latter. *Lunulicardium fragile* (Hall) is the most abundant fossil in the black shale, and with it occurs *Styliolina fissurella* (Hall), though not very commonly, except in certain places. *Lingula spatulata* (Vanuxem) is a fairly common and well preserved shell, passing through several variations. *Orthoceras* and *Bactrites* are represented by small species, and these with *Coleolus aciculum* (Hall) are frequently replaced by iron pyrites. *Goniatites* are rare, a few small specimens having been found, including *G. lutheri* (Clarke). *Spirifer tullius* (Hall) is fairly well represented for a normal Hamilton species. Of crustacean remains, a small ostracod—*Entomis* (?) has alone been found. Plant remains in an unidentifiable condition occur frequently. The included limestone bands represent accumulations of enormous numbers of the small tapering pterepod tubes known as *Styliolina fissurella* (Hall). To the unaided eye the limestone has a compact appearance, with indications of a finely crystalline texture on the broken surfaces. Viewed under a magnifier, the rock appears finely crystalline, and if sufficiently magnified, is seen to be made up of the very fine delicate needle-like shells. Occasionally these are large enough to be clearly visible under an ordinary magnifier, or even to the naked eye. Most commonly, however, a considerable magnification is needed to show the shells clearly.

The only other fossil observed in these beds is *Lingula spatulata* (Vanuxem), which is not uncommon, and of average size.

The Styliolina Limestone.—This is a continuous stratum from four to six inches thick, and of a somewhat concretionary character. It forms the bed of the stream under the bridge, and for the greater part of the distance fronting the section. (Plate IV.). Its concretionary character is brought out by the differential solution which it has undergone, an irregular undulating surface resulting. A part of this is, however, original structure, as shown by the overlying shales which conform to it. Near the lower end of this section the stream has cut down through this rock, exposing it in its full thickness, together with the "Conodont" limestone and a part of the underlying Moscow shales.

The Styliolina limestone is usually very compact, without any appearance of crystalline structure. It is highly argillaceous, giving off a strong clay odor when breathed upon. This fact accounts for the great amount of solution which the rock has suffered on the exposed surfaces. These surfaces invariably present a dissolved appearance, which is not unlike an artificially smoothened mass of moulding clay, which still shows the finger marks upon it. This solution has brought out in relief the contained organic remains other than *Styliolina* and the otherwise smooth surface frequently exhibits small projecting fragments and joints of crinoid stems, black shining "conodonts" and other minute organisms. This is especially true of the under side of the bed, which thus exhibits a close relation to the next underlying bed. The whole of the limestone is made up of the exuviae of *Styliolina fissurella* (Hall) which frequently are visible to the unaided eye. The shells lie in all positions, a fact prominently brought out by thin sections. (Fig. i).

The Styliolina (Styliola) layer was first described by Clarke* from Ontario county and adjoining districts. It there lies about twenty feet above the base of the Genesee formation and varies in petrographical character in its different outcrops. Clarke has estimated that the rock contains at least 40,000 individuals of the *Styliolina* to a cubic inch, which, when the whole extent of this limestone bed is taken into consideration, indicates an almost incredible numerical development of these shells. According to Clarke's investigations† the shells have been filled by calcic carbonate, deposited in even concentric layers on the inside of the shell, a longitudinal section of a shell thus having the appearance of vein infiltration. Many shells also have an external coating of calcic carbonate, which like the internal filling, has a crystalline structure.‡

Plant remains are not uncommon in the Styliolina stratum, these being usually the trunks and other woody parts of coniferous trees, most of which may probably be referred to the genus *Dadoxylon* (Unger). These tree trunks are supposed by Sir William Dawson to have been carried by river floods into the sea, like modern drift wood, and there buried in the growing lime stones and shales, and finally to have been replaced by mineral matter.

The genus *Dadoxylon* (Unger) is referred by Dawson to the yews,§ while Shenk‖ classes it with *Cordaites*. Speaking of these trees Dawson says¶: "It" (the wood) "often shows its structure in the most perfect manner in specimens penetrated by calcite or silica, or by pyrite, and in which the original woody matter has been resolved into anthracite or even into graphite. These trees have true woody tissues, presenting that beautiful arrangement of pores or thin parts enclosed in cup like discs, which is characteristic of the coniferous trees, and which is a great improvement on the barred tissue" (of lycopodiaceous trees) ". . . . . . . affording a far more strong, tough and durable wood, such as we have in our modern pines and yews." A remarkable fossil wood was described by Dawson under the name *Syringoxylon mirabile*°, from a small fragment collected by Prof. Hall—"from a limestone in the upper part of the Hamilton group" at Eighteen Mile Creek. The limestone referred to is probably the Styliolina, or perhaps the "Conodont." The wood is that of an angiospermous exogen, the

*J. M. Clarke, Bull. 16, U. S. Geol. Surv., p. 14.

†Loc. cit., p. 15.

‡For a detailed description of the interesting optical phenomena exhibited in sections of these shells, see Clarke, Bull. 16, U. S. Geol. Surv., p. 16.

§Geol. Hist. of Plants, 1888, p. 78.

‖Zittel Handb., d. Pal. 2te Abth., p. 870.

¶Loc. cit., pp. 79 and 80.

°Quart. Journ. Geol. Soc., Vol. XVIII., p. 305, 1862.

specimen constituting, according to Dawson, the sole representative of this class of trees in the Palaeozoic, implying "the existence in the Devonian Period of trees of a higher grade than any that are known in the Carboniferous system."*

The fossil wood, as it occurs in the limestone, is always much compressed, and its determination is attended with considerable difficulty. Nevertheless the specimens are interesting as examples of "petrified woods" related to, and in a sense ancestral to, the fossil woods of the Tertiary and Post-tertiary forests of the west, which have furnished so many beautiful and often brilliantly colored specimens for our cabinets.

The Conodont Bed.—This limestone is from two to two and one-half inches thick, and full of fossils, which on the weathered surfaces stand out in relief. The rock is concretionary, with thin masses of shale occupying the deeper hollows. In some places masses of bituminous shale lie between it and the overlying Styliolina limestone, while in others again the two are in contact. The rock is more coarsely crystalline than the Styliolina limestone, and is always readily distinguished from the latter.

The Conodont bed is interesting on account of the numerous fish remains which it contains, these being usually the plates and jaws of Placoderms, the spines of Sharks and more rarely the scales of Ganoids. Most of the remains are fragmentary, though small perfect plates and scales are occasionally found. When weathered in relief they have a highly dissolved appearance. These fish remains are not confined to the Conodont bed, but frequently pass upward into the lower portion of the Styliolina limestone.

Another characteristic class of fossils in this rock and the one which has given in it's name, is that of the so-called "Conodonts." These are minute jaw-like bodies, black and lustrous, covering the weathered surfaces of the rock in great

*Loc. cit.

numbers. In form they are very variable, no two probably being exactly alike. A number of species have been described by Hinde from this bed, and they are all illustrated in Part II. They are composed of carbonate and phosphate of lime, and were regarded by Pander and others as the teeth of Myxinoid fishes. According to Zittel and Rohen*, however, they must be regarded as jaws of Annelids.

The Conodont bed was described and named by Hinde†, who discovered its position in this and the adjoining sections of Eighteen Mile Creek. He referred it to the Upper Hamilton, which was clearly erroneous, as all its affinities, lithological and palaeontological are with the Styliolina of the Genesee. This is well shown by the fact that in places the rock loses its distinctive character and is made up of local accumulations of *Styliolina fissurella* (Hall).

Normally the rock is composed of the fragments of crinoid stems, and probably some other calcareous remains, mingled with those of fish plates and corneous conodonts. Grains of a green mineral, probably glauconite, are common, and pyrite likewise occurs in considerable abundance. In a thin section, fine quartz grains appear at intervals. Altogether the limestone may be regarded as a fragmental rock, composed of the broken remains of organisms, with a very small admixture of transported material.‡

Besides the fossils already mentioned, imperfect specimens of (?) *Ambocoelia umbonata* (Conrad) have been noticed in the rock, but in general, the shells, if they occur, are so poorly preserved as to be unidentifiable.

---

*Zittel and Rohen, "Ueber Conodonten." Sitzungsber. Bay. Akad. Wissensch. Bd. XVI., 1886.

†Quart. Journ. Geol. Soc. Vol. 35, p. 352, et seq.

‡Since the above has gone to press, my friend, Dr. Theodore G. White of Columbia College has examined, at my request, thin sections of the Conodont limestone. He has kindly furnished me with the following note concerning the petrographic character of this rock: "The sections strongly resemble in appearance the silicate bunches occurring in the Archaean or Algonkian limestones at Port Henry, N. Y., near the contact with the crystalline rocks and ore bodies. The texture of the rock is distinctly crystalline and the mineral fragments do not seem to be water rounded. *Magnetite* is very abundant through the sections, accompanied by *pyrite*. *Biotite* ranks next in abundance and forms a large proportion of the mass of the rock. Scattered throughout the sections are long shreads of a fibrous mineral, white in color, scarcely polarizing and giving no interference figure. The extinction angle is 25° to 28°, which would indicate that the mineral was probably *cyanite*. It contains grains of the magnetite, as does also the biotite. *Quartz*, *calcite* and *hornblende* are present in lesser amounts. One distinct and very perfect spherulite was observed."

In addition to the above, the rock contains the organic remains already noted.

The Conodont, the Styliolina, and the overlying eighteen inches of bituminous shale and limestone (b) may be designated collectively as the *Styliolina band*.

The fauna of this band appeared again under more favorable conditions during the deposition of the Naples shales, when the Goniatites were much more abundant. It did not, however, reach such a luxuriant development in this region, either in its first or its second appearance, as was the case in the Genesee Valley. Clarke has noticed over fifty species from the Styliolina band of that region, besides numerous Conodonts and fish remains*. Careful exploration of these beds in the region about Eighteen Mile Creek will undoubtedly reveal a richer fauna than is now known, though the number of species and individuals will probably always be much smaller than that characterizing the fauna in the Genesee Valley.

The Conodont limestone is seen in this section only near the lower end, where the stream has cut through the Styliolina limestone. Large blocks of the rock are scattered about in the bed of the stream near the lower end of the section, and for some distance below. With them are blocks of the Styliolina limestone, of Corniferous limestone, and occasionally of Encrinal limestone, these latter two having been carried by floating ice from the bridge, where they were brought for purposes of construction.

Underlying the Conodont bed are about two inches of shale, which are divisible into an upper chocolate colored band, frequently bearing *Styliolina fissurella* (Hall) and occasionally *Conodonts*, and a lower, almost unfossiliferous gray band, which splits into thin laminae, with smooth surfaces, having a talcose feel. Besides the *Styliolina*, the chocolate colored slate contains numerous small, flattened disclike bodies, of a black carbonaceous appearance, the spores of plants allied to modern rhizocarps. These spores, (macrospores) when viewed under the microscope, present thick, rounded rims, and a more or less irregularly depressed centre. They are frequently thickly scattered through the shales, giving to them, in part at least, their bituminous

*Am. Geol., Vol. VIII., p. 86 et seq.

character.* Similar spores occur in vast numbers in Devonian shales and limestones of various parts of the United States and Canada, and to them the name *Sporangites* (*Protosalvinia*) *huronensis* was given by Dawson. Allied spores have been discovered in widely separated localities all over the world, and they are not infrequently found in such quantities as to suggest that they may play a not unimportant role in the accumulation of vegetable carbon. In the Devonian shales of this country they probably constitute one of the sources of petroleum and natural gas. Spores are occasionally found in the gray portion of the shale, but they are very rare.

The spores are, as a rule, readily separated from the shale, and may be mounted either in balsam or dry. When viewed under the microscope by transmitted light, the discs appear of an amber or orange hue, translucent and structureless, except for minute spots, which are regarded as pores in the thick walls. The size varies; the ordinary specimens having a diameter of from one seventy-fifths to one one-hundreds of an inch (one-third to one-fourth of a millimeter). Some of the spores, however, are larger. Flocculent carbonaceous matter often occurs, associated with these macropores, probably representing the more or less decomposed microspores.

These shales mark the base of the Genesee stage, and, since the Tully limestone is absent, the base of the Upper Devonian.

The Moscow Shales. These, the upper shales of the Middle Devonian, are exposed near the lower end of Section 1, where about a foot is visible. The top of the series is formed by a gray concretionary limestone band, four inches thick and highly argillaceous. It is a very refractory rock, and of a uniform texture throughout. Fossils are common, but they are chiefly of three species which characterize this horizon. These are:

Liorhynchus multicostus (Hall).
Schizobolus truncatus (Hall).
Ambocoelia praeumbona (Hall).

*According to Newberry, the carbonaceous matter of the bituminous shales is mainly derived from the broken down and carbonized tissues of algae and other low plants. See his paper on this subject in the Annals of the New York Academy of Sciences, Vol. II., No. 12, 1883.

The first of these is a form common at various levels in the Hamilton group. Nowhere, however, does it occur so abundantly and so well preserved as at this level, and it is especially in the concretionary limestone bed that this fossil shows its characteristic outline and convexity of valves. It is a form eminently characteristic of the Hamilton stage, giving way in the Genesee to a form with few, almost obsolete plications, the *L. quadricostatus* (Vanuxem), which however, apparently did not flourish in this vicinity. *Schizobolus truncatus* (Hall) (Fig. 85, Pt. II.) is a characteristic Genesee fossil, not commonly occurring below that formation. In fact, this appears to be the first locality from which this fossil has been recorded as occurring in the Hamilton beds, and its occurrence here is in direct accord with the slow change from Hamilton to Genesee conditions which took place in this portion of the Interior Devonian Sea.* It is a noteworthy fact that this species has not been found in the Genesee shales of this region, though it seems to be a characteristic fossil of that formation in the Genesee Valley and eastward. It usually occurs in the limestone bed as separate valves, not infrequently showing the interior of the valves. Where the true surfaces of the valves are exposed, either internal or external, these commonly have a bluish-gray color, which seems to be characteristic, and due to the corneous character of the shell.

Ambocoelia praeumbona (Hall) (Fig. 127, Pt. II.) while a characteristic Hamilton fossil, is, in this region entirely restricted to the upper part of the Moscow shales. It is an abundant and well-preserved form in the concretionary limestone bed, retaining its normal convexity in both valves. The specimens vary considerably in size, and occur usually as separate valves, their surface characters commonly obliterated through the exfoliation of the outer layers of the shell. Brachial valves are quite as common as pedicle

*See Chapter III.

valves, and are at once recognized by their semi-elliptical outline, slight convexity and straight hinge line.

These three species occupy the rock almost to the exclusion of every other form, and constitute a distinct association of fossils, which is characteristic of the upper part of the Moscow shale of this region. The fauna thus produced constitutes the "Schizobolus fauna," named so after its most characteristic member, and, inasmuch as it contains typical Hamilton and typical Genesee fossils, it is a true *transition fauna* from the Middle to the Upper Devonian of this region.

The most fossiliferous portion of the rock is that portion having the character of individual concretions. The more continuous portion of the bed, while containing these fossils, is nevertheless comparatively barren.

The limestone rests on gray calcareous shale, readily splitting into thin layers, and moderately fossiliferous. On the surfaces to which air and water have access whitish or yellowish granules can usually be observed scattered thickly over the shale and the fossils. Sometimes these are so closely crowded as to give the rock an oolitic appearance. Under a lens these granules appear dull, rounded or disclike, but under a microscope they appear to be bunches or aggregates of small crystals. Analysis shows them to be crystals of gypsum (hydrous sulphate of calcium). The origin of these crystals is explained by the occurrence of pyrite grains and nodules in considerable number in the shale. These by oxidation form sulphate of iron, which reacts with the calcium carbonate in the shale and produces calcium sulphate. Free sulphuric acid is likewise formed, which reacts with the calcium carbonate to form calcium sulphate, water and carbon dioxide. The calcium sulphate, from the presence of water during its formation will be hydrated. The formation of the gypsum is probably going on constantly, just as the alum is constantly forming on the exposed laminae of the Genesee and other bituminous shales.*

*See the reactions given in Chapter II.

PLATE V. (*a*).—View of a part of Section 1, showing the Styliolina limestone at the base, the Genesee shales and the Naples shales.

(*b*).—View of the lower end of Section 2. The projecting bed is the Styliolina limestone. The concretionary layer limiting the Schizobolus fauna in the underlying Moscow shales is shown. —Photographed by A. W. GRABAU.

This shale well repays careful study, for in it occur a large number of those minute problematical bodies, the "Conodonts." They are readily detected by the use of a lens, and from the nature of the rock in which they are imbedded, they are in an excellent state of preservation, and afford interesting objects for microscopic study.

Ambocoelia praeumbona (Hall) occurs in considerable numbers in some portions of this shale, but the specimens are smaller on the average than those found in the calcareous bed above. *Liorhynchus multicostus* (Hall) also occurs, the specimens occasionally attaining great size. Some of the specimens of this species from these shales, approach much more closely to the typical *L. quadricostatus* (Vanuxem) of the Genesee than any of those found either above or below. Besides these, the minute pteropod *Styliolina fissurella* (Hall) occurs, often in considerable numbers, on the laminae of the shale.

Section 2 (G).

PLATE V.

This section is a very short one, being scarcely more than three hundred and fifty feet in length. It is cut in the left bank of the stream, and extends in the same general direction as the preceding one. The dip of the strata is greater than that of Section 1, being about 2.5 degrees to the southeast. A large portion of this section is covered by the decomposed shale which the rains have carried down from above, and on which a strong growth of vegetation has become established, obscuring the rocks underneath. In consequence of this, the upper strata are well exposed only near the up-stream end of the section, but from the steepness of the bank at this point the study of these strata is attended with considerable difficulty.

The Black Naples Shales appear at the top of this section, and they are again exposed in a "dug way" which leads from the terrace, just beyond the section, to the top of the bank. The whole of the Gray Naples or Cashaqua shales is exposed in this section and the concretions are numerous. Those of the Goniatite stratum are frequently found at the foot of the section, where they have fallen on being loosened by frost action and the disintegration of the bank. The specimens of *Goniatites* in these concretions, as in those of Section 1, are much compressed, and only the outline and the degree of involution of the respective species are as a rule discernable.

The Genesee shales show the same characteristic as in Section 1. The upper bituminous portion projects in masses bounded by joint planes, and where these masses have fallen after the removal of the support, smooth walls remain, on which frequently may be observed an efflorescens of alum. The shales usually present the rusty surfaces on their laminae which result from the oxidation of the pyrite. The lower portion of the Genesee is, as everywhere in this region, represented by about eight feet of grayish shale with a few bituminous bands, and grades below into the Styliolina band. This has much the character noticed at Section 1, except that the Styliolina limestone is about ten inches thick. In the black shale of the "band" spores are not uncommon, while *Lunulicardium fragile* (Hall) and *Styliolina fissurella* (Hall) are the only other abundant fossils. The Conodont limestone is chiefly represented in the upstream end of the section. Here it is about three inches thick, less compact than at Section 1, and rich in crinoid joints, which on the weathered surfaces stand out in relief. This causes the rock to contrast strongly with the overlying Styliolina limestone, which always has a dissolved appearance, owing to the uniformity of its texture. Near the middle of the section, the Conodont bed dwindles in thickness to less than an inch, and finally appears only as a thin coating on the under side of the Styliolina limestone.

From the erosion of the soft Moscow shales the Conodont and Styliolina limestones together project for some distance beyond the bank, frequently forming an overhanging shelf, which in the course of time will break down, carrying with it large masses of the overlying shale. (See Fig. b, Pt. V.).

About four feet of the Moscow shales are exposed near the lower end of the section. The concretionary limestone bed which capped the shale at Section 1, is here represented by a layer of scattered concretions which contain a few fossils, principally *Liorhynchus multicostus* (Hall). About a foot below this is a second layer of concretions, double in many places, and more continuous than the upper one. The shale between these two layers of concretions contains the Schizobolus fauna, *i. e. Schizobolus truncatus* (Hall), *Liorhynchus multicostus* (Hall) and *Ambocoelia praeumbona* (Hall). The first of these is quite common and well preserved. Large individuals of the other two are common, but the shells exfoliate so strongly that the original surface characters are seldom preserved in the specimens obtained.

About four inches below the lower bed of concretions, or from fourteen to sixteen inches below the top of the Moscow shales, occurs a band of pyrite concretions, some of which are of considerable size.* They are highly impure, and when oxidized show as a brown band in the cliff. *L. multicostus* (Hall) occurs abundantly down to the pyrite layer, after which it becomes rare. *Ambocoelia praeumbona* (Hall) is common, however, throughout the exposed portion of the shale in this section.

In the lower beds of this section a dwarfed form of *Spirifer tullius* (Hall) occurs, a species which, in this region, appears to be wholly restricted to the upper Moscow shales. *Schizobolus truncatus* (Hall) occurs occasionally, but fossils on the whole, are rather uncommon. The characteristic association, however, of three species restricted to the upper Moscow shale, namely: *Spirifer tullius* (Hall), *Ambocoelia praeumbona* (Hall) and *Schizobolus truncatus* (Hall),

*My attention was first called to this band and its persistence in the other sections by Prof. I. P. Bishop.

establish a distinct fauna—the *Spirifer tullius fauna*—which occupies the upper four feet of the Moscow shales of this region.* The Schizobolus fauna (or faunule) is merely the last phase of this fauna, where *Spirifer tullius* (Hall) has disappeared, while *Schizobolus truncatus* (Hall) and *Liorhynchus multicostus* (Hall) have reached a great numerical development.

Between Sections 1 and 2, the Moscow shale is exposed in various portions of the stream bed.

Section 3 (F).

Plate VI.

This section extends almost due north and south, and it forms a projecting point, the termination of a semi-circular wooded rock wall, which itself is an extension of Section 1. In front of this cliff is an extensive "flat" or terrace, rising four feet or more above the river bed. The portion of the cliff showing the rocks is only about five hundred feet long. It is kept clear of talus by the stream, which washes its base. The most prominent rock of the cliff is the black fissile and much jointed upper Genesee shale, which here as everywhere, projects from the bank. The Gray Naples or Cashaqua shales appear above it, and in some parts of the section, a portion of the Black Naples (Gardeau) shales can be seen. The lower Genesee shales form the greater portion of the remainder of the cliff, while only a slight thickness of the Moscow shales appears. The Styliolina projects as a shelf from the bank, and on its under side frequently patches of the crystalline Conodont limestone appear, never, however, exceeding a fraction of an inch in thickness. The beds dip about one degree to the south.

Of the Moscow shales, eighteen inches are exposed at the lower (southern) end of the section, and three feet at the upper (northern) end. The shale embraces a very con-

*For a complete list of the species of this fauna see "Faunas of the Hamilton Group of Eighteen Mile Creek and Vicinity."

PLATE VI.—View of the lower end of Section 3. The upper portion of the Moscow shales is exposed at the foot of the section. The projecting Styliolina band, the gray and much-jointed black Genesee shales, and a portion of the Cashaqua shales appear above it. —Photographed by A. W. GRABAU.

tinuous layer of calcareous concretions, one-half foot below the top at the upper end and one foot below the top at the southern end. This layer, therefore, dips to the south at a higher angle than does the Styliolina bed. It corresponds to the lower of the two layers of concretions noticed in Section 2, the shale over it containing the Schizobolus fauna. In the shale beneath the concretions, a considerable variety of fossils occur, most of which, however, are but sparingly represented. The characteristic Hamilton trilobite *Phacops rana* (Green) is not uncommon, while a minute pteropod, the *Tentaculites gracilistriatus* (Hall) occurs in great abundance in a layer less than half an inch think. This species occurs by the hundreds on the shale laminae, closely resembling the *Styliolina fissurella* (Hall), and showing a similar longitudinal line of compression. The concentric rings or annulations, however, which are characteristic of the genus, serve to distinguish it at once. *Spirifer tullius* (Hall) is also a frequent and characteristic fossil.

Just beyond the lower end of the section, in the bed of the stream, appears a small anticlinal fold, the axis of which extends nearly north and south. The fold indicates a lateral compression of the strata, as a result of which they were crushed and uplifted. The line of weakness thus produced probably determined the course of erosion, which has removed the overlying rock. In the shale thus crushed occur a large number of the spiny brachiopod *Productella spinulicosta* (Hall), none of which, however, retain their original outline. The long slender curved spines appear, however, in great numbers on the shale, an occurrence nowhere else observed. (Fig. 112, Pt. II.).

Section 4 (E).

Plate VII.

This section is cut into the left bank of the stream, beginning opposite the southern end of Section 3, and extending in a general north-west direction. Opposite it is the deepest portion of the creek, and when the water is high, it is practically impossible to pass along the foot of the cliff. The greatest height of the section is seventy-seven feet, but it becomes much lower towards its down-stream end. The dip of the strata, as determined from the Styliolina limestone, is about four degrees to the south-east, giving an average rise of one foot in one hundred and fifty. The section has a length of about six hundred feet.

At the upper end of the section, between twenty-five and thirty feet of the Black Naples (Gardeau) shales are exposed, the line of demarkation between them and the underlying Cashaqua shales being very distinct. (See Fig. a, Pl. VII.). The whole of the latter shales are exposed, including seven distinct courses of concretions. The line of separation between the Cashaqua and the Genesee shales is not so strongly defined, the latter, however, exhibiting their characteristic jointing and fissility. (Fig. b, Pl. VII.). The Styliolina limestone has a thickness of ten inches, its upper portion having a shaly character. At the upper end of the section it forms the basal layer, projecting as an extensive shelf beyond the bank. Its surface here is very uneven, showing the same semi-concretionary character exhibited under the bridge at Section 1, and wherever a large area of its surface is exposed. At the lower end of the section the Styliolina limestone is about four feet higher, and frequently projects from the bank when the shale beneath has been worn away. The disintegration and falling of the shales above furnish material for the accumulation of a talus on this shelf, which may remain in this position long enough for vegetation to grow. Sooner or later, however, the undermining is carried so far that the projecting limestone blocks break off, and with their loads of debris, tumble into the stream. The Conodont limestone is not represented in this section.

The whole four feet of the upper Moscow shales, which contain the Spirifer tullius fauna, are exposed at the lower

PLATE VII. (*a*).—View of the upper end of Section 4. The base of the section is formed by the Styliolina limestone, above which are visible the gray and black Genesee, and the Cashaqua and Gardeau shales.

(*b*).—View of the Genesee shales of Section 4, showing the characteristic jointage of the black shales. —Photographed by A. W. GRABAU.

end of the section. The lowest portion of this mass of shale contains chiefly *Ambocoelia praeumbona* (Hall), which for the first time made its appearance in this region, and continued to the close of the Hamilton or Mesodevonian period. The characteristic species of this fauna all occur in these shales, the type species *Spirifer tullius* (Hall) having its best development near the middle of the series. The layer of concretions which marks the downward limit of the Schizobolus sub-fauna (faunule), appears again in this section. It is usually double, and very continuous. At the upper end of the section it is twelve inches below the Styliolina limestone, while at the lower end it is only four inches below that rock. The point of first appearance of this layer in Section 4 is just opposite the southern end of Section 3. In both places the layer is a foot below the Styliolina band, and approaches it as we go northward.

The shale between this layer and the Styliolina limestone is especially rich in *Liorhynchus multicostus* (Hall), which occurs by the hundreds between certain of the shale laminae. Many of the specimens are of great size, but the shell commonly breaks away, while the specimens usually present a compressed, semi-crushed appearance. The other members of the Schizobolus sub-fauna are by no means rare. The layer of pyrite nodules noticed in Section 2 is sparingly represented here, occuring in a similar position.

At the lower end of the section the Genesee shales form the top of the bank, which is here much lower than elsewhere. Beyond the end of the section, where a roadway leads to the top of the bank, is the mouth of "Fern brook" ravine, which is cut back nearly to the main road, and terminates in a vertical wall, over which, in wet weather, the drainage of a considerable portion of country descends as a fall. In this ravine only the Upper Devonian shales are exposed, and it is a place more frequented by the botanist than by the geologist.

Between this section and the next, there is a long reach of the stream, banked by no well cut sections. There are numerous exposures in the bed of the stream, however, and these allow an examination of the shale underlying that which bears the Spirifer tullius fauna. The greater portion of these "middle Moscow" shales is barren, and one may search for hours without finding a single specimen. Near the middle of the mass, however, about eight or nine feet below the Styliolina band, occurs a thin layer containing an abundance of the nearly circular brachiopod *Orbiculoidea media* (Hall). Associated with this species are specimens of *Schizobolus truncatus* (Hall), this being the lowest position in the Hamilton strata, in which this species has been found.

As we approach the bottom of the Moscow shale, fossils become abundant again, the first to do so being the trilobite *Phacops rana* (Green), of which very good and large specimens may be obtained. These lower Moscow beds should be explored when the water in the stream is low, the shale in the stream *bed* being much more accessible than that in the *bank* at Section 5. Just before reaching this latter section, the stream descends over the hard Encrinal limestone bed, which separates the Moscow shales from the Hamilton shales proper.

It is above this fall, in the bed of the stream, that the lower Moscow shales are best exposed. The fossiliferous portion comprises about five feet of the shale, which is characterized by an association of species, differing from that at other levels. The robust, short winged, sparingly plicated *Spirifer* called in the old reports *S. zigzag* (Hall) from the zigzag surface striae, but the correct name for which is *S. consobrinus* (D'Orb.) is entirely restricted to these shales, and gives its name to the fauna. Besides the type species, the *Spirifer consobrinus fauna* comprises a large number of species which are common only at this level, while a few are entirely restricted to it.* In the shale

*For a complete list of the fossils of this fauna see the author's paper on the "Faunas of the Hamilton Group, etc."

immediately above the Encrinal limestone occur vast numbers of the small *Ambocoelia umbonata* (Conrad), with the sinus or depression in the centre of the convex valve. (Fig. 125, Pt. II.). This fossil in some places almost makes up the rock, and for a few inches in thickness scarcely any other fossils occur. Occasionally crushed specimens of *Athyris spiriferoides* (Eaton) occur with it, this fossil when first exposed having a white or calcined appearance. A little higher up, the large flat *Stropheodonta perplana* (Conr.) occurs in considerable numbers, and with it a small patella-like brachiopod—the *Pholidops hamiltoniæ* (Hall). The small conical coral *Streptelasma rectum* (Hall) is also found. Other corals occur, making up the "coral layer," which is so well exposed in Section 5, under which it will be described. The shale from two to three feet above the Encrinal limestone is rich in two small species of *Chonetes*, which are very similar to each other, and both of which are characterized by the possession of laterally projecting spines. These are *C. deflecta* (Hall) and *C. mucronata* (Hall). The type species, *Spirifer consobrinus* (D'Orb.) is likewise abundant in this portion of the rock. Above this *Ambocoelia umbonata* (Conr.) gradually disappears, while the coarser brachiopod *Atrypa reticularis* (Linn.) and the corals *Streptelasma rectum* (Hall) and several species of *Cystiphyllum* become quite abundant. A few crinoids also occur. The trilobite *Phacops rana* (Green) occurs throughout the five feet of shale containing this fauna, and it is the last to disappear. Finally, it too, is no longer represented, and the shale is barren to the base of the Spirifer tullius fauna, except for the thin band with *Orbiculoidea media* (Hall) already noticed.

Section 5 (D).

Plates VIII and IX.

This is by far the longest and most interesting section in the gorge. It lies on the right side of the stream, and begins some little distance above the, fall formed by the outcrop of the Encrinal limestone. The length of the section below the fall is about 2200 feet, and the chord of the crescent described by it, extends approximately, east 20 degrees north, by west 20 degrees south, which is about the direction of the strike of the strata in this region. This accounts for the fact that the strata appear horizontal in the section. The dip may be observed at the fall near the head of the section. On the right side of the fall the limestone commonly projects above the water, while on the left side it is a foot or more below the ordinary water level.

In the section appear representatives of the strata from the black Naples (Gardeau) shales to the Hamilton shales. The former are represented by their lower five or ten feet only, which form a vertical face under the influence of the perfect jointing developed in them. The gray Naples or Cashaqua shales are represented in their entirety, and form a more or less sloping bank under the vertical cliff of Gardeau shales. Beneath the gray Naples shales, another vertical cliff is formed by the black Genesee shales, which in many places overhang the rock below, presenting smooth joint faces, and projecting prisms and parallelepipedons, nearly separated from the main wall and dangerously insecure. Frequent falls of rock from a height of about thirty feet, furnish abundant material for examination, at the same time making the collecting of the fossils from the extremely rich Hamilton fauna at the base of the cliff, a hazardous undertaking.

The Genesee shales in their fresh condition, are heavy bedded, and large blocks will hold together quite firmly. On weathering, however, probably by the oxidation of the pyrite grains which are plentifully scattered through the rock, they become more fissile, so that ultimately large slabs of excessive thinness can be readily separated. It is probable that the pyrite grains are spread more thickly on the bedding planes, or at any rate that they are most prone to

PLATE VIII.—View of the upper end of Section 5, showing the falls caused by the outcropping of the Encrinal limestone.
—Photographed by I. P. BISHOP.

oxidize along these, where water and oxygen find a ready access. Nodules of pyrite, often of quite large size, are common in this shale.

The gray Genesee shales, being calcareous, weather more readily than the black, which, from the absence of soluble material offer peculiar resistance to the chemical action of the atmosphere. Hence the portion of the cliff formed by the lower Genesee shales recedes rapidly through weathering, while that portion formed by the upper black Genesee shales recedes only by the fall of the undermined portions.

The Styliolina limestone appears in the bank seventeen feet above the top of the falls. It has an average thickness of six or seven inches, and in character does not vary much from the outcrops in other sections. It frequently projects beyond the underlying shales, while blocks which have fallen to the base of the cliff are not uncommon.

The whole of the Moscow shales are exposed in this section, lying between the Styliolina limestone above, and the Encrinal limestone below. Their thickness is nearly seventeen feet, and they usually form an almost perpendicular wall. A smooth face occasionally appears where a joint crack has cut the rock in the direction of the face of the section. This feature, however, is not characteristic, the calcareous shales, probably from their more tenacious nature, being much less fissured than the bituminous shales.

Five inches below the Styliolina limestone is a layer of concretionary limestone, gray, compact and practically non fossiliferous. This apparently corresponds to the layer of concretions noted in a similar position in the preceding sections. A few layers of scattered concretions appear in the shale below this concretionary limestone.

The most interesting portion ot these shales is the "coral layer" of the Spirifer consobrinus fauna. This layer appears in the bank eighteen or twenty inches above the Encrinal limestone, and can be traced the whole length of the section.

It is about three inches thick, and in most places consists entirely of an accumulation of cyathophylloid or cup corals. These are mostly of the genera *Heliophyllum* (*H. halli* E. & H.) *Cystiphyllum* and *Zaphrentis*, and nearly all lie prostrate. Frequently three or four lie above each other, as if they had been carried in by a strong flood and spread over the sea bottom. They show, however, no signs of wear, the delicate bryozoans and small corals which encrust many of them, showing that little, if any disturbance has occurred here since the growth of the corals. They therefore indicate a flourishing coral reef or forest, which was suddenly overwhelmed, probably by the influx of muddy waters, and was completely destroyed, without, however, undergoing any mechanical abrasion. The appearance of these large corals seems to have driven out the small *Streptelasma*, for this coral, adapted probably to muddy waters, occurs above and below the coral layer, but not in it.

Associated with the corals, and becoming the sole occupants of the bed in the absence of the corals, are a number of brachiopods, usually of robust character. These are *Spirifer audaculus* var. *eatoni* (Hall), *Atrypa reticularis* (Linn.) and *A. aspera* (Dalman). The latter form is restricted to this bed, and is abundant in all its outcrops. A curious feature, however, is, that nearly every specimen has lost its spines, while the same species in the Genesee Valley, where it is associated with the same species of corals, nearly always retains its spines. That the loss of the spines in this region is due to protracted maceration before final burial seems likely, and would be in direct accord with the slight thickness of the Moscow shales in this region.*

The Encrinal Limestone. This rock appears for the first time near the upper end of Section 5, where it causes the fall in the stream. Above this point it quickly dips below the Moscow shales, and is not seen in any of the upper sections.

---

*See Chapter III.

The thickness of the stratum is one and one-half feet, varying but little in different parts of the section. Its upper portion is of a somewhat shaly character, and highly fossiliferous. More than fifty species of fossils have been obtained from this portion of the stratum, many of them being either rare or unrepresented outside of it. One of the most striking species is a large pelecypod, which is found in considerable numbers in the upper part of the limestone, near the lower end of the section. This is the *Mytilarca oviformis* (Conrad), a large mussel shell which is not found outside of this bed. The shell is commonly removed, the "mould" of the interior alone remaining. The rock is composed chiefly of the finely comminuted remains of calcareous organisms, among which crinoid stems and joints predominate. Weathering brings the coarser of these out in relief, a character often observable on the moulds of such shells as the *Mytilarca*.

Although fossils are numerous, perfect specimens are difficult to obtain. This is due to the fact that the outer layer of the shells tends to adhere to the rock on being split out. This exfoliation is not restricted to shells alone, but occurs in the trilobites and other organisms as well. It is only where weathering has removed the surrounding matrix that the perfect surface characters become visible. The lower, more solid and more crystalline portion of the bed contains chiefly corals, among which the honeycomb coral—*Favosites hamiltoniæ* (Hall) predominates. It usually forms rounded heads six inches to a foot in diameter, sometimes containing petroleum, probably the result of the decomposition of the original animal matter.

The rock is pyritiferous in places, sometimes so to a considerable degree. On its under side occurs a coating of iron sulphide, probably in the form of the mineral marcasite, which occasionally has a thickness of an inch. From the oxidation of this mineral, the rock is stained a reddish brown color. This feature diminishes the value of the rock as a building stone, for structures built of it will invariably show the characteristic but undesirable iron stain. This can be seen in various buildings in the vicinity of the creek on the lake shore road. The rock of this section was formerly quarried and used for constructive purposes, in part at least, on the railroad bridges at North Evans. That the rock had a tendency towards the formation of concretionary masses is indicated by the occurrence of one of these on the under side of the bed, about half way down the section. This mass is cylindrical, three inches in diameter, and lies just below the limestone bed. It is of similar composition, and lies approximately parallel to a joint plain.

Among the more important fossils of the rock *Spirifer sculptilis* (Hall) should be mentioned, a form readily recognized by its few angular plications and the zigzag concentric lamellæ. This species is entirely restricted in this region to the Encrinal limestone, and may be regarded as the typical fossil of the fauna, which is named after it, the Spirifer sculptilis fauna.*

The fauna contains a number of gasteropods not found outside of it, as well as a number of others, (*Platyostoma* (*Diaphorostoma*) *lineata* (Conrad), various species of *Platyceras*, etc.,) which occur both above and below. Trilobites are common and of large size, the predominating form being *Phacops rana* (Green). The pelecypods are few and poorly preserved, but the brachipods are well represented. *Orthis* (*Rhipidomella*) is very common, and so are the *Stropheodontas*. One of the important fossils almost entirely restricted to the bed is *Tropidoleptus carinatus* (Conrad), of which large specimens may be obtained. The little *Vitulina pustulosa* (Hall) and the equally neat *Centronella impressa* (Hall) occur side by side in the upper part of the rock, and have not been noticed outside of it. Another characteristic Terebratuloid is the *Cryptonella planirostra* (Hall), which however is not wholly confined to this rock.

*For a list of the fossils of this fauna see my paper on the "Fauna of the Hamilton Group," etc.

PLATE IX.—View of Section 5, showing the Hamilton shales, with the Demissa bed at the base. Above this appear the Encrinal limestone, the Moscow shales, the projecting Styliolina limestone, the jointed Genesee shales, and in the upper, sloping portion of the bank, the lower Naples (Cashaqua) shales. —Photographed by I. P. BISHOP.

The Lower Shales, or the Hamilton Shales Proper. Only about a foot of these is exposed at the base of Section 5, but this foot of shale contains a large number of interesting fossils. Immediately below the Encrinal limestone the shale is practically barren for a thickness of three or four inches. Even calcareous matter seems to be absent from it, and the shale is soft, light colored and easily cut with a knife. If it is exposed to the atmosphere and the heat of the sun, it hardens, by the evaporation of the water which it contains, but on soaking, it becomes a tenacious mud. This character is due to the leaching out of the calcareous matter by the waters which carried sulphuric acid, derived from the oxidation of the iron sulphide on the under side of the Encrinal limestone. Below this decalcified mass of shale is a bed an inch or less in thickness, which is made up mainly of three classes of fossils, viz: A small, flat, branching bryozoan, *Stictopora incisurata* Hall, a small brachiopod with matted spines all over its exterior, *Nucleospira concinna* Hall and a large number of the joints of crinoid stems. These three forms occur in such numbers, and they are usually so firmly cemented, that the bed becomes a solid limestone. Where it has been exposed for a considerable length of time, the fossils have weathered out completely, so that they may be picked up in a perfect state of preservation. This bed has been called the Stictopora bed. It is the highest true Hamilton bed which has a distinct association of fossils. Throughout it, and in almost every bed below, the typical Hamilton brachiopod *Spirifer mucronatus* (Conrad) occurs. This is frequently furnished with long mucronate points or lateral extensions, and in the Stictopora bed it is represented mainly by the separated valves. The species is practically restricted to the Hamilton shales*, where it is abundant, only a few fragmentary specimens having been obtained from the higher beds. It therefore constitutes the index species of this lower fauna—the Spirifer mucronatus

*It occurs however, in the transition shales of the Marcellus.

fauna, which is by far the richest of any of the faunas of this region.

The most fossiliferous bed in this fauna is the one exposed at the very base of Section 5, about a foot below the Encrinal limestone. This bed has been called the Demissa bed, from the fact that the brachiopod *Stropheodonta demissa* (Conrad) occurs in it in great numbers and is practically restricted to it. It has furnished more than sixty species of fossils, though its total thickness is not over four inches. It may be explored at low water continuously along the base of the cliff, as well as in the shallower portions of the stream below the fall. The occurrence of *Stropheodonta*, especially *S. demissa* (Conrad) and the large *S. concava* Hall, as well as large numbers of *Spirifers*, including the large and robust *S. granulosus* (Conrad), make it conspicuous. This latter species occurs also in considerable numbers in the Encrinal limestone, but it has not been observed in the Moscow shales. It does not occur, at Eighteen Mile Creek, in the shales below the Demissa bed.*

Near the lower end of the section occurs an oblique thrust fault, which has brought up about a foot of the shale underlying the Demissa bed. The shearing plane passes obliquely upwards from left to right,(as seen from the opposite bank). The inclination from the horizontal is 24°, thus giving the fault a hade of 66°. The fault is of interest as indicating a compressive force, the same probably which caused the anticlinal fold at Section 3, and the other thrust faults to be noted later.

Section 6 (C).

PLATE XI.

This section is cut in the left bank of the stream and extends in a general north and south direction. Its height is about sixty-two feet above the stream bed, and its total

*For a list of the fossils in the Demissa bed, see "Faunas of the Hamilton Group," etc. They are all included in the descriptions in Part II.

PLATE X.—View of the "corry" in Section 7, showing an example of gorge cutting in an early stage. The backward cutting of the falls produces the gorge, and the downward cutting of the stream the V-shaped trench seen above. The Encrinal limestone is seen near the middle of the cliff.

—Photographed by A. W. GRABAU.

PLATE XI. (*a*).—View of Section 6, showing four feet of Hamilton shales at the base; the Encrinal limestone, the Moscow shales, the Styliolina band, the Genesee shales and a portion of the Cashaqua shales.

(*b*).—View of the Encrinal limestone of Section 6, showing the undermining of the bed, and the recently fallen blocks. —Photographed by A. W. GRABAU.

length about seven hundred feet. The highest beds exposed are the gray Naples (Cashaqua) shales, which, as usual, contain many concretions. The shale has crumbled under the action of the atmosphere until the whole upper portion of the cliff is soil-covered and overgrown with vegetation. The Genesee shales appear much less prominently in this section than in any of the preceding, nevertheless the characteristic jointed structure of the upper shales appears half way up the bank. The Styliolina limestone projects from the bank, and as usual, forms a prominent line of demarcation between the Middle and Upper Devonian strata of this region. The Moscow shales, seventeen feet thick, form a vertical cliff in some portions of the section. In the main, however, they are more or less covered up by the talus which has accumulated on the shelf formed by the projecting Encrinal limestone. This latter stratum has a thickness of twenty-two inches in this section, and exhibits the same coating of oxidized iron sulphide on the under side, which characterizes its other exposures. The many fallen blocks at the base of the cliff, as well as the dangerously far-projecting portions of the bed in the cliff, testify to the continued activity of the stream in the wearing away of the softer shales beneath. (Plate XI, fig. b). These blocks are collected from this section and used for purposes of construction. Fossils are not so numerous in the bed at this section, as they are at Section 5, nevertheless some very fine specimens of *Actinopteria decussata* Hall have been obtained from it. Corals are common, especially the honeycomb—*Favosites hamiltoniæ* Hall. The average northward rise of the limestone in this section is one foot in forty-seven, giving an approximate southward dip of five degrees. This allows nine feet of the Hamilton shales to be exposed at the lower end of the section, while at the upper end the exposure is only three feet.

Here is the first good opportunity to examine the Hamilton shales in their relation to the overlying limestone, and it becomes at once apparent that the most fossiliferous beds are those near the top of the series, namely the Demissa and Stictopora beds. As the water became purer towards the close of the deposition of the Hamilton shales, the brachiopods, which occurred sparingly during the greater part of the time, underwent a luxuriant development, all the important and characteristic species growing in great profusion. The change of conditions, however, which succeeded, drove out most of them, and when the water became pure enough for the growth of the limestone-building corals and crinoids, a quite distinct assemblage of species appeared. (See further, Chapter III.).

In the lower beds the fossils are scattered, from some, they appear to be entirely absent. Down to about three feet below the Encrinal limestone, the shale contains species such as are found in greater abundance in the Demissa bed. Associated with these is *Athyris spiriferoides* (Eaton), which here reached its last abundant development. Below this, down to about four feet below the Encrinal limestone, fossils are very rare, with the exception of the two species of minute needle-like pteropods, *Styliolina fissurella* (Hall) and *Tentaculites gracilistriatus* Hall, both of which occur in vast numbers on some of the shale laminæ. With them occur several species of minute ostracod crustaceans, among which the *Primitiopsis punctulifera* (Hall) predominates.

Still descending, we find the fossils somewhat more abundant, but in no case do they approach the numerical development found in the Demissa bed. The only constant and abundant species throughout these shales is the type species of the fauna, the broad-winged *Spirifer mucronatus* (Conrad).

Nine feet below the Encrinal limestone, or at the base of the section at its lower end, and forming a portion of the stream bed, is a layer of large, flat calcareous concretions, occasionally united into a continuous bed; but chiefly composed of separate masses. These contain a large number of

PLATE XII.—View of the upper part of Section 7, looking up-stream. The talus covered Hamilton shales appear in the lower part of the cliff. The Encrinal limestone projects above them, and blocks of this have fallen to the foot of the cliff. Near the middle of the bank are seen the Moscow shales, and the Styliolina limestone projecting above. The top of the cliff is formed of the Genesee shales.

—Photographed by I. P. BISHOP.

Athyris spiriferoides (Eaton), all in a perfect state of preservation. The same fossil occurs in the shale between the concretions, and when thus found, it presents its original gibbous character. Above or below this layer, however, this fossil usually occurs in a compressed condition from the settling down of the shale masses on lithifying, thus showing well, how the presence of such concretions in a bed, may protect the fossils from the compression incident upon the lithification of the containing rock. This layer furnishes most of the specimens of this brachiopod, which is nowhere else so characteristic as at Eighteen Mile Creek.

Section 7 (B).

Plates XII and XIII.

This section extends north-west from a point directly north of the northern end of Section 6, to the bridge on which the Lake Shore road crosses the creek. It is cut into the right bank of the stream, and has a total length of about twelve hundred feet. Near the middle of the section a small lateral stream has cut a V-shaped gully down to the Styliolina limestone, over which the water falls in wet weather. Below this is a larger V-shaped recession, a diminutive "corry," which here marks the beginning of a lateral gorge. (Plate X.).

The lower portion of the section is covered by a talus of fine shale particles, derived from both Moscow and Hamilton beds. At the foot of the cliff are large fragments of limestone and shale, with fossils, as well as a debris of foreign material. The difference in the steepness of the bank, between this section and the preceding one, forms an interesting study, the small amount of undercutting in Section 7 being due, as already noted, to the shallowness and width of the stream, which two features combine to dissipate the force of the current, and also to the presence of the large rocks at the foot of the cliff, which act as a barrier to the inroads of the current.

The Upper Devonian strata of this section include several feet of the black Genesee shales, the gray Genesee shales, and the Styliolina band. The Genesee shales are usually talus-covered and overgrown with vegetation. The Styliolina limestone is somewhat more shaly in this section than in the preceding ones, but as usual, projects some distance from the bank. No good opportunity for the study of the Moscow shales is afforded, for they are practically inaccessible. The large cup corals which are common in the talus at the foot of the section are all derived from the coral layer in the lower Moscow shale. They may be seen in place by climbing the bank in the little "corry" near the centre of the section. The Encrinal limestone appears near the middle of the section, forming a prominent band. It rises north-westward at the average amount of one foot in sixty-three, giving an approximate south-easterly dip of less than one degree to the strata.

On the Lake Shore road, at the descent to the bridge from the north, the Encrinal limestone formerly caused a distinct shelf or ridge, which extended across the road. The earlier visitors to the Eighteen Mile Creek sections will remember the distinct bump which the carriage or omnibus, which brought them, experienced in passing over this rock. At the present time the rock has either been taken out or covered over, so that the characteristic bump is no longer experienced.

Where the rocks first become exposed at the upper end of the section, about sixteen feet of the Hamilton shales appear. At the bridge, thirty to thirty-five feet of these shales are exposed, but the lower portion of the cliff is covered by talus. The layer of concretions bearing the *Athyris spiriferoides* (Eaton), first noted in Section 6, appears throughout in this section, remaining at the average distance of nine feet below the Encrinal limestone. From its disintegration, the talus at the foot of the cliff is rich in this fossil, this being the best locality for collecting it. Many specimens will be found

PLATE XIII.—View of Section 7, looking down stream, showing the "corry" on the right. The same strata are seen as in Plate XII.
—Photographed by I. P. BISHOP.

overgrown with delicate Bryozoa and *Aulopora* corals, which furnish an additional incentive for collecting them.

A large number of concretions occur in this lower shale, among which the horn-shaped forms with smooth slicken-sided exterior are characteristic. These are often mistaken for organic remains, chiefly cup corals, and are prized as such by the inexperienced collector. An axis or core of iron pyrites will usually be found as the nucleus of these concre-cretions. Frequently the strata above and below, as well as on the sides, appear crowded out of position, as if by the growth of the concretion. As before noted, however, this crowded appearance is probably due to the settling down of the strata around the resistant body.

A few feet below the layer bearing the *Athyris spiriferoides* (Eaton), pelecypods occur plentifully. A large number of species have been obtained, many of which have not been noticed elsewhere in this region. At the base of the cliff, near the mouth of the "corry" *Liorhynchus multicostus* Hall again occurs in abundance in some concretion bearing beds. Another concretionary layer containing *A. spiriferoides* (Eaton) occurs twenty feet below the Encrinal limestone. Throughout the exposed portion of the shales, fossils occur in considerable number and variety. Brachiopods always predominate, the most abundant being *Spirifer mucronatus* (Conrad). Good specimens of the trilobite *Phacops rana* (Green) are occasionally found; but on the whole, only the smaller species of organisms are abundant. Thus, *Chonetes lepida* Hall, and *Ambocoelia umbonata* (Conrad), as well as the little *Pholidops hamiltoniæ* Hall, are abundantly scattered through the shales. *Liorhynchus multicostus* Hall is common in the lower ten or fifteen feet.

About twenty-five feet below the Encrinal limestone occurs a thin argillo-calcareous bed, less than two inches thick. This contains large numbers of *Modiomorpha subalata* (Conrad), a characteristic Hamilton pelecypod, and one which occurs throughout the lower shales. In this bed, however, it occurs in great abundance, almost to the exclusion of every other form. The bed is not well exposed in this section owing to the talus, but in the east branch of Idlewood Ravine, which mouths in the main gorge below the bridge, it appears both in the bed and banks of the ravine.

Section 8 (A).

PLATE XIV.

This is the lowest section in the gorge, occurring in the left bank and extending from near the mouth of the creek halfway to the bridge. Its total length is not over one thousand feet, and it extends north forty degrees west, by south forty degrees east. Its height is about fifty-six feet above the normal lake level.

Only middle Devonian strata are exposed in this section, the Moscow shales forming the top member. The greater portion of these are exposed near the upper end of the section, but owing to the rise of the strata north-westward, only a few feet occur at the lower end of the section. The Encrinal limestone occurs throughout, and large blocks of it are found at the foot of the section. The lowest bed exposed at the upper end of the section is an argillaceous limestone, which in places becomes shaly, and the total thickness of which is about a foot. This contains very few fossils, *Spirifer mucronatus* (Conrad) and a few pelecypods being the only ones observed. Underlying it are about six feet of shale, which become exposed at the lower end of the section. These contain few fossils, principally *Spirifer mucronatus* (Conrad) and *Phacops rana* (Green). Below them, and exposed only near the lower end of the section are the "Trilobite beds." These are three in number. The upper one is a foot thick, shaly and often fissile, yet sufficiently calcareous to be distinct from the overlying shale. It is very rich in trilobites, though usually the heads and tails alone

PLATE XIV.—View of Section 8, looking down stream. The Trilobite beds appear at the base of the section, near its lower end. The Encrinal limestone projects from the bank near the top. Blocks of Encrinal limestone lie at the foot of the section.

—Photographed by I. P. Bishop.

are common. The thorax, from its jointed condition, is subject to greater destruction, and hence is not commonly preserved. Nevertheless, complete and perfect specimens are occasionally obtained. The trilobite most common in this bed is the ordinary Hamilton species *Phacops rana* (Green), though *Cryphaeus boothi* Green, the form with long spines on both sides of the head, and with fringed tail, also occurs. Other fossils are rare in this bed. Below it, is a somewhat more compact calcareous layer three to four inches thick and rather concretionary. In this layer fossils are rare. Under it occurs the second trilobite layer, eight inches thick and, like the upper one, it is a calcareo-argillaceous, and somewhat arenaceous bed, sometimes becoming quite gritty. This contains more fossils than the upper bed, but the trilobites of both species are the only abundant forms. Below this, and separating it from the lowest trilobite bed—which latter is only exposed at low water at the extreme lower end of the section—are two or three inches of fissile shale, in which *Athyris spiriferoides* (Eaton) is especially abundant. With it occurs a large number of the small cup coral *Streptelasma rectum* Hall, these two, with an occasional specimen of *Spirifer mucronatus* (Conrad), forming the only important fossils of the bed.

Only about six inches of the lowest trilobite bed are exposed, the total thickness of that bed being about a foot. Both species of trilobites are abundant, and good specimens may be easily obtained.

Nowhere in the entire Hamilton group of this region are trilobite remains so abundant. The conditions of the sea must have been particularly favorable for their development at that period, so that their remains became entombed by the thousands. That they were but slowly buried seems to be indicated by the separated portions of the body, a condition probably brought about by long continued maceration before burial. Trilobites probably never lived in very deep water, and both the nature of the rock and the scattered position of the remains indicate shallow water with a distinct current, though with probably a small amount of mechanical sediment.

Several small thrust or reversed faults may be noted in this section. They have mostly affected the trilobite beds, and the calcareous bed six feet above them. The vertical displacement is never more than a few inches, yet the occurrence of these faults in connection with that of Section 5, and another one on the lake shore, present a problem of extreme interest.

GENERAL REMARKS.

At several places in the gorge, gas bubbles up through fissures in the rock. Near the upper end of Section 5, above the falls, bubbles of gas constantly escape from the water. In the gorge above the railroad bridges, opposite the village of North Evans, gas escapes from a fissure in the rock in such quantity as to give a steady flame when lighted. The occurrence of such gas springs has led to the sinking of a well in the gorge near the head of Section 6. The supply of gas thus received has diminished but little during a number of years of steady flow.

The origin of the gas is probably to be sought for in the bituminous shales, some of the springs undoubtedly deriving their supply from the deeply-buried black Marcellus beds. The gas well, however, draws its main supply from Silurian strata, which are tapped several hundred feet below the surface.

The Mouth of the Stream. An interesting problem in the shifting of the mouth of a stream by current and wave action is presented by Eighteen Mile Creek. Running out from the left bank is a long sand bar, which effectually closes the mouth of the gorge, and compels the stream to find its outlet at another point. The bar formerly extended

PLATE XXI.—View of the mouth of Eighteen Mile Creek, the Idlewood Cliff on the right, and the sand bar on the left. (Compare Plate XXII.). —Photographed by I. P. BISHOP.

nearly 2000 feet northward, and the mouth of the stream was shifted to that point. Since then, the stream has broken through the bar at several places, shifting its mouth every season, and leaving partially closed outlets to be filled in subsequently by the waves. The map (Plate II.) represents the temporary conditions which existed in August, 1895. (See also Plate XXI.).

CHAPTER II.

THE GEOLOGY OF THE LAKE SHORE SECTIONS.

All along the lake shore from Eighteen Mile Creek, north to Bay View, and south to the county line, there are numerous exposures of the strata described in the preceding chapter, as well as others which lie above and below these. The exposures are in the cliffs, which, with few exceptions, front the lake, rising sometimes to a height of nearly a hundred feet. The cliffs commonly rise with a vertical face from the beach. Many of them are washed by the waves the year round, and consequently kept in a perpendicular or even overhanging condition, while others experience the cutting of the waves only during storms or in seasons of unusually high water. In this latter case a talus of shale fragments usually accumulates at the foot of the section, and this not infrequently becomes a rich collecting ground for the palaeontologist, for here the weathered out fossils may be found in great numbers, and usually in a perfect state of preservation. The stratigraphist, however, avoids collecting from these natural "dump-heaps," or at least does not attach much stratigraphic value to his collections, for he finds in them a commingling of the fossils of the various beds exposed in the section, a condition which is unfavorable to the proper discrimination between successive faunas.

The sections are by no means of uniform height. This can be best appreciated by the diagrammatic representation of these sections given on Plate V. of the Geological Report of the Fourth District of New York. In this plate Professor Hall gives a semi-pictorial representation of the shore of Lake Erie from Black Rock to Sturgeon Point, with the omission of the eight miles of beach and low swamp-land between Buffalo and Bay View (Comstock's tavern). By reference to this plate it will be seen that the highest cliff is just south of Eighteen Mile Creek, in the first section of the "South Shore Cliffs."

This irregularity in the height of the cliffs, is, of course, produced by erosion, which has swept away the rocks in some places, and left them in others. In general terms, the sections as seen on the lake shore represent a profile of the topography, which was impressed upon the country during long cycles of preglacial erosion. The low drift-filled portions, where no rock is exposed, probably in all cases represent broad valleys cut out by some preglacial stream. Some of the irregularities in height, however, are only apparent, and due to the varying directions in which the sections are cut. To this latter cause must also be attributed the varying dips observed in different parts of the sections, as these sections sometimes extend in the direction of the strike of the strata, or again obliquely across it. In no portion of the sections is the true dip exposed, which, as was noted in Chapter I., is to the south-east.

The shore of Lake Erie presents a succession of crescents, the projecting points usually being headlands of rock, which frequently extend into the water, and so form an obstacle to walking on the beach. Excepting such instances however, the beach is of a character, which allows easy travelling on it. Wherever it is sandy, it is usually much compacted and firm, and will even permit the advantageous use of a bicycle. But when the beach is composed of shingle, as on the more exposed portions of the shore, the case is different, for the pebbles are usually smooth flat shale fragments, which slip over each other, and make walking a rather tiresome undertaking, while the use of a bicycle is impossible.

In the following descriptions of the sections on the Lake Shore, the names applied to them are those by which they are designated in the paper on the "Faunas of the Hamilton Group" of this region, to which the student is referred for many points not here discussed. If access to the volume on the Geology of the Fourth District can be had, a thorough study of the sections as given on Plate V., should be made.

A. The South Shore Cliffs.

Plates XV to XX.

The first of these cliffs extends from the mouth of Eighteen Mile Creek south-westward for a distance of about three miles, beyond which a low and sandy stretch separates it from the next cliff. The northern half of this section, or that portion between Eighteen Mile Creek and Pike Creek, is of the greatest interest to the student, as it includes, besides all the beds found in the lower gorge of Eighteen Mile Creek, a number of interesting structural and dynamic phenomena, which will be described below. This portion of the section comprises several crescents, and as the strata dip at about forty feet to the mile, or approximately one foot in one hundred and thirty,* the appearance of faults is produced, wherever the central portion of the farther crescent is seen directly behind the projecting salient between the two adjacent crescents.

About forty feet of the Hamilton shales are exposed in this section near the mouth of Eighteen Mile Creek. The Trilobite beds would probably be exposed at the base of the section, if the talus were removed. The other beds noted in the Eighteen Mile Creek sections, can be seen in the northern half of this section, when not covered by talus. The shale is full of fossils, mainly brachiopods, among which *Spirifer mucronatus* (Conrad) predominates. The shells may be picked out of the weathered bank with ease, and usually occur with the valves separated, so that specimens showing the muscular impressions and other internal features are among the frequent treasures to be met with in collections from these banks. The talus is especially rich in *Athyris spiriferoides* (Eaton). These are furnished by the disintegrating concretionary layer, nine feet below the

---

*This estimate is based on the fact, that at the mouth of Eighteen Mile Creek, the Encrinal limestone is about forty feet above water level, while at the "uplift," a little over a mile to the south, in a straight line, this rock has reached the level of the lake. The inaccuracy comes from the greater actual length of the section when the curves of the crescents are considered. The dip thus obtained is only the apparent, and not the true dip.

PLATE XV.—View of the first section of the South Shore Cliffs, looking southward from the mouth of Eighteen Mile Creek. The Encrinal limestone appears as a prominent southward dipping band in the cliff. —Photographed by I. P. BISHOP.

Encrinal limestone. Specimens of *Spirifer granulosus* (Conrad) are also common. They are derived from the Demissa bed, which also furnishes the specimens of *Stropheodonta demissa* (Conrad), though these are of less frequent occurrence.

The Encrinal limestone is the most prominent stratum in the bank. It appears for the first time a few hundred feet south of the northern end of the cliff, and gradually descends, until near the middle of the section, at Pike Creek, it passes below the level of the lake. It has the same thickness and character as in the Eighteen Mile Creek sections, and also has the coating of iron sulphide on the under side, which is characteristic of all its outcrops. Professor Hall states that this coating was formerly "wrought to some extent on the supposition that it was silver."*

From the constant wearing away of the soft Hamilton shales, the Encrinal limestone becomes undermined, so that large blocks break off annually and fall to the beach, where they accumulate in considerable numbers. Not infrequently, these blocks of limestone are full of fossils, chiefly corals, some of which stand out in relief through differential solution. They tempt the collector with visions of choice specimens for the cabinet, but he is apt to be disappointed in his attempt to obtain them, unless he has a good hammer, a number of well-tempered chisels, and plenty of time and patience. A sledge hammer is the most desirable tool in such cases. Unless the collector is properly equipped, he had better not attempt the working of this refractory rock, for he is sure to end in spoiling his tools, his temper, and worse than all, the specimens, which he should leave for some one better prepared.

The Moscow shales have much the same character which they exhibit in the Eighteen Mile Creek sections. Their thickness hardly diminishes, and they usually contain a fair proportion of concretions. The coral layer appears in the

*Geol. Rep't, 4th Dist. N. Y., 1843, p. 472.

lower portion of the mass in the same position, and with the same fossils as at Section 5. It alone furnishes the specimens of large *Cyathophylloids* and *Atrypa aspera* Dalman, which are so common in some portions of the talus. The specimens of *Streptelasma rectum* Hall are likewise furnished by beds of the lower Moscow shale.

The Styliolina limestone rapidly thins out towards the south, so that, at the middle of the section, it is scarcely an inch in thickness, being at the same time very shaly. The Genesee shales, in this section, appear in their full thickness, which, according to Professor Hall, is twenty-three feet and seven inches, including the Styliolina band.* The lower portion of this shale is more homogeneous in this section, partaking in color and texture more of the character of the upper beds. The bituminous character of the shale as a whole is strongly marked, plant remains and even coal seams being of not infrequent occurrence. Large masses of the rock are usually found on the beach, and in them the characteristic fossil *Lunulicardium fragile*† Hall, is often found in great numbers. Pyrite grains are scattered throughout the shale in large quantities, and these on oxidizing produce the usual result of thin, iron-stained shale laminae, which frequently have iridescent surfaces.

One of the interesting products of the oxidation of the pyrite, is found in the sulphuretted water, which trickles from the bank at various places. On exposure to the air, the sulphuretted hydrogen, with which the water is charged, is commonly decomposed, (see below) and sulphur is deposited. This is well seen in a small cavernous indentation in the bank, midway between Eighteen Mile and Pike Creeks, where the shale walls are covered with a thin coating of sulphur.

*Rep't 4th Geol. Dist. N. Y., 1843, p. 221.

†This is the *Avicula fragilis* Hall of the Geol. Rep't of the 4th Dist., 1843,

Mr. S. H. Emmens has tabulated the following steps in the oxidation of pyrite.* Part of the sulphur of the pyrite is converted by the oxygen and the moisture of the atmosphere into sulphuric acid, leaving a residue of iron monosulphide. This is then attacked by the sulphuric acid and ferrous sulphate results, while at the same time sulphuretted hydrogen is evolved. The reactions are as follows:†

(*1.*) $Fe\,S_2 + O_3 + H_2O = Fe\,S + H_2S\,O_4$.
(*2.*) $Fe\,S + H_2\,S\,O_4 = Fe\,S\,O_4 + H_2S$.

If the sulphuretted hydrogen comes in contact—as it naturally must in passing through the rock—with oxydizing pyrite, and if, as Emmens holds, sulphurous anhydrite ($S\,O_2$) is formed, together with the sulphuric acid, the hydrogen sulphide will react with the sulphurous anhydrite and form water and free sulphur. The reactions would be tabulated thus:

a. $Fe\,S_2 + O_2 = Fe\,S + S\,O_2$.
b. $S\,O_2 + 2\,H_2S = 2\,H_2O + 3\,S$.

or, as given by Emmens:

(*3.*) $Fe\,S_2 + O_2 + 2\,H_2S = Fe\,S + 2\,H_2O + 3\,S$.

This sulphur may be in part deposited, and in part again oxidized to sulphuric acid, thus:‡

(*4.*) $S + O_3 + H_2O = H_2S\,O_4$

this latter again attacking the monosulphide ($Fe\,S$).

The third and fourth reactions probably do not take place in these shales, the hydrogen sulphide being directly decomposed by the atmosphere, with the formation of sulphur and water, the former being deposited where the oxidation takes place. Thus:

$2\,H_2S + O_2 = 2\,H_2O + S_2$.

The ferrous sulphate will absorb oxygen, and sulphuric acid, if the latter is in excess, and form ferric sulphate, according to the following reactions:§

(*5.*) $2\,Fe\,S\,O_4 + O + H_2S\,O_4 = Fe_2\,(S\,O_4)\,3 + H_2O$

which would be the final result of the oxydation. But if the amount of sulphuric acid is insufficient, or if the ferrous sulphate is carried in solution and spread over the surface of the shales, it will oxidize in part to ferric hydrate or limonite, which stains the shales. The reaction, according to Emmens, is:

$Fe\,S\,O_4 + 6\,O. + H_2O = 4\,Fe_2(S\,O_4)_3 + 2\,Fe_2O_3\,.\,H_2O.$

*Stephen H. Emmens: "The Chemistry of Gossan," Engineering and Mining Journal, Dec. 17, 1892, p. 582.

†‡Emmens, loc. cit.

§Loc. cit.

If lime is present in the shales, this will react with the ferric sulphate to form calcium sulphate and ferric oxide; the latter being insoluble, will be deposited where formed.* The reaction is:

$$Fe_2(SO_4)_3 + 3\,CaCO_3 = 3\,CaSO_4 + Fe_2O_3 + 3\,CO_2.$$

The calcium sulphide will be hydrated and deposited as gypsum, as was noted in some portions of the upper Moscow shales.

The ferrous sulphate may react directly with the calcium carbonate of the shales, giving calcium sulphate and ferric carbonate. The former is hydrated and deposited as gypsum, while the ferrous carbonate is carried off in solution. This may account for the absence of much iron stain on the shales in which the gypsum crystals are formed. Eventually on exposure to the atmosphere, the ferrous carbonate will oxidize to insoluble ferric hydrate, which will be deposited.

Concretions are not uncommon in this shale. They are usually of iron pyrite, or at least have a pyrite nucleus. Occasionally they have a septarian structure, with veins of crystalline calcite, siderite, or more rarely, barite. The gray Naples or Cashaqua shales, appear between the Genesee below, and the black Naples or Gardeau shales above. They are readily recognized by their gray color, the numerous rows of concretions, and the sloping, more or less weathered face which they present. The rocks above and below form perpendicular banks, and consequently whatever vegetation grows on the face of the cliff, is chiefly confined to the portion formed by the Cashaqua shales. The upper (Gardeau) shales, are exposed in the first half mile of the cliff, after which they are absent for a greater distance, the banks decreasing to less than half their original height.

This decrease in height begins at the "uplift," a thrust fault of considerable magnitude, when the general undisturbed character of the strata of this region is taken into consideration. The fault appears in a recession of the bank, which is due to the weakening of the strata by the fault, and consequently the greater readiness with which they succumb to the attack of the waves. The vertical displacement of the

*In this manner shells are often entirely replaced by limonite.

PLATE XVI.—View of the "uplift" in the South Shore Cliffs, a mile and a half south of the mouth of Eighteen Mile Creek. The flexure passes into a fault in the rigid strata. The Moscow shales are shown below, and the much-jointed Genesee shales appear above.
—Photographed by I. P. BISHOP.

strata in this fault, is about four feet*, and the thrust plane passes obliquely upward from right to left. The upper strata, *i. e.* the Genesee, which, with the Hamilton beds are alone involved, are flexed and broken, some portions standing on end, the whole having the appearance of a monoclinal fold. The Moscow shales are much fractured along the shearing plane, and present the characteristic features of the "crushed zone" of such displacements. The Encrinal limestone is completely broken, the right hand portion being raised four feet above the left hand portion. Professor Hall who described and figured this fault†, found striæ on the faces of one of the oblique fissures, a feature not unusual in such displacements. (See Plate XVI.).

The crushed zone has afforded a suitable avenue of escape for the sulphuretted waters from the Genesee shale, and the odor of the sulphuretted hydrogen is very strong near the fault, while deposits of sulphur are not uncommon on the face of the cliff.

Just before reaching the "uplift" the Encrinal limestone descends almost to water level. Beyond the uplift it quickly returns to this level, forming a floor of rock for some distance along the shore, and finally dipping below the water. The coral layer of the lower Moscow shale appears to advantage in this portion of the cliff, numerous large cyathophylloids characterizing it.

From the uplift, to Pike Creek, the bank is low, scarcely rising above thirty feet, and is made up of the Moscow and Genesee shales. At Pike Creek less than half of the Moscow shales is exposed, their final disappearance below the lake level occurring about a quarter of a mile beyond the mouth of that creek.

The mouth of Pike Creek presents an interesting feature, due to the combined wave and stream erosion. The opening

*Hall, Rep't 4th Geol. Dist., 1893, p. 295.
†Loc. cit., p. 295, fig. 141.

in the rock wall is very broad, and in the centre is a mass of shale completely separated from the main bank, and rising like the sea-stacks of the English and Scottish coast from the general platform of rock, which forms the bed of both the stream and the lake. The illustration given below—(Plate XVII.), represents the stack as it appeared in 1888. The dead tree at its further end has long since fallen, through the continued crumbling of the rock, as will be noticed in the photograph reproduced in Plate XVIII. A reference to Plate V. of the Report on the Geology of the 4th District will show that these conditions did not exist in 1843. Only a single mouth is indicated for Pike Creek, which is the opening shown in the right of the illustration (Plate XVII.). The other and smaller one between the stack and the main bank was cut, according to the testimony of the residents, within the last thirty or forty years.

In the ravine of Pike Creek, the Genesee shales alone are exposed, the bed of the stream furnishing a good opportunity for the exploration of these strata. For some distance beyond Pike Creek, the Genesee shales form the top of the cliff. Farther on, the gray Naples (Cashaqua) shales appear again in the cliff, rising to a height of about fifty feet. The Genesee shales disappear below water level about two miles south of the mouth of Eighteen Mile Creek. Before the section comes to an end, the black Naples (Gardeau) shales again make their appearance, the Cashaqua shales dipping below the water near the end of the section.

Several of the projecting points of this portion of the cliff can not be rounded by the pedestrian on the beach, unless he is willing to wade in water sometimes waist-deep. These projecting headlands afford interesting examples of the carving and undercutting action of the waves, which, during storms, hurl pebbles against the foot of the cliff. The smooth, cavernous indentations are excellent illustrations of phenomena frequently noted on a larger scale, on

PLATE XVII.—View of the mouth of Pike Creek in the Spring of 1888. The stack has been separated from the main bank on the left by the stream and wave cutting within very recent times.
—Photographed by H. C. Gram, Jr.

PLATE XVIII.—View of the mouth of Pike Creek in the autumn of 1897, showing the changes produced by sub-ærial denudation. (This view is not taken from the same point as the preceding one). The lower part of the stack consists of the Moscow shales and the upper of the Genesee shales. —Photographed by I. P. BISHOP.

the rocky shore of New England, and the rock bound coasts of other regions.

Beyond the first of these projecting points, another thrust fault of similar character to the "uplift," appears in the bank. As in the case of the latter, this fault passes upward into a monoclinal fold, while the lower strata alone are fractured, portions of them being turned on end.

From the point where the shale appears again in the bank, something over three miles below the mouth of Eighteen Mile Creek, as far as Sturgeon Point, the cliffs are comparatively low, and composed wholly of the black Naples or Gardeau shales. Septaria are common in these shales, and they often reach a large size. One of these which, I observed in the bank some years ago, was perfectly elliptical in outline, its length and thickness being twelve and ten inches respectively. It had been split in two by a joint crack, and the septarian structure was clearly visible. The shale above and below curved around the concretion, this being caused by the settling of the whole mass upon the shrinking of the clay beds during the process of lithification.

Before reaching Sturgeon Point, the shale disappears, and the banks for some distance are composed of sand and clay, with occasional outcrops of the shale near the water's edge. Septaria of great size are common on the beach. At Sturgeon Point the shale appears again in the bank, and is visible for some distance. It is black, highly bituminous, and contains plant and fish remains. The latter are of great interest, and are occasionally found in a very good state of preservation.

The following notes on the fish-remains found up to date at Sturgeon Point, were kindly furnished by Mr. F. K. Mixer, who has for many years studied the fish horizons of this vicinity:

"The first of the remains described from the shales at Sturgeon Point, was the dorso-median plate of a new species of *Dinichthys*, which by its discoverer and describer, Dr. E. N. S. Ringueberg, was named *D. minor*.* This name being pre-occupied, *D. ringuebergi* was substituted for it by Newberry.† In 1886, Dr. Herbert Upham Williams described and figured two new species, both of the genus *Palæoniscus* De Blainville.‡ These were *P. riticulatus* H. U. Williams and *P. antiquus* H. U. Williams. With these were found remains of, probably, *Dinichthys ringuebergi* Newberry (*D. minor* Ringueberg). Since that time a number of remains have come to light from these shales,§ among which the following may be mentioned: 1.—A specimen showing both rami of the mandible of a *Dinichthys*, which may be referred to *D. minor* Newberry with a good deal of reservation, since the terminal portion is completely crushed, and beyond the recognition of the characteristic features. Its size is intermediate between that of *D. minor* Newb. and that of *D. newberryi* Clarke. 2.—A specimen of an undescribed *Dinichthys*, considerably weathered. 3.—A specimen which appears to be the terminal tooth of *D. minor* Newb., but smaller than the usual form. Besides these there are specimens referable to *Mylostoma variabilis* Newberry, *Callognathus serratus* Newberry, and a large scale which appears to belong to a species of *Holoptychius*, but further examination may result in placing it in a new genus. These remains of fishes are not found in any great abundance. They have to be carefully looked for over a considerable area at Sturgeon Point, and they are found most frequently associated with two species of *Lingula*—*L. concentrica* Conr., (probably a variety of *Schizobolus truncatus* Hall) and *L. spatulata* Vanux., with *Goniatites*, *Lepidodendra*, *Calamites* and Conodonts. The larger specimens of fish remains are usually so much weathered, that their identification becomes, if not impossible, yet a matter of extreme difficulty."

Beyond Sturgeon Point the shale disappears again, and unconsolidated material takes its place. In many places the bank is low, and largely composed of sand dunes, in others it is a sand and clay cliff, which bears evidence of being constantly eroded by the waves. Trees and shrubs have slid down the bank, and are now growing from it at all angles.

At "Dibble Point," beyond the mouths of the Sister Creeks, the shales appear again in a low cliff. They vary in color from dark gray to black, and are full of septaria, most of

*Am. Journ. Science, Vol. 27, p. 476, 1884. With figures.

†The Palæozoic Fishes of North America by J. S. Newberry. Mon. XVI., U. S. Geol. Surv., p. 60.

‡Bull. Buff. Soc. Nat. Sciences, Vol. V., No. 2, pp. 81-84; one plate.

§Mainly through the labors of Mr. Mixer himself.

PLATE XIX.—View of the stack at Pike Creek and the cliff beyond. The beach in the foreground consists of "flat gravel," derived from the shale cliffs.

—Photographed by I. P. BISHOP.

PLATE XX.—View of the cliff south of the mouth of Pike Creek. A few feet of the Upper Moscow shales are exposed at the base of the cliff, where they are cut into by the waves. The Genesee and Gray Naples shales form the main portion of the cliff. The beach consists largely of transported material from the drift.

—Photographed by I. P. BISHOP.

which are of gigantic size, individuals six, eight, or even ten feet in diameter being common. Many of them exhibit grotesque imitative forms, and are often taken for prehistoric monsters, which some freak of nature has preserved in all their grotesqueness. These concretions are of similar size to those found in the gorge of Eighteen Mile Creek near the forks, and it is possible that the same bed is represented in both localities. Another small fault occurs in this cliff.

The septarium-strewn beach finally gives way once more to a sandy and pebbly beach, behind which the banks again consist of unconsolidated material, which completely conceals the underlying shale beds.

Beyond Muddy Creek the shales appear again. The bank is at first only eight feet high, but soon rises to the height of thirty feet or more. This is at Harrison's Point, a rocky headland, the base of which is washed by the waves the year round. The cliff beyond, descends perpendicularly to the water, and ordinarily passage along its base is impossible. These conditions continue for some distance, after which the cliffs are again fronted by sand and gravel beaches. Several of the points beyond this, however, project far out into the water, so that ordinarily travel on the beach is impracticable. Near Cattaraugus Creek the banks are low, and for the most part composed of unconsolidated material.

It will be observed that the highest members of the Genesee stage, *i. e.* the Naples (Gardeau) flags, are not exposed in the section along the lake shore. This is due to the fact that the sections extend in a general south-west direction, which does not vary much from the direction of the strike of the strata in this region. Consequently most of the sections exhibit strata having a very low dip, and therefore no great stratigraphic ascent has been made by the time the county line is reached. The flagstones of this stage, as well as the sandstones of the lower Chemung stage (the Portage sandstones) are however, found in the higher south-eastern portions of the county, where they are exposed in ravines and water courses, and uncovered in quarries.

B. The North Shore Cliffs.

North of the mouth of Eighteen Mile Creek, there are five sections, which are of sufficient importance to require separate and detailed descriptions.

THE IDLEWOOD CLIFF.

Plate XXII.

This section extends from the mouth of Eighteen Mile Creek northward to the old drift-filled gorge noted above. The cliff is usually steep, but much weathered, and many places are thickly overgrown by vegetation. The beach at the foot of the cliff is very broad, and the waves ordinarily do not reach the cliff. In consequence, a strong talus has accumulated at the foot of the cliff, thus obscuring many of the lower strata.

At Idlewood, the cliff has a total height of something over sixty feet. At the top, six feet of the Moscow shales are exposed, these therefore, including the whole of the shale bearing the Spirifer consobrinus fauna. If care is taken to collect all the fossils when excavations are made, preparatory to the erection of new cottages, a most complete series of specimens of this fauna may be obtained. The natural exposures in this cliff are such, that the Moscow shales can not be readily examined. The Encrinal limestone is exposed in the cliff at Idlewood, its average thickness being one foot and a half. It may be traced for some distance northward, after which it is not seen again until near the northern end of the next section. The calcareo-argillaceous layer first noticed at the upper end of Section 8 in Eighteen Mile Creek, forms a prominent band on the face of the cliff, ten or twelve feet above the base. About seven feet above it, the Modiomorpha subalata bed is seen, forming a distinct band one inch wide, on the cliff. At the base of the cliff the three

PLATE XXII.—View of Idlewood Cliff and the mouth of the gorge of Eighteen Mile Creek. The Trilobite layers, and the hard bed seven feet above them, are prominent in the cliff. The south shore cliff is shown in the distance, and the sand bar, stretching from it across the mouth of Eighteen Mile Creek, is seen on the right. A foot bridge connects the bar with the Idlewood Cliff. —Photographed by I. P. Bishop.

PLATE XXIII.—View of Wanakah Cliff, looking north. About forty feet of the Hamilton shales are shown at the base, succeeded by the Encrinal limestone, which projects from the bank. The Moscow shales, Styliolina limestone and Genesee shales appear above these. Encrinal limestone blocks occur on the beach.
—Photographed by I. P. BISHOP.

Trilobite beds appear, having all the characters, and the same species of fossils, as those noted in their exposures in the gorge of Eighteen Mile Creek. The lowest bed, not fully exposed there, exhibits its full thickness of one foot in this section. In some places the shale underlying the lowest Trilobite bed is seen, bearing *Athyris spiriferoides* (Eaton), and *Spirifer mucronatus* (Conrad). At the lower end of this section the Trilobite layers appear on the beach, where they form a distinct shelf or platform, at the water's edge.

Altogether this section is not a good one at the present time, though some years ago, when a cutting was made into it for a roadway, it afforded an excellent opportunity for collecting fossils.

WANAKAH CLIFF.

PLATES XXIII AND XXIV.

This cliff begins north of the drift-filled gorge, on the land of Mr. Albert Meyer. It extends northward for about a mile and a half, and terminates in a bluff seventy-five feet high. The northern end of the bluff drops off quite suddenly, and a long stretch of low clay banks, with occasional outcrops of shale on the beach, succeeds this section, and separates it from the next one.

The cliff at the southern end is very low, and much broken. There is considerable accumulation of debris at the base, which has to be removed if the lowest strata are to be examined. The Trilobite beds appear prominently in the bank, the base of the lowest being some eight or ten feet above normal water level. In their total thickness these beds do not differ much from the Eighteen Mile Creek outcrops, but in the subdivisions into shaly and calcareous beds, some variations are observable. The most important strata, however, occur again, *i. e.* the lower bed (one foot thick), and the shale next above, (with *Athyris spiriferoides* (Eaton), and *Streptelasma rectum* Hall). Half way up the bank appears the calcareous layer noted in other sections as lying about six feet above the upper Trilobite bed. This contains many robust specimens of *Spirifer mucronatus* (Conrad), but few other fossils are found. Mr. Albert Meyer has, however, obtained some interesting fish remains from a fragment of rock which probably came from this bed.

About five feet of the shales below the Trilobite beds are exposed. The upper two feet of these are highly fossiliferous. The fossils are mainly brachiopods, of the genera *Spirifer*, *Stropheodonta*, *Rhipidomella*, *Athyris*, *Chonetes*, etc. Below this the shale is less fossiliferous, down to about five feet below the lowest Trilobite bed. Here a hard calcareous layer occurs, an inch or two in thickness, in which fossils are very abundant. The large *Spirifer granulosus* (Conrad), which was found to be characteristic of the Demissa bed, and of the Encrinal limestone, occurs here in considerable numbers. Many other fossils occur with it, among which may be mentioned *Tropidoleptus carinatus* (Conrad), which is almost absent from the shale between this bed and the Encrinal limestone, but is abundant in the latter rock. Less than a foot below this bed is another of similar character, which however, is usually covered by the debris on the beach. In this bed the little Favositoid coral, *Pleurodictyum stylopora* (Eaton) is met with for the first time, this being the highest bed in which the fossil occurs in this region. *Spirifer granulosus* (Conrad) is also common in this bed, and besides these, twenty other species of fossils have been obtained from it. Among them should be mentioned a specimen of *Goniatites uniangularis* Conrad, completely replaced by iron pyrites, as well as a number of specimens of *Orthoceras* similarly replaced. This bed is the upper one of three, in all of which *Pleurodictyum stylopora* (Eaton) is common, and to these beds it is restricted in this region. These strata have, therefore, been named the Pleurodictyum beds,* and will later be described more at length.

*Faunas of the Hamilton Group, etc.

PLATE XXIV.—View of the northern end of Wanakah Cliff. The Hamilton shales, Encrinal limestone, and Moscow shales are shown. The beach on the left is underlain by the Trilobite beds. Erie Cliff appears in the distance. —Photographed by I. P. BISHOP.

In a little ravine near the center of the section, a good opportunity is afforded for the exploration of the Modiomorpha subalata bed, which is twenty-five feet below the Encrinal limestone. This bed appears near the center of the cliff as a well-marked band one inch wide, whence it can be traced in the bank of the ravine, to a little beyond a foot bridge, where the layer produces a small fall or rapid in the bed of the stream. *Modiomorpha subalata* (Conrad) is extremely abundant, while the other fossils in this bed are rare. *M. subalata* occurs in the beds above and below, but nowhere in these shales is it so abundant, or so well preserved. The floor of the old Devonian sea must have been thickly covered with these ancient mussels, which formed a bed similar to those near our modern shores. The Trilobite beds, and the calcareous layer above them, likewise appear in the floor and banks of the little ravine.

Beyond this ravine, the cliff rapidly increases in height, until in its last third, it has a height of seventy-five feet or more. It there forms one of the finest sections anywhere to be seen in this region. The perpendicular face of the cliff, the projecting Encrinal limestone half way up, and the overhanging prismatic blocks of black Genesee shale on top, are the most striking features, and all combine to make the height of the cliff seem greater than it actually is. At the northern end of the section the Trilobite layers appear on the beach, forming a shelf at the water's edge. The middle bed is highly fossiliferous, while the shale just below is full of *Streptelasma rectum* Hall. The apparent northward dip of the Trilobite beds is due to the direction in which the section is cut, which in its lower part is more east and west than north and south.

Large slabs of Encrinal limestone occur on the beach, containing *Heliophyllum confluens* Hall, several species of *Zaphrentis*, and a large number of crinoid stems. *Stropheodonta concava* Hall is also common in the limestone.

ERIE CLIFF.

PLATE XXV.

This section is best approached from Hamburgh-on-the-lake station. To the right of the road which leads from the station to the shore, is Avery's Creek,* a small stream, which has cut several sections in the rock. Near the railroad crossing, the hard layer, six feet above the Trilobite beds, appears in the bank, included by shale above and below. Farther down the stream, the Trilobite layers are exposed in the bed of the stream, where they are the cause of rapids. They contain essentially the same fauna as at Eighteen Mile Creek and the sections on the Lake Shore, except that the trilobites are somewhat less abundant. The beds here are subdivided as follows in descending order:

Argillo-arenaceous limestone	3 inches
Shale with few fossils	3 "
Limestone similar to above	4 "
Fissile shale	8 "
Arenaceous limestone, somewhat shaly and very fossiliferous	12 "
Total	30 inches

In the middle bed the rare trilobite *Homalonotus dekayi* (Green) was found. The two feet of shale next below the Trilobite beds contain a rich fauna, which recalls the fauna of the Demissa bed in the upper Hamilton shales. *Spirifer mucronatus* (Conrad) is very common, and *Athyris spiriferoides* (Eaton), and *Streptelasma rectum* Hall are likewise abundant. *Rhipidomella penelope* Hall is one of the rarer forms found here, *Tropidoleptus carinatus* (Conrad) being another. *Rhipidomella leucosia* Hall and *R. cyclas* Hall are among the forms seldom found above this shale. Altogether more than thirty species of fossils occur, most of which are brachiopods.†

*The stream is named after Mr. Truman G. Avery, the proprietor of the land through which it runs.

†For a list of the fossils obtained from these and the lower beds see the author's paper on the Faunas of the Hamilton Group of Eighteen Mile Creek and vicinity. —Ann. Rept. State Geol. N. Y. 1896.

PLATE XXV.—View of the mouth of Avery's Creek, and a part of Erie Cliff. Only the Transition shales of the Upper Marcellus are shown.
—Photographed by I. P. BISHOP.

Below this shale occurs a hard calcareous layer less than an inch in thickness. This is especially rich in bryozoans, which sometimes make up the bed. The shale below this bed is less fossiliferous and fissile than that above. About a dozen species of fossils occur, but all of them are rare. Among them is *Homalonotus dekayi* (Green).

About four feet below the Trilobite layers is another hard calcareous layer, something over an inch in thickness. This is full of fossils, among which *Spirifer granulosus* (Conr.) predominates. It corresponds to the layer noted in a similar position at the upper end of Wannakah Cliff.

Less than a foot below this calcareous layer, or about five feet below the Trilobite beds, appears the first or upper Pleurodictyum bed. The second and third are immediately below it, all of them being exposed in the bed of the stream, beyond the last bend, or not very far from Mr. Avery's barn. None of the beds have a very great thickness, the lowest and thickest not exceeding four inches. As already noted, the little coral *Pleurodictyum stylopora* (Eaton) is wholly restricted to them, and occurs in great numbers, being especially common in the middle one of the three beds. With it occurs *Spirifer granulosus* (Conrad), which is frequently overgrown with bryozoa and corals.

Altogether these are the richest beds in the lower Hamilton shales, holding the relation to the lower portion of these shales which the Demissa bed holds to the upper portion. Their chief interest lies in the presence of *Pleurodictyum stylopora* (Eaton), which is thus seen to be entirely restricted to the lower portion of the Hamilton shales of this region. The lowest of the three beds is of further interest, as it contains besides the *Pleurodictyum*, two other fossils, which are not found outside of it.* These are *Nautilus magister* Hall and *Ambocoelia umbonata* var.

*It should be noted, however, that the second of these, *Ambocoelia umbonata* var. *nana* Grabau, has been noticed in the bed just below, the few specimens found, however, differed considerably from the normal characters of the variety.

nana Grabau (var.). The *Nautilus* is of especial interest from the large size of the specimens obtained, which often measure six or eight inches in greatest diameter. The specimens occur in the concretionary masses of which this bed is composed, and from the nature of the rock and the brittleness of the fossils, great care is needed in freeing them from the matrix. This is by far the largest and finest fossil found in the region, and its restriction to this, the lowest bed of the Hamilton shales proper, is of great interest. This bed has therefore been named the Nautilus bed.* It was from this bed that the original specimens described and figured in Volume V. of the Palaeontology of New York, were obtained, and so far as known, this species has not been found elsewhere.

Ambocoelia umbonata var. *nana* is a small representative of the species, the brachial valve differing in its greater convexity and its general resemblance to that of *Spirifer subumbonus* Hall. The proportions differ from the normal for the species, and the surface is marked by numerous elongated pits, as in *A. spinosa* Clarke. This variety occurs in great numbers, and characterizes the rock where-ever found.

Another fossil which is practically restricted to this bed, and which occurs in great numbers, associated with the preceding, is *Camarotoechia dotis* Hall. These shells are usually found in an excellent state of preservation, and where differential weathering has left them in relief, details of structure appear clearly. Sometimes the rock is made up of these shells and the little *Ambocoelia*, and in such instances it is a comparatively pure limestone, though ordinarily it partakes more of the nature of a calcareous claystone. Other fossils are extremely rare, and occur mainly in the shaly portions of the bed.

*Faunas of the Hamilton Group, etc.

The position of this bed is about seven feet below the base of the lowest Trilobite bed, and its outcrop in the ravine is almost opposite Mr. Avery's barn.

The Transition Beds. With the Nautilus bed the base of the Hamilton shales is reached. Underlying it are thirty feet of shales which contain a mixed Hamilton and Marcellus fauna, and they are therefore regarded as transition beds between the Marcellus and Hamilton. The shales are capped by a bed of somewhat arenaceous limestone, six inches in thickness and very fossiliferous. This bed lies immediately below the lower Pleurodictyum or Nautilus bed, its position being about fifty feet below the base of the Encrinal limestone. It forms the top of the fall in the ravine just below the bridge on which the Lake-shore turnpike crosses. Here the bed is full of *Orthoceras* (*O. exile* Hall) and of gastropods (*Bellerophon leda* Hall, *Loxonema hamiltoniæ* Hall and *L. delphicola* Hall). The small productoid brachiopod with the truncated beak—*Strophalosia truncata* Hall—is the most abundant fossil in this bed, and as it seldom occurs outside it in this region, it becomes a convenient form from which to name the bed. The name Strophalosia bed has been adopted for it,* this name at the same time indicating the geological position of the bed, since the *Strophalosia truncata* Hall is a characteristic Marcellus fossil.† The Strophalosia bed appears in the cliff both above and below the mouth of Avery's Creek. Passing southward, we find, after crossing the mouth of a second small ravine, which opens near Avery's Creek, that the cliff has a height of only twenty feet or thereabouts, and is entirely made up of the transition shales, which also form the walls of the ravine of Avery's Creek below the falls. Several layers of concretions occur in these shales, but fossils

*Faunas of the Hamilton Group, etc.

†This is the bed lettered (a) on Plate V. of the Report on the Fourth Geological District by Professor James Hall. The position of Avery's Creek is there indicated by the depression marked "13 miles from Black Rock." The bed is referred to on pp. 190 and 191 of that report, where it is spoken of as the westward extension of the "thick mass of sandy shale, so abounding in conchiferous molluska in the eastern part of the State, ... which in the central part is still in great force."

as a rule are rare. *Spirifer mucronatus* (Conr.) occurs in the upper portion, and with it a number of other Hamilton fossils, all of which, however, have been found in true Marcellus shales. Lower down, the characteristic Marcellus and Genesee pelecypod *Lunulicardium fragile* Hall appears, and with it its constant associate, the minute pteropod *Styliolina fissurella* (Hall). The eminently characteristic Marcellus fossil *Liorhynchus limitaris* (Conr.) is sparingly represented in the lowest beds. Some little distance below the mouth of Avery's Creek, the Strophalosia bed appears in the bank again, and with it the overlying lower Pleurodictyum or Nautilus bed. Both beds gently descend towards the south, until near the end of the section, they pass below the lake level.

This portion of the cliff affords a good opportunity for collecting the fossils from these beds, especially the *Nautilus magister* Hall. Specimens of the latter were formerly obtained in numbers on the beach at the foot of the cliff, and the supply is probably still a fairly good one.

North of the mouth of Avery's Creek the cliff rises to a height of something over thirty feet, a portion of it projecting out into the water, so that one can not pass along the beach for any distance. At the northern end of the section, however, one can descend in a dry ravine* to the beach, and walk southward along the beach to the projecting point. The Strophalosia and Nautilus beds are seen everywhere in the section near the top of the cliff, forming together a band about a foot in thickness. The beach is strewn with the fragments of these beds which have fallen from above, and a good collection of the specimens may be obtained with little labor. *Pleurodictyum* is especially abundant, the specimens usually being free from the matrix. The cliffs are very picturesque, and present good examples of wave and frost erosion. All the lower portion of the cliff consist

*Marked "Davis" on Plate V. of the Geol. Rep't 4th District, 1843.

PLATE XXVI.—View of the north end of Athol Springs Cliff, showing the Transition and the Upper Marcellus shales, traversed by two sets of parallel joints.
—Photographed by I. P. Bishop.

of the Transition shales, in the upper part of which, Hamilton species predominate, while the lower portion contains mainly Marcellus species.

ATHOL SPRINGS CLIFF.

PLATE XXVI.

This cliff extends from the dry ravine, which runs to the lake-shore from Lake-side Cemetery Station, to the Fresh-Air-Mission Hospital at Athol Springs. In the ravine few exposures are found, but some outcrops of the Trilobite and Pleurodictyum beds occur. In the cliff, for some distance above the ravine, the Strophalosia bed appears near the top of the section; but the overlying beds are too much obscured by talus and vegetation, to be visible. The whole of the Transition shales appear below the Strophalosia bed.

The Upper Marcellus Shales.—The Transition shales are limited below by a hard layer, containing an enormous number of pteropods, chiefly of the two species *Styliolina fissurella* (Hall) and *Tentaculites gracilistriatus* Hall. The two species appear very much alike on the rock, owing to the fact that both exhibit the longitudinal "fissure" due to compression. *Tentaculites* however, as noted before, is readily distinguished on close inspection, from *Styliolina* by the raised annulations. Where the surface of the rock has weathered, the pteropods appear in vast numbers, and in great perfection. This layer appears for the first time on the beach about the center of the section. It rises northward, until near the Hospital it forms the top of the cliff, which here has a height of from fifteen to twenty feet. At this point the cliff projects into the water, and in climbing over it, an opportunity is afforded for the examination of the pteropod-bearing bed. This bed marks the top of the Marcellus shales in this cliff. The shales below it contain only characteristic Marcellus fossils. The predominating species are: *Tentaculites gracilistriatus* Hall, *Styliolina fissurella* (Hall), *Lunulicardium fragile* Hall, and *Liorhyn-*

chus limitaris (Conrad). Several other species occur, but on the whole fossils are rare, and a day's search may furnish only a very meagre collection. A small specimen of *Nautilus marcellensis* (Vanux.) was found in the Pteropod bed. This fossil has heretofore been known only from the Goniatite limestone, between the lower and upper Marcellus of Central New York.

About six feet below the top of the Marcellus, occurs a hard layer, about two inches thick, containing *Ambocoelia umbonata* (Conrad) in considerable numbers. This bed appears about ten feet above the water in the cliff behind the Hospital. In the shale below it, carbonized plant remains occur occasionally. The cliff is succeeded by a long stretch of low, sandy shore, with no rock outcrops.

BAY VIEW CLIFF.

PLATE XXVII.

This cliff extends southward for about two thousand feet from the Bay View House (formerly Comstock's tavern). The cliff, where highest, does not exceed fifteen feet in height, while the greater portion is much lower. The outline of the cliff is a zigzag one, this being due to the two sets of joint cracks, which traverse the rock, and intersect at nearly right angles. The Marcellus shales alone are exposed in this cliff, and fossils are few, consisting chiefly of the pteropods *Styliolina fissurella* (Hall) and *Tentaculites gracilistriatus* Hall. *Lunulicardium fragile* Hall and *Chonetes lepida* Hall, are occasionally found. *Chonetes mucronata* Hall, and a few other Marcellus species also occur.

At the southern end of the section, the hard layer with *Ambocoelia umbonata* (Conrad) appears about ten feet above the water. It is here two inches thick. Six inches above, is a similar layer one inch thick, the two appearing as prominent bands wherever the section is fresh.

A little to the north of the Bay View House, the shale disappears, and the beach from this point to the Niagara

PLATE XXVII.—View of Bay View Cliff, showing the jointed Marcellus shales, overlain by glacial detrilus.
—Photographed by I. P. Bishop.

River, a distance of about eight miles, is low and sandy. The country for some distance back from the lake, is low, level farm or swamp land. The shale appears in the bed of Smoke's Creek, near West Seneca, containing *Liorhynchus limitaris* (Conr.). The exposure is about a mile and a half from the shore, and its consideration does not properly belong here.

General Summary of the Lake Shore Sections.—Taking a general view of the lake shore cliffs, we notice that they furnish a continuous section from the Marcellus to the upper Naples shales. Of the former, less than twenty feet are exposed, these representing the upper olive shales of the formation. The greatest thickness of the Marcellus in Western New York, according to Professor Hall, is not over fifty feet.* The thickness of the rock in Erie County is probably somewhat less.

Resting on the Marcellus shales, are the thirty feet of Transition rock, terminated by the Strophalosia bed. These are by some included in the Hamilton stage, but their relation is probably more with the Marcellus, and they are here placed with the latter. The whole thickness of the Lower or Hamilton shales—about fifty feet—is exposed, beginning with the Nautilus bed.

The noteworthy beds included in the Hamilton shales are as follows: First, at the base, the three Pleurodictyum beds, (the lowest of which is the Nautilus bed). Second, the three Trilobite beds, beginning between nine and ten feet from the base. Third, the lithologically similar bed, six feet above these, or eighteen feet from the base, (noteworthy mainly on account of its persistence). Fourth, the Modiomorpha subalata bed, twenty-five feet from the base. Fifth, the Athyris spiriferoides layer forty-one feet from the base. Sixth and seventh, the Demissa and Stictopora beds, between four inches and a foot from the top.

---

*Rep't 4th Geol. Dist. 1843, p. 179.

The Encrinal limestone, eighteen inches to two feet thick, is well exposed. The whole of the Upper or Moscow shales (seventeen feet) are exposed. The divisions into lower Moscow (shales bearing the Spirifer consobrinus fauna), middle Moscow (barren shales), and upper Moscow (shales bearing the Spirifer tullius fauna), are retained throughout.

The whole of the Genesee shales—twenty-three feet and seven inches thick (Hall), are exposed, beginning at the base with the Styliolina layer. The subdivision into lower gray and upper black shales is not as marked, as in the gorge of Eighteen Mile Creek. The whole thickness of the gray Naples or Cashaqua shales is exposed, this, according to Hall being thirty-three feet. Probably less than one hundred feet of the upper Naples or Gardeau shales are exposed in these sections, the lower half of which consist of black and fissile shales, while the upper, remaining exposed portion, consists of alternations of olive and gray or black shales, with septaria in the lighter colored beds.

This may be tabulated as follows:

UPPER DEVONIAN (CHEMUNG GROUP).	CHEMUNG STAGE.	Not exposed.
	GENESEE STAGE.	Naples shales { Gardeau.......100 ft. (estimated). Naples shales { Cashaqua.... 33 " (Hall). Genesee shales and Styliolina limestone...... 23.5 " (Hall).
MIDDLE DEVONIAN (HAMILTON GROUP).	HAMILTON STAGE.	Moscow shales.................... 17 ft. Encrinal limestone.............. 1.5 " Hamilton shales.................. 50 "
	MARCELLUS STAGE.	Transition shales................ 30 ft. Upper Marcellus shales....... 20 " (exposed.) Lower Marcellus, (not exposed).
		Total, . . . 275 feet.

CHAPTER III.

SEQUENCE OF GEOLOGICAL EVENTS.

Let us picture to ourselves the succession of the geological events which occurred in this region since Lower Devonian times.

The Lower Devonian in this part of the country was a limestone making age, when the pure, and presumably warm waters of the great interior Palæozoic sea, which stretched from the Adirondacks to the Rocky Mountains, was inhabited by corals, crinoids, and other pure water animals. Miles upon miles of coral reefs stretched across what is now the State of New York, and westward to the Mississippi River, and beyond. All that portion of the "vast American Mediterranean Sea," as Dana has called it, was inhabited by myriads of coral-building polyps, which constructed a reef, comparable to the Great Barrier Reef of Australia. This ancient reef was a barrier reef for the Devonian continent of North America, which lay to the north, and which consisted of the old Archæan lands, with the additions made during Cambrian, Ordovician and Silurian times.

This ancient coral reef now constitutes the Corniferous limestone, which can be traced from Buffalo eastward nearly to the Hudson River, and westward into Missouri and Iowa, with a northern spur running up into the peninsula of Michigan. Northern Illinois and Wisconsin, at that time, seem to have been above water. (Dana). Similar coral reefs were forming in the seas which covered portions of New England and Canada.

Dull-colored and unattractive as these ancient coral reefs may seem to-day to the ordinary observer, they nevertheless had beauty once, beauty comparable, if not superior, to that seen in existing coral reefs.* The visitor to the Bahamas, who looks through his water-glass at these marine flower-gardens, can form some conception of the beauty which once existed in the coral reefs of the Devonian Sea. He sees to-day the large coral masses, consisting of huge brain corals, multicolored Astræans and branching Madrepores, whose surfaces are covered with myriads of tiny polyps; and, waving over all, the graceful Gorgonias, the sea-whips and sea-fans, as they are so aptly called. Then let him be transported back, in imagination, some millions of years, to the coral reefs which then grew where now are some of the most important states of the Union. The Mæandrinas and Astræans were then represented by large heads of *Favosites*, which grew sometimes in such abundance that their remains constitute a large portion of the reef. The Madrepores and other branching corals were not represented, but in their stead grew multitudes of cup-corals, chiefly single, horn-like or funnel-like structures, not infrequently a foot in length, and supporting at their growing ends, polyps, which rivalled in size the modern sea-anemones of our coast. And beauty of color there probably was, as well as beauty of form, though only the latter is suggested in the remains. Waving over the bottom in place of the modern Gorgonia fronds, were those graceful and remarkable creatures, the crinoids, whose modern representatives, dredged principally in tropical seas, are objects of exquisite beauty. Swaying on their stems, with their much-divided arms outspread, flower-like, they must have presented a striking spectacle. In modern tropical waters, the multicolored fishes swimming in and out among the gorgeous coral masses, quickly attract the attention of the observer. There were fishes in the Devonian seas, but they were strange, uncouth creatures, predaceous

*Some conception of the luxurience of life and wealth of form in coral reefs can be obtained from an inspection of Mr. W. Saville Kent's photographs of living corals, reproduced in his book on the "Great Barrier Reef of Australia." The coloring is absent from these plates, but as far as the character of the corals and their association in the reefs are concerned, the plates are superb, and next to seeing the reef itself, the student can do no better than to study these photographs carefully. The coloring is reproduced in the chromo-lithographs appended to the volume. The student will also be surprised to find how universally the corals are exposed at low tide, a condition which one would ordinarily regard as fatal to the animals.

sharks and plate-covered ganoids, which probably had no great beauty of color. Their strange forms, however, and their frequently formidable size, made up for their lack of coloration, and they probably were among the most striking tenants of those waters. Shells were by no means uncommon, and though many of the modern brachiopods are dull-colored, it is highly probable that some, at least, of the many Corniferous species, showed tints approximating those of tropical gastropods and lamellibranches of the present day.

Thus, shut off from the destructive forces of the outer ocean by the Devonian land, which then existed to the east and south-east, this great interior sea was peopled with a multitude of organic forms, and the luxuriance of the life can only be imagined from the results which have been left behind. It is an interesting fact that this great Devonian coral reef seems to have been absent from Pennsylvania and the Southern States, and it is possible that this is due to the fact, that the water at that time was deeper over this area. For it is now generally recognized that corals flourish best in comparatively shallow water, and limestones are no longer regarded as necessarily of deep water origin. It is highly probable that the great Corniferous coral reef was built in shallow water, far enough away from land to be out of reach of the sediment carried down by streams. The reef probably grew southward, where the breakers, rolling in from the open ocean on the south-west, supplied pure water and ample nourishment for the polyps and other organisms.

How long these conditions continued, is difficult to say. That the time occupied for the growth and accumulation of the Corniferous coral reef was equal in length to that occupied in the accumulation of the much thicker shales succeeding it, will appear, when it is remembered that five to ten feet of fragmental rocks will accumulate during the time required for the formation of one foot of limestone.* We

*Dana, Man. Geol.

may place the time anywhere from a few hundred thousand to a million years or more. Eventually, however, the period came to an end, and the crinoids, corals, and other evidences of pure water disappeared. The limestone areas were invaded by mud-bearing currents, which apparently caused the local extinction of the reef-building corals. Thus we find, at the opening of the Hamilton period, that in place of the former wealth and beauty of the coral reef, organic life presents a more sombre tone.

The cause of this change in sedimentation was the shoaling of the water, so that extensive areas, formerly covered by the sea, became dry land, while other areas were converted into great mud-flats, laid bare at low tide. With the shoaling of the water, the influx of abundant fresh water from the land was probably combined, so that these shallower portions of the sea became fresh or brackish, rather than salt. We have here an approximation to the conditions which later gave rise to the extensive coal-swamps, and the black shales may be regarded as partial attempts at coal-making. As Professor William B. Rogers once said: "Nature tried her hand at coal-making during these epochs."

If we wish to gain a conception of these regions as they appeared after the beginning of the Middle Devonian period, we need only look at the extensive mud flats, which are laid bare at low tide on our shores, and notice the black carbonaceous mud, in which mussels and periwinkles lie buried by the thousands, waiting for the returning tide to restore them to activity. Some such conditions prevailed at the opening of the Mesodevonian period over all this region. Coarse sediment was absent, suggesting feeble currents in the shallow waters. Only fine silt and mud was spread out by the tidal currents, and the vegetation on these mud flats was slowly buried, and underwent a partial decay. Occasionally somewhat more gritty sediments were carried in, and at such times the pelecypods (*Lunulicardium fragile*, *Actinopteria muricata*, etc.) seem to have flourished in great numbers. The black carbonaceous muds hardened to form the black, bituminous, Marcellus shales, which immediately overlie the Corniferous limestone.* These shales, in many places, are full of fossils, chiefly brachiopods and pelecypods, indicating that these ancient mud-flats had their tenants similar to the mud-flats on the modern sea-coast. Streaks of coaly matter show how abundant was the vegetation, which, by its incomplete decay, gave rise to the bituminous matter in these shales.

During the Marcellus (Minuta) epoch, there were several minor oscillations, which, however, as their record is not revealed in any of the sections discussed in the preceding chapters, will be passed over. It may simply be remarked that after the accumulation of a number of feet of the black shale, more calcareous shales were formed, indicating the deepening of the water. Deeper water conditions were finally established towards the close of the Marcellus (Minuta) epoch, as recorded in the first sections on the lake shore. The pure water of the Corniferous (Acuminatus) epoch, however, was not re-established until very much later, and then only over limited areas.

In our own region, as the waters became deeper and purer, new forms of life appeared, probably through immigration from other regions where they originated. In the gradual appearance of these species in the Transition shales, we have recorded the long struggle to which the new-comers were subjected before they finally became established. By the time that the thirty feet of Transition shales had accumulated above the Marcellus beds, the water had become pure enough for the sudden development or immigration of the fauna of the Strophalosia bed. Silt and gritty material were still carried in, and constitute a large proportion of the material in the bed, but there was no longer any paucity of living forms. *Strophalosia*, *Bellerophon*, *Loxonema* and *Orthoceras* flourished in great numbers, and their shells

*These can be well seen in the beds of Cayuga and other creeks.

constituted a large proportion of the accumulation formed. These conditions, however, did not continue very long, for this fauna was soon driven out and replaced by the first of the true Hamilton faunas, which began with the development of corals, brachiopods, and large Nautili. It thus appears that the change from the Marcellus to the Hamilton conditions was a slow and gradual one, consisting in the deepening and purification of the water. Hamilton species gradually appeared, and although the change from the Strophalosia bed to the Nautilus bed is an abrupt one, the way for this change was being prepared during the long preceding ages. Not so, however, at the beginning of the Mesodevonian period, for the change from the Corniferous coral reef to the Marcellus mud-flats was sudden, resulting in the extinction of numerous forms of life, many of which disappeared forever. What became of the fauna of the Strophalosia bed at the opening of the Hamilton (Spiriferoides) epoch, is not known. The survivors probably migrated eastward, where the conditions continued more favorable.

At the commencement of the Middle Devonian period, the character of the sea-bottom, and the relative depth of the ocean, became more varied. In the west, owing probably to the absence of coincident subsidence and deposition, the conditions continued to remain uniform into the Upper Devonian. In the extreme east, however, subsidence went on at a uniform and continuous rate. This accounts for the fact that the beds are much thicker in the eastern portion of the State of New York than they are on Lake Erie or westward. For thick beds of fragmental material can not accumulate unless there is coincident subsidence, the sea floor sinking at a uniform rate, and thus making room for the material constantly brought in by the streams. While, however, the subsidence was greater in its totality and more continuous in the east, than in the west, it was more sudden in the Erie County region, so that, at the opening of the Hamilton period, the water over the present Erie County was deeper and purer than it was in the region of the present Genesee valley, where the Marcellus conditions continued into, and through the Lower Hamilton time. Farther east, *i. e.* nearer to the source of supply of the fragmental material, the water was still shallower and sands accumulated, the increase in the coarseness of which, was proportionate to their nearness to the old shore-line. It is an interesting fact, that in these near-shore formations we have a littoral fauna, consisting mainly of gastropods and pelecypods, brachiopods, which are the predominating forms in the deeper western waters, being almost entirely absent.

When we compare the fauna of the Hamilton shales in the region about Eighteen Mile Creek with that of the corresponding shales in the Genesee Valley, we will be impressed by the numerical preponderance, in species and individuals, of the life in the more western area. This indicates more favorable conditions in the Eighteen Mile Creek region, and consequently a greater luxuriance of life. The subsidence of fifty feet which occurred in this region during the deposition of the Hamilton shales was not uniform throughout, as is indicated by the alternations of coarser and finer material, and to some extent also by the variation of the faunas, and the fluctuation in the number of fossils in the various beds. That these local topographic faunas were influenced by local topographic changes, will be conceded, even though the precise changes can not be determined, just as the changes on modern shores can not always be determined, though their effects in the disappearance or reappearance of faunas may be quite marked. It is certain that many species, which flourished at the beginning of the Hamilton epoch, soon disappeared, and did not again occupy this region. An example is the great *Nautilus magister*, which flourished at the opening of the Hamilton epoch, but the remains of which are only found in the lowest true Hamilton bed, showing that the species disappeared at the end of the time occupied in the formation of that bed. The species associated with *Nautilus magister*, practically shared its fate, none of the characteristic forms of the Nautilus bed appearing in any higher horizon, with the exception of *Pleurodictyum stylopora*, and perhaps a few straggling individuals of *Camarotoechia dotis*. *Pleurodictyum stylopora* is another example of a species which became extinct in this region shortly after the opening of the Hamilton conditions, in the early times of which it flourished in great numbers.* Many of the species which lived at the beginning of the Hamilton epoch in this region, (many of which had undoubtedly immigrated from other localities) disappeared after the cessation of conditions favorable to their existence. While the mature individuals died, their more adaptable offspring migrated by successive stages, and finally became established in other localities. Towards the close of the Hamilton epoch, however, when the conditions favorable to the existence of the species again appeared, the species slowly returned. We find, therefore, the upper beds of the Hamilton shales, *i. e.* the Demissa and Stictopora beds, filled with species which are common in the Pleurodictyum beds and the shales just above.

It is not to be presumed, that during the time-interval which elapsed between the deposition of the lower and upper Hamilton beds, the migrated faunas made no attempt to return. The fact that such attempts were actually made seems to be indicated by the few straggling representatives of these faunas, such as *Tropidoleptus carinatus* and others, which occur at intervals in the beds overlying those in which they make their first appearance. But while a few individuals may have existed, the species never multiplied, until the time when the associated species which existed side by side with it during the earlier ages, returned. The causes for this may have been manifold, such as lack of proper food,

*It must be noted, however, that this species occurs in higher horizons farther east, and this may indicate an eastward migration after the conditions had become unfavorable in the west. On the other hand the eastern representatives of this species in the Moscow shale may have come from the same favorable locality from which the western forms had migrated at the opening of the Hamilton epoch, the species becoming entirely extinct in this region at the end of that time.

insufficiency of calcareous material in the water, increased or diminished depth or temperature, unfavorable currents, or other injurious physical conditions. The existence of other creatures, which preyed upon the species, may also have been the cause of the paucity of individuals. In this latter case the reappearance of the species in great numbers in the later beds, may have been due to reinforcement of the survivors from without, by the immigration of numerous individuals, so that by sheer force of number they survived the wholesale destruction, which formerly kept them down.

The sequence of changes during the continuance of the early Hamilton epoch was something as follows: The epoch opened with the formation of the Nautilus bed, the water being comparatively pure and free from coarse sediment. On the floor of the shallow ocean, grew millions of tiny brachiopods, which in places were closely packed, growing over and on each other and making clusters, in appearance recalling those of our modern mussel beds. Over these beds crawled the great Nautili, with their coiled and probably highly-colored shells. Brachiopods probably formed the food of these creatures, though many soft-bodied and shellless animals undoubtedly existed, of which no trace has been preserved. Here and there may have appeared a Nautilus floating on the surface or swimming vigorously to escape some hungry shark, which had wandered into the region. Scattered over the sea floor among the brachiopods were the tiny coral heads of the *Pleurodictyum*, the polyps probably with brilliant colors. Trilobites crawled about, but they were not very common. Gastropods likewise occurred, as well as a few pteropods, but pelecypods seem to have been absent altogether. With the beginnig of the second Pleurodictyum bed the conditions changed. The Nautilus became extinct, the waters probably shoaled somewhat, and brachiopods continued to increase in number and variety, the earlier species, however, having disappeared. Bryozoa began to grow, and often formed large fronds, while gastropods and pelecypods became common. The *Pleurodictyum* still continued to exist in great numbers for some time, but finally it too disappeared. After that, the sea was peopled chiefly by brachiopods and bryozoa, while trilobites continued to increase in number. Before long, a rich brachiopod fauna had developed, and the deposition of the sediment went on at a somewhat accelerated pace. Another change occurred, and the rich brachiopod fauna disappeared. With this was brought to a close the deposition of the fossiliferous shales underlying the Trilobite beds. Then came a time of more shallow water, when gritty sediments were deposited along with the lime and mud. Here trilobites found conditions more favorable to their existence, and for a long time they continued to people the waters in great numbers. Occasionally they were kept down for a time, by unfavorable changes, and in their stead, other forms, such as *Athyris* and *Streptelasma* flourished. Eventually, however, they regained their vitality and again increased rapidly.

Then there came a time when the muddy waters allowed but little development of life, so that the shales succeeding the Trilobite beds are comparatively barren. When, however, the conditions recurred which favored the great development of the trilobites, these latter did not return. Probably by this time the great Placoderms had found their way into these waters in considerable numbers, and to them may be due the destruction of the trilobites. It is known from the specimen (before referred to) discovered by Mr. Myer, that these fishes were present at that time, and as they were ground feeders, the supposition lies near that they preyed upon the crawling trilobites and other bottom forms, and thus kept the water comparatively free from invertebrate life.

For a long time after this, animal life was scarce in the Hamilton sea of this region, brachiopods alone occurring in anything like abundance. Then came the arrival of numberless mussels (*Modiomorpha*), which at once began to settle down and appropriate the ground for themselves. These new-comers may have appeared from without, or they may indicate the sudden increase in numbers of the few forms which existed during the preceding ages. In any case, their development was rapid and complete, and so was their extermination. Thus was formed the mussel-bed which now appears in the sections twenty-five feet below the Encrinal limestone. After the mussels had virtually disappeared, except for a few stragglers, which remained on the scene of their former occupancy, brachiopods once more appeared in numbers, and continued thus for a very long period of time. At one time numberless individuals of *Athyris spiriferoides* appeared on the scene, and their appearance seems to have driven out most of the other forms of life, as recorded in the Athyris spiriferoides bed. Later, however, these returned again, but before they finally re-established themselves, some unexplained changes took place, which temporarily established conditions similar to those which prevailed during the later Marcellus epoch. The two pteropods, *Styliolina fissurella* and *Tentaculites gracilistriatus*, became the sole occupants of the water, and as they probably were pelagic animals, their occurrence in these shales may be explained by the assumption of the existence of currents, which carried them in from the open sea.

At last, when the Hamilton age was near its end, the rich fauna of the Demissa bed appeared. This sudden development of forms, many of them appearing for the first time, can only be explained by supposing immigration to have taken place. An interesting feature of this bed is the occurrence of two brachiopods, *Stropheodonta plicata* and *Spirifer asper*, both of which belong normally to the Hamilton fauna of Iowa. This fact would indicate, that at some time during the later Hamilton age, fairly uniform conditions extended westward from this region to Iowa, and perhaps beyond.

Before the close of the age, the water had become pure enough for the growth of crinoids, the remains of which, together with the fronds of the branching bryozoan *Stictopora incisurata*, and the shells of the small brachiopod *Nucleospira concinna*, make up the greater portion of the "Stictopora" bed. The age closed with the deposition of a few inches of mud, in which few remains were buried.

The conditions, however, were now favorable for the re-establishment of a coral reef, which began by the growth of large heads of *Favosites hamiltoniæ*. Cup corals soon made their appearance again, though they were of different species from those found in the Corniferous reef. This was to be expected, for the many vicissitudes which the old Corniferous corals passed through, would undoubtedly effect specific if not generic modification. Crinoids, too, reappeared, though the genera and species were widely different from those which grew on the Lower Devonian coral reef. The Encrinal limestone is this much modified coral reef, which by its slight thickness indicates a comparatively short period of duration.

This reef was also of less areal extent than its predecessor in early Devonian times. The Encrinal limestone is not recognized in the eastern portion of the State of New York, and it has not been traced westward. In Illinois, Iowa, Michigan, Ohio, Indiana and other central states, however, the Hamilton is chiefly represented by limestones, often of considerable thickness, and in these, corals of various kinds abound, thus showing that the Encrinal limestone represents only a temporary eastward extension of the coral reefs which were forming in the clearer waters of the Central Interior Sea.

With the close of the short Encrinal limestone age, the corals did not become suddenly overwhelmed as was the case with the Corniferous reef. In fact, we find that after an interval, a number of corals appeared which did not grow on the coral reef proper in this immediate region.* They did not flourish long however, but were soon overwhelmed and disappeared. Some of them, such as *Cystiphyllum* and the adaptable *Streptelasma* continued at intervals for some considerable length of time. Aside from these, however, the Hamilton fossils are not common in the Moscow shales of this region. True, there are some adaptable species, such as *Phacops rana*, which are to be met with everywhere, but the great majority of species had left this region, migrating, during the uniform conditions of the Encrinal limestone age, probably to the eastward. At any rate, most of them re-appeared in the Upper or Moscow shales in the Genesee valley. In this latter region the shales are also much thicker, aggregating nearly three hundred feet, while in our own vicinity seventeen feet constitute the whole thickness of these shales.† The cause of the slight development of these shales in the region under consideration, was the comparatively stationary character of the sea bottom, in other words, the absence of subsidence. The water more-over, was shallow over Erie County, the evidence for which is found in the character of the fossils and in the shale itself, in the plant remains which occur in it, and in a fragment of a water-worn shell and a similarly worn pebble which were found.‡

Throughout the Moscow time, the water probably continued shallow, and life was scarce. The mud flats were probably never exposed at low tide, but their component material was worked over and over by the tidal currents, so that no perfect lamination was developed. On a sandy sea floor, such conditions would have formed oscillation ripples, but the fine mud did not admit of such impressions, or if they were formed, their preservation in the shale was an improbability.

*At Morse Creek, near Athol Springs, *Heliophyllum*, which among others is here referred to, occurs in the Encrinal limestone.

†For a comparison of the Hamilton faunas of Eighteen Mile Creek with those of the Genesee Valley, see "Faunas of the Hamilton Group, etc."

‡The shell was a *Spirifer granulosus*, which does not normally occur in the Moscow shales of this region, but is common in the Encrinal limestone.

Life finally disappeared almost completely from this region, and for a long period the waters were practically uninhabited. The Upper Devonian conditions were ushered in slowly, some of the Genesee species appearing early during the Moscow age. This indicates that the change from the upper Middle to the lower Upper Devonian was a gradual one, and that abrupt changes did not occur, either in physical conditions or in life.

Meanwhile, during the whole progress of the Hamilton period in the east, there were regions in the west and south-west, where neither the limestone nor the shale-forming conditions of this period existed. In these regions, bituminous shales were deposited from the close of the Lower Devonian, far into the Upper Devonian. The changes in physical geography which allowed the development of the Hamilton beds in New York State after the deposition of the Marcellus beds, did not occur in the south-west, and with the continuance of the same physical conditions, the material deposited as well as the life continued very uniform throughout. The "black shale" of Ohio and other states represents these deposits, which continued uniformly, during all the time that the Hamilton beds were being laid down over New York. This enables us to understand why the species of fossils which flourished in the Marcellus epoch, should return during the Genesee epoch, while during the intervening Hamilton epoch they were absent.

If the centre of distribution of these animals, which found their natural habitat under conditions necessary for the formation of the fine black shales, was in the southwest, and there continued undisturbed during the whole of the Middle and later Devonian periods, new emigrants could travel eastward when the favorable conditions were, in part at least, restored. In Central New York a limestone making age, that of the Tully limestone, preceded the Genesee age, and while it continued, deposition was almost at a standstill in the west. The Tully limestone at some places in

Central New York has a thickness of nearly twenty feet, but its average thickness is only about half that. Towards the west it becomes thinner, until at Canandaigua Lake it is represented by a calcareous band three or four inches thick.* This limestone contains an association of fossils, which cause it to be referred to the Genesee stage, of which it forms the basal member. It is succeeded by the black Genesee shales, containing a number of fossils which had been characteristic of the black Marcellus shales. Twenty feet of these shales occur in the Genesee Valley, while at Eighteen Mile Creek there is scarcely a trace of them. At Section 1, the thin bed of spore-bearing shale is the only representative of this series, and even this does not occur everywhere. It is very possible, however, that during the time that the Tully limestone and the black shale above it, were forming in central New York, the transition beds of the upper Moscow shale were deposited in the Eighteen Mile Creek region, and that the Schizobolus fauna of these shales (if not the whole Spirifer tullius fauna) was, in a limited sense, contemporaneous with the Tully and lower Genesee faunæ of Central New York.

After the close of the Moscow age, when the transition beds had been deposited in this region, and the few inches of spore-bearing shale were laid down upon them, a subsidence, somewhat widely spread through Western New York, occurred, which brought with it the purification of the waters, which had hitherto been laden with fine carbonaceous silt. In the region about Eighteen Mile Creek, the beginning of this purification of the water is marked by the appearance, in a circumscribed favored spot, of a colony of crinoids, which seem to have flourished there for a considerable period, so that their remains accumulated to a depth of from two to three inches, as indicated by the thickness of the "Conodont" limestone. That the water was not very deep at this time, is shown by the highly comminuted condition

*Hall, Rep't 4th Geol. Dist., p. 214.

of the remains, which indicate a considerable amount of wave action, as well as by the grains of sand which occur in the rock.

While the crinoids flourished in this spot, and while similar conditions probably existed elsewhere, there came, perhaps from Ohio and the south-west, representatives of the great Placoderms which had ruled for many generations in those waters. These fishes seem to have found the area where the crinoids flourished, an exceptionally good feeding ground if we are to judge from the frequency of their remains in the rock. Living among the crinoids was a vast number of marine worms, the record of whose existence is now found in the "Conodonts," so plentiful in the rock. These bodies, as already noted, probably represent the œsophageal teeth of animals similar to our modern Annelida and Gephyrea.

As the subsidence continued, and the water became purer over larger areas, there began the deposition of the countless millions of shells of the minute pteropod *Styliolina fissurella*, which as noted above, in many places completely make up the Styliolina limestone. The conditions which favored the deposition of this limestone, were quite uniform over the greater portion of what is now Western New York. The character of the rock indicates that it was deposited at a distance from shore, where comparatively little sediment was carried, so that, as on the death of the pelagic animals, the shells slowly sank down from the surface, they accumulated by the millions on the ocean floor and formed a limestone bed of great purity. The accumulation of this inconceivably vast number of minute shells must have been a process of extreme slowness, even if we suppose that large numbers of the animals were carried to this region by favorable currents. It must be noted, however, that in many localities this bed contains a considerable amount of foreign matter, showing that some deposition of detrital material was going on.

While this long age continued, it not infrequently happened that trunks of trees, which grew on the land to the northward, were carried out into the comparatively quiet water, where, becoming water-logged, they finally sank, and after a long time, were buried in the growing deposit of shells. Eventually, however, this long limestone making age came to a close, by the gradual shoaling of the water, and the return of the mud-bearing currents. While at first there were some oscillations in the region, mud deposits alternating with deposits of shells, the conditions finally became uniform, and for a long period of time the Genesee mud-flats with their paucity of animal life, and their richness of vegetable life, constituted the characteristic feature of this portion of the Devonian sea. Of course subsidence of the sea floor went on throughout this period, but it was a very slow subsidence, so that the filling in by the fine mud, went on at the same rate, the relative depth of the water remaining the same.

Not until the close of the Genesee age did the subsidence become more rapid, and when this occurred, the deposits became once more of a calcareous nature, giving rise to the thirty feet of calcareous and concretion-bearing Cashaqua or lower Naples shales.

While these shales were being deposited, the water was inhabited, amongst other animals, by *Goniatites*, the shells of which are found in some of the concretionary layers. These animals may have come to this American Interior Devonian sea by immigration from the seas which then covered Europe, or they may have arisen independently. This latter is hardly conceivable, for parallelism of development between America and Europe would probably not have resulted in identity of species. As already noted, the few members of the fauna in which *Goniatites intumescens* and other *Goniatites* are the predominating species in this region, mark only a westward extension of the fauna which found its more perfect development in the region now occupied by the Genesee River.

Eventually shallow, brackish, or nearly fresh water conditions returned, and the black shales, which succeed the gray, were deposited. These deposits became more and more sandy as time progressed, and eventually culminated in more or less argillaceous sandstones. The faunas of the Genesee shales returned in a more or less modified condition, fishes being especially prominent. As the shoaling of the water continued, sands were deposited exclusively, and so the thick beds of Chemung sandstones were formed, succeeded later by beds of subcarboniferous conglomerate. Then the mud making conditions, which had at intervals occurred, and during the existence of which the carbonaceous shales were deposited, returned with greater perfection and greater permanency. Continuing long, they permitted a luxurient growth of vegetation, which, becoming buried in detrital deposits, has given us the Pennsylvania coal-beds. Similar conditions existed in other regions, where beds of coal also accumulated. The Pennsylvania coal-beds may be regarded as the record of the consummation of that coal-making tendency, which was so continuously exhibited during the middle and later Devonian, in this region, but which, at no time preceding the coal-measure (meso-carbonic) period, produced results which were in any way comparable to those produced during these later ages.

The sandstone beds of the Chemung period were probably the last beds to be spread over the Erie County region, which shortly after the commencement of the Carbonic era became dry land. The shore-line was transferred to somewhere in the vicinity of the boundary line between New York and Pennsylvania, nearly all the area comprised within the latter state being under water. It was in this great bay-like indentation, and in another one which stretched north into Michigan, that the chief coal-beds were deposited.*

*Dana in the 4th Edition of his Manual of Geology, gives on p. 633 an instructive map of the outlines of the land at the beginning of the Carbonic era.

Post-Devonian Events.—We have now traced the history of this region from the time of the Lower Devonian to near the close of the Upper Devonian time, when it was raised into dry land. The changes which were going on outside of this area after its elevation, are out of place in this discussion. The interval which elapsed between the close of the Devonion era and the beginning of the Quaternary era, can be passed over briefly. It was a long interval, during which the atmosphere, the rivers, and the sea exerted their combined influences to destroy the new-formed land again. Much of the material deposited in the Carbonic sea was derived from the erosion of the land, which had been formed in the age just preceding.

It was during this interval of time that the slight crust-movements occurred, which gave rise, on the one hand, to the faults and folds, and on the other to the joint-cracks which traverse these rocks. The beds which at first were horizontal, or nearly so, were tilted until they stood at the present angle. The lithification of the beds, probably commenced while they were still submerged, continued, and ultimately, the shales and sandstones as we see them to-day, were produced.

At the end of this long period of erosion, we find some interesting topographical features, which are no longer in existence. A broad and deep river valley had been carved out of the strata where Lake Erie is now. A stream—the Idlewood River—coming from the south-east, entered this valley through a gorge, half a mile north of the mouth of the present Eighteen Mile Creek. Then came the great "Ice Age," and all the country was buried beneath the accumulating mantle of snow and ice. When, through its increased thickness, and through melting at its southern end, this great ice sheet began to move, it scratched and polished the bed rocks, by means of the pebbles and sand frozen into its under side.*

*The glacial history of this region is too intricate, and involves the detailed consideration of regions outside of those treated of in these chapters; therefore its complete discussion will not be taken up in this paper. See Gilbert's History of Niagara Falls, National Geographic Monographs, Vol. I., No. 7, and numerous papers in various Journals referred to in the appendix.

Eventually the long reign of the ice came to an end, and the glaciers slowly melted away, leaving behind the debris, which had been brought from the regions to the north. Thus, when the land was again uncovered, a mantle of drift was spread over it, filling the ravines and smaller valleys which had been cut by the pre-glacial streams. The great valley now occupied by Lake Erie was filled up to a considerable extent, and its continuation through the Dundas valley into the valley of Lake Ontario was cut off by the drift. The old channel of the preglacial Idlewood River was also filled in by drift. All this, however, did not appear at first, for as long as the ice filled the Ontario valley, the drainage of the water, resulting from the melting ice, was impossible in the present direction, and it accumulated, forming a long lake at the front of the ice sheet. This lake, which Spencer has named Lake Warren, increased in size until its waters finally began to overflow across the lowest point on the southern watershed, which happened to be near where Chicago now stands. Thus the drainage of this great lake was into the Mississippi, for a long time. The beaches built by this old lake can be seen a short distance behind the present beach of Lake Erie, running southward through Hamburgh, and crossing the present gorge of Eighteen Mile Creek beyond the forks.* When, through continued melting of the ice, the Mohawk, and later the St. Lawrence valleys were opened, the drainage went by these channels, and the water in Lake Erie was lowered to near its present level. Then the waves began their work of cutting into the land leaving the cliffs, now exposed on the shore, which in some places are formed of the bed rock, and in others of the drift-heaps left by the ice in the valleys.

*Leverett, Am. Journ. Science, July, 1895, gives a map of the beaches.

Much of the sand now found in the beaches along the shore of Lake Erie was derived from the drift deposits left by the ice. Only a comparatively small portion of this beach material has a local origin, having been worn by the waves from the shale cliffs. The material thus derived, is readily recognized by the flat thin character of the pebbles composing it, a feature which early caused it to be known by the name of "flat gravel." (See Plate XIX.).

The cliffs of unconsolidated material are of course much more readily eroded by the waves, than the shale cliffs. The active destruction of the drift cliffs can be seen at a great many points along the lake shore, and it is frequently emphasized by the trees, which, losing their foot-hold as the cliff is being undermined, slide down the banks.

The sands derived from the cliffs are carried away by the long-shore currents, and deposited where the force of these currents diminishes. Thus, bars are thrown across the mouths of all the streams and inlets, and sand-spits run out from the headlands, menacing the safety of the coast navigator.

The beaches between the headlands vary in the character of their material, as well as in the angle of the slope facing the water. Where the water deepens rapidly off-shore, so that the large breakers roll in and reach the shore, the material of the beach is usually coarse gravel, and the front slope a steep one, the beach often assuming a terrace form. Where, however, the water is shallow for a considerable distance from shore, or where a submerged sand-bar causes the breaking of the great waves long before they reach the shore, the beach is usually of a sandy character, and the slope a gentle one. In the first case (that of the deep water) the fine material is carried out by the undertow, so that only coarse material remains. This will naturally retain the steep slope given it by the great waves. In the second case (that of the shallow water) the sands dropped by the long-shore currents are washed on to the shore by the "swash" following the breaking of the off-shore waves. Hence the slope of the sand-beach will be comparatively gentle and uniform.

Where the drift contains boulders, these are usually left by the waves on the beach, a feature well illustrated in many of of the sections, particularly that of the old gorge of the Idlewood River. In such instances it frequently happens that shore ice will transport some of these blocks, which may eventually come to rest at the foot of a cliff, where there are other blocks, derived from the cliff itself. Thus, Corniferous limestone boulders from the drift, have been mingled with the blocks of Encrinal limestone from the cliffs at various portions along the shore, and there is danger of mistaking the former for the latter, unless this fact is borne in mind. Blocks and slabs of shaly limestone may also be frequently found projecting from, or lying on drift covered banks, and the fossils contained in these, differ from those found in the adjoining cliffs. Such rock masses are commonly derived from the Corniferous limestone in the northern part of Erie County.

At Stony Point, about three miles north of the Bay View cliff, Corniferous limestone boulders are exceedingly abundant on the beach. With them occur boulders of Niagara limestone, brought by the ice from Niagara County, as well as boulders of Waterlime from North Buffalo. These boulders constitute a portion of an old glacial moraine, which can be traced inland to West Seneca, where it is cut by the railroads, and exhibits the limestone blocks in the unconsolidated banks. The name "Limestone Ridge" which has been applied to this moraine, is derived from the presence of these limestone boulders.

Sand dunes are found at a great many places along the shore of Lake Erie. They are commonly low, but occasionally, as in the Crystal Beach dunes on the Canadian shore, they rise to considerable heights. These sand dunes are met with behind those beaches which are not bounded by shale or drift cliffs. It is here that the winds meet with little obstruction, and they can sweep the dry sands inland, until friction and the rise of the land prevent further advance. Low, swampy ground is commonly found behind such dunes, and the beach in front of them is usually a firm gently sloping sand beach.

The present shore features of Lake Erie are of post-glacial origin, and came into existence since the establishment of the present St. Lawrence drainage system. The gorge of Eighteen Mile Creek, as we know it, was cut since that time by the stream carrying the drainage from the high lands in the southern part of Erie County.

Thus the stream which we have been studying in such detail, was one of the last features to appear in the present landscape. It is still actively eroding its banks, and revealing fresh sections from which to study the past history of this region.

PART II.

PALÆONTOLOGY.

"The crust of our earth is a great cemetery, where the rocks are tombstones, on which the buried dead have written their own epitaphs."

—*Agassiz.*

NOTE.

The following new species are described herein :

Hadrophyllum woodi : p. 129.
Monotrypa amplectens : p. 137.
Habrocrinus pentadactylus : p. 143.
Platyostoma lineata, var. ; *emarginata :* p. 274.

The following illustrations are original :

Figures 1, 5, 8, 10, *10C*, 11, *15*, *16*, 17, 18, 22-25, 27-30, 32, 66, 78, *81*, *84*, *85*, *89*, *90*, *104*, *122*, *141*, 151, 168, *200A*, *218*, 228a, *261*. Those printed in italics were drawn by Miss Elvira Wood, Instructor in Palæontology in the Massachusetts Institute of Technology. The remainder were drawn by the author, except Fig. 228a, which was drawn by Mr. John A. Hutchinson. The other pen-and-ink drawings are copies by Miss Wood (Figs. 10A–10C, 15, 16, 77A, 124, 126, 128, 182A, 198, 207, 210-212, 215, 217, 219, 225C, 229, 230, 232, 233, 236–260, 262, 263) ; by Mr. Hutchinson (Figs. 52, 64, 65, 66A, 68–72, 74, 194-197, 199, 200, 201–206, 208, 209, 214, 214A, 216, 220, 225B, 226-228, 231, 234, 235); by the author, and by others. The source is in each case credited as follows: "after Hall," " after Clarke," etc. The illustrations marked "from Hall," etc., were reproduced directly from the lithographs.

CONTENTS OF PART II.

INTRODUCTION.

Palæontology* deals with the past organic life of the earth. It is concerned with the structural characters, the systematic position, the mode of life, and the geographic as well as geologic distribution of former animals and plants. Palæontology also deals with questions concerning the development of organic forms, and the causes which have determined such development.

The data upon which the conclusions of palæontologists are based are derived from the study of fossils and from a comparison of these fossils with living animals and plants. The term Fossil is commonly applied to the remains of animals and plants which were buried before the beginning of the present geologic epoch.† This definition is an arbitrary one, and is not based on any distinction in character between the remains which were buried before, and those which were buried during, the present geologic epoch. Thus the marine shells in the post-glacial elevated clays of northern New England and Canada differ in nowise from those of the same species buried in the modern deposits off the present coast. In the former case, the strata have been elevated several hundred feet; while in the latter case, they still retain their original position, or, at least, have experienced no appreciable disturbance. In like manner, many of the Miocene and Pliocene shells are not only of the same species as those recently buried on neighboring shores, but the changes which they have undergone, since burial, are frequently not greater than those experienced by shells buried in modern accumulations. The difference in the alteration is merely one of degree, and with proper discrimination, specimens can be selected which show all grades of

---

*** Gr. *palaios*, ancient; *onta*, beings; *logos*, discourse.**

† Zittel — Text-book of Palæontology.

change, from the unaltered state of shells in modern mud-flats to the crystalline condition of an ancient limestone fossil, in which the original structure has been completely lost. It is, then, obvious that palæontologists should follow geologists, and extend the term fossil to include all remains of animals and plants preserved from the time of the earliest fossiliferous strata to the present. As Geikie says: "The idea of antiquity or relative date is not necessarily involved in this conception of the term. Thus, the bones of a sheep buried under gravel and silt by a modern flood and the obscure crystalline traces of a coral in ancient masses of limestone are equally fossils." *

Geologic time is continuous, and the development of life is progressive. No break divides the present from the past, and the geologic phenomena of the present epoch are controlled by the same laws which governed those of past time. Fossilization is a mere accident by which some animals and plants are preserved, and it resolves itself into a process of inhumation, neither the nature of the organism nor the time or mode of burial being of primary significance. These are of first importance in determining the degree of preservation which the fossil is to experience, and, consequently, the nature of the record which is to remain; but they do not affect the process of fossilization, which is merely the burial of the dead organism. Thus, the idea of change is not necessarily involved in the concept of a fossil, although it is true that few organisms long remain buried without undergoing some chemical change. Examples of the preservation of organisms in an almost unchanged condition are nevertheless known, the most conspicuous being the mammoths frozen into the mud and ice of Siberia, and retaining hair, skin, and flesh intact; and the insects and other animals included in the amber of the Baltic, where they have remained unchanged since early Tertiary time. Ordinarily, however, the flesh of the buried animal soon decays, and, consequently, no record of the soft parts is retained. In plants, the decay

* Text-book of Geology, 3d Ed., p. 645.

is less rapid, and the buried vegetable remains may be indefinitely preserved in the form of carbonaceous films.

The hard parts of animals are best preserved as fossils. Such are the shells and other external skeletal structures secreted by a variety of animals—as crustacea, molluscs, echinoderms, corals, and so forth; and the bones, teeth, and other hard structures of the vertebrates. Besides the actual remains of animals and plants, any evidence of their existence which is preserved is commonly included under the name of fossil. Thus, impressions made by living animals and plants in the unconsolidated rock material, and structures built by animals from inorganic material, are fossils if properly buried. Examples of the first are the foot-prints of vertebrates; the tracks and trails of jelly-fish, worms, molluscs or crustacea; the burrows of worms, borings of animals in stones or shells, and the impressions made by seaweeds in motion. Among the second class are worm tubes, built of sand grains; foraminiferal shells, built of foreign particles; flint implements and other utensils of primitive man; the relics of the Swiss Lake Dwellers; Roman and other ancient coins buried in the peat bogs; and, in fact, all artificial productions of early man or other animals which have become entombed by natural agencies. Thus, three classes of fossils may be recognized, viz:

1. Organic remains and their impressions.
2. Trails, tracks, and burrows of organisms.
3. Artificial structures.

Mere burial, however, does not in all cases insure preservation, even of the hard parts of animals. The fossil must be protected from subsequent destruction. The subsequent destruction of fossils is usually most complete in those beds which have been subjected to alteration by heat during mountain building disturbances, and in such cases the fossils are usually no longer distinguishable. This has been the fate of many organic remains, which have thus been completely destroyed.

SOLUTION AND THE FORMATION OF MOLDS AND CASTS.

Carbonated, or otherwise acidulated waters will dissolve calcareous fossils, if the strata in which they are embedded are pervious to the water. Thus, a mold of the *exterior* of a dissolved shell, for example, may remain in the rock, while a mold of the *interior*, formed by the mud or sand which found its way between the valves, will remain within the mold of the exterior. If the rock is under pressure, it may happen that the two molds are pressed against each other, and the stronger features of one may become superimposed upon the weaker features of the other. Thus, fossil mussels may show the external striæ impressed on the internal mold, showing at the same time the muscular impressions in relief. Occasionally the space between the two molds, i. e. that formerly occupied by the shell, may be filled by infiltrations, and a *cast* of the original shell may thus be produced.

MECHANICAL DEFORMATIONS.

These are very common, and they are apt to give a false impression of the form of the fossil. Distortion by vertical compression is the characteristic method of deformation of fossils in undisturbed strata. This pressure is due to the shrinking of the strata on solidifying, and is especially marked in shales. Most fossils have probably been affected to some extent by such compression, and frequently the resulting deformation is very marked. When the fossils are protected by a limestone concretion formed about them, they probably remain unaffected by such pressure. In laterally compressed beds the distortion may render the fossil unrecognizable, while in beds in which cleavage is developed, this may affect the fossil as much as the rock.

All remains of animals and plants commonly undergo more or less alteration after burial. The amount of alteration which will occur during a given time varies in general in inverse proportion to the relative amount of mineral matter in the fossil. The flesh of animals, as already noted, will commonly disappear quickly, not even an impression remaining. The presence of petroleum in corals and in cavities of shells, however, indicates a probable result of the decomposition of buried fleshy portions of animals. A more complete preservation of soft organic tissues is brought about by the process of

CARBONIZATION.

This occurs in plants and in those animals which have a chitinous skeleton, e. g., Hydrozoa; a carbonaceous film, seldom showing structure, will usually remain.

The most important changes which buried hard structures of animals undergo are as follows:

1. Infiltration.

Skeletal structures are commonly more or less porous, and the first change which is likely to occur is the filling of the pores by mineral matter, usually by carbonate of lime, though infiltration of silica often occurs. The filling of the pores occurs upon the decay and removal of the perishable organic matter which occupied them. The structure then is solid, and completely "petrified" or turned to stone.

Fossils made solid by infiltration of carbonate of lime are commonly among the best preserved organic remains, for they will retain, in an unaltered condition, the minutest structural features. This is the normal condition of the fossils in limestones and shales, and hence specimens obtained from such rocks are in the best condition for critical study. All classes of organisms are, however, not equally well preserved by this process. Very porous structures, such as the plates of echinoderms (e. g., crinoid stems and plates), are commonly affected by the crystallization of the infiltrated calcite. Such crystallization usually affects the whole plate, thus obliterating the original microscopic structure, though the external form may be perfectly retained.

Shells of brachiopods and molluscs preserved by the infiltration of calcite are among the least altered remains, and corals thus affected commonly retain all the details of their structure. If the infiltrating mineral is silica, it will commonly lead to a complete silicification.

2. Replacement.

This occurs when another mineral takes the place of that of which the skeleton originally consisted. It is commonly a process of *silicification*, where silica replaces the original substance, though *calcification* of originally siliceous structures is known to occur in sponges and Radiolaria (Zittel). Silicification may conveniently be considered as occurring in two ways. The first obtains when the decaying organic tissue is directly replaced by silica, as in fossil wood. This is a process of molecular substitution, where a molecule of silica takes the place of a molecule of the wood, the interchange probably being due to some form of chemical reaction. In such cases the microscopic structure of the wood is usually retained in great perfection. The other mode of silicification involves the replacement of the mineral matter of the shell or other hard structure by silica, a process which must be preceded by, or concurrent with, solution. In this latter case the beginning of silicification is usually marked by the appearance, on the surface of the fossil, of a series of concentric rings (Beekite rings) surrounding a central elevation. This method of silicification commonly destroys the microscopic structure of the organic remains, but it gives them a mechanical and chemical stability, which will insure the perfect preservation of the external forms, and, furthermore, allow the fossil to weather out in relief.

Fossils are also replaced by iron pyrites (or marcasite), by iron oxide, and by other minerals. Such replacements involve a chemical reaction between the replacing and original substances. Pyritized fossils are among the most exquisitely preserved organic remains, but they are subject to disintegration on exposure.

PALÆONTOLOGY IN ITS RELATION TO GEOLOGY.

(Stratigraphy.)

Fossils may be studied in various ways, and with several ends in view. The simplest use which can be made of them is that of geological indices, or "medals of creation," each characteristic, to a certain extent, of the particular geologic horizon in which it is found. This is the empirical method of study, for it is only by experience that we learn to recognize particular fossils as characterizing particular formations. It is the method most frequently employed, and it is sufficient for the purpose of identifying a stratum over a limited area, or of correlating, in a general way, formations at widely separated localities. Studied in this way, fossils become "finger-marks" by which to recognize the position of a given formation in the geological scale.

In order that such identification and correlation may be successfully accomplished, intimate acquaintance with the fossils on which the correlation depends is required. It is, furthermore, important that the geologist who proposes to use fossils should have a clear knowledge of the relative stratigraphic value of the species to be used; in other words, he must know which species are to be depended upon as indicative of a given horizon. Species of animals or plants which are thus characteristic of definite geologic horizons are known as "Index Fossils,"* and the precision with which they indicate the geologic horizon is, in general, inversely proportional to the distance between the localities in which the formations are to be correlated. Single strata can be identified only over very limited areas by their index fossils,—usually only over the area characterized by a uniform lithologic condition of the stratum. Thus, it is only within a radius of perhaps fifteen or twenty miles from Eighteen Mile Creek that the brachiopod *Stropheodonta demissa* is characteristic of the upper beds of the Hamilton shales, and that the coral *Pleurodictyum stylopora* is characteristic of the lower beds of the Hamilton. But within these limits

* German "*Leitfossilien*."—See further, Chapter III.

these fossils are practically reliable guides to the position of these strata, as they are not found above or below them.

But if we attempt correlation by index species over greater areas we shall have to be less precise. Thus, *Stropheodonta demissa* and *Pleurodictyum stylopora*, together with a number of other species, such as *Spirifer granulosus*, *Stropheodonta concava*, etc., are practically confined to, and indicative of, the Hamilton stage of Western New York. But while these species are sure guides to the identification of the Hamilton stage over this area, they can not be used in correlating even the greater subdivisions of this stage. Thus, in the region about Eighteen Mile Creek the species mentioned are entirely confined to the Hamilton shales below the Encrinal limestone, not a single specimen having been found in the Moscow shale above that bed. But in the Genesee Valley these species are entirely confined to the Moscow shales above the Encrinal limestone, none having been observed below that bed. Consequently, detailed correlation by these species alone is impossible.

In the intercontinental correlation of formations, the greatest caution is necessary in the selection of index species, and it not infrequently happens that a characteristic species of a particular horizon in one country may be wholly restricted to a different horizon in another country. *Tropidoleptus carinatus* and *Vitulina pustulosa* are examples of this. These two brachiopods are eminently characteristic of the Hamilton or Middle Devonian group of North America, occurring in it wherever this group is typically developed. They are again characteristic of beds in the Amazon River district, which by some are placed in the Middle, and by others in the Lower Devonian group. In Bolivia they characterize the Icla shales, which are considered Lower Devonian, and in South Africa these species are reported from beds of the same horizon (Ulrich). *Tropidoleptus carinatus* has also been reported from the Lower Devonian of the Bosphorus and the Rhine district. *Leptocœlia flabellites* is commonly found associated with these species in foreign countries, but in North America it is restricted to the base of the Lower Devonian group. (Lower Helderberg and Oriskany beds.)

Index species which have been successfully employed in intercontinental correlation are *Spirifer disjunctus* for the upper, and *Goniatites intumescens* and *Rhynchonella* (*Hypothyris*) *cuboides* for the lower, part of the Upper Devonian group.

While general correlation by index species is thus possible, much detailed work is necessary to establish the proper relations between the beds occupied by these species at the several localities. The nature of the sediment, and the physical conditions indicated by it, and by the fossils themselves, must be taken into consideration, and the causes for, and directions of, the migrations of the faunas must be investigated. This method of investigation in correlative geology is still in its infancy, and it requires for its proper prosecution a thorough palæontological training. The results to be obtained are certain to be of far-reaching importance to both geologist and biologist.

PALÆONTOLOGY IN ITS RELATION TO BIOLOGY.

(Palæobiology.)

The study of fossils, from a purely biological point of view, has made such progress within the last fifty years, and the results obtained have been of such importance, as to raise palæontology from a subordinate geological study to the rank of an independent science. Not only have important discoveries in comparative anatomy, morphology, and systematic zoölogy and botany been made by the study of fossils, but it has become possible to trace out actual lines of genetic descent in the organic realm. This has been accomplished by the detailed study of particular classes of organisms and the comparison of the several transient stages in the life-history of the individual with the persistent adult characteristics of those members of the same class which preceded them in time. Such detailed study has been carried on among the cephalopods by Hyatt and others in this country, and by Würtenberger, Branco, Karpinsky and others in Europe. Jackson has studied the pelecypods and the Palæozoic Echini, and Beecher the brachiopods and trilobites. The principle on which this work is based is embodied in the law first clearly enunciated by Louis Agassiz and Carl Vogt: that the stages in the cycle of individual life can be correlated with the characteristics of the adult in allied types which appear earlier in the geologic record. According to the modern interpretation of such phenomena, this correspondence indicates a genetic relation, the later forms having descended from the earlier, and each recapitulating in its own life-history, more or less perfectly, the life-history of the group to which it belongs.

Investigations in this direction require the study of young and intermediate as well as adult individuals. Immature forms may frequently be found associated with the mature individuals in the strata, and they can be obtained by processes described in the next chapter. For the details of the methods of investigation in Biologic Palæontology the student is referred to the works of Hyatt, Jackson, Beecher, Clarke, Schuchert, J. P. Smith, and others.

CHAPTER I.

HOW TO COLLECT AND PREPARE FOSSIL INVERTEBRATES.

(A.) Collecting Fossils.

Outfit. The outfit needed for collecting fossils is a very simple one. It consists of the following articles:

1. *A Collecting Bag*, basket or other receptacle for carrying the fossils. The dimensions of the leather bag commonly used by geologists and palæontologists are 13 x 13 x 4 inches. It opens at one end, where it is protected by a flap, which may be secured by a buckle. It has an additional pocket for a note-book, and has a strap for carrying it on the shoulder. The common canvas hunting-bag, obtainable at any gun store, is well suited for this work, and has the additional advantages of being light and cheap.

2. *Hammers*. A mason's or bricklayer's hammer, with a square face and a peen end, which tapers with the cutting edge transverse to the handle, and a small square-faced and sharp-edged trimming hammer, are needed. The former is used to pry up the shale laminæ, and is especially useful in the beds of the streams, while the latter is used to trim off most—not all—of the superfluous rock.*

3. *Chisels*. Several stone-cutter's chisels of different sizes, for cutting the fossils from the limestone, are needed.

4. *Wedges*. Two or three large steel wedges, for prying up large slabs of rock, are exceedingly useful.

5. *Lens*. The collector should always be provided with a fairly good lens of large field.

6. *Note-book*. Some form of note-book, for recording observations on the spot, should be taken into the field. Those with the paper bound on the end instead of the side are more convenient.

---

* The hammers here described can be obtained from Fayette R. Plumb, Philadelphia, Pa., under styles G. and N., at $1.25 and $0.60 respectively.

7. *Labels.* Blank paper for labels should always be at hand. It is desirable to have the field labels cut to uniform size.

8. *Wrapping Paper and Twine.* A good supply of these most necessary articles should be taken. This should comprise tissue paper, newspapers, and strong brown paper, such as can be obtained at any country grocery store. The twine should be strong, but not too thick.

9. *Boxes.* A number of cigar boxes, tin tobacco boxes, and small spool, pill or other paper boxes should be taken for the more delicate fossils.

10. *Cotton Batting.* A supply of this article for use with the boxes is necessary.

Field Work. The rock from which fossils are to be collected in this region are shales and limestones. The former, when calcareous, are usually rich in fossils; but when bituminous or gritty, fossils are usually scarce. The limestones are often made up of fragments of fossils, but the variety is commonly not very great.

Collecting from the Shales. It is next to useless to attack a vertical shale bank, as it is difficult to extract the fossils entire, even if they are exposed. A better plan is to follow down the stream bed, and pry up the layers, in descending order. If this is impracticable, the bank has to be attacked as best may be. Joint cracks will assist in prying out large masses, which may then be split up. In prying out such masses, however, care must be taken that the overlying beds are not too much disturbed, as dangerous falls of rock from above may result. This caution is especially necessary where the fissile bituminous shales (Genesee and Black Naples) are undermined. In such cases it is prudent to pry out the piece quickly and cautiously, and then take it to a place of safety, where it can be split up. The shales are most easily split up while still wet. After they have dried in the sun they become very brittle, and it is difficult to get perfect specimens from them. The shale mass is to be split, first, with the peen end of the hammer, or with a flat chisel, and after that with a small prying instrument. A pocket-knife is very serviceable. The thin shale pieces can be easily reduced to the proper size by breaking with the fingers, or by cutting with a chisel; trimming with the hammer should be avoided. The ultimate trimming and cleaning is to be done in the laboratory. If the specimen is broken, the parts should be wrapped separately and then together, the gluing being left for the laboratory.

Collecting from the Weathered Shale. When exposed to rain and sun for some time the shale becomes reduced to clay, and the fossils weather out free. In such cases the collector should get down on hands and knees and crawl over the ground, carefully picking up all the good specimens and all the doubtful ones. A small pair of pointed pincers will be found useful for picking up the smaller fossils. When the rock is weathered deeply, it will be found advantageous to carry away a quantity of the clay in bulk, to be looked over in the laboratory. The fossils, as they are picked up, should be placed on a layer of cotton batting, in a box, and not be disturbed again until they reach the laboratory.

Collecting from the Limestone. Such rocks as the Encrinal limestone will usually yield their fossils on the blow of the hammer. The rock should be split, if possible, parallel to the bedding plane. If portions of fossils are visible the bulk of the surrounding rock should be trimmed with the hammer, and the further cleaning and developing reserved for the laboratory. *Do not try to break out the fossils in the field.* You will probably end by breaking the fossil. It is better to carry some additional rock. When the rock is weathered, the fossils usually stand out in relief, and they may often be obtained by careful manipulation with hammer and chisel. Some rock should always be taken with the specimens, as they can seldom be wholly freed from the matrix without losing in appearance, if not in value. If extensive collections are to be made from the limestones, a sledge hammer is desirable.

Collecting from the Concretions. The calcareous and pyrite concretions often yield good fossils. These may not appear on breaking the concretion, because the splitting seldom occurs in the right plane. Geikie suggests putting the nodule into the fire and dropping it, when quite hot, into cold water.*

Collecting from the Talus. This resolves itself into simply picking over the loose material at the foot of the cliff and selecting desirable specimens. Good material is often obtained in this manner; but it is of little value for stratigraphic purposes, as the various beds here have their fossils commingled. Fossils from the talus should always be marked as such. Not infrequently their position in the bank can be ascertained, as in the case of the large cup-corals, which all belong to the lower Moscow shale. I have frequently found among the talus heaps, rock fragments which have no local outcrops, but belong farther north, having been brought down in the drift during the glacial period, as noted in Chapter III., Part I. This will serve to show how unreliable talus specimens are, as distinct geologic horizons may easily be confounded.

Wrapping and Packing. Wrap each specimen separately in newspaper, or, if very delicate, in tissue paper, and then in newspaper. Small, delicate, free fossils should be placed between layers of cotton batting in boxes. When all the specimens from one bed are wrapped, make a package of them by wrapping them up in a piece of brown paper and securely tying them with twine. With the specimens should be packed a label, on which a record of the bed and locality is made, and which bears a number corresponding to the entry in the note-book. The legend on the label should also be written upon the outside of the package, preferably with an indelible pencil. Never neglect the labeling and recording in the note-book, as otherwise much of the value of the collection may be lost. Also make the notes extensive and at the time of collecting. *An experienced collector will never trust*

* Text-book of Geology, 3d Ed., 1893, p. 673.

his memory. When the packages are all securely tied and labeled, set them in a stout wooden box,* and mark the contents on the outside of the box. Never ship specimens in a box which is not completely filled and firmly packed.

(B.) Preparing Fossils for Study.

Outfit. The laboratory outfit varies according to the amount and character of the work to be done. Much must be left to the ingenuity of the worker; but the following tools are indispensable:

1. *Trays.* Both wooden and pasteboard trays are needed. The wooden trays should not be less than two inches deep, should fit one upon the other, so as to prevent dust from getting into them, and should not be too large for easy transportation. A wooden rim nailed around the outside of the top of each tray, so that a portion projects above the upper rim of the tray, will be found an excellent device for making the pile of trays stable, for keeping out dust, and for aid in carrying the tray. In place of the trays, wooden drawers may be used. The paper trays should be shallow — not over an inch deep, and of different sizes. Pasteboard box covers, and the boxes themselves with the rims cut down, are suitable. The trays in which the fossils are to be permanently kept should be of uniform quality, and in size they should be multiples of one another, and made to fit into the drawers which are to contain the collection permanently.

2. *Tools for Cleaning.*

a. *Brushes.* A variety of brushes is required. Several coarse bristle brushes, of various sizes and stiffness, are needed for washing the fossils. Finer brushes, such as nail-brushes and tooth-brushes, are needed for developing. A fine camel's-hair brush, for picking up delicate specimens, is convenient. A long, narrow brush of fine brass wire is useful for cutting soft sandy matrix from the fossils.

* Soap boxes are excellent for this purpose.

b. *Cutting Forceps.* The ordinary cutting forceps obtainable at any hardware store will be found exceedingly useful. The kind with the cutting edge at right angles to the long axis of the tool is best.

c. *Pincers.* Several small pincers, such as are used by watchmakers, are serviceable for picking up small specimens.

d. *Cutting and Graving Tools.* These should be picked out to suit the nature and delicacy of the work to be done. A number of fine-pointed steel gravers in handles are necessary. At least one of these should have a chisel edge. Dentists' tools are excellent for cleaning and preparing fossils.

e. *Chisels and Mallets.* Small stone-cutters' chisels and a small mallet are useful for trimming limestone specimens.

f. *Sand Bag.* A stout canvas bag, partly filled with fine quartz sand, is necessary to prevent the specimens from being shattered, and to prevent the marring of the underside of the specimens.

g. *Trimming Hammers.* These should be of small size, and should have square faces.

h. *Lenses and Microscope.* Several lenses of different power are needed. Among them should be a watchmaker's eye-glass, which can be attached to the eye, and will thus leave both hands free for work. A compound microscope is needed for the study of small specimens.

i. *Glass Slides and Balsam.* These are needed to mount the microscopic specimens obtained by washing the clays.

j. *Alcohol Lamp.* A small alcohol lamp or Bunsen burner is frequently needed.

k. *Dishes, Beakers and Bottles.* These should be selected to suit the convenience of the manipulator.

l. *Glue.* Liquid fish glue will be found suitable for mending broken specimens.

m. *Field Tickets.* Small colored tickets, only large enough to write a number on, are used to ticket all specimens after cleaning. The number on the field label is to be written on the ticket.

n. *Moulding Material.* Gutta-percha, which comes in thin sheets and can be obtained at any rubber store, is useful for taking impressions from the moulds of fossils. "Modeling composition No. 2, medium"—a dentist's wax of a red color, and obtainable in half-pound boxes at any dentists' supply store—will frequently be found more useful than gutta-percha.

o. *Chemicals.* Hydrochloric acid, caustic potash (sticks), and vinegar are necessary for cleaning and etching.

Laboratory Work. As soon as the specimens are unpacked, place them in the paper trays, making sure that *each tray* is provided with a copy of the proper field label. The specimens may be roughly assorted, but they must never be left without labels. The clay is washed off by use of the coarse brushes, and the superfluous rock is removed with the cutting forceps, or other tools. If the specimen is broken, clean the parts and then glue them together, placing them on a bed of sand until dry. The sand will support the unequal parts, and prevent them from separating, as they would if unsupported. In cleaning specimens with chisel and mallet always place them on a sand bag.

To remove hard clay or shale from delicate specimens, where cutting is impossible, place small tablets of caustic potash, cut from the sticks, upon the shale matrix, and leave it for some hours. The calcareous shale will be disintegrated and can be washed off. Repeat this until the specimen is clean. After that, wash the specimen thoroughly for some days in several changes of water, to which a few drops of hydrochloric acid have been added, to remove all the potash, otherwise the specimen may, in the course of time, disintegrate. Specimens from the Encrinal and the other limestone beds may be cleaned with acid, the final etching being done with dilute vinegar.

Obtaining Fossils from the Disintegrated Shales. The shales have frequently disintegrated into clay. To obtain the small fossils from these the following method of procedure is recommended: "Palæozoic fossiliferous clays, which are to be washed for small and young fossils, should be first dried in an oven or in the sun, and then well soaked in water for a day or more before washing. A deep pan or bucket serves well for this purpose, using the hands to stir the mass around, but do not get too much mud in suspension, since in pouring off the muddy water many of the smaller organisms are liable to be carried away. . . . . . After the washed earth has been dried, it should be sifted, to facilitate picking, into three grades, using sieves of 6, 18, and 38 meshes to the inch. The coarser material can be assorted with the unaided eye, but the finer grades will have to be selected under a low-power lens. A moistened camel's-hair brush is the best tool with which to pick up these smaller organisms. If the brush is held in the end of a small vial, a twirl of the fingers will readily remove the attached fossil." *

Highly fossiliferous shales, such as that of the Demissa bed, may be disintegrated by drying them well in an oven and then soaking in water until they crumble. Repeated drying and soaking will reduce most of the material to clay, after which the fine mud is to be washed away. The final process consists of boiling the material in a dish for about half an hour, frequently changing the water, until no more mud appears.

Washing the Clay for Microscopic Organisms. The following method is recommended for obtaining microscopic organisms from the clays resulting from the disintegration of the shales:

"In preparing most of the samples of clay, we would put about one ounce of the material and the same amount of common washing soda into a druggist's two-quart, clear-glass packing bottle, not over one-fourth filled with water, and let it remain twelve to twenty-four hours, frequently shaking the bottle, so as to thoroughly break up the clay. Now fill the bottle with water, and after twenty-five minutes

* Schuchert, Bull. 39, U. S. Nat. Mus. Part K., p. 20.

carefully pour off the upper three-fourths of it. Again fill with water, and in twenty-five-minutes decant as before; repeating this at twenty-five-minute intervals until the upper three-fourths of the water in the bottle, after a twenty-five-minute rest, will be nearly clear. A large amount of the fine sand, clay, and soda has by this process been washed, and the action of the soda has broken up the clay and removed most of the adhering material from the fossils. Now mount a few microscopic slides from the residuary sands, etc., at the bottom of the bottle, by taking up with a pipette (a piece of small glass tubing makes the best pipette) a small amount of the material; scatter very thinly over the middle of the slides; dry them thoroughly over an alcohol lamp, or in some better way, and, while hot, cover the dry material with a few drops of Canada balsam, keeping the slides quite warm until the balsam will be hard when cold. As these "trial slides" are seldom of any value, it is not necessary to use cover glasses if the balsam is hardened as above directed. A careful examination of these slides under the microscope, with a good quarter- or half-inch objective, will decide as to the value of the material under observation; and if it proves to be only sand, pour it all out, wash the bottle, and again try the same process with another sample of clay. But if the slides show a few good fossils, the next step is to separate them as much as possible from the mass of sand, etc., with which they are associated. In this, as in the first washing, specific gravity will do most of the work. Pour off most of the water and put the shells, sand, etc., into a four-ounce beaker (or glass tumbler), wash out the bottle, fill the beaker about three-fourths full of water, and, after it has rested ten minutes, pour three-fourths off the top through a glass funnel into the bottle, repeating this five or six times. As in the first washing, mount and examine a few slides from the material at the bottom of the bottle, mounting and preserving slides, if found to be of value. If nothing of value is found, pour out the contents of the bottle and fill up again as before from the beaker, after five minutes' rest, repeating these washings, and examinations at shorter resting intervals, of, say, three, two, and one minute, or less, until nothing but the coarsest sand remains in the beaker. . . . . . . Each layer of clay, as deposited by its specific gravity, has now been examined, and most of the fossils are contained in some one, or possibly two, of them. Nineteen-twentieths of the original sample of clay have been washed away and in the selected one-twentieth that remains there may be one fair fossil to 100 grains of sand."*

In the above process, all glassware, etc., must be perfectly clean, and the water used must be first filtered, otherwise organisms foreign to the rock under investigation may appear. In the final disintegration of the shale for this purpose, it is well to boil it for a few minutes in a rather strong solution of washing soda.

Hardening of Fossils. Some of the more delicate fossils from the shales require hardening, to preserve them permanently. This may be done by warming the fossil and then dipping it into hot thin glue, or the fossil may be well soaked in a very thin solution of white shellac, and then laid aside to dry. This latter method is preferable.

To make Artificial Casts from Natural Molds. In many cases the fossil has been removed in one way or another, and nothing but the mold remains. In such cases a cast made with gutta-percha will often give the surface features of the fossil with even greater detail than could be seen on the original specimen. A small piece of gutta-percha is to be softened in hot water, and pressed into the moistened mold with the thumb, which must be wet, to prevent sticking. Considerable pressure is required, and the squeezed-out borders should be folded in again, in order to insure a perfect cast. "Modeling composition for dental purposes, No. 2, medium," is often better than gutta-percha. It is likewise made soft by heating in hot water.

*Woodward and Thomas, Geol. of Minnesota, Final Report. Vol. III.: Pt. I., pp. 25 and 26.

To obtain the best results with the fossils of the Stropha losia and Nautilus beds and similar impure argillaceous limestones, the following process, devised by J. M. Clarke, is recommended: "Let small fragments exposing fossils in section be placed in dilute muriatic acid, until the calcareous matter is removed to a sufficient depth from the surface to leave all impressions of fossils at the surface perfectly clear. The argillaceous or other impurity of the matrix left after the reaction will be exceedingly soft, but retain the impressions, whether external or internal, with exceeding delicacy of detail. The fragments may then be carefully removed from the acid and washed, by placing for a moment in pure water. They should then be thoroughly dried, and afterwards hardened, by cautiously soaking in a very weak solution of glue, care being taken that this solution be sufficiently thin to enter all the ornamental or structural cavities and interstices of the impressions. After again drying, soft, clean, and clear squeezes are to be taken with soft gutta-percha. To preserve the hardened matrix, such squeezes must be taken rapidly, lest the heat of the gutta-percha soften the glue and cause adhesion. If, however, the destruction of the matrix is not of moment, the gutta-percha may be withdrawn at will, and the adhering dirt soaked and washed off at leisure." *

* 14th Ann. Rep't, N. Y. State Geol., 1894, p. 100. Footnote.

TABLE D.

Classification of the Animal Kingdom.

SUB-KINGDOM.	TYPE.	SUB-TYPE.	CLASS.*
B. METAZOA,	IX. Vertebrata,		5. Mammalia. 4. Aves. 3. Reptilia. 2. Amphibia. 1. Pisces.
	VIII. Protochordata,		
	VII. Arthropoda,	II. *Tracheata*,	3. Insecta. 2. Arachnoidea. 1. Myriopoda.
		I. *Branchiata*,	1. Crustacea.
	VI. Mollusca,		6. Cephalopoda. 5. Pteropoda. 4. Gastropoda. 3. Amphineura. 2. Scaphopoda. 1. Pelecypoda.
	V. Molluscoidea.		2. Brachiopoda. 1. Bryozoa.
	IV. Vermes,		3. Annelida. 2. Gephyrea. 1. Nemathelminthes.
	III. Echinodermata,	III. *Echinozoa*,	2. Holothuroidea. 1. Echinoidea.
		II. *Asterozoa*,	2. Asteroidea. 1. Ophiuroidea.
		I. *Pelmatozoa*,	3. Crinoidea. 2. Blastoidea. 1. Cystoidea.
	II. Cœlenterata,		2. Anthozoa. 1. Hydrozoa.
	I. Porifera,		1. Spongiæ.
A. PROTOZOA,			1. Rhizopoda.

* Under the Classes, only those are given which are preserved in a fossil state.

CHAPTER II.

DESCRIPTIONS OF THE GENERA AND SPECIES OF INVERTEBRATES FOUND IN THE MARCELLUS, HAMILTON, GENESEE, AND NAPLES BEDS OF EIGHTEEN MILE CREEK AND THE LAKE-SHORE REGION OF ERIE COUNTY, NEW YORK.

Class Hydrozoa. Owen.

This class includes the simplest polyps, of which the fresh-water Hydra is an example. The body consists of a hollow tube, the walls of which are composed of two cellular layers,—*ectoderm* and *endoderm*. with a non-cellular layer, the *mesoglœa*, between them. These layers meet at the mouth, which is the only opening into the gastric space enclosed by the body wall. Tentacles, furnished with nettle-cells, surround the mouth.

A few hydroids are simple forms, but the majority are united into colonies, which frequently assume a branching or tree-like character, a polyp occupying the end of each branch. Reproduction is usually carried on by specially modified polyps—the *gonopolyps*, which produce jelly-fish or medusæ. These latter may remain attached to the colony or become free-swimming.

Some hydroids are entirely unprotected, no hard structures being developed, and these, consequently, leave no remains. The majority of species, however, secrete a horny or chitinous covering—the *periderm*, which invests the whole stock, and in one group is expanded, at the ends of the branches, into cups or *hydrothecæ* into which the polyps can withdraw. This chitinous periderm may be preserved in the form of a carbonaceous film.

Some hydroid colonies secrete a calcareous covering which has much the aspect of coral, and is frequently classed as such (e. g., Millepora). Most hydroid colonies are permanently attached to rocks, seaweeds, or other objects of support.

Note.—For a detailed account of the structure of living Hydrozoa, see any advanced text-book of zoölogy or anatomy. The fossil genera are discussed in Zittel's Text-book of Palæontology (Eastman's translation), where an extensive bibliography is given.

Genus DICTYONEMA. Hall.

[Ety.: *Dictyon*, net; *nema*, thread.]

(Pal. N. Y., Vol. II., p. 174.)

Colony forming a network of anastomosing branches, the whole commonly flattened on the rock, but originally forming a funnel- or fan-shaped expansion. The branches proceed from a common acute base, divide frequently, and are at intervals united again by transverse dissepiments. The outer surfaces of the branches are striated; the inner bear hydrothecæ, although these are seldom seen in the flattened specimens.

DICTYONEMA HAMILTONIÆ (?). Hall. (Fig. 1.) (Canadian Organic Remains, Decade II., 1865, p. 58, named but not described.)

*Distinguishing Characters.** — Irregularly branching. Branches freely anastomosing, and uniting by transverse thin dissepiments. Fenestrules irregular, elongate, and greatly varying in size. Surface roughly striate.

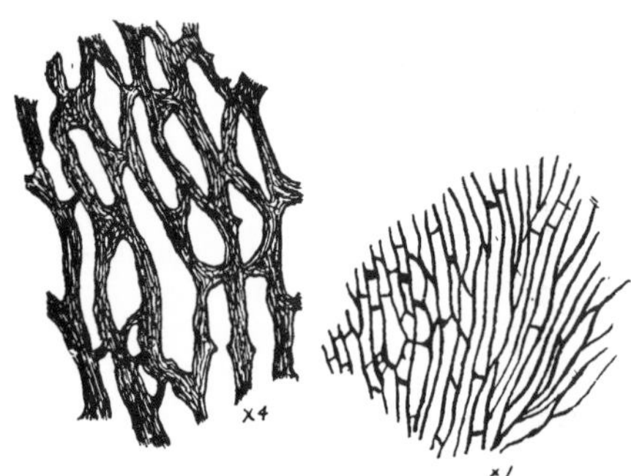

FIG. 1. *Dictyonema hamiltoniæ* (?) Idlewood Cliff. Natural size. and a portion enlarged four diameters. Stud. Pal. Col. Harvard Univ. Cat. No. 230. (Original.)

A specimen (Fig. 1) was taken from the Idlewood Cliff, by Dr. R. T. Jackson. It probably came from the Trilobite beds. Another specimen was obtained from the first South Shore Cliff, probably from the same beds.

CLASS ANTHOZOA. EHRENBERG.

The Anthozoa or coral polyps are marine animals ranging from low water to 300 and sometimes even 1,500 fathoms (Zittel). Both simple and colonial forms occur, the latter predominating at the present time, while the former were especially abundant in Palæozoic time. The "Rugose corals" or Tetracoralla, are the best represented among the fossils, commonly occurring as simple forms, though compound "heads" are by no means uncommon.

The simple *Rugose corallum* is well represented by the little *Streptelasma rectum* (Fig. 2), common throughout the Hamilton shales. It consists of numerous radiating *septa*, disposed in several cycles, and united round their outer margins by a wall or *theca* (*pseudotheca*). This is formed by the lateral expansion or thickening of the septa in that region. The exothecal prolongations of the septa are visible on the exterior of the

* The description here given applies only to the specimen illustrated. It is provisionally referred to Hall's species; the final determination must await the description of the type specimens of that species. As the above name has been adopted in the literature, it seems undesirable to replace it by another.

corallum as *costæ*. These, in the species referred to, as well as in others, commonly show the peculiar tetrameral arrangement characteristic of the septa of this group. On or near the convex longitudinal surface of the corallum a median, or "cardinal," septum appears, from which the secondary septa pass off in a pinnate manner. (Fig. 2a.) Ninety degrees towards either side occur the "alar" septa. (Fig. 2b.) These are parallel * to the secondary septa which branch off from the cardinal septum. They have a single series of secondary septa branching off from them on the side away from the *cardinal quadrants*. The two remaining, or *counter quadrants*, are filled with parallel septa, which branch off, in a pinnate manner, from the alar septa, and are completed in front by the *counter septum*, to which they are all parallel.

One of the four "primary septa"—commonly the cardinal septum—may be aborted, leaving a groove or fossula. Between the septa various endothecal tissues may be developed, such as cross-plates, or *dissepiments* connecting adjoining septa; *tabulæ* or floors, more or less dividing off the whole inner space, irrespective of the septa; and *cysts*, which form a vesicular tissue more or less regularly disposed (Cystiphyllum). The cup or calyx may be limited below by a continuous floor, by dissepiments, or otherwise, or it may be limited only by the margins of the septa, the spaces between the septa being open to the bottom of the corallum. The costæ are commonly covered by a concentrically wrinkled *epitheca*, which forms the outermost wall of the corallum.

In colonial forms the adjacent corallites commonly become prismatic from crowding. The separate thecæ may be retained, or they may become obsolete, the corallites becoming confluent. The epithecal covering in these forms is commonly confined to the free margins of the outer corallites, and surrounds the whole colony as a *peritheca*.

Reproduction takes place by ova and by budding. In certain aberrant forms, e. g., *Favositidæ*, *Monticuliporidæ*, etc., the septa are obsolete, or nearly so, but tabulæ are well developed.†

NOTE.—An account of the structure of the polyp may be obtained from any text-book of zoölogy. Zittel's Text-book of Palæontology (Eastman's translation) should be studied for this as well as the succeeding groups. The descriptions of species are still very imperfect, especially as far as the Devonian species are concerned. The only available work treating of them is the now rare volume in the Palæontology of New York series, entitled "Illustrations of Devonian Fossils," and even this is incomplete, inasmuch as it is unaccompanied by descriptions. The various sources from which the following descriptions are drawn are indicated in the references under each species. The most complete work extant is that of *Milne Edwards et Haime; Histoire Naturelle des Corallaires*, 3 volumes, and atlas; Paris, 1857–60. This classic the student will do well to consult; also the "*Monographie des Polypiers Fossiles des Terrains Palæozoiques*," by the same authors, Paris, 1851.

---

* Parallel as seen in the *costæ*.

† As no true *Hexacoralla* occur in the formations treated of in these pages, an account of their structure is omitted.

GENUS STREPTELASMA. HALL.

[ETY.: *Streptos*, twisted; *elasma*, lamella.]

(Pal., N. Y., Vol. I., p. 17.)

Corallum simple, turbinate and often curved. Septa numerous, those of the earlier cycles all reaching the center, where they are twisted into a *pseudo-columella;* those of the last cycles short. Dissepiments present. Epitheca well developed.

STREPTELASMA RECTUM. Hall. (Fig. 2.) (Ill. Dev. Foss., Pl. XIX.)

Distinguishing Characters.—Rather small size; conical outline; rapidly tapering toward the base; twisting of the septa near the center of the calyx, and formation of a solid axis or pseudo-columella; slight development of dissepiments; height, 3 or 4 cm.; diameter of calyx, 1.5 to 2 cm.

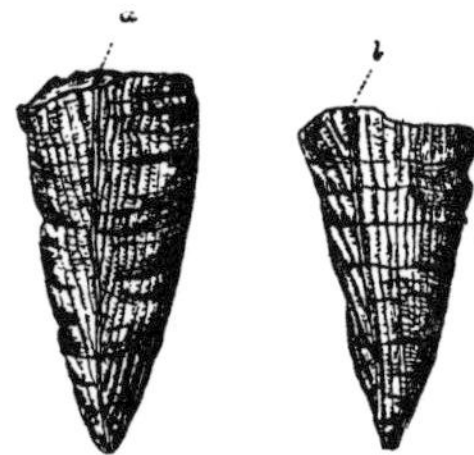

FIG. 2. *Streptelasma rectum* (after Hall). (*a*) cardinal septum; (*b*) alar septum.

Found in the lower Moscow shales near the head of Section 5; also in the Demissa bed at Section 5, and in the Trilobite beds and the shales below them down to the Nautilus bed, at Section 8, on the Lake Shore, and in the bed of Avery's Creek. It is usually abundant.

STREPTELASMA UNGULA. Hall. (Fig. 3.) (Ill. Dev. Foss., Pl. XIX.)

Distinguishing Characters.—Smaller size than *S. recta;* less degree of tapering; curved or horn-shaped outline; slight twisting of septa at the center.

FIG. 3. *Streptelasma ungula* (after Hall).

Found in the lower Moscow shales, between Sections 4 and 5.

GENUS ZAPHRENTIS. RAFINESQUE.

[ETY.: *Za*, very; *phrentis*, diaphragm.]

(An. Des. Sci. Phys. Brux., Vol. V., p. 234.)

Corallum simple, conical or turbinate, or conico-cylindrical, with a deep calyx, and well-developed septa, the primary ones reaching to the center. Dissepiments and tabulæ occur, the latter usually well developed. A deep fossula marks the abortion of one of the four primary septa. Costæ and a thin epitheca occur.

NOTE.—It is probable that several species of Zaphrentis occur in the Hamilton of this region; only one is here given, however, as definitely identified.

ZAPHRENTIS SIMPLEX. Hall. (Fig. 4.) (Ill. Dev. Foss., Pl. XXI.)

Distinguishing Characters.— Smooth and gently curving, regularly tapering outline, often abruptly deflected at the base; septa scarcely reaching the center; tabulæ strong, curving down near the margin; dissepiments few.

FIG. 4. *Zaphrentis simplex* (after Hall).

Found in the coral layer of the lower Moscow shales, at Section 5; also in the Encrinal limestone (?) on the Lake Shore, where it is rare.

GENUS AMPLEXUS. SOWERBY.

[ETY.: *Amplexus*, encircling.]

(Mineral Conchology, Vol. I., p. 165.)

Corallum simple, conical, or cylindrical, with a well-developed epitheca, and a circular, moderately deep calyx. Septa strong, short, never reaching the center, which is occupied by horizontal tabulæ, frequently bent down at the periphery. A well-developed fossula is present.

This genus differs from Zaphrentis mainly in the smooth central area of the calyx, which is formed by the tabulæ in the absence of the septa.

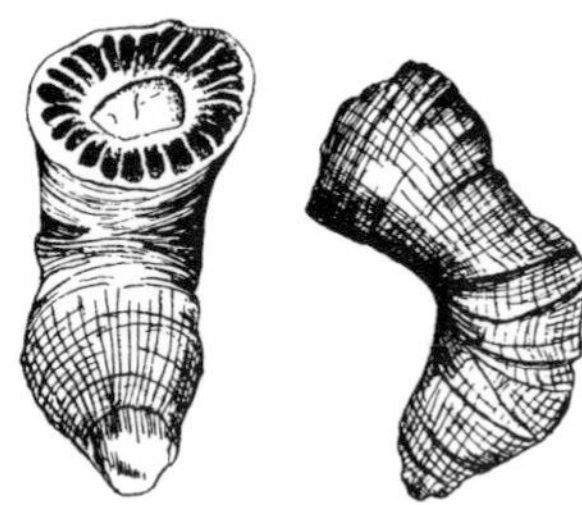

FIG. 5. *Amplexus hamiltoniæ.* Front and side view of a specimen from Morse Creek, showing irregular form, discontinuous septa and central tabulæ. The center of the calyx is broken. Natural size. Stud. Pal. Coll. Harv. Univ. Cat. No 231. (Original.)

AMPLEXUS HAMILTONIÆ. Hall. (Fig. 5.) (Ill. Dev. Foss., Pl. XIX.)

Distinguishing Characters.—Elongated cylindrical, gently tapering form, often abruptly bent at the base; strongly wrinkled epitheca; comparatively slight development of septa; well-developed tabulæ, bent down near the thin wall.

Found frequently in the Moscow shale, three to five feet above its base, between Sections 4 and 5, and at Morse Creek.

AMPLEXUS (?) INTERMITTENS.* Hall. (Fig. 6.) (Ill. Dev. Foss., Pl. XXXII., Figs. 8-13.)

FIG. 6. *Amplexus (?) intermittens* (after Hall).

Distinguishing Characters.—Small size; irregular form, varying from cylindrical, with sudden expansions, to regularly conical outline; well-developed septa, which reach to the center, and frequently unite before reaching it.

Found in the lower Moscow shale, between Sections 4 and 5. It is comparatively rare.

GENUS HELIOPHYLLUM. HALL.

[ETY.: *Helios*, sun ; *phyllon*, leaf.]

(Dana's Zoophytes, 1848, p. 356.)

Simple or compound, the individuals conical, or turbinate, with shallow calyx, and surrounded by a thin epitheca. Septa alternating in length, the longer extending to the center, all supplied with supporting lamellæ, which curve from the periphery upwards and inwards, so as to describe a convex upward-curve, and appear in the calyx as crossbars or carinæ.

HELIOPHYLLUM HALLI: E. and H. (Fig. 7.) (Ill. Dev. Foss., Pl. XXIII.)

* This species is probably not an Amplexus, nor does it seem to belong to any described genus.

Distinguishing Characters.—Simple corallum; cylindrico-conical or turbinate outline with moderate curvature at the base; circular and moderately profound calyx; small fossula; well-pronounced, but rather small, carinæ; strongly wrinkled epitheca.

Found abundantly in the coral layer of the lower Moscow shales, at Sections 5 to 7, and on the Lake Shore; also in the Demissa bed of Section 5 (one specimen).

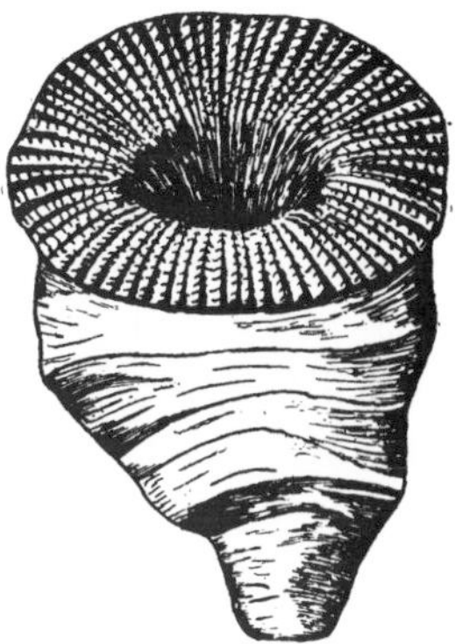

FIG. 7. *Heliophyllum halli* (after Hall).

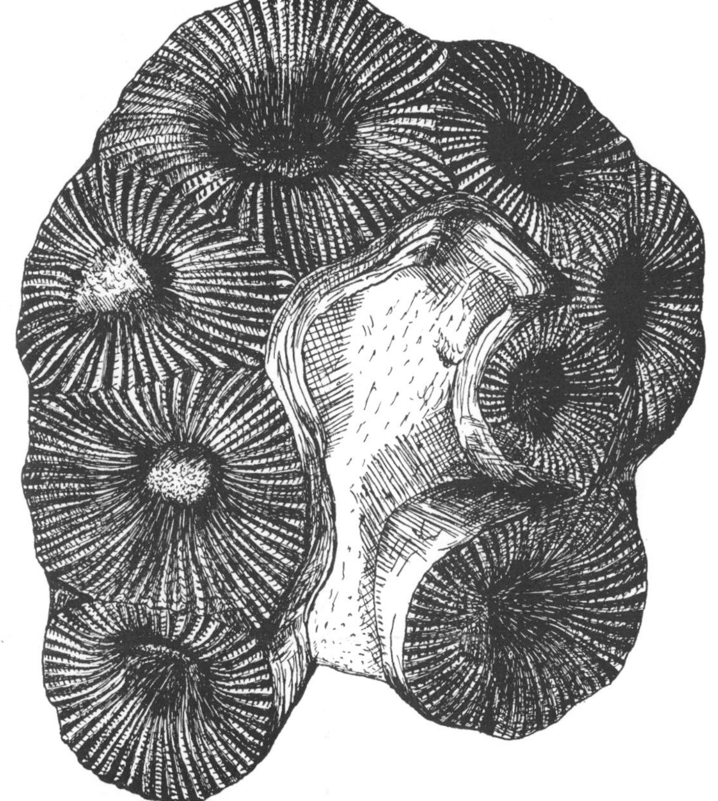

FIG. 8. *Heliophyllum confluens.* From a specimen in the Student Palæontological collection of Harvard University. Cat. No. 232. (Original.)

Heliophyllum confluens. Hall. (Fig. 8.) (Ill. Dev. Foss. Corals., Pl. XXVI.)

Distinguishing Characters.—Compound or confluent growth, often forming heads of considerable size; strongly wrinkled peritheca surrounding the colony, and the free parts of individual corallites where separated; moderately deep calices; well-developed carinated septa.

Found only in the Encrinal limestone, on the Lake Shore. (Also at Morse Creek.) It is rare.

Genus CYSTIPHYLLUM. Londsdale.

[Ety.: *Kustis*, cavity; *phyllon*, leaf.]

(Murch. Sil. Syst., p. 691, 1839.)

Chiefly simple coralla, varying in outline from depressed turbinate to cylindrical; often irregular in growth. Septa rudimentary and frequently obsolete, the floor of the calyx being formed by the upper portion of the vesiculate filling. Entire interior of corallum filled with vesicular tissue, disposed in more or less regular series, and presenting in section a rough tabulate appearance. An epitheca is present. Frequent constrictions occur in some forms, indicating periodic rejuvenation.

Fig. 9. *Cystiphyllum conifollis.* Showing the prevailing form and irregularities (after Hall).

Cystiphyllum conifollis. Hall. (Fig. 9.) (Pal. N. Y. Ill. Dev. Foss., Pl. XXX., Figs. 3–9.)

Distinguishing Characters.—Slender cylindrical form; irregular, intermittent growth; coarse wrinkled epitheca; moderate-sized cysts arranged in a cup-like manner; rather shallow calyx with simulation of septa by the radial arrangement of the cysts.

Found in the coral layer of the lower Moscow shales, at Sections 5, 6, 7; also on the Lake Shore. Occasionally it occurs in the Demissa bed.

Cystiphyllum americanum. E. and H. (Fig. 10.) (Pol. Foss. d. Terr. Pal., p. 464.)

FIG. 10. ?*Cystyphyllum americanum.* A specimen from the coral layer of Section 5. Natural size. Stud. Pal. Coll. Harv. Univ. Cat. 233. (Original.)

Distinguishing Characters.— Elongated, cylindrico-turbinate, straight or slightly curved form; thin, but strongly wrinkled, epitheca; moderate depth of calyx, with faint indications of septal ridges about its sides; irregular vesicular tissue, dense near the wall, coarser near the center.

Found in the coral layer and above it in the lower Moscow shales, at Section 5.

CYSTIPHYLLUM VARIANS. Hall. (Fig. 10A.) (Ill. Dev. Foss., pl. XXIX., 1876.)

Distinguishing Characters.— Irregular cylindrical or conical form, varying greatly; coarse, wrinkled epitheca, which, near the base, is often produced into irregular projections which serve to cement the coral to a shell or other foreign object; moderately deep funnel-shaped calyx, its floor formed by the upper surfaces of the cysts, septa in the form of radiating ridges. Interior structure cellulose, the cysts of moderate size and arranged in cup-in-cup manner.

Found in the Hamilton group of Eighteen Mile Creek. (Coll. Am. Mus. Nat. Hist. New York.)

FIG. 10A. *Cystiphyllum varians.* A small specimen (after Hall).

Genus CYATHOPHYLLUM. Goldfuss.

[Ety.: *Kuathos*, cup; *phyllon*, leaf (septum).]

Corallum simple or compound; the individuals conical, conico-cylindrical, or prismatic and closely crowded, forming astræi-form heads. Septa well developed, radially arranged, the larger extending to the center, where they are twisted into a pseudo-columella. Costæ absent. Tabulæ present, but only in the center of the visceral chamber, the outer area being filled with vesicular dissepiments. Exterior covered with an epitheca. Asexual reproduction by calicinal or lateral gemmation.

Fig. 10B. *Cyathophyllum conatum.* Lateral and calicinal view of a small specimen (after Hall).

Cyathophyllum conatum. Hall. (Fig. 10B.) (Ill. Dev. Foss., Pl. XXXI., 1876.)

Distinguishing Characters.—Irregular, cylindrical or conico-cylindrical growth, often variously bent; frequent constrictions, leaving the septate rim of the older calice projecting around the base of the newer one; well developed alternating, radiating septa; rather smoothly wrinkled epitheca; numerous closely crowded irregular tabulæ bending down at the periphery; well developed dissepiments in peripheral zone.

Found in the Hamilton group of Eighteen Mile Creek. (Coll. Am. Mus. Nat. Hist. New York.)

Genus HADROPHYLLUM. E. and H.

[Ety.: *Hadros*, mighty; *phyllon*, leaf (septum).]

(Brit. Foss. Corals, p. lxvii., 1850.)

Corallum simple, short, cushion-shaped, with the lower part covered by an epitheca. Calyx superficial, with three septal fossulæ, that of the cardinal septum being the largest. Septa stout, numerous, approaching radial arrangement which is however imperfect. Tabulæ and dissepiments wanting.

Hadrophyllum woodi. sp. nov.* (Fig. 10C.) (Compare *Amplexus* (?) *intermittens*.)

* Named in honor of Miss Elvira Wood, Instructor in Palæontology, Mass. Inst. Technology.

Fig. 10 C. *Hadrophyllum woodi.* Type specimen Morse Creek : natural size. (Original.)

Distinguishing Characters.—Corallum small, turbinate, regularly expanding from the base. Calyx superficial, sub-circular. Cardinal septum aborted, forming the main fossula, which is very broad. The two septa bounding the cardinal septum reach the center, and the remaining septa of the cardinal quadrants unite with these. Alar septa reach center. Lateral fossulæ not formed by the abortion of septa, but by the union, among themselves, of the septa in the counter quadrants, and their separation from the alar septa. Counter septum not reaching the center. A pseudo-columella is formed by the junction of the longer septa in the center.

Found in the lower Moscow shale at Eighteen Mile and Morse creeks (rare).

GENUS CRASPEDOPHYLLUM. DYBOWSKY.

[ETY.: *Kraspedos*, an edge; *phyllon*, leaf.]

(Beschr., von neuen Devonischen Arten der Zoantharia Rugosa, p. 153.)

Corallum simple or fasciculate; corallites commonly cylindrical, each with a moderately-deep calyx and well-developed epitheca. A secondary central wall is present, which is not crossed by the septa, the longer of which join it to the outer wall. Inner area with tabulæ, outer with dissepiments. Upper edges of septa carinate.

CRASPEDOPHYLLUM ARCHIACI. Billings. (Not figured.) (*Diphyphyllum archiaci.* Billings. Canadian Journal, Vol. V., p. 260, Fig. 8.)

Distinguishing Characters.—Heads consisting of parallel nearly straight cylindrical corallites, nearly or quite in contact with each other; young stems added by lateral or marginal gemmation; central tube small, apparently wanting in some corallites; dissepiments numerous; epitheca showing numerous lines of growth, and sharp-edged annulations. Some corallites exhibit sudden constrictions of growth.

Found in the Hamilton group (Encrinal limestone ?) on the shore of Lake Erie. (Coll. Am. Mus. Nat. Hist. New York.)

CRASPEDOPHYLLUM SUBCÆSPITOSUM. (Nicholson.) (Fig. 11.) (*Heliophyllum subcæspitosum*, Nicholson, Geological Magazine, London, Dec. II., Vol. I., 1874, p. 58, Pl. IV., Fig. 9.)

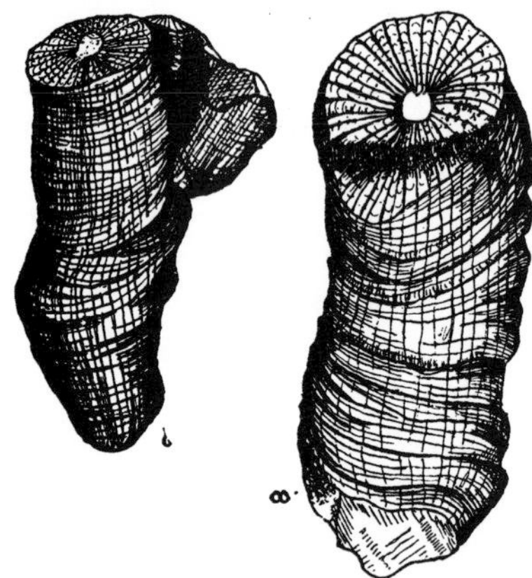

FIG. 11. *Craspedophyllum subcæspitosum.* Encrinal limestone. (*a*) Single branch, Eighteen Mile Creek; (*b*) Specimen with several branches. Morse Creek. Stud. Pal. Coll. Harv. Univ. Cat. 234. (Original.)

Distinguishing Characters.—Cylindrical corallites, which sometimes slightly expand towards the calyx; simple or compound form, the latter consisting of two or three buds around the parent corallite; parallel position of corallites; wrinkled epitheca; secondary wall and carinæ.

Found in the Encrinal limestone, at Section 5; also at Morse Creek.

GENUS FAVOSITES. LAMARK.

[ETY.: *Favus*, honeycomb.]

(Hist. des An. sans Vert., Tome 2, p. 204.)

Corallum massive, more rarely branching, commonly forming heads which may be a foot or more in diameter. Corallites prismatic, thin, united by their walls, which are perforated by equi-distant pores. Septa rudimentary or obsolete. Numerous more or less regular tabulæ divide the intrathecal space. Peritheca present.

FIG. 12. *Favosites argus.* Outline of a small specimen, and enlargement of a portion of the surface (after Hall).

FAVOSITES ARGUS. Hall. (Fig. 12.) (Ill. Dev. Foss., Pl. XXXIV.)

Distinguishing Characters.—Hemispheric, pyriform, or sub-globular form; two sizes of cell apertures, the larger circular and with prominent crenulated rims or peristomes, the smaller angular.

Found in the Demissa bed (?), at Eighteen Mile Creek.

Favosites hamiltoniæ. Hall. (Fig. 13.) (Ill. Dev. Foss., Pl. XXXIV.)

Distinguishing Characters.—Hemispherical heads, often of large size; the base covered by peritheca; slender corallites; somewhat distant mural pores, in two rows; rather closely crowded tabulæ, some of which are horizontal, others bent down at the angles.

Fig. 13. *Favosites hamiltoniæ.* A fragment of a head slightly enlarged, showing the columnar corallites and the mural pores (after Hall).

Found in the Encrinal limestone, at Section 5, and the Lake Shore; also at Morse Creek, at which place heads, a foot or more in diameter, occur.

Genus PLEURODICTYUM. Goldfuss.

[Ety.: *Pleura*, side; *dictyon*, net.]

(Petref. Germ., Vol. I., p. 209.)

Corallum depressed, discoidal, lower surface covered by a concentrically wrinkled peritheca. Corallites small, prismatic, funnel-shaped below; septa faint or obsolete, a scanty development of tabulæ occurring; mural pores irregularly distributed.

Pleurodictyum stylopora. (Eaton.) (Fig. 14.) Ill. Dev. Foss., Pl. XVIII.)

Distinguishing Characters.—Flat base, covered by peritheca; faint septa; crenulated margins of calices; irregular convex or concave tabulæ; diameter one to two inches.

Fig. 14. *Pleurodictyum stylopora* (after Hall).

Found in the Pleurodictyum beds of Avery's Ravine and the Lake Shore (usually abundant).

Genus AULOPORA. Goldfuss.

[Ety.: *Aulos*, pipe; *poros*, pore.]

(Goldf. Petrefact. Germ., p. 82.)

Corallum prostrate, the corallites adhering to foreign bodies by the whole of the lower surface. Corallites slender, joined, the cavity of each communicating with that of the one from which it springs; septa rudimentary or absent; tabulæ curved.

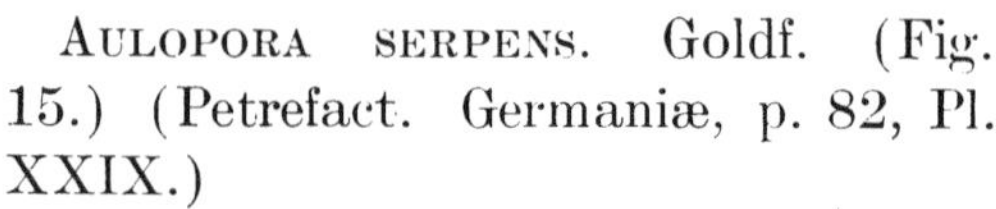

Fig. 15. *Aulopora serpens.* Attached to a shell of *Athyris spiriferoides.* From Section 8, Eighteen Mile Creek. From a specimen in the Student Palæontological Collection, Harvard University. Cat. 235. (Original.)

AULOPORA SERPENS. Goldf. (Fig. 15.) (Petrefact. Germaniæ, p. 82, Pl. XXIX.)

Distinguishing Characters.—Budding somewhat below the calices; one or two buds from each corallite; anastomosing of corallites, forming enclosed meshes of various sizes and forms. Found on brachiopods in the Demissa bed, at Section 5, and in the Athyris bed, at Section 7 (rare).

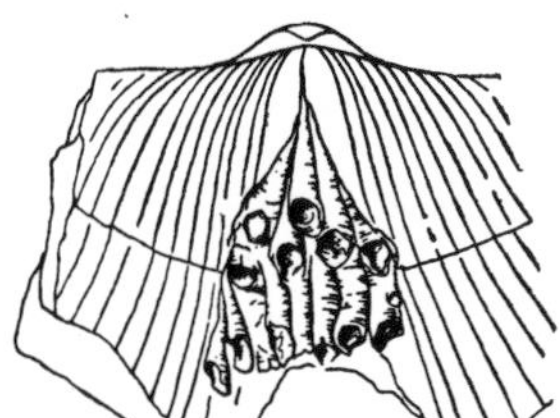

Fig. 16. *Aulopora tubœformis.* Attached to *Spirifer granulosus;* Pleurodictyum bed, at Avery's Creek. Student Palæontological Collection, Harvard University. Cat. 236. (Original.)

AULOPORA TUBÆFORMIS. Goldf. (Fig. 16.) (Petrefact. Germ., p. 83, Pl. XXIX.)

Distinguishing Characters.—Large curved corallites, which are enlarged at the mouth, budding from near center of preceding corallite; no intergrowth of corallites, but occasionally a lateral union occurs by the erect portion of the walls.

Found in Avery's Ravine, four feet below the Trilobite beds, on brachiopod shells (rare).

GENUS CERATOPORA. GRABAU.

[ETY.: *Ceras*, horn ; *poros*, pore.]

(1899: Proc. Bost. Soc. Nat. History, Vol. XXVIII, No. 16.)

Corallum compound, increasing by lateral gemmation; erect or prostrate, but never attached above the base; septa absent, or represented merely by vertical ridges or costæ seen on the outside of the corallum. Calyx deep, funnel-shaped, thin-walled, and continued downwards in a narrower tube, formed by the thickening of the walls, through the addition, internally, of concentric layers of sclerenchyma,

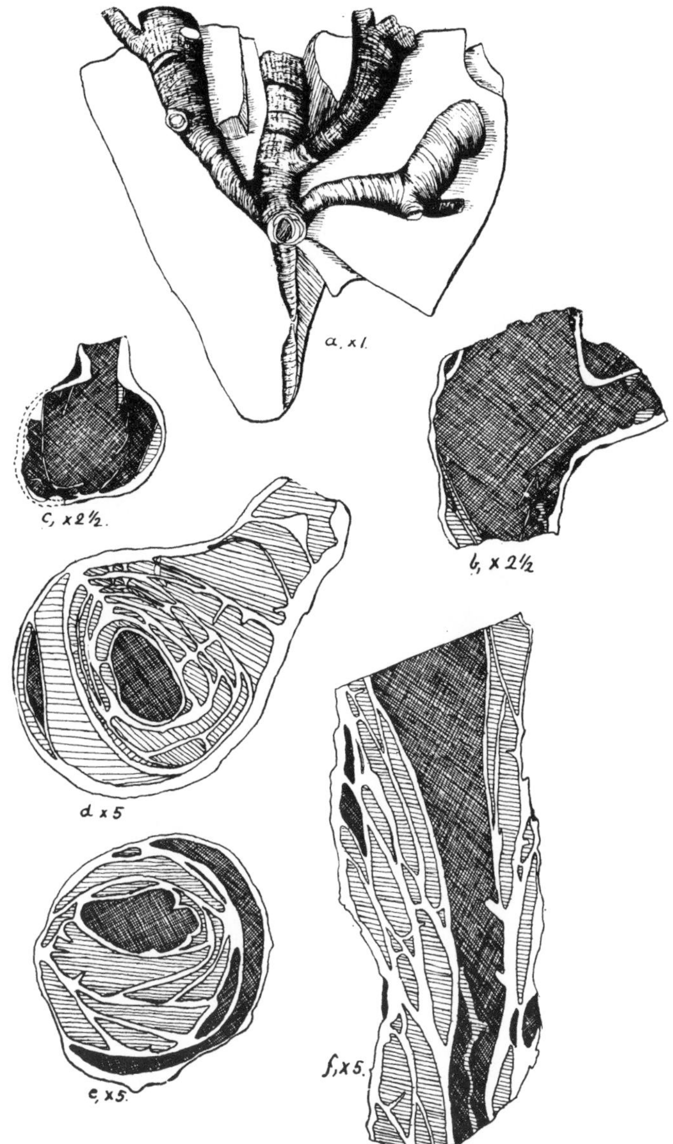

Fig. 17. *Ceratopora jacksoni.* (*a*) The type specimen natural size; (*b*) longitudinal section of a calyx, showing bud, and absence of cysts in the upper part, x 2½; (*c*) cross-section of calyx, and bud, x 2½; (*d*, *e*) cross-sections of corallites, showing the cysts and the central living chamber, also the spines or trabeculæ, x 5; (*f*) longitudinal section of a corallite, x 5. The dark shading indicates cavities filled with mud, the light shading those filled by crystalline calcite. (Original.)

and through the formation of coarse cysts. No true tabulæ are known; the polypites in some of the species apparently remained connected throughout the life of the colony, while in others the cavities of the corallites are separated by a spicular partition. Surface formed by a wrinkled epitheca.

CERATOPORA JACKSONI. Grabau. (Fig. 17.) (1899. Proc. Boston Soc. Nat. History, Vol. XXVIII, p. 415, Pls. I., II.)

Distinguishing Characters.—Erect, irregular, and frequently-branching corallum; cylindrical or trumpet-shaped corallites; coarsely wrinkled epitheca with costal ridges; coarse, irregular internal cysts, arranged semi-concentrically, with frequent projecting spine-like processes.

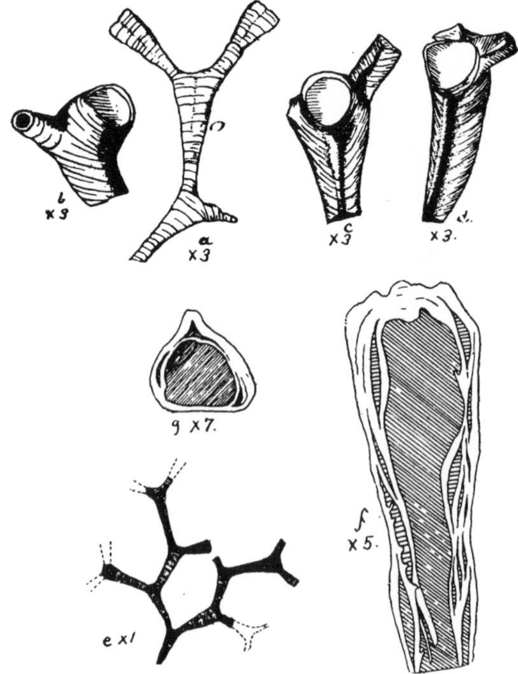

FIG. 18. *Ceratopora dichotoma.* (*a–d*) Specimens viewed from different positions, showing the flattened under side, the calyx, carination, and lines of growth, x 3; (*e*) specimen seen from below, showing the characteristic mode of branching—natural size; (*f*) longitudinal section of the procumbent portion of a corallite, showing the living chamber and the cysts, x 5; (*g*) transverse section of procumbent tube, showing central cavity, cysts, and hollow carina, x 7. (Original.)

Found in the Demissa bed, at Section 5, Eighteen Mile Creek (common). It is often overgrown with bryozoa. Also found at Morse Creek. This species is readily recognized by its cylindrical corallites, numerous irregular branches and coarse cysts, which are well shown in cross-section.

CERATOPORA DICHOTOMA. Grabau. (Fig. 18.) (1899. Proc. Bost. Soc. Nat. History, Vol. XXVIII., p. 418, Pls. II. to IV.)

Distinguishing Characters.—Free prostrate habitat; lower flattened, and upper convex or sloping and carinated surfaces; abruptly upturned calices; regular dichotomous branching, with branches diverging at right angles; triangular cross-section of main tube; circular cross-section of calyx; large inner cavity lined with moderate-sized cysts and trabeculæ; wrinkled epitheca.

Found in the lower Moscow shales, three to five feet above the Encrinal limestone. Also in the Demissa bed, at Section 5; and in the Lower shales, seven feet below the Encrinal limestone, at Section 6; and between nine and twenty-one feet below that bed, at Section 7.

This species is readily recognized by its regular branches, its flattened lower surface, triangular cross-section, upturned, round calyx, and central carination. The specimens vary greatly in size, those of the Demissa bed being the largest. They are usually found with the calices embedded in the shale, the flat face alone being exposed.

GENUS TRACHYPORA. E. AND H.

[ETY.: *Trachys*, rough; *poros*, pore.]

(1851: Edwards and Haime, Pol. Foss., d. Terr. Pal., p. 305.)

Corallum dendroid, with cylindrical stems. The corallites are polygonal, with very thick walls, the calices being rounded and superficially far apart. Mural pores few, irregularly distributed; septa represented by rows of spines; tabulæ present at remote intervals.

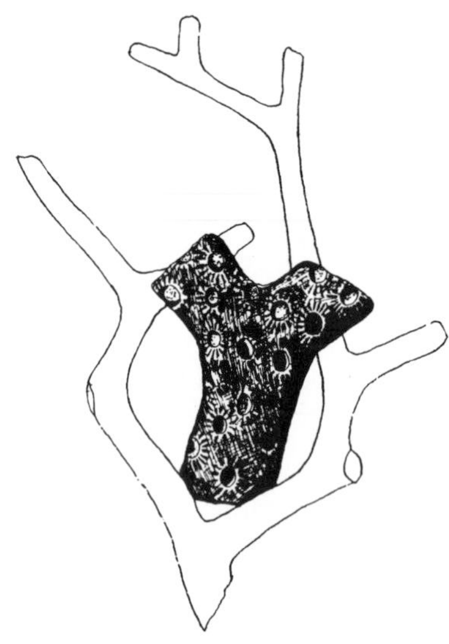

FIG. 19. *Trachypora limbata.* Branch natural size, and a portion enlarged to show the calices (after Hall).

TRACHYPORA LIMBATA. (Eaton.) (Fig. 19.) (Ill. Dev. Foss., Pl. XXXIII. *Striatopora limbata.*)

Distinguishing Characters.—Rather irregularly disposed oval calices; moderately strong peristomes, with radiating ridges running out upon the thickened walls; corallites abruptly bent outwards.

Found on the " . . . south Shore of Lake Erie, near Eighteen Mile Creek." (Eaton, Geol. Text-book, p. 39.) Common at Morse Creek.

GENUS MONOTRYPA. NICHOLSON.

[ETY.: *Monos,* one ; *trypa,* hole.]

(1879 : Nicholson, Tabulate Corals of the Paleozoic Period, p. 293.)

Corallum composed of long, slender, prismatic corallites, which are of two kinds, not conspicuously different from each other. The large tubes are aggregated into clusters or "monticules," and very slightly differ in size from the smaller ones. The smaller tubes occupy all the spaces between the monticules. All the corallites of both kinds are thin-walled, regularly polygonal, and similarly tabulate, the tabulæ being remote and few in number, and not uncommonly disposed at corresponding levels in contiguous tubes.

MONOTRYPA FRUTICOSA. (Hall.) (Fig. 20.) (*Chætetes fruticosus.* Hall. Ill. Dev. Foss., Pl. XXXVIII.)

Distinguishing Characters.—Tubes passing upwards and gently bending outwards from a central imaginary axis; numerous small, low, monticules, scattered over the surface of the branches; calices of monticules larger than those on remainder of branches; tabulæ remote, except near the surface, where they are numerous.

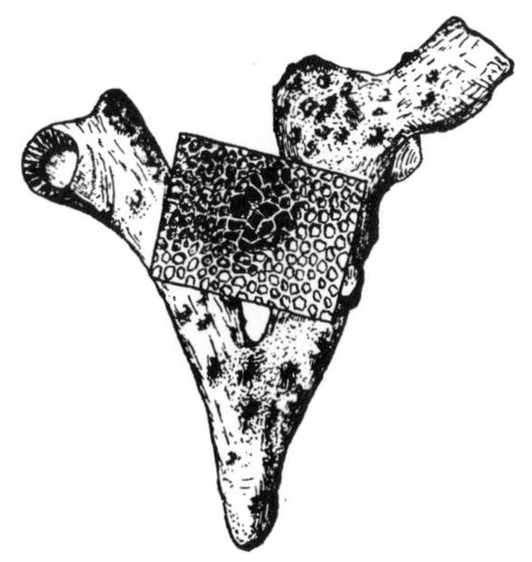

Fig. 20. *Monotrypa fruticosa.* A specimen of the natural size, and a portion of the surface enlarged (after Hall).

Found in the Moscow shale, three to five feet above the Encrinal limestone, at Section 5; also in the Demissa bed of Section 5; between ten and fifteen feet below the Encrinal limestone, at Section 7, and in the Pleurodictyum beds of Avery's Creek (rather rare).

Monotrypa (?) furcata. (Hall.) (Fig. 21.) (*Chætetes furcatus.* Hall. Ill. Dev. Foss., Pls. XXXVII. and XXXVIII.)

Distinguishing Characters.—Branching form similar to the preceding, from which it differs chiefly in the absence of the monticules, and in the transversely-ridged appearance of the corallites. (On a number of specimens, apparently of this species, spines or acanthopores occur at the angle of junction of the corallites, a feature which would demand the removal of the species to another genus. See Ulrich, Paleozoic Bryozoa, Palæontology of Illinois, Vol. VIII., Part II., Section 6, 1890.)

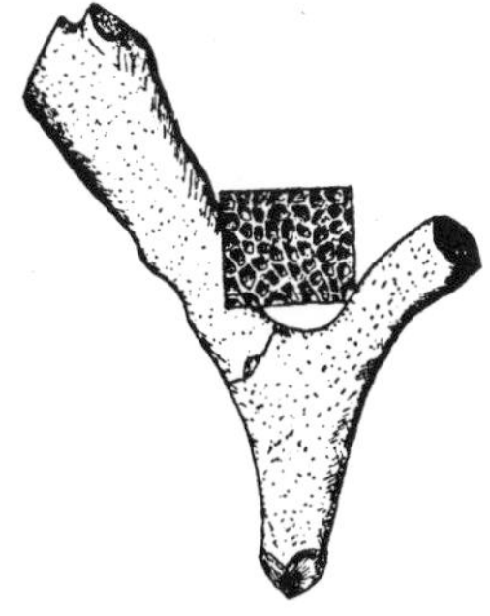

Fig. 21. *Monotrypa* (?) *furcata.* A specimen of the natural size, and a portion of the surface enlarged (after Hall).

Found in the Demissa bed, at Section 5, and two to four feet below the Trilobite beds, at Avery's Creek.

Monotrypa amplectens. sp. nov. (Fig. 22.)

Distinguishing Characters.—Encrusting habit; uniform, rather large, and regularly distributed monticules, the calices of which are larger than those of the main mass; small, new

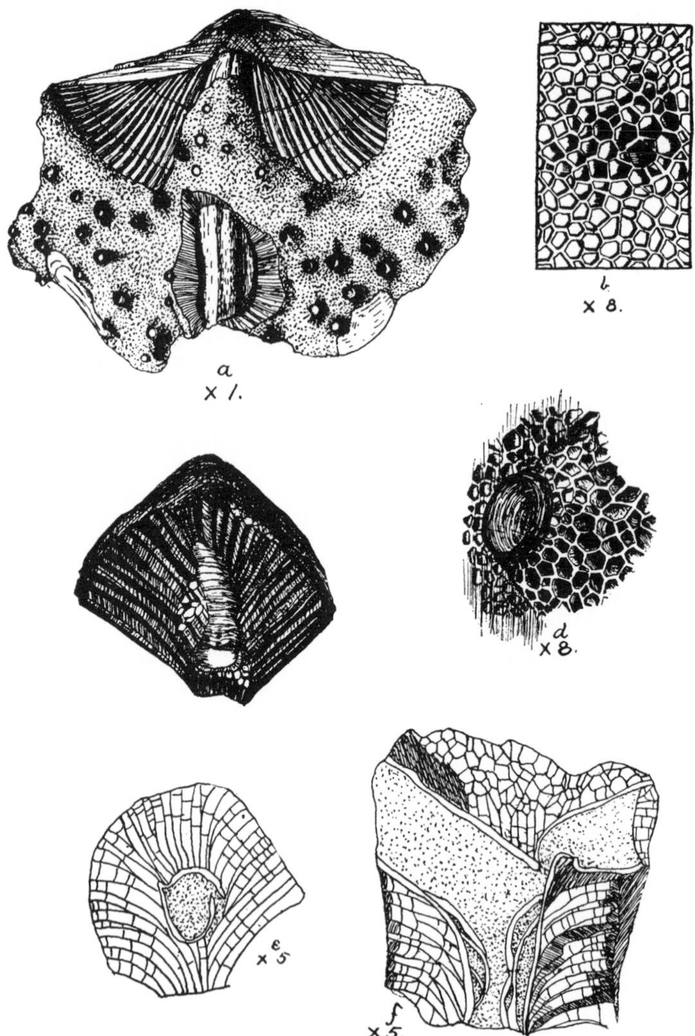

FIG. 22. *Monotrypa amplectens.* (*a*) Shell of *Spirifer granulosus* with *Aulopora tubæformis* attached to it, the whole overgrown with *Monotrypa amplectens*; the calices of the Aulopora appear like craters above the surface of the Monotrypa colony; natural size; (*b*) a portion of the surface enlarged, showing the larger corallites of the monticules, x 8; (*c*) a portion much enlarged, showing a buried branch of the Aulopora: (*d*) a calyx of Aulopora enlarged, showing the relation of the Monotrypa to it, x 8; (*e*, *f*) sections showing specimens enclosing a branch of Ceratopora, also showing tabulæ, x 5. (Original.)

individuals appear between the larger corallites of the monticules, occasionally between those of the interspaces. Corallites with fine transverse striæ; walls of uniform thickness throughout; tabulæ at irregular intervals, remote in older parts of tube, more closely set in outer portions.

This coral is almost always found encrusting *Aulopora tubæformis*, which in turn grows on shells of *Spirifer granulosus*. These shells when full-grown apparently became free, and rolling over, so as to lie on the pedicle valve, allowed the growth of the Aulopora on the upturned brachial valve —particularly on the mesial fold. No shell with the coral on the pedicle valve has been observed. All the specimens obtained showed the Monotrypa growing on the Aulopora in various stages of development. The specimen (Fig. 22a) shows the most advanced stage, where the Monotrypa has completely enveloped the Aulopora, as well as the greater portion of the shell. It has forced the Aulopora to depart from its normal method of growth (compare Fig. 16), which is prostrate, and bend upward, at right angles, its calices appearing on the surface, like a series of crater-like rims, rising above the monticules of the Monotrypa. The two types probably lived together as commensals, judging from the constant association, although in places the Aulopora becomes completely overgrown by the Monotrypa. This may indicate a choking of the former by the latter, or it may mean burial after death. In several parts of the specimen (Fig. 22a) the encrusting corals near the front have grown beyond the edge of the shell, and there assumed the cylindrical outline of the colony, similar to that of *M. fruticosa.*

Found in the middle and upper Pleurodictyum beds of Avery's Creek and Wanakah Cliff; also in the calcareous bed, above the Pleurodictyum bed, at Avery's Creek.

Class Crinoidea. Miller.

The crinoids, or sea-lilies, are marine invertebrates, represented in the modern seas by a number of genera and species, which range from shallow water to a maximum depth of about 3,000 fathoms. They are gregarious in habit, and usually of very local distribution. A typical crinoid consists of a dorsal cup or *calyx*, placed upon a *stalk*, by means of which it is attached, and bears a fringe of *arms*, variously divided and furnished with jointed appendages or *pinnules*. The calyx is composed of a number of plates, which have a definite arrangement, in horizontally disposed series (Fig. 25). The lowest of these are the *basals*, though in many forms an additional series, the *infrabasals*, may underlie and alternate with the basals. Next above the basals, and alternating with them in position, are the *radials*, five in number, so called because they are in line with the rays or arms. Referring the position of the inferior plates to that of the radials, we find that the basals are always situated *interradially*, while the infrabasals are situated *radially*. Above the radials lie the *brachials*. These vary greatly in number and kind, sometimes articulating directly with the radials, in which case all the brachials are free, and sometimes having their lower series fixed and immovable, thus forming a part of the calyx. The brachials lying directly upon the radials are the *costals;* of these there may be one or more series, when they are distinguished from below up as *primary* (cost.^{1}), *secondary* (cost.^{2}), etc. The uppermost costal of each ray is commonly axillary, i. e., pentagonal in outline, with two upper joint edges inclined from each other. On these rest the *distichals*, of which there are ten in each series. Secondary distichals (dist.^{2}) may rest upon the primary ones (dist.^{1}), and may in turn support the *palmars*, of which there would be twenty in a normal series. Above these, on further division, are the *post-palmars*, which are often very numerous. Two types of arms can be distinguished, those composed throughout of one series of plates (uniserial), or those made up of a double series (biserial), the plates of which usually interlock to a greater or less extent. These latter are the more specialized, always beginning uniserially.

Between the radials are often found additional plates, the *interradials*, which may vary in number.

Between the distichals of one ray may occur the *interdistichals*, which are situated *radially*. Between the distichals of adjacent rays may occur the *interbrachials*, and these will be situated *interradially*. An anal interradius is present in unsymmetrical forms. The *tegmen* forms the cover, or ventral part, of the calyx, and is composed of plates either closely anchylosed, or held together by a leathery membrane. In the Palæozoic *Camerata* the plates of the ventral disc fit closely and they are considerably thickened, forming a very rigid, more or less convex, vault, from which may arise the plated anal proboscis.

The mouth of Palæozoic crinoids is usually beneath the tegmen, the only external opening in the tegmen being that of the eccentric anus. From the mouth, radiating grooves or canals commonly pass outward to the arms, in which they are continued. These are the ambulacral grooves, along which the food, caught on the arms, is conveyed to the central mouth. These grooves may be open or covered by plates. Within the cavity of the calyx are the viscera.

The stalk, or *stem*, is composed of a varying number of joints, which are circular, elliptical, or angular in cross-section (Fig. 29). The joint nearest to the calyx is the last formed one. Frequently, a certain number of the joints bear root-like extensions, or *cirri*. The stem and cirri are pierced by an axial canal, round or pentagonal in cross-section. The stem was in most cases attached by a root (Fig. 29, *m-o*).

NOTE.—For a more detailed account of the structure of the crinoids, and for a discussion of their development and affinities, see Zittel's "Text-book of Palæontology" (Eastman's translation), pp. 124-133. The magnificent work of Wachsmuth and Springer, "The Crinoidea Camerata of North America," published by the Museum of Comparative Zoölogy,* at Cambridge, will be found exhaustive and indispensable to the advanced student of crinoids.

Specific descriptions are usually scattered through scientific publications; those of the division *Camerata* may, however, be found in the monograph of Wachsmuth and Springer, above referred to.

GENUS GENNÆOCRINUS. W. AND S.

[ETY.: *Gennaios*, of noble birth; *krinon*, lily.]

(1882: Proc. Acad. Nat. Sci., p. 334.)

Calyx deeply indented at the arm region. Plates thin, ornamented with radiating striæ. Axial canal large, pentalobate. Basals three, small. Radials and costals similar, the former five, the latter 2x5. Costals hexagonal and heptagonal, respectively. Above the distichals the branching is from alternate sides, arms branching off at one side, and brachials of a higher order at the other. Arms eight. Interradials numerous. Tegmen of small plates; no anal proboscis.

GENNÆOCRINUS NYSSA. (Hall.) (Fig. 23, *a-d.*)

(*Actinocrinus nyssa*. Hall. 1862. 15th Rep't N. Y. State Cab. Nat. Hist., p. 129.)

Distinguishing Characters.—Calyx wider than high; lobed at arm region; arms given off in clusters; semi-globose calyx; striated plates, a ridge passing to each face of the plate, and another to each angle; ridges of adjoining plates form triangles; ridges of radial plates increase in prominence towards distichals, having at the arm bases almost the width of the arms; short flat basals; radials and costals as long as wide, decreasing rapidly in size upwards; second

*Mem. Mus. Comp. Zoöl., Vol. XXIV.

costals less than half the size of the radials. Distichals 2x10, comparatively small, wider than long, the second ones axillary.

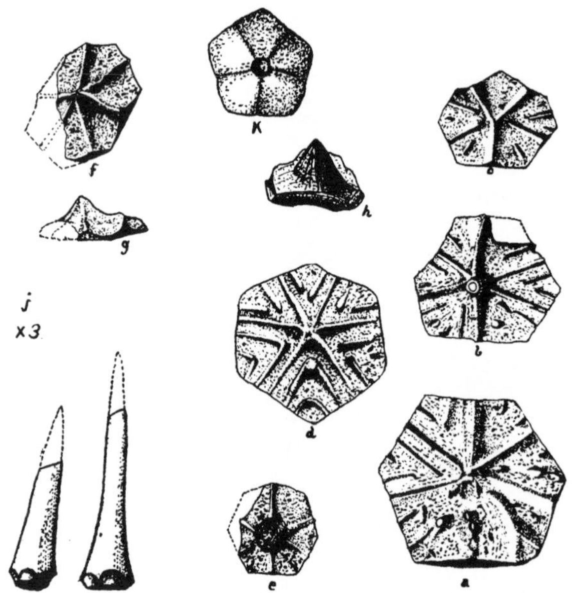

FIG. 23, *a–d*. *Gennæocrinus nyssa*. (*a*) radial; (*b*, *c*) brachial; (*b*, cost. 1, *c*, cost. 2); (*d*) interradial.

FIG. 24, *e–g*. *G. eucharis*. (*e*) Plate of unknown position, bearing tubercle or spine; (*f*, *g*) interradial (?) plate; (*h*) tegminal spine of unknown species; (*i*) spines of *Dorycrinus* (?) sp.; (*k*) part of calyx of unknown affinities. (All enlarged. Original.)

Found as dissociated plates in the Demissa and Stictopora beds of Section 5 (rather rare).

GENNÆOCRINUS EUCHARIS. (Hall.) (Fig. 24, *e–g*.)

(*Actinocrinus eucharis*. Hall. 15th Rep't, N. Y. State Cab. Nat. Hist., p. 130.)

Distinguishing Characters.—Low basals, large radials; cost.[1] hexagonal, cost.[2] pentagonal, small; ten or eleven interradials in each interradius, except the anal interradius, which contains a greater number; strong, radiating surface-ridges on plates; center of plates nodose.

Found in the Demissa bed of Section 5, as detached plates (rare).

GENUS DORYCRINUS. ROEMER.

[ETY.: *Dory*, spear; *krinon*, lily.]

(1854: Archiv. für Naturgesch. Jahr. XIX., Bd. I., p. 207.)

This genus seems to be represented in the Hamilton beds of this region by strong tegminal spines, which were found in the Demissa bed. (Fig. 24, *i.*) The genus, as restricted by Wachsmuth and Springer, has, to my knowledge, not been recorded from so low an horizon.

The spinose tegminal plate (Fig. 24, *h*) and the calyx base (Fig. 24, *k*) have not been identified.

GENUS HABROCRINUS. D'ORB.

[ETY.: *Habros*, splendid; *krinon*, lily.]

(1851: *Abracrinus* D'Orbigny,—Cours elém. de Paléont, Vol. II., Fasc. II., p. 144. *Habrocrinus* (D'Orb.) Angelin,—Iconographia crinoideorum, p. 3.)

Basals three, equal; costals 2 x 5, the distichals supporting the arms. Anal interradial plate very large, heptagonal, and followed by a second between two inter-brachials, above which follow numerous other plates. Arms uniserial, long, heavy, and simple throughout.

HABROCRINUS PENTADACTYLUS. sp. nov. (Fig. 25.)

Distinguishing Characters. — Obconical form, uniformly enlarging from base upwards; rather large basal plates; large radials and smaller costals; strong, carinate, rounded

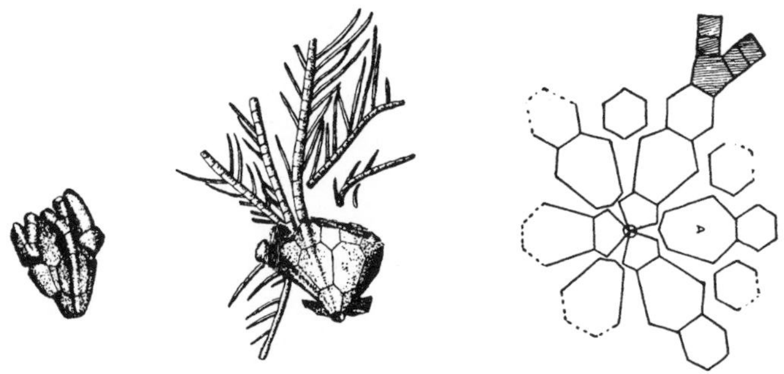

FIG. 25. *Habrocrinus pentadactylus.* Two specimens enlarged, with an analysis of the calyx. (a.) Anal interradius. The shaded portion is added from the smaller of the two specimens. (Original.)

ridges extending from the base to the ten arms, along the five rays.

Found in the Moscow shale of Section 5, two feet above the base (two specimens).

NOTE.—This species is the first of the genus noted above the Silurian, as well as the first representative of the genus in America; the other species being known from Gotland and England.

GENUS PLATYCRINUS. MILLER.

[ETY.: *Platys*, flat; *krinon*, lily.]

(Miller, Natural History of Crinoidea, p. 73, 1821.)

Calyx composed of three unsymmetrical and frequently anchylosed basals, succeeded by five large radials, laterally united by close sutures, their upper margins crescent-shaped. The costals are small and axillary, the single series being often entirely hidden. The distichals commonly in two rows, the upper axillary, and bearing the palmars. The first row of interradials is on a level with the arm bases, and is in part interbrachial, and in part interambulacral. The succeeding interradials are all interambulacral. Anal interradius of numerous plates. Arms simple, dividing and becoming biserial, i. e., composed of a double row of plates. Proboscis often present. Stem elliptical and twisted, with a minute axial canal.

PLATYCRINUS ERIENSIS. Hall. (Fig. 26.) (15th Rep't N. Y. State Mus. Nat. Hist., p. 119, Pl. I.)

FIG. 26. *Platycrinus eriensis* (after Hall).

Distinguishing Characters.—Small cup-shaped calyx; comparatively large column facet, bordered by a thick rim; anchylosed basals; radials wider than high, with prominent articulating surface above; first costal quadrangular; second costal axillary, pentagonal; sub-angular arm joints; strong pinnules; granulose plates.

Found "in the shales of the Hamilton group, near Hamburgh, Erie County, N. Y." (Hall.)

GENUS TAXOCRINUS. PHILLIPS.

[ETY.: *Taxus*, yew tree; *krinon*, lily.]

(1843: Morris Cat. Brit. Foss., p. 90.)

Calyx with dicyclic base; three infra-basals, small, unequal, fused with top stem-joint; five small basals; five radials; costals 2 x 5 to 3 x 5; interbrachials numerous. On the truncated larger posterior brachial occurs a primary anal, followed by numerous small secondary anals. All the plates, from the radials upwards are united by loose sutures or by muscular articulation.

TAXOCRINUS NUNTIUS. Hall. (Compare Fig. 27.)

(*Forbesiocrinus nuntius*. Hall. 15th Rep't N. Y. State Mus. Nat. Hist., p. 124.)

Distinguishing Characters.—Costals 2 x 5, increasing rapidly in width from the radials; distichals 3 x 10 decreasing in width from below upwards; (d^3) axillary; palmars four in one branch, seven in the next one, upper palmars axillary; strongly granulose or papillose surface; strong ridge on center of plates; stout obtuse spine on center of axillary plates.

Found "in the shales of the Hamilton group, associated with *Platycrinus eriense*, *Spirifer granuliferus*, *S. mucronatus*, *Strophodonta demissa*, *Orthis penelope*, and other characteristic Hamilton fossils in Erie County, N. Y." (Hall.) This association suggests the Demissa bed.

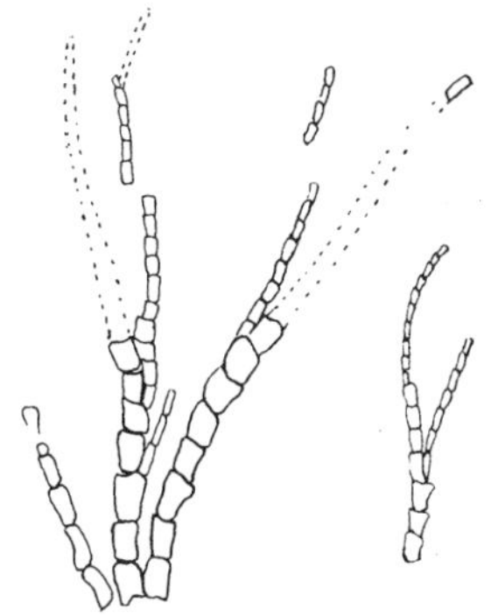

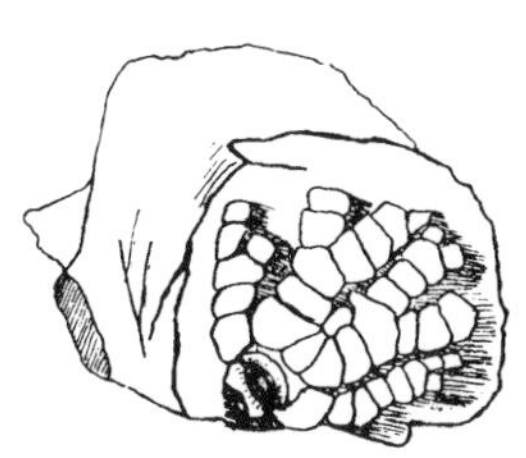

FIG. 27. *Taxocrinus nuntius* (?). Calyx and fragments of arms, x 2, 3. (Original.)

The description here given is condensed from that of Hall. So far as I am aware, the species has not been figured. The following illustration

(Fig. 27) represents a calyx obtained from the Demissa bed, which is with some hesitation referred to this species. The median ridge, on the center of the plates is strong, but ill defined, and the spine of the bifurcating second costal is represented by a blunt tubercle. A small anal interradial appears on the exposed side of the specimen, and above this primary interradial, appears a secondary one, much smaller. In the original description of *T. nuntius* Hall states . . . . . "interradial and anal plates, apparently none." From the description we may gather that the type specimen was an imperfect one, and it may have been that the azygous side, if present, was not exposed.

The specimen figured is somewhat crushed and distorted.

What appears to be arms of this, or a closely-related species, were obtained on a slab of shale at Section 7, from between nine and twelve feet below the Encrinal limestone. They are figured herewith.

Genus ANCYROCRINUS. Hall.

[Ety.: *Ankura*, grapnel ; *krinon*, lily.]

(15th Rep't N. Y. State Mus. Nat. Hist., p. 89.)

This genus was founded on what appears to be the base of a stem enlarged into a bulb, from which four ascending processes diverge, giving the whole a resemblance to an anchor. From the center the main stem ascends.

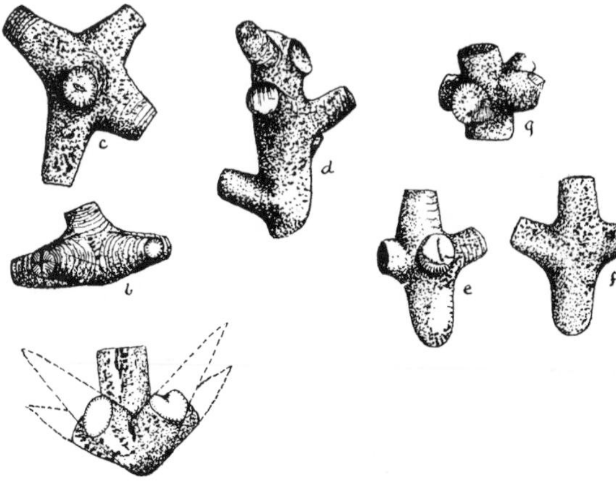

Fig. 28. *Ancyrocrinus bulbosus.* (*a*) Normal specimen with spines restored; (*b-g*) variously deformed individuals: (*b, c*) specimen with flat base and four irregular prongs; (*d*) specimen with numerous prongs diverging at different levels; (*e, f*) specimen with prolonged base and three prongs: (*g*) specimen with broken base, prongs diverging nearly at right angles. Student Palæontological Collection, Harvard University, Cat. 237. (Original.)

ANCYROCRINUS BULBOSUS. Hall. (Fig. 28.) (15th Rep't N. Y. State Mus. Nat. Hist., p. 90.)

Distinguishing Characters.—Bulbiferous lower end; oblique ascending processes; column round below, obtusely quadrangular above. Found in the Moscow shale, three to five feet above the Encrinal limestone, at Section 5; and also in the Demissa bed of Section 5 (rare).

CRINOID JOINTS AND STEMS. (Fig. 29.)

These bodies are of common occurrence. The Encrinal limestone is in places almost made up of their fragments (hence the name), though few calices have been found in that

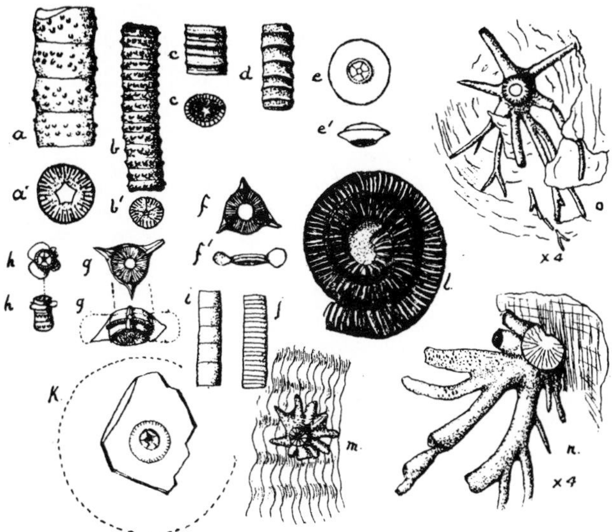

FIG. 29. *Crinoid Stems, Joints and Roots.* (*a*, *b*) Stems ornamented with tubercles; (*c*, *d*) stems with annulations; (*e*) joint with beveled margin; (*f*, *g*) joints with three vertical expansions or wings; (*h*) part of stem, with only one joint ornamented by expansions; (*i*, *j*) smooth stems, with thick and thin joints respectively; (*k*) fragment of a large joint with a knife-edge bevel, the dotted line shows original size; (*l*) a coiled stem; (*m*–*o*) "roots" attached to shells, etc. (All natural size except *n* and *o* which are x 4. Original.)

rock. The stems are extremely abundant in the Demissa and Stictopora beds, but are comparatively rare elsewhere. A number of species are represented, but no attempt at identification has been made. Not infrequently nodal joints occur, which have a projecting knife-edge margin (Fig. 29, *k*), and others with three projecting vertical plates. (Fig. 29, *f*, *g*.) Various modes of ornamentation, such as tubercles, rings, and spinous processes, occur, though frequently the stem is quite plain. (Fig. 29, *i*, *j*.) A remarkable example of a closely-coiled stem from the Demissa bed is illustrated in Fig. 29, *l*. It was coiled in a single plane, resembling much a non-involute cephalopod shell. The coiling probably occurred during the life of the animal, the stem having been severed from the root by some accident.

ROOTS.—These are occasionally met with, attached to the shells of brachiopods, on corals, and on other objects of support. (Fig. 29, *m*–*o*; see, also, Fig. 30.)

CLASS ANNELIDA. MAC LEAY.

The annelids, or typical worms, are soft-bodied, marine, fresh-water, or terrestrial animals, whose remains can seldom be preserved in a fossil state. It is only the tube-building order (*Tubicola*) which leaves any satisfactory remains. In these the tube is either a calcareous secretion of the animal, or it is composed of agglutinated sand and other foreign particles, being, in each case, wholly external. The peculiar bodies known as *Conodonts* are supposed to be the jaws of annelids. Worm burrows are often preserved by sand or mud infiltration, a cast of the burrow appearing in the strata.

NOTE.—The anatomy of recent worms is treated of at length in most text-books of zoölogy, to which the student is referred for further information.

The literature on *Conodonts* is scattered. Pander's Monographie der Fossilen-Fische des Silurischen Systems des Russisch-Baltischen Gouvernements (1851), treats of them at length, they being there considered as fish teeth. A paper by Zittel and Rohen entitled "Ueber Conodonten," and published in the *Sitzungsbericht der Bayrischen Akademie der Wissenschaften*, Bd. XVI., 1886, discusses them in detail, and brings out their annelid affinities. Hinde's paper is quoted below.

TUBES.

GENUS SPIRORBIS. LAMARK.

[ETY.: A spiral whorl.]

(1801: *Syst. An. sans Vert.*, p. 326.)

Minute, spirally-coiled calcareous tubes, which are cemented to some foreign substance by one side. Surface smooth or ornamented with concentric striæ or annulations, or with tubercles or spines. Living species (marine) commonly adhering to algæ.

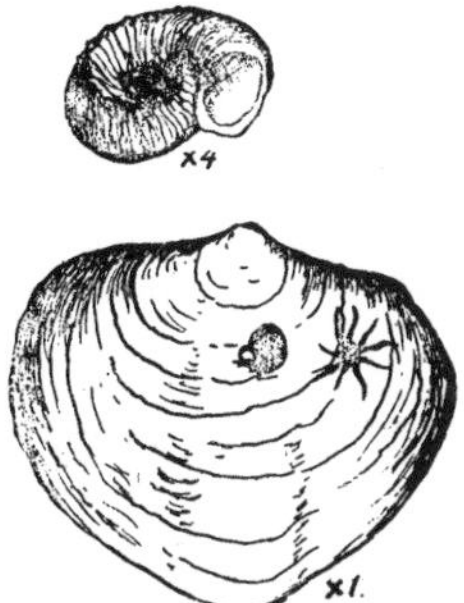

FIG. 30. *Spirorbis angulatus.* Attached to a shell of *Athyris spiriferoides.* Natural size and enlarged. (Original.)

SPIRORBIS ANGULATUS. Hall. (Fig. 30.) (15th Rep't N. Y. State Mus. Nat. Hist., p. 84.)

Distinguishing Characters.—Two or more volutions, outer one robust; subangular sides; upper angular surface sometimes nodose; aperture round or oval, usually nearly rectangular to the plane of volution.

Found in the Demissa bed, and occasionally in the shales below, at Sections 5 to 8, and on the Lake Shore (rather rare).

GENUS AUTODETUS. LINDSTRÖM.

(1884: On the Silurian Gastropoda and Pteropoda of Gotland, p. 185.)

Tube a sinistral (left-handed) coil, somewhat resembling a gastropod shell. The form is that of a truncated cone, whose exterior is smooth, seldom showing any traces of the internal coil, though covered with a fine undulose and sometimes rugose concentric striation. The apical extremity is flattened into a broad cicatrix of attachment, which sometimes has one-half the width of the body-whorl. Usually attached to a brachiopod shell. Walls of the tube thick, somewhat cellular in the thickest portions.

AUTODETUS LINDSTRŒMI. Clarke. (Fig. 31.)

(Am. Geol., Vol. XIII., p. 334, Figs. 1, 2, 3, May, 1894.)

Distinguishing Characters.—Rapid expansion of shell; cicatrix of attachment less than one-third the diameter of the body-whorl. Found in the Hamilton shales, at Hamburgh, N. Y. (Clarke.)

FIG. 31. *Autodetus lindstrœmi.* Lateral and top view, and section, x 3 (after Clarke).

GENUS CORNULITES. SCHLOTHEIM.

[ETY.: *Cornu*, horn; *lithos*, stone.]

(1820: Schlotheim Petrefactenkunde, p. 378.)

Tube gently tapering, flexuous, the small end usually bent. The tube either wholly or in part adhering to other objects. Walls thick cellular, composed of imbricating rings. Surface ornamented by annulations and longitudinal striæ. Interior presenting a succession of annular constrictions, giving a scalariform character to the cast.

FIG. 32. *Cornulites hamiltoniæ*. The type specimen enlarged eight diameters. (Original.)

CORNULITES HAMILTONIÆ. sp. nov. (Fig. 32.) (Compare Pal. N. Y., Vol. VI., p. 52, Fig. 12.)

Distinguishing Characters.—Uniform curvature of base, which makes nearly or quite a right angle with the main portion of the tube; uniform rounded annulations; attachment by whole surface. Found in the Pleurodictyum beds of Avery's Creek.

CONODONTS.

GENUS PRIONIODUS. PANDER.

[ETY.: *Prionion*, small saw; *odous*, tooth.]

(1851: Monograph. d. Foss. Fische, d. Sil. Syst., p. 28.)

"Jaw" with a narrow basal portion, which supports numerous delicate denticles; and an elongated tapering tooth, which extends below the basal portion.

PRIONIODUS ERRATICUS. Hinde. (Fig. 33A.) (Quart. Journ. Geol. Soc., Vol. XXXV., p. 359, Pl. XV.)

Distinguishing Characters.— Short, narrow, slightly-arched base; larger cylindrical curved main end-tooth, projecting obliquely outward, forming an obtuse angle with base. Denticles five, small, upright.

FIG. 33A. *Prioniodus erraticus*, x 13 (after Hinde).

Found in the Conodont bed of the Genesee, at Section 1. (Hinde.)

PRIONIODUS ABBREVIATUS. Hinde. (Fig. 33B.) (Quart. Jour. Geol. Soc., Vol. XXXV., p. 359, Pl. XV.)

FIG. 33B. *Prioniodus abbreviatus*, x 13 (after Hinde).

Distinguishing Characters.—Short, stout base; long, nearly straight, cylindrical, blunted main end-tooth; denticles two, small, blunt, with knobs at their summits.

Found in the Conodont bed of the Genesee, at Section 1. (Hinde.)

PRIONIODUS CLAVATUS. Hinde. (Fig. 33C.) (Quart. Journ. Geol. Soc., Vol. XXXV., p. 360, Pl. XV.)

FIG. 33C. *Prioniodus clavatus*, x 13 (after Hinde).

Distinguishing Characters.—Arched, narrow, stout base, convex in section; main central tooth straight, cylindrical, and blunted; denticles similar to central tooth, four on one side, two on the other.

Found in the Conodont bed of the Genesee, at Section 1. (Hinde.) Upper Moscow shale, Section 1 (rare).

PRIONIODUS ANGULATUS. Hinde. (Fig. 33D.) (Quart. Jour. Geol. Soc., Vol. XXXV., p. 360, Pl. XV.)

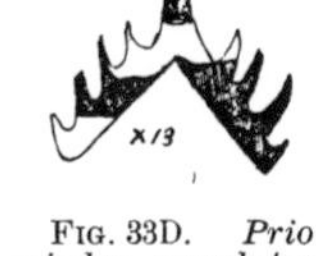

FIG. 33D. *Prioniodus angulatus*, x 13 (after Hinde)

Distinguishing Characters.—Narrow, thin, arched base, the two halves meeting at an acute angle; main tooth central, long, straight, compressed, with median longitudinal groove; denticles, four on each side, slightly curved; delicate and brittle.

Found in the Genesee shale, at North Evans, Section 1 (?). (Hinde.)

PRIONIODUS ACICULARIS. Hinde. (Fig. 33E.) (Quart. Jour. Geol. Soc., Vol. XXXV., p. 360, Pl. XV.)

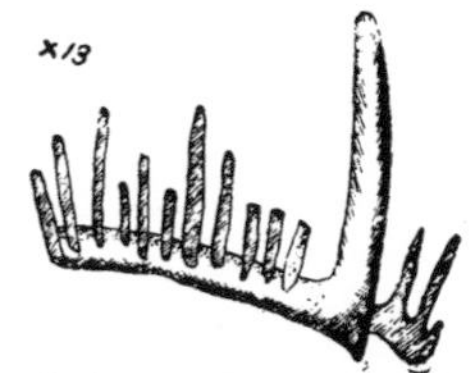

FIG. 33E. *Prioniodus acicularis*. Two styles of teeth, x 13 (after Hinde).

Distinguishing Characters.—Wide, thin, polished and transparent, straight or slightly arched basal portion. Main tooth near one end large, slightly curved, compressed; denticles, two on one side, eleven to thirteen on the other, delicate, slender, acutely pointed, and slightly inclined.

Found in the Genesee shale, at North Evans, Section 1 (?). (Hinde.)

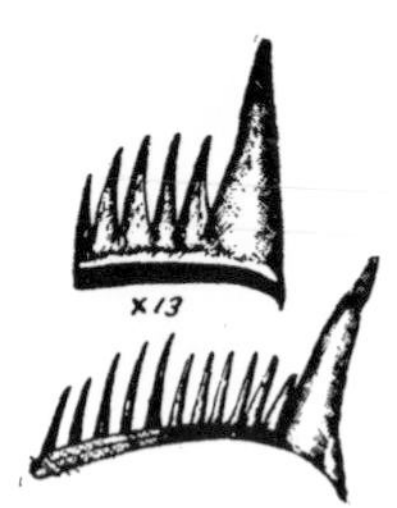

FIG. 33F. *Prioniodus armatus*, x 13 (after Hinde).

PRIONIODUS ARMATUS. Hinde. (Fig. 33F.) (Quart. Jour. Geol. Soc., Vol. XXXV., p. 360, Pl. XV.)

Distinguishing Characters.—Narrow, slightly curved basal portion; main end-tooth large, triangular, depressed convex, its anterior end produced downward into a short spur; denticles, five to eleven, straight, compressed.

Found at North Evans, in the Genesee shale, Section 1 (?). (Hinde.)

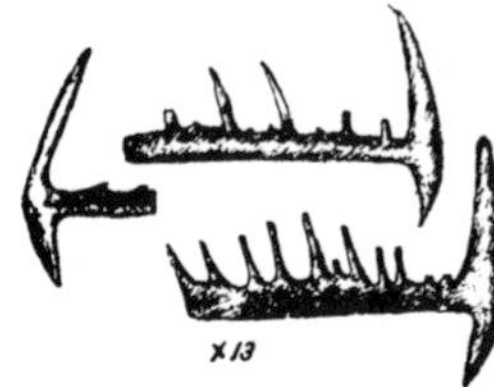

FIG. 33G. *Prioniodus spicatus*, x 13 (after Hinde).

PRIONIODUS SPICATUS. Hinde. (Fig. 33G.) (Quart. Jour. Geol. Soc., Vol. XXXV., p. 361, Pl. XVI.)

Distinguishing Characters.—Narrow, straight basal portion; straight or slightly curved main end-tooth, produced below in a spur; denticles of two sizes, alternate, of variable number.

Found in the Genesee shale, at North Evans, probably Section 1. (Hinde.)

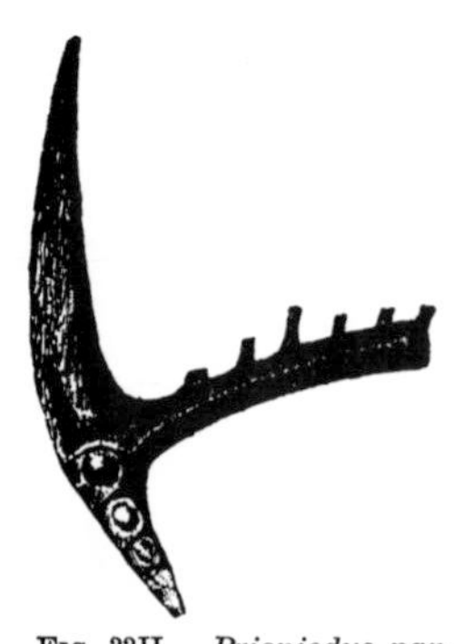

FIG. 33H. *Prioniodus panderi*, x 13 (after Hinde).

PRIONIODUS PANDERI. Hinde. (Fig. 33H.) (Quart. Jour. Geol. Soc., Vol. XXXV., p. 361, Pl. XVI.)

Distinguishing Characters.—Narrow base; very large, slightly curved, depressed, convex main end-tooth prolonged below into a stout, long spur, which bears what appears as bases of four denticles; denticles six.

Found in the Conodont bed of the Genesee, at Section 1. (Hinde.)

PRIONIODUS (?) ALATUS. Hinde. (Fig. 33I.) (Quart. Jour. Geol. Soc., Vol. XXXV., p. 361, Pl. XVI.)

FIG. 33I. *Prioniodus* (?) *alatus.* x 7 (after Hinde).

Distinguishing Characters.—Base narrow, arched; large triangular, depressed, convex main end-tooth, with reëntrant base; denticles five, short, blunt, indistinctly marked off from base.

Found in the Conodont bed of the Genesee, at Section 1. (Hinde.)

GENUS POLYGNATHUS. HINDE.

[ETY.: *Polys*, many; *gnathus*, jaw.]

(Quart. Jour. Geol. Soc., Vol. XXXV., p. 361.)

This name was proposed by Hinde for animals possessing numerous, variously-formed conodonts, and minute, tuberculated plates.

POLYGNATHUS DUBIUS. Hinde. (Fig. 34.) (Quart. Jour. Geol. Soc., Vol. XXXV., p. 362, Pl. XVI.)

The very variable teeth associated by Hinde under the above name (from being found together in a patch one-fourth inch in diameter) are, by him, divided into *pectinate* teeth (Fig. 34, *a–g*), *fimbriate* teeth (Fig. 34, *h, i*), and

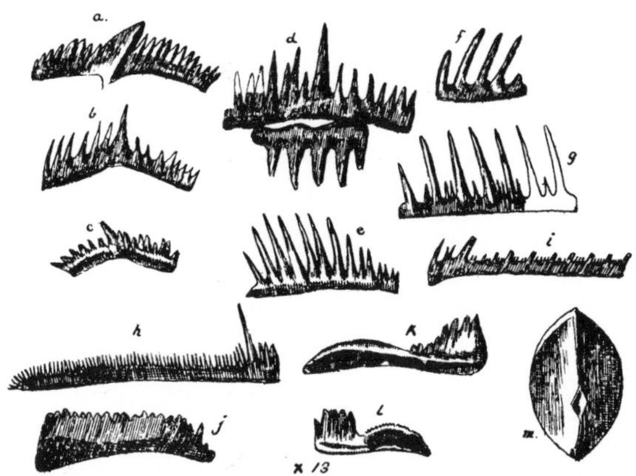

FIG. 34. *Polygnathus dubius.* (*a–g*) Pectinate teeth; (*h, i*) fimbriate teeth; (*k, l*) crested teeth; (*m*) plate. All x 13 (after Hinde).

crested teeth (Fig. 34, *k*, *l*). Hinde's figures are here reproduced.

PECTINATE TEETH, *A*. (Fig. 34, *a–d*.)

Distinguishing Characters.—Narrow, slightly arched base; main central tooth sometimes produced below in a spur; denticles slender and acute, fourteen to twenty.

Found in the Conodont bed of the Genesee stage, at Section 1 (abundant); in the Genesee shale, Section 1 (?) (Hinde); and in the upper Moscow shale, at Section 1 (rare).

PECTINATE TEETH, *B*. (Fig. 34, *e–g*.)

Distinguishing Characters.—Straight, almost linear, base; teeth all similar, central one longest, sometimes as many as fourteen; occasionally smaller denticles between.

Found at North Evans, in the Genesee shale. (Hinde.)

FIMBRIATE TEETH. (Fig. 34, *h*, *i*.)

Distinguishing Characters.—Straight, narrow, elongate base, pointed at one end; delicate main tooth near blunt end; denticles, three on one side; very many extremely minute ones on the other side, often varying in size at regular intervals.

Found in the Genesee shale, at North Evans, Section 1 (?). (Hinde.)

CRESTED TEETH. (Fig. 34, *k*, *l*.)

Distinguishing Characters.—(*A*) Compressed base of nearly uniform width; one end abruptly contracted; crenulations (denticles) about twenty. (Fig. 34, *k*.)

(*B*) Part of base narrow and thickened, with sometimes a row of minute crenulations on upper edge; remainder of base small; flattened crest; with five to eight denticles. (Fig. 34, *l*.)

Found in the Genesee shale, at North Evans, Section 1 (?). (Hinde.)

PLATES.—Small, elliptical, smooth-edged plates, with one surface slightly convex, bearing a longitudinal ridge, and having a granulose surface on one side and a smooth one on the other, were found associated with the above teeth at North Evans, by Hinde. (Fig. 34, *m*.)

POLYGNATHUS NASUTUS. Hinde. (Fig. 35.) (Quart. Jour. Geol. Soc., Vol. XXXV., p. 364, Pl. XVI.)

Distinguishing Characters.—Narrow, elongate, straight base; broad, flattened main tooth, projecting in a line with the base; spur blunt, with three spines; denticles twenty, of various lengths.

FIG. 35. *Polygnathus nasutus*, x 13 (after Hinde).

Found at North Evans, in the Genesee shale, at Section 1 (?). (Hinde.)

POLYGNATHUS PRINCEPS. Hinde. (Fig. 36.) (Quart. Jour. Geol. Soc., Vol. XXXV., p. 365, Pl. XVI.)

Distinguishing Characters.—Relatively large size; narrow, elongated base; teeth similar, eleven, large, robust, somewhat oval in section; longest in the center.

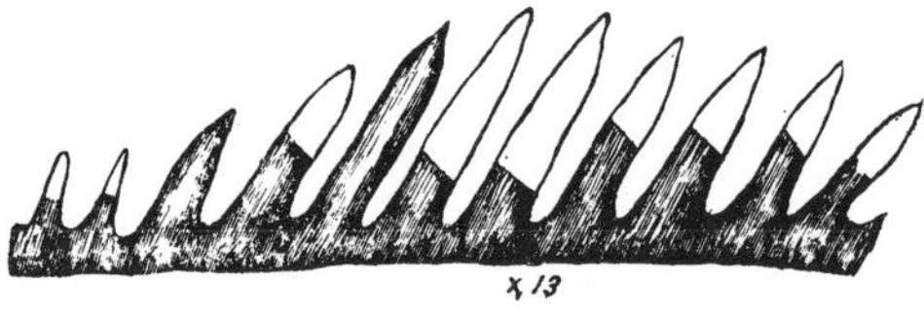

FIG. 36. *Polygnathus princeps*, x 13 (after Hinde).

Found in the Conodont bed of the Genesee, at Section 1. (Hinde.)

POLYGNATHUS SOLIDUS. Hinde. (Fig. 37.) (Quart. Jour. Geol. Soc., Vol. XXXV., p. 365, Pl. XVII.)

Distinguishing Characters.—Base short, very thick, wide; teeth sub-equal, short, stout, obtuse, seven to eleven, closely arranged.

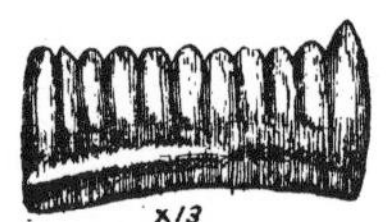

FIG. 37. *Polygnathus solidus*, x 13 (after Hinde).

Found in the Conodont bed of the Genesee, at Section 1. (Hinde.)

POLYGNATHUS CRASSUS. Hinde. (Fig. 38.) (Quart. Jour. Geol. Soc., Vol. XXXV., p. 365, Pl. XVII.)

Distinguishing Characters.—Narrow, curved, and relatively thick base; with a prominent ridge, bearing six obtuse crenulations; posterior crest with two stout teeth.

FIG. 38. *Polygnathus crassus*, x 13 (after Hinde).

Found in the Conodont bed of the Genesee, at Section 1. (Hinde.)

PLATES.

Polygnathus pennatus. Hinde. (Fig. 39.) (Quart. Jour. Geol. Soc., Vol. XXXV., p. 366, Pl. XVII.)

Fig. 39. *Polygnathus pennatus*, x 13 (after Hinde).

Distinguishing Characters.—Elongate, oval outline; depressed longitudinal furrow; slender central keel, produced beyond main portion, and bearing tubercles; lateral ridges.

Found in the Conodont bed of the Genesee, at Section 1 (abundant). (Hinde.)

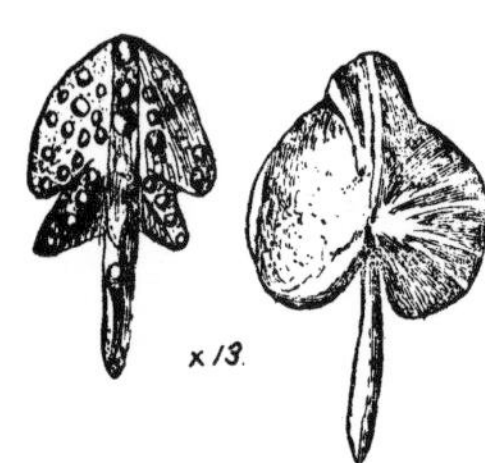

Fig. 40. *Polygnathus tuberculatus*, x 13 (after Hinde).

Polygnathus tuberculatus. Hinde. (Fig. 40.) (Quart. Jour. Geol. Soc., Vol. XXXV., p. 366, Pl. XVII.)

Distinguishing Characters.—Lobate form; produced and tuberculated central keel; converging rows of tubercles; reverse side smooth.

Found in the Conodont bed of the Genesee, at Section 1. (Hinde.)

Fig. 41. *Polygnathus cristatus*, x 13 (after Hinde).

Polygnathus cristatus. Hinde. (Fig. 41.) (Quart. Jour. Geol. Soc., Vol. XXXV., p. 366, Pl. XVII.)

Distinguishing Characters.— Oval outline, depressed convex expression; prominent crenulated keel; two rows of tubercles on either side of keel.

Found in the Conodont bed of the Genesee, at Section 1. (Hinde.)

Polygnathus truncatus. Hinde. (Fig. 42.) (Quart. Jour. Geol. Soc., Vol. XXXV., p. 366, Pl. XVII.)

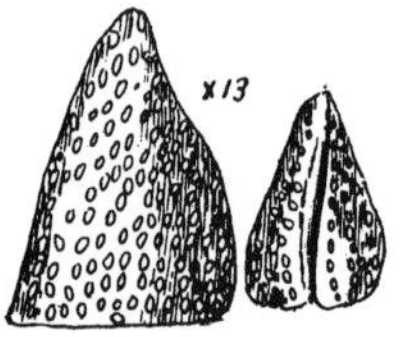

Fig. 42. *Polygnathus truncatus* and *P. truncatus*, var. x 13 (after Hinde).

Distinguishing Characters. — Sub-triangular outline of plate; median keel, not extended; convex, tuberculated surface.

Found in the Conodont bed of the Genesee, at Section 1. (Hinde.)

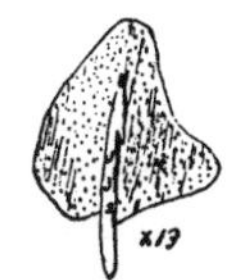

Fig. 43. *Polygnathus punctatus*, x 13 (after Hinde).

POLYGNATHUS PUNCTATUS. Hinde. (Fig. 43.) (Quart. Jour. Geol. Soc., Vol. XXXV., p. 367, Pl. XVII.)

Distinguishing Characters.—Flat, thin, unsymmetrical form; keel produced, but not reaching tip of plate, with two or three nodes; surface of plate minutely tuberculated.

Found at North Evans, in the Genesee shale, at Section 1 (?). (Hinde.)

Fig. 44. *Polygnathus linguiformis*, x 13 (after Hinde).

POLYGNATHUS LINGUIFORMIS. Hinde. (Fig. 44.) (Quart. Jour. Geol. Soc., Vol. XXXV., p. 367, Pl. XVII.)

Distinguishing Characters.—Elongate form; tongue-like, deflected, transversely-ridged process; upward curving sides of plate, with central trough between; keel arising from bottom of trough, produced, with crenulated crest; lateral surfaces tuberculated.

Found in the Conodont bed of the Genesee, at Section 1 (abundant). (Hinde.)

POLYGNATHUS PALMATUS. Hinde. (Fig. 45.) (Quart. Jour. Geol. Soc., Vol. XXXV., p. 367, Pl. XVII.)

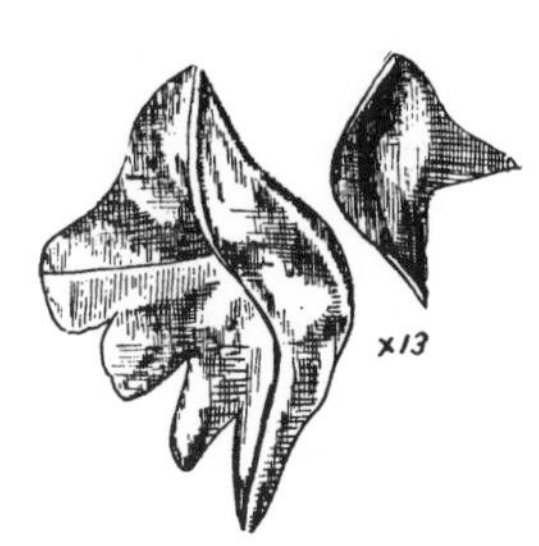

Fig. 45. *Polygnathus palmatus*, x 13 (after Hinde).

Distinguishing Characters.—Unsymmetrical, lobed outline; depressed central portion; longitudinal and sometimes transverse keel, extending to depressed center; smooth surface.

Found at North Evans, in the Genesee shale (very abundant). (Hinde.)

POLYGNATHUS (?) SIMPLEX. Hinde. (Fig. 46.) (Quart. Jour. Geol. Soc., Vol. XXXV., p. 367, Pl. XVII.)

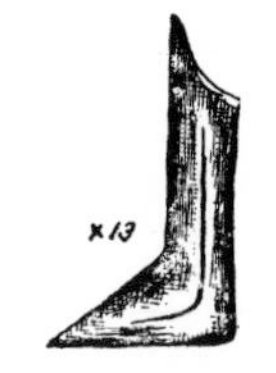

FIG. 46. *Polygnathus* (?) *simplex*, x 13 after Hinde).

Distinguishing Characters.— Body shaped like a tenter-hook, nearly oval in section; hook pointed, opposite end smooth, rounded like an articular surface; prominent median ridge extending from point to opposite end.

Found in the Conodont bed of the Genesee, at Section 1 (very abundant). (Hinde.)

CLASS BRYOZOA. EHRENBERG.

The Bryozoa, or Polyzoa, are marine or fresh-water invertebrates, almost always occurring in colonies, which increase by gemmation. Each *zoöid* of the colony is enclosed in a membranaceous, or calcareous, double-walled sac, the *zoœcium,* into which it can withdraw. The animal possesses a mouth, an alimentary canal, and an anal opening, and, in addition to these, a fringe of respiratory tentacles — the *lophophore.* The colony is commonly attached to foreign bodies, which it either incrusts or from which it arises as an independent frond.

In the Palæozoic genera the cell apertures are often surrounded by elevated rims, or *peristomes.* In many forms a portion of the posterior wall of the tube is more or less thickened, and curved to a shorter radius, projecting often above the plane of the aperture. This forms the *lunaria,* and their ends may project into the tubes as *pseudo-septa.* In the interapertural space may occur angular or irregular cells, the *mesopores,* while on many portions of the surface, tubular spines (*acanthopores*), or nodes (rounded, knob-like elevations), may occur. At intervals, in many genera, rounded elevations, or *monticules,* are found, which may, or may not, be destitute of cells. *Maculæ* or irregular blotches, destitute of cells, also occur in many forms. Many species bear a superficial resemblance to certain corals, particularly the Monticuliporoids.

NOTE.—The anatomy of recent Bryozoa (Polyzoa) may be found in the text-books of zoölogy. An admirable and comprehensive discussion of the structural features of living Bryozoa will be found in the introduction to Simpson's "Hand-book of North American Palæozoic Bryozoa," published in the 14th Annual Report of the State Geologist of New York, 1894. In the "Hand-book" itself, the Palæozoic genera are described and illustrated. Ulrich's systematic description of the Bryozoa, in Zittel's Text-book of Palæontology (Eastman's translation), will be found of great value, and also his "Palæozic Bryozoa." (Geol. Surv. Ill., Vol. VIII., 1890.)

Genus FENESTELLA. Miller.

[Ety.: *Fenestella*, little window.]

(1839: Lonsdale in Murchison's Sil. System, Pt. II., p. 677.)

Bryozoum, consisting of a calcareous branching frond, forming cup-shaped or funnel-shaped expansions. The branches fork, and are connected by transverse bars or dissepiments, thus enclosing spaces or fenestrules. The cell apertures occur on one side of the branches. They are surrounded by rims or peristomes, and are arranged in two parallel rows, while between them occurs a ridge (carina), or a row of nodes.

Fenestella emaciata. Hall. (Fig. 47.) (36th Ann. Rep't N. Y. State Mus. Nat. Hist., p. 68, 41st Rep't, do., Pl. VIII.)

Distinguishing Characters.—Large, funnel-shaped frond; longitudinal striations of branches on the non-celluliferous face, with thin, oblique dissepiments; angular character of branches, and dissepiments on celluliferous face; closely and regularly disposed cell apertures.

Found in the Demissa bed, at Section 5 (common).

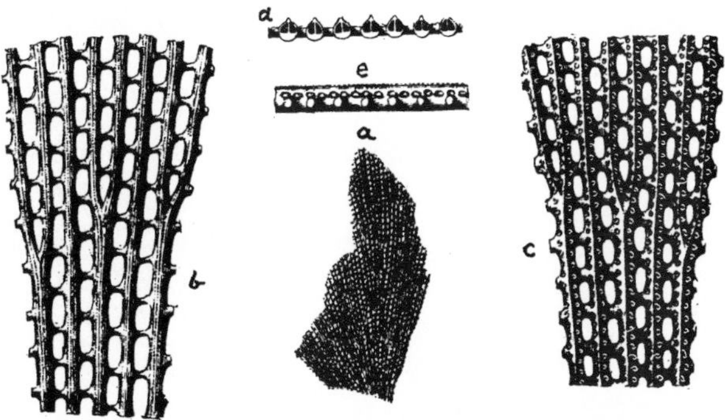

Fig. 47. *Fenestella emaciata* (from Hall). (*a*) Fragment of frond, reduced; (*b*) an enlargement from the non-celluliferous face, showing the striated granulose branches, and the oblique dissepiments, 4 x; (*c*) an enlargement from the celluliferous face, showing the form and disposition of the cell apertures, 4 x; (*d*) a transverse section of the branches, 4 x; (*e*) a lateral view of the branches, showing the dissepiments and position of the apertures, 4 x.

Fenestella planiramosa. Hall. (Fig. 48.) (36th Ann. Rep't N. Y. State Mus. Nat. Hist., p. 62; Rep't State Geol., 1887, Pl. I.)

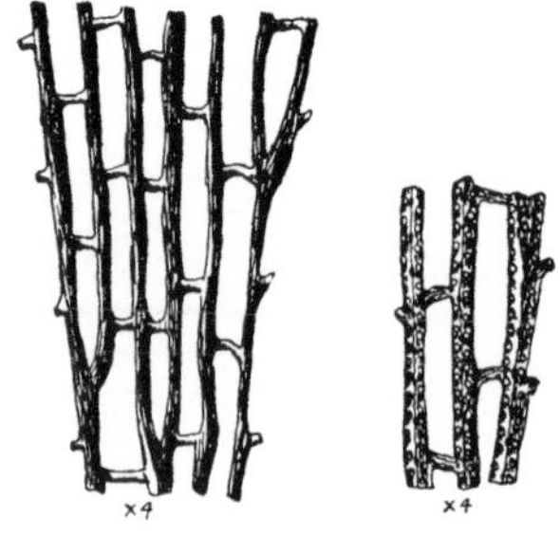

FIG. 48. *Fenestella planiramosa.* The non-celluliferous and celluliferous sides, x 4 (after Hall.)

Distinguishing Characters.—Apparent flat expansion of the frond; irregularly-forking branches; slender, rather distant (2 to 5mm.) dissepiments; striated branches of non-celluliferous face; angular branches of celluliferous face, with sharp carina, nodes, or spinules; cell apertures in double row, except just below a fork, where three rows occur.

Found in the Demissa bed, at Section 5 (rare).

GENUS LOCULIPORA. HALL.

[ETY.: *Loculus,* cell; *poros,* pore.]

(1887: Pal. N. Y., Vol. VI., p. 33.)

Bryozoum funnel shaped, with sinuous or zig-zag branches, which reunite at intervals, or are connected by very short dissepiments of about the same width as the branches. The cell apertures completely surround the fenestrules; the center of the branches and dissepiments are marked by a prominent expanded ridge, or carina, on the celluliferous face.

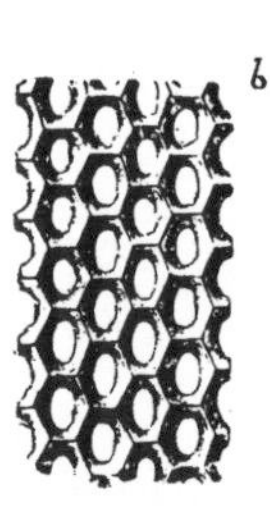

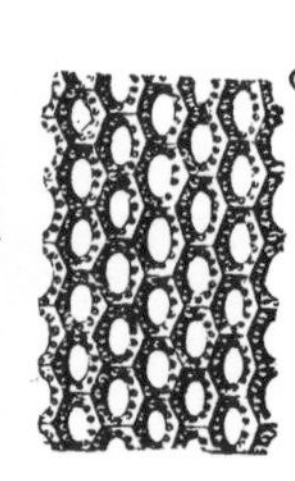

FIG. 49. *Loculipora perforata* (from Hall). (*a*) A large fragment showing the general appearance and manner of growth; (*b*) an enlargement from the non-celluliferous face, showing the angular, slightly-carinated branches connected by dissepiments, 4 x; (*c*) an enlargement of the celluliferous face, showing the angular branches and the disposition of the cell apertures around the fenestrules, 4 x.

LOCULIPORA PERFORATA. Hall. (Fig. 49.) (36th Rep't N. Y. State Mus. Nat. Hist., p. 65; 41st Rep't N. Y. State Mus. Nat. Hist., Pl. X.)

Distinguishing Characters.—Reticulated aspect of fronds; oval fenestrules; nine to ten apertures to each fenestrule, completely surrounding it. (On account of the expansion of the carina to nearly the middle of the branches, this face may appear like the non-celluliferous face, especially when embedded in rock.)

Found in the Demissa bed, at Section 5 (common).

GENUS RETEPORINA. D'ORBIGNY.

[ETY.: *Rete,* net; *poros,* pore.]

(1850: Prodome de Pal., T. I., p. 101.)

Bryozoum fenestelloid, with sinuous and anastomosing branches. The non-celluliferous side has the appearance of a net-work, with oval fenestrules; while the celluliferous side shows sinuous branches, with a double row of apertures on each.

RETEPORINA STRIATA. (Hall.) (Fig. 50.) (6th Ann. Rep't N. Y. State Geol., p. 45, Pl. III. 1886.)

FIG. 50. *Reteporina striata.* Non-celluliferous and celluliferous sides, enlarged, x 4 (after Hall).

Distinguishing Characters.—Reticulated appearance of frond; frequently a prominent node at point of junction of branches; sinuous branches of celluliferous face, apparently connected by wide, depressed dissepiments; thin, elevated and crenulated carina between apertures.

Found in the Demissa bed, at Section 5.

GENUS UNITRYPA. HALL.

[ETY.: *Unus,* one; *trypa,* perforation.]

(1885: Rep't N. Y. State Geologist for 1884, p. 36.)

Bryozoum consisting of fenestelloid fronds, with two rows of apertures, separated by a carina on the celluliferous face of each branch. The carinæ are prominent, high, thickened near the top, and those of adjacent branches are connected by thin obliquely-placed, or abruptly-bent, transverse plates or *scalæ*.

Unitrypa scalaris. Hall. (Fig. 51.) (6th Ann. Rep't N. Y. State Geol., p. 60, 1886; Report of 1897, Pl. XI.)

Distinguishing Characters.—Straight parallel and rigid branches; ladder-like appearance of carinæ and scalæ, the former projecting above the latter; very oblique scalæ, with their summits nearest the base of the frond.

Found in the Demissa bed, at Section 5 (rare).

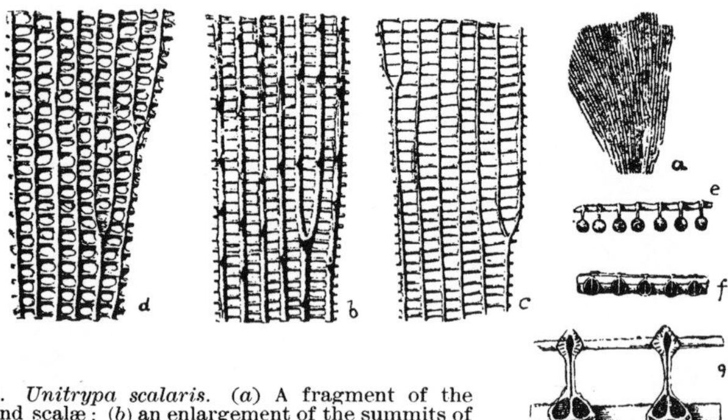

Fig. 51. *Unitrypa scalaris.* (*a*) A fragment of the carinæ and scalæ; (*b*) an enlargement of the summits of the carinæ and scalæ, showing nodes on the carinæ, x 4; (*c*) an enlargement showing very thin carinæ and scalæ, x 4; (*d*) an enlargement, showing the under side of the carinæ and scalæ, x 4; (*e, f*) transverse sections of different fronds, x 4; (*g*) a transverse section further enlarged, showing the rhomboidal form of the branches, in section at the base, where they are connected by the tranverse dissepiment; the branches are continued upward into the carinæ, which are expanded at the summit, and connected by the transverse "scalæ" (from Hall.)

Genus POLYPORA. McCoy.

[Ety.: *Polys*, many; *poros*, pore.]

(1845: Carb. Foss. Ireland, p. 206.)

"Bryozoum having the same manner of growth and general aspect as Fenestella, but having the cell apertures disposed in three or more ranges, entirely covering the celluliferous face of the branches, which are without a median keel or carina." (Simpson, Pal. Bryoz., p. 502.)

Polypora multiplex. Hall. (Fig. 51A.) (Rep't State Geol. for 1886, p. 66, ibid. 1887, Pl. XI.)

Distinguishing Characters.—Large infundibuliform fronds, with frequent longitudinal folds or undulations. Non-celluliferous face; moderately slender, sharply angular, straight and rigid, or more or less zig-zag branches, with a slight carina; comparatively strong, sharply angular dissepiments, on a plane with the branches, and slightly expanding at their junction, with a slight carina similar to and uniting with that of the branches; elongate to broadly oval fenestrules; celluliferous face; rounded character of branches

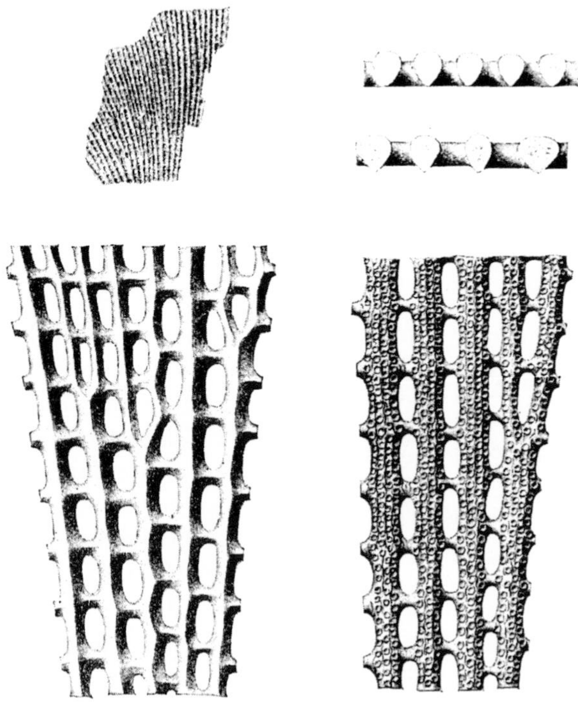

Fig 51A. *Polypora multiplex*. Portion of a frond natural size; enlargement of the non-celluliferous face, showing angular branches connected by slender dissepiments, x 6; enlargement of celluliferous face, showing form and disposition of cell apertures, and the striæ or ridges between the ranges of apertures, x 6; transverse sections of different fronds, showing variation, x 6 (from Hall).

and dissepiments, the latter slender and much depressed, obscure, and sometimes obsolete; narrow fenestrules, adjacent branches frequently almost or quite in contact; cell apertures in two to four ranges, circular or oval, closely arranged; smooth interspaces; strong elevated peristomes.

Found in the Hamilton group at Alden, Erie Co. (Hall), and at Eighteen Mile Creek. (Coll. Am. Mus. Nat. Hist., New York.)

Genus RHOMBOPORA. Meek.

[Syn.: Orthopora. Hall. Ety.: *Rhombus*, rhomb; *poros*, pore.]

(1872: Meek, Pal. Eastern Nebraska, p. 141.)

Bryozoum consisting of solid branches, with cylindrical cells, which pass outward from an imaginary axis; cells with transverse plates or tabulæ; apertures separated by ridges, which are often broad, and either continuous or unite to form rhombic or polygonal cell spaces. Ridges bearing short spines or nodes, and containing tubuli near the surface, from the growth of the nodes.

Rhombopora (?) transversa. (Hall.) (Fig. 52.) (Pal. N. Y., Vol. VI., p. 187, Pls. LV., LVI.) (Simpson uses this species to illustrate the genus. See Hand-book Pal. Bryozoa, Pl. XIX.)

Distinguishing Characters.—Diameter of branches about 1.75 mm.; oval cell apertures in longitudinal rows, diagonal rows, or irregularly disposed; flat or slightly concave interapertural space, with small, prominent nodes or granules surrounding the apertures; peristome prominent.

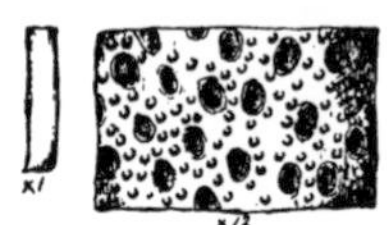

Fig. 52. *Rhombopora* (?) *transversa*. A fragment natural size, and a portion of a branch enlarged, x 12 (after Hall and Simpson).

Found in the "Hamilton group, at West Hamburg, Erie County, N. Y." (Hall.)

Rhombopora polygona. (Hall.) (Not figured.) (Pal. N. Y., Vol. VI., p. 176.)

Distinguishing Characters.— Infrequent bifurcations; widely diverging branches with diameter of 1.25 to 1.50 mm.; oval cell apertures, alternating in adjacent rows, so as to make diagonal series at forty-five degrees to the axis; angular or rounded, granulose interspaces, with conical nodes at the angles.

Found in the "Hamilton group, West Hamburg, Erie County, N. Y." (Hall); also four to five feet below the Encrinal limestone, at Section 6, Eighteen Mile Creek (rare).

Rhombopora hexagona. (Hall.) (Fig. 53.) (Pal. N. Y., Vol. VI., p. 178, Pls. LV., LVI. Simpson, Pl. XIX., Fig. 12.)

Distinguishing Characters.—Rhombic or hexagonal outline of the cell spaces; areas surrounding the cell apertures (*vestibular area*) smaller than in preceding species; nodes at angles absent; granules fewer and more prominent than in preceding species.

Fig. 53. *Rhombopora hexagona.* Fragment natural size, and a portion enlarged, x 12 (after Hall and Simpson).

Found in the "Hamilton group, Eighteen Mile Creek, Shore of Lake Erie, Erie County, N. Y." (Hall.)

Rhombopora reticulata. (Hall.) (Fig. 54.) (Pal. N. Y., Vol. VI., p. 179, Pls. LV., LVI.)

Distinguishing Characters.— Infrequent bifurcations; rhomboidal cell spaces; oval apertures; rather small vestibular areas; dividing ridge angular, with a row of minute granules along the crest and prominent spinules at the intersections.

Fig. 54. *Rhombopora reticulata.* Fragment natural size, and a portion enlarged, x 12 (after Hall and Simpson).

Found in the "Hamilton group, West Hamburg, Erie County, N. Y." (Hall.)

Rhombopora tortalinea. (Hall.) (Fig. 55.) (Pal. N. Y., Vol. VI., p. 180, Pl. LVI.)

Distinguishing Characters.—Somewhat sinuous growth; infrequent bifurcations; branches with diameter of .60 to .75 mm., and frequently diverging at an angle of ninety degrees; oval apertures more or less regularly disposed in nine or ten longitudinal rows, separated by rounded, sinuous, or twisted ridges, bearing small nodes.

Fig. 55. *Rhombopora tortalinea*, x 12 (after Hall and Simpson).

Found in the "Hamilton group, Hamburg-on-the-Lake, Erie County, N. Y." (Hall.)

Rhombopora lineata. (Hall.) (Fig. 56.) (Pal. N. Y., Vol. VI., p. 181, Pls. LV., LVI.)

Distinguishing Characters.— Branches often diverging at angles of ninety degrees, diameter about .6 mm.; elongate, oval, distant, cell apertures, disposed in eight or nine longitudinal and parallel rows; thin, scarcely elevated, peristome; prominent granulose ridges between the

Fig. 56. *Rhombopora lineata.* Natural size, and enlarged, x 12 (after Hall and Simpson).

rows; ridges more prominent and straight than in the preceding.

Found in the "Hamilton group, West Hamburg, Erie County, N. Y." (Hall, explanation of plates.)

RHOMBOPORA IMMERSA. Hall. (Fig. 57.) (Pal. N. Y., Vol. VI., p. 185, Pl. LVI.)

FIG. 57. *Rhombopora immersa*, x 12 (after Hall and Simpson).

Distinguishing Characters.—Oval, alternating apertures, disposed in longitudinal rows; obsolete peristomes; prominent longitudinal ridges, slightly narrower than cell apertures; comparatively prominent node, and shallow pit at base of each aperture.

Found in the "Hamilton group, West Hamburg, Erie County, N. Y." (Hall, explanation of plates.)

GENUS ACANTHOCLEMA. HALL.

[ETY.: *Acantha*, spine; *klema*, twig.]

(1887: Pal. N. Y., Vol. VI., p. 72.)

Bryozoum consisting of slender branches, with cylindrical cells arising from a filiform axis at the center of the branch. The oval cell apertures are in longitudinal or diagonally intersecting rows, with ridges between. Nodes or spines commonly occur. When hollow spines occur between the apertures, the space below is occupied by tubuli.

ACANTHOCLEMA SCUTULATUM. Hall. (Fig. 58.) (Pal. N. Y., Vol. VI., p. 190, Pls. LV., LVI.)

FIG. 58. *Acanthoclema scutulatum*. Fragment of the natural size; enlargement of a perfect specimen, and of a slightly macerated specimen, showing nodes and pits between the apertures (after Hall and Simpson).

Distinguishing Characters.—Ridges unite between cell apertures; vestibular area rhomboided; at intersections of ridges are prominent conical hollow nodes; when worn or macerated, a crescentic opening appears at base of each aperture; branches diverging at angle of sixty to ninety degrees; diameter about .70 mm.

Found in the "Hamilton group, West Hamburg, Erie County, N. Y." (Hall, explanation of plates.)

Genus STREBLOTRYPA. Ulrich.

[Ety. : *Streblos*, turned about; *trypa*, opening.]

(1890: Geo. Surv. Ill., Vol. VIII., p. 403.)

Bryozoum resembling Rhombopora in structure and form, but having angular pits between the ends of the apertures, and irregular cells, or mesopores, in the inter-apertural spaces.

Streblotrypa hamiltonense. (Nicholson.) (Fig. 59.) (Pal. N. Y., Vol. VI., p. 191, Pl. LV.)

Distinguishing Characters.—"Cells tubular, arising from a filiform axis at the center of the branch . . . ." [This character would place the species under Acanthoclema (Hall), under which genus it was described in Vol. VI., Pal. N. Y.]; oval cell apertures in longitudinal parallel rows, often alternating, separated by prominent longitudinal ridges; ridges usually slightly sinuous; two angular pits between apertures.

Fig. 59. *Streblotrypa hamiltonense.* Natural size, and fragment enlarged, x 12 (after Hall and Simpson).

Found in the "Hamilton group, West Hamburg, Erie County, N. Y." (Hall.) Found also at Avery's Creek, in the shale below the Trilobite beds (rare).

Genus FISTULICELLA. Simpson.

[Ety.: *Fistula*, pipe; *cella*, cell.]

(1894: 14th Rep't N. Y. State Geol., p. 606.)

"The manner of growth and general appearance is the same as that of Lichenalia, but the cells are circular and without pseudosepta or lunaria." (Type *F. plana*, Hall.)

Fistulicella plana. Hall. (Fig. 60.) (Pal. N. Y., Vol. VI., p. 215, Pl. LVIII.)

Distinguishing Characters.—Thin, lamellate expansions, incrusting or free; circular apertures, regularly or irregularly disposed; circular or elongate, depressed maculæ, without cells; adjacent apertures slightly larger than those on general surface.

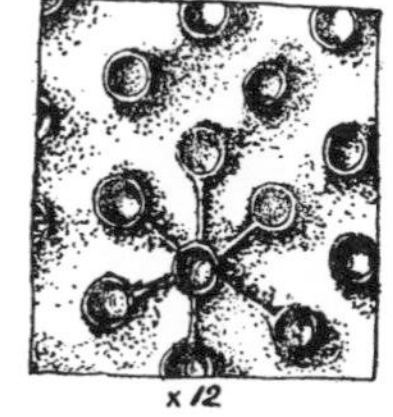

Fig. 60. *Fistulicella plana.* Enlargement of a portion of the surface, x 12 (after Hall and Simpson).

A single fragment of a free frond was found in the Demissa bed of Section 5, at Eighteen Mile Creek.

GENUS FISTULIPORINA. SIMPSON.

[ETY.: *Fistula*, pipe ; *poros*, pore.]

(1894: 14th Rep't N. Y. State Geol., p. 555, Pl. XXI.)

Bryozoum consisting of free or incrusting flat and spreading fronds, or of masses made up of successive layers. The cells are tubular and open by circular or oval apertures, which are furnished with granular or spinulose rims or peristomes, and are irregularly disposed. The space between the cells is occupied below by irregular vesicles and near the top by irregularly superimposed vesicles, or by mesopores with tabulæ. Space between apertures occupied by angular pits, and often, also, by nodes or spines. Base covered by strong epitheca. The genus differs from Fistulipora in its circular cell apertures, "and in the absence of pseudosepta and lunaria."

Ulrich's genus Cyclotrypa, published in Zittel's Palæontology (Eastman's translation), p. 269, is a synonym, Simpson's name having priority according to the date on the title page.

FISTULIPORINA SCROBICULATA. (Hall.) (Fig. 61.) (Pal. N. Y., Vol. VI., p. 212, Pl. LVIII.)

FIG. 61. *Fistuliporina scrobiculata.* A portion of the surface magnified, x 12 (after Hall and Simpson).

Distinguishing Characters.—Cell apertures distant from each other something more than their diameter; strong granulose peristomes; large mesospores, frequently equal to cell-apertures, with slightly elevated margins; large sterile (poreless) blotches or maculæ, 1 to 2 mm. in diameter, occur at intervals; adjacent apertures not larger than others.

Found in the "Hamilton group, Eighteen Mile Creek, Erie County, N. Y." (Hall.)

FISTULIPORINA SEGREGATA. (Hall.) (Fig. 62.) (Pal. N. Y., Vol. VII., p. 219, Pl. LIX.)

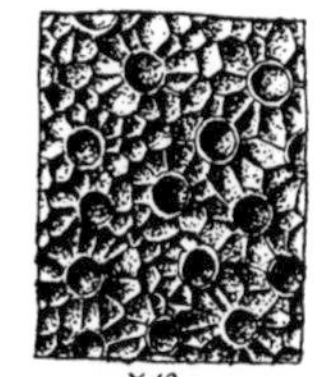

FIG. 62. *Fistulipora segregata.* A portion of the surface enlarged, x 12 (after Hall and Simpson).

Distinguishing Characters.—Thin, lamellate expansion of fronds; under surface with thin epitheca; broadly oval or circular, irregularly disposed, cell apertures; interspaces equal to or greater than diameter of aperture; strong, distinct, smooth peristome; comparatively large mesopores in two or three series between apertures, their margins lower than the peristomes; low, rounded monticules, destitute of cell apertures in their center.

Found in the "Hamilton group, at Eighteen Mile Creek, Erie County, N. Y.," also "West Hamburg, Erie County, N. Y." (Hall.)

FISTULIPORINA MICROPORA. (Hall.) (Fig. 63.) (Pal. N. Y., Vol. VI., p. 220, Pls. LVII., LIX.)

Distinguishing Characters.—Thin, lamellate expansion of frond, incrusting crinoid stems, etc.; vesiculose intercellular tissue; broadly oval to nearly circular irregularly disposed cell apertures, with thin, smooth peristomes, ranging from contact to a cell-diameter apart; minute mesopores (about ten in space of 1 mm.) in one, rarely two, series between apertures, their margins equal in elevation to the peristomes; general delicate appearance of surface of frond.

FIG. 63. *Fistulipora micropora.* Part of surface enlarged, x 12 (after Hall and Simpson).

Found in the "Hamilton group, at Eighteen Mile Creek, Erie County, N. Y." (Hall); and also in the "Hamilton group, at West Hamburg, Erie County, N. Y." (Explanation of plates.)

FISTULIPORINA MINUTA. (Rominger.) (Fig. 64.) (Pal. N. Y., Vol. VI., p. 222, Pl. LIX.)

Distinguishing Characters.—Thin, lamellate expansion of frond, which is free or incrusting; very thin, concentrically wrinkled epitheca; irregularly disposed, comparatively large vesicles occupying the intercellular space; oval to obscurely

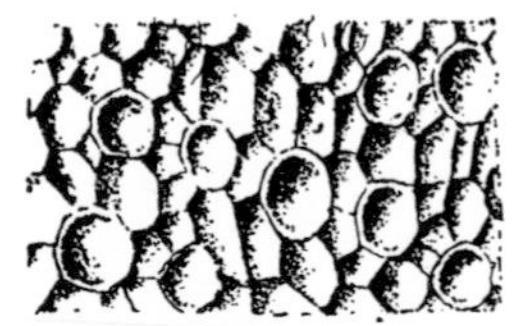

FIG. 64. *Fistuliporina minuta.* Portion of surface enlarged, x 18 (after Hall and Simpson).

sub-polygonal irregularly disposed cell apertures, with moderately strong nodose or spinulose peristomes; mesopores with margins of same height as the peristomes, with minute nodes at the angles; low rounded monticules, with apertures and mesopores like those on the rest of the frond.

Found in the "Hamilton group, at West Hamburg, Erie County, N. Y." (Hall, explanation of plates.)

FISTULIPORINA DIGITATA. (Hall.) (Fig. 65.) (Pal. N. Y., Vol. VI., p. 229, Pl. LIX.)

Distinguishing Characters.—Thin, lamellate expansion of incrusting frond; finger-like growth (digitate expansion); closely and irregularly (sometimes somewhat regularly) disposed oval apertures, with thin, smooth, slightly elevated peristomes; minute mesopores, usually in a single series between apertures; numerous strong conical nodes, occupying places of mesopores.

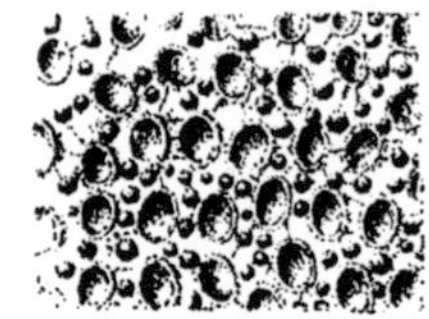

FIG. 65. *Fistuliporina digitata.* Portion of the surface enlarged, x 18 (after Hall and Simpson).

Found in the "Hamilton group, at West Hamburg, Erie County, N. Y." (Hall.)

GENUS PALESCHARA. HALL.

[ETY.: *Palaios*, ancient; *eschara*, scar; Eschara, a genus of Bryozoa.]

(1872: 26th Ann. Rep't N. Y. State Mus. Nat. Hist., p. 107.)

"Zoarium consisting of thin expansions incrusting other bodies. Cells polygonal, in contact, with frequent maculæ (or monticules) of larger cells." (Hall, Pal. N. Y., Vol. VI., p. xviii.)

PALESCHARA INTERCELLA. Hall. (Not figured.) (3d Ann. Rep't N. Y. State Geol., p. 5.)

Distinguishing Characters.—Extremely thin, incrusting corals, etc.; cells in contact, irregularly or diagonally disposed; quadrangular, square, or oblong, smaller interstitial cells; broad, slightly elevated monticules, with larger cells in the center; triangular spinules at angles of cell rims, sometimes on sides.

Found in the Demissa and Stictopora beds, at Section 5.

PALESCHARA RETICULATA. Hall. (Fig. 66.) (3d Ann. Rep't N. Y. State Geol., p. 6.)

Distinguishing Characters.—Thin incrustation; pentagonal, hexagonal, or quadrangular cells, .35 mm. in diameter, in contact, and variously disposed; general appearance of surface often reticulate; minute interstitial cells; monticules 4 or 5 mm. distant; central space with cells .45 or .50 mm. in diameter; marginal spinules in well-preserved specimens.

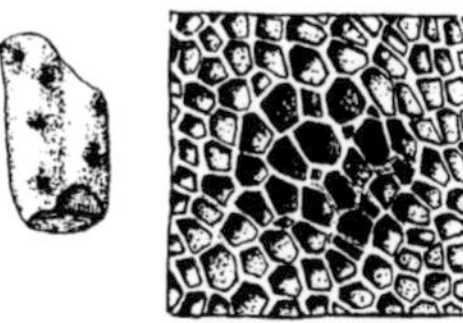

FIG. 66. *Paleschara reticulata.* A frond encrusting a coral; natural size, and a portion of the surface enlarged, showing the monticules. From the Demissa bed. (Original.)

Found in the Demissa bed, at Section 5.

PALESCHARA AMPLECTENS. Hall. (Not figured.) (3d Ann. Rep't N. Y. State Geol., p. 7.)

Distinguishing Characters.—Extremely thin incrustation, commonly on crinoid stems; quadrangular to hexagonal cells, 2 mm. in diameter; minute marginal nodes or spinules; no monticules or maculæ, but cells all of same size.

Found in the Demissa bed, at Section 5 (rare).

GENUS LICHENALIA. HALL.

[ETY.: From resemblance to a lichen.]

(1852: Pal. N. Y., Vol. II., p. 171.)

Zoarium massive, or growing in circular or flabellate expansions, celluliferous on one side, the other covered with an epitheca. Cells arising from the epitheca, with transverse tabulæ, and circular or trilobate, sometimes operculate, apertures, which are often denticulate, and have the posterior portion of the peristome arched and elevated. Space between apertures smooth. Intercellular spaces vesicular.

LICHENALIA STELLATA. Hall. (Fig. 66 A.) (Pal. N. Y., Vol. VI., p. 195, Pl. LVIII.)

Distinguishing Characters.—Free or incrusting lamellate expansions, or masses, formed by superposition of successive layers of growth; tubular cells, recumbent for a short distance, but chiefly at right angles or oblique to surface; oval or nearly circular cell apertures, usually a little oblique to the surface; prominent rounded monticules, bearing an elongate depression in the center, which is destitute of cells; large cell apertures adjacent to the depressions; radiating rows of apertures, giving the monticules a stellate appearance.

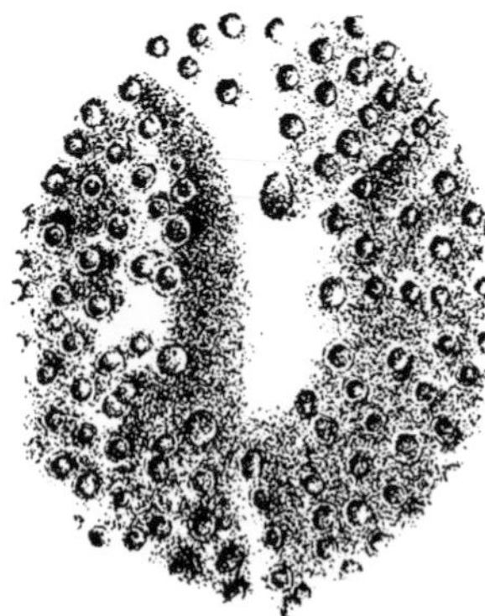

FIG. 66A. *Lichenalia stellata.* Portion of the surface enlarged, x 6 (after Hall and Simpson).

Found in the Demissa bed of Section 5 (massive specimens).

GENUS STICTOPORA. HALL.

(1847: Pal. N. Y., Vol. I., p. 73.)

[ETY.: *Stictos*, punctured; *poros*, pore.]

Bryozoum consisting of thin, flat branches with a lenticular cross-section, and attached by a spreading base to foreign objects. Cells in two series, separated by a median wall or mesotheca, each series having its apertures on one of the flat sides. Margin without cells.

FIG. 67. *Stictopora incisurata.* Natural size and a portion enlarged (after Hall and Simpson).

STICTOPORA INCISURATA. Hall. (Fig. 67.) (Pal. N. Y., Vol. VI., p. 241, Pl. LX.)

Distinguishing Characters. — Elongate oval to nearly circular apertures in longitudinal diverging lines, increasing by interstitial additions; marginal apertures largest; peristomes strong;

ranges of apertures separated by longitudinal ridges, which often continue out on the non-celluliferous spaces.

Found in the Encrinal limestone (rare); in the Stictopora bed, at Section 5, etc. (abundant); in the Demissa bed (common); in the shale down to and in the Pleurodictium beds and the shales below, at Sections 5 to 8; and on the Lake Shore and in Avery's Creek (often abundant).

STICTOPORA SINUOSA. Hall. (Fig. 68.) (Pal. N. Y., Vol. VI., p. 247, Pl. LXI.)

Distinguishing Characters.—Broadly oval to nearly circular, distant, apertures; strong peristomes, more elevated on posterior part; strong, sinuous interrupted ridges between the apertures.

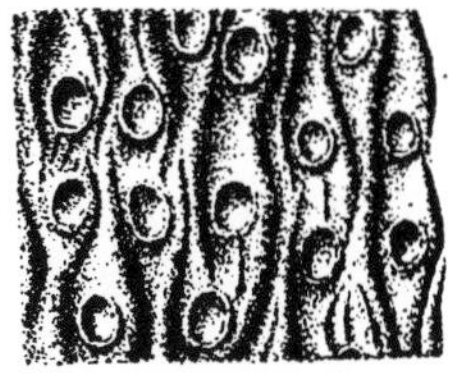

FIG. 68. *Stictopora sinuosa.* Portion of surface enlarged, x 18 (after Hall and Simpson).

Found two feet below lowest Trilobite bed, in Avery's Creek (one specimen).

STICTOPORA RECTA. Hall. (Pal. N. Y., Vol. VI., p. 253.) (Not figured.)

Distinguishing Characters.—Width of branches from 1 to 1.25 mm.; parallel margins; no expansion before bifurcating; narrow or obsolete non-celluliferous space; bifurcations at intervals of about 6 mm., branches diverging at angle of forty-five degrees; oval apertures in five or six parallel longitudinal rows, separated by less than length of apertures; prominent granulose or nodulose ridges separating rows, equal in width to apertures, and frequently obscuring them; numerous irregularly disposed granules.

FIG. 69. *Stictopora palmipes.* Natural size, and a portion enlarged, x 18 (after Hall and Simpson).

Found in the "Hamilton group, at West Hamburg, Erie County, N. Y." (Hall.)

STICTOPORA PALMIPES. Hall. (Fig. 69.) (Pal. N. Y., Vol. VI., p. 255, Pl. LX.)

Distinguishing Characters.—Small size; intermediate, lateral, palmate branches or lobed expansions between regular bifurcations, not over 1.50 mm. long by 1 mm. wide; oval apertures; slight peristomes; strongly nodose longitudinal ridges.

Found in the "shales of Hamilton group, at West Hamburg, Erie County, N. Y." (Hall, type.)

STICTOPORA PERMARGINATA. Hall. (Fig. 70.) (Pal. N. Y., Vol. VI., p. 258, Pl. LXIII.)

FIG. 70. *Stictopora permarginata.* Portion enlarged, x 18 (after Hall and Simpson).

Distinguishing Characters.—Narrow or obsolete non-celluliferous margins; oval cross-section; thick peristomes of irregularly scattered apertures; absence of ridges.

Found in the "Hamilton group, at West Hamburg, Erie County,. N. Y." (Hall, type.)

GENUS TÆNIOPORA. NICHOLSON.

[ETY.: *Tainia*, ribbon; *poros*, pore.]

(1874: Geol. Mag. Lond. N. S., Vol. I., p. 120.)

Bryozoum consisting of narrow flattened branches, which are often rhombic in cross-section. Cells on both sides, with rounded apertures. In the center there is usually a prominent longitudinal keel, while the cell apertures are more prominent than in Stictopora.

TÆNIOPORA EXIGUA. Nicholson. (Fig. 71.) (Pal. N. Y., Vol. VI., p. 263, Pl. LXII.)

Distinguishing Characters.—Comparatively wide non-celluliferous margin; strong central, and similar lateral (branch) ridges; minute circular apertures; prominent peristomes.

Found at "West Hamburg, Erie County." (Hall.) Found also in the Stictopora and Demissa beds, at Section 5, Eighteen Mile Creek (rare).

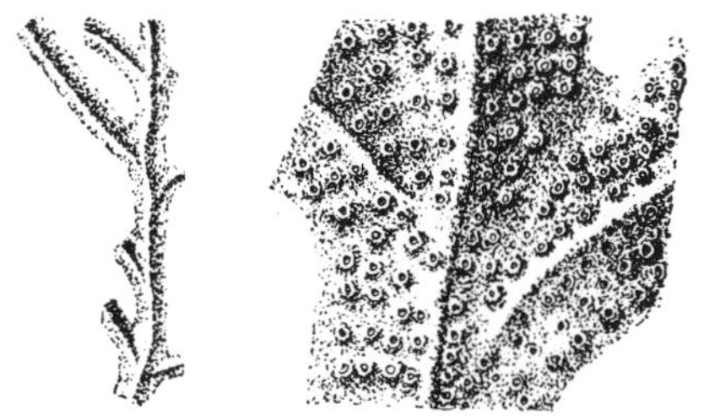

FIG. 71. *Tæniopora exigua.* Natural size, and a portion enlarged, x 6 (after Hall and Simpson).

GENUS ACROGENIA. HALL.

[ETY.: *Akros,* sharp; *genea,* growth.]

(1881: Trans. Albany Inst., Vol. X., p. 193.)

"Zoarium" (Bryozoum) "ramose, proliferous; consisting of flattened branches, two proceeding from the truncate termination of the previous one, and continuing growth in the same manner. Branches striated below, flattened and celluliferous above. Intercellular structure vesiculose. Apertures arranged in longitudinal rows." (Hall, Pal. N. Y., Vol. VI., p. xx.)

ACROGENIA PROLIFERA. Hall. (Fig. 72.) (Pal. N. Y., Vol. VI., p. 267, Pl. LXIII.)

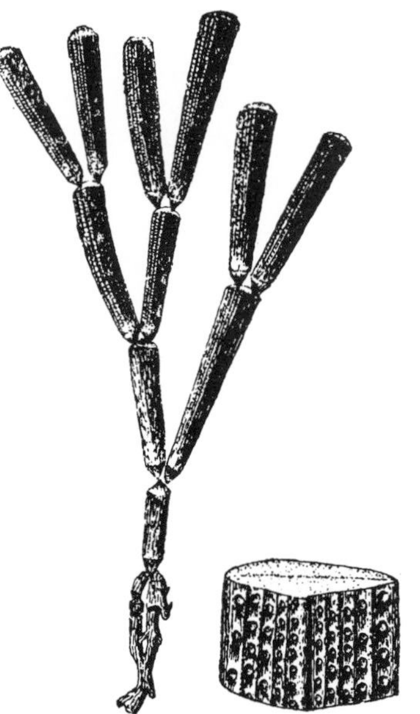

FIG. 72. *Acrogenia prolifera.* Natural size, and a portion enlarged, x 6 (after Hall and Simpson).

Distinguishing Characters.—Peculiar growth and jointage; small circular apertures; weak peristomes; prominent lunaria; continuous ridges separating apertures.

Found in the "Hamilton group, Eighteen Mile Creek, Erie County, N. Y." (Hall, explanation of plates.)

Genus PTILODICTYA. Lonsdale.

[Ety.: *Ptilon*, feather; *dictyon*, net.]

(1839: Murchison's Silurian System, p. 676.)

"Zoarium" (Bryozoum) "pointed below, articulating into a spreading base; above, a leaf-like expansion, which is sometimes lobed at the distal extremity, celluliferous on both faces, divided by a mesial lamina. Margin without cells. Apertures circular or subquadrate. No intercellular tissue, although some species show minute interapertural pits or tubuli on the surface of the stipe." (Hall, Pal. N. Y., Vol. VI., pp. xix., xx.)

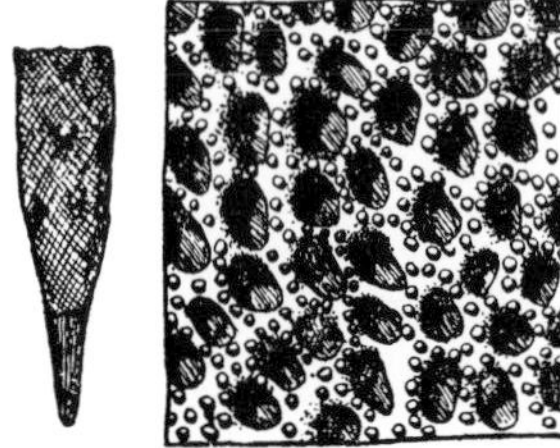

Fig. 73. *Ptilodictya plumea.* Natural size, and portion of surface enlarged (after Hall and Simpson).

Ptilodictya plumea. Hall. (Fig. 73.) (Pal. N. Y., Vol. VI., p. 271, Pl. LXI.)

Distinguishing Characters.—Flattened wedge-shaped form; circular or broadly oval apertures; obsolete peristomes; elevated, granulose, interapertural space; low convex monticules, with somewhat larger apertures; striated cylindrical basal portion.

Found at "Hamburg-on-the-Lake, Erie County, N. Y." (Hall); and in the Demissa bed, at Section 5, in Eighteen Mile Creek (rare).

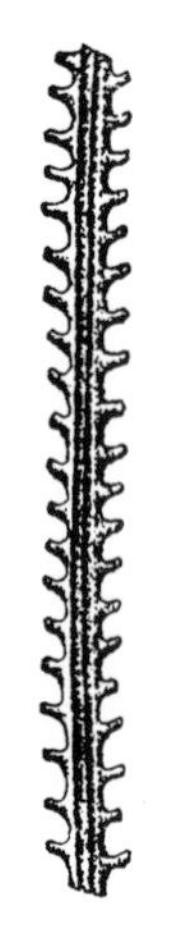

Fig. 74. *Glauconome carinata.* Enlarged, x 6 (after Hall and Simpson).

Genus GLAUCONOME. Goldfuss.

[Ety.: Mythological name.]

(1826: Petrefacta Germaniæ, Vol. I., p. 100.)

"Zoarium consisting of a main stem or rachis, from which proceed simple lateral branches at regular intervals, and occasionally branches having the same manner of growth as the primary rachis; celluliferous on one side. Cell apertures in two ranges, often separated by a longitudinal carina." (Hall, Pal. N. Y., Vol. VI., p. xxiv.)

GLAUCONOME CARINATA. Hall. (Fig. 74.) (Pal. N. Y., Vol. VI., p. 273, Pl. LXVI.)

Distinguishing Characters.—Small size; broad central rachis; thin, short, lateral branches; flattened, non-celluliferous face, with three prominent ridges or carinæ; circular apertures; comparatively strong peristomes; prominent carina between ranges of apertures.

Found in the "Hamilton Group, in Eighteen Mile Creek, Erie County, N. Y." (Hall, type.)

GENUS BOTRYLLOPORA. NICHOLSON.

[ETY.: *Botryllos*, cluster; *poros*, pore.]

(1874: Geol. Mag. N. S., Vol. I., p. 160.)

Bryozoum consisting of small discoidal bodies, which occur either singly or in clusters, and adhere to foreign bodies by their under surface, which is covered by a concentrically wrinkled epitheca. The cells are tubular and rectangular to the surface, in double rows, forming radiating ridges. Central depressed space of the body non-celluliferous.

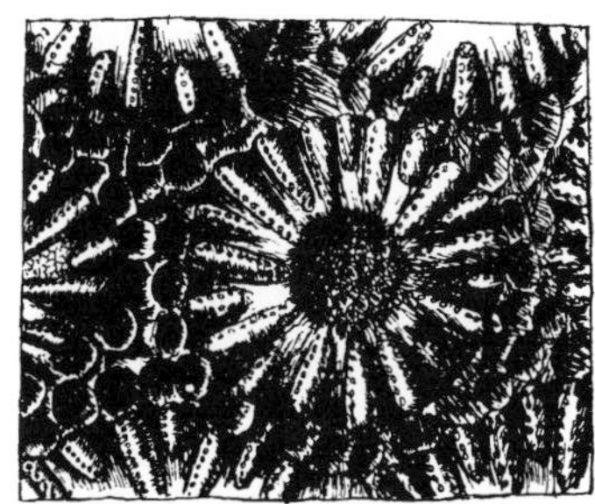

FIG. 75. *Botryllopora socialis.* Portion of a colony enlarged (after Hall and Simpson).

BOTRYLLOPORA SOCIALIS. Nicholson. (Fig. 75.) (Pal. N. Y., Vol. VI., p. 282, Pl. LXIV.)

Distinguishing Characters.— Alternate ridges extending to central area, others one-half to two-thirds that distance; minute circular apertures often in contact or inosculating.

Found in the shale below the Trilobite beds, in Avery's Creek, and on the Lake Shore (not common). Demissa bed, at Section 5 (rare).

Genus REPTARIA. Rolle.

[Ety.: *Repto*, to creep.]

(1851: Leonhard and Bronn, Neues Jahrbuch, p. 180.)

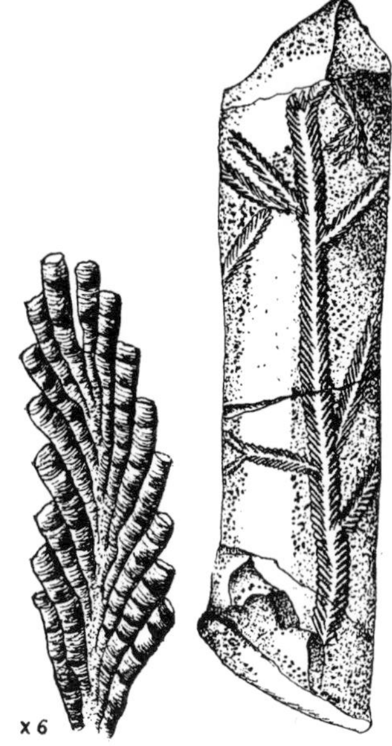

Fig. 76. *Reptaria stolonifera*. Frond incrusting Orthoceras, natural size; and a portion enlarged, x 6 (after Hall and Simpson).

Bryozoum creeping and adhering to foreign bodies. A central stem or rachis gives off lateral tubes, and at irregular intervals, branches. The tubes are slightly sinuous and nearly parallel with the rachis below, but farther up they diverge more and more.

Reptaria stolonifera. Rolle. (Fig. 76.) (Pal. N. Y., Vol. VI., p. 274, Pl. LXV.)

Distinguishing Characters.—Incrusting habit; equal lateral tubes, of similar length; slight annulations of tubes; last cell terminal.

Found in the Demissa bed, at Section 5, attached to an Orthoceras (one specimen).

Genus HEDERELLA. Hall.

[Ety.: *Hedera*, ivy.]

(1881: Trans. Albany Inst., Vol. X., p. 194.)

"Zoarium parasitic, consisting of a filiform tubular axis, with opposite or alternate lateral budding of simple tubular cells; also of lateral extensions, continuing in the same manner of growth as the initial axis."

Hederella canadensis. (Nicholson.) (Fig. 77.) (Pal. N. Y., Vol. VI., p. 277, Pl. LXV.)

Distinguishing Characters.—Sub-cylindrical cell tubes, transverse section oval; tubes usually alternating; tubes either in contact with main axis, or diverging from it; general prolific development of tubes.

Found incrusting brachiopods, in the shale four feet below the lowest Trilobite bed, in Avery's Ravine (rare).

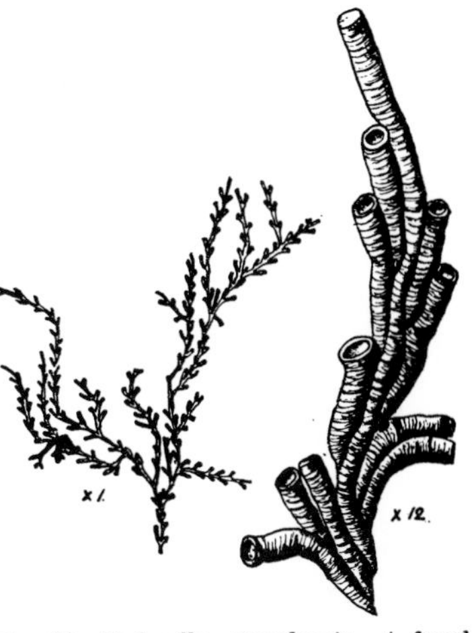

Fig. 77. *Hederella canadensis.* A frond natural size, and a portion enlarged, x 12 (after Hall and Simpson).

HEDERELLA FILIFORMIS. (Billings.) (Fig. 77A.) (*Aulopora filiformis.* Billings, Can. Journ., Vol. IV., p. 119. Pal. N. Y., Vol. VI., p. 278, Pl. LXV.)

Distinguishing Characters.—Parasitic procumbent habit; attached for its entire length; elongate sub-cylindrical primary axis, with lateral simple tubular cells, and occasionally tubular branches; sinuous or tortuous character of cells, with apertures abruptly turned outwards; cell tubes of greater diameter and less length than *H. canadensis.*

Found incrusting shells and corals in the Hamilton group of Eighteen Mile Creek. (Coll. Am. Mus. Nat. Hist. New York.)

Fig. 77A. *Hederella filiformis.* Natural size and enlarged, x 6 (after Hall and Simpson).

CLASS BRACHIOPODA. CUVIER.

The Brachiopoda are marine animals, sparingly represented in the modern seas, but most prolifically developed in the Palæozoic and early Mesozoic waters. The soft parts are enclosed in a bivalve shell, for which reason they are often, though erroneously, classed with the Mollusca, their true affinities being decidedly with the worms and Polyzoa.

The valves of the brachiopod shell are dorsal and ventral, and not right and left as in the lamellibranch Mollusca; they are unequal, and each one is symmetrical with reference to a median line (longitudinal axis) drawn through its apex. The larger valve (in most species) has its beak variously truncated, or furnished with an opening or *foramen*, for the emission of the fleshy "*pedicle*," by means of which the animal fixes itself to rocks, shells, or other substances. *

Certain genera, such as Crania, do not conform to this general method of fixation, but cement their shell directly to the foreign object, while others, e. g., Pholidops, appear to have led a free existence. In many of the discinoid genera, such as Orbiculoidea, etc., the pedicle passed through an opening in the lower valve; while in Lingula, the pedicle protruded between the two very nearly equal valves. In all cases the valve giving emission to the pedicle is spoken of as the *pedicle valve* (ventral valve of many authors, dorsal valve of some).

The opposite valve in the more specialized genera bears on its interior two short processes, or *crura*, which arise from the hinge plate. To these may be attached a calcareous "*brachidium*," which functions as a support for the delicate fleshy "arms." In a large number of forms this brachidium is absent, and the fleshy arms are directly supported by the crura, but their relation to the valve in question is similar to that obtaining in the brachidium-bearing forms. This valve is designated the "*brachial*" valve (dorsal valve of many authors, ventral valve of some). In all the forms in which the valves are articulated with each other (*Brachiopoda articulata*) such articulation is produced by *teeth* arising from the pedicle valve, and lodged in *sockets* in the brachial valve. The beak of the brachial valve is commonly furnished with a more or less pronounced "*cardinal process*," which, at its free end, presents a surface for the attachment of the *diductor*, or opening muscles, the opposite ends of which are attached near the center of the pedicle valve, where they often leave pronounced *scars*. A contraction of these muscles pulls on the cardinal process, which pull, as it is exerted *behind* the plane of articulation, will draw the beak of the brachial valve toward the interior of the pedicle valve, and thus cause a separation of the valves at the *front* or opposite end from the beak. *Adductor muscles* passing from valve to valve, and also commonly leaving scars, close the valves again.† Below the cardinal process, and often merged with it, is an elevated *hinge-plate*, whose surface often serves for muscular attachment.

Beneath the beak of each valve frequently occurs a flat "*cardinal area*," bounded above by the *cardinal slopes*, and below by the articulating margin or *hinge-line*. This area is commonly divided in the center by a triangular fissure (*delthyrium* in the pedicle valve, and *chilyrium* in the brachial valve). This occurs also in genera where no "*area*" is present, e. g., *Cryptonella*, *Athyris*, etc. It is commonly covered either by a single plate, or by two plates which join in the center. These are the *deltidium* or *pedicle plate* in the pedicle valve, when single, or the *deltidial plates*, when double, and the *chilidium* in the brachial valve.‡

---

* This foramen frequently becomes obsolete in mature or old shells by the deposition of secondary calcareous material below it.

† In the inarticulate genera, i. e., Lingula, Orbiculoidea, etc., a more complicated muscular system exists, by means of which the valves can be partially rotated, and thus separated.

‡ In Orbiculoidea the triangular fissure is a feature of early growth only, being in the later stages closed below by the growth of the shell. A secondary plate, or "*listrium*," also covers the aperture beneath the beak.

The important surface features of the shell are: the *lines of growth*, the radiating *plications* or *striations*, the *fold* or medial elevation, and the *sinus* or medial depression, the fold commonly occurring in the brachial, and the sinus in the pedicle, valve.

The following diagram represents the principal features of the shell, and gives its orientation.

NOTE.—For an account of the anatomy of the animal, any text-book of zoölogy may be consulted. Zittel's text-book of Palæontology (Eastman's translation) is standard. For the best account of the animal and the shell, as well as detailed descriptions of the genera, the student is referred to the admirable hand-book of the Brachiopoda, by Hall and Clarke, entitled "An introduction to the study of the Brachiopoda," and published in the reports of the State Geologist of New York, for 1891 and 1893. Vol. VIII., Pts. I. and II., of the Palæontology of New York, should also be within the reach of the student.

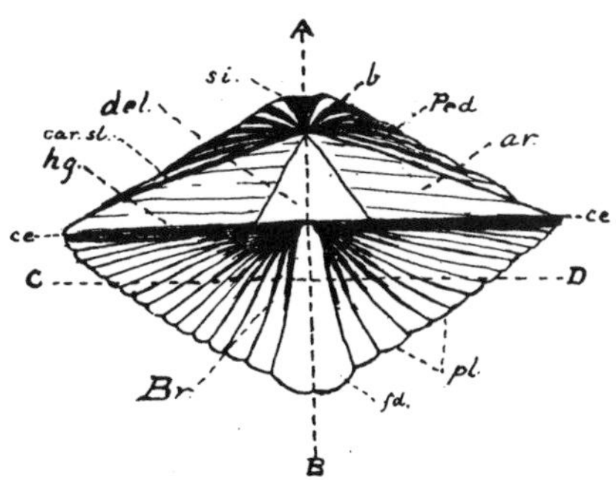

FIG. 78. Diagram of *Spirifer*. (*A*, *B*) Longitudinal axis marking the height; (*C*, *D*) Transverse axis marking the width; (*B*) anterior (front) end; (*A*) posterior or beak end; (*ar.*) cardinal area; (*b*) beak (or umbo); (*Br.*) brachial valve; (*car. sl.*) cardinal slopes; (*ce*) cardinal extremities; (*del.*) delthyrium; (*fd.*) mesial fold of brachial valve; (*hg.*) hinge-line; (*Ped.*) pedicle valve; (*pl.*) plications; (*si.*) mesial sinus of pedicle valve. (Original.)

The specific descriptions will nearly all be found in Vol. IV. of the Palæontology of New York, and for a more detailed study that volume should be consulted. For classification, synonomy, and distribution consult "A Synopsis of American Fossil Brachiopoda," by Charles Schuchert. Bull. 87, U. S. G. S. In the preparation of the following brief descriptions the above-named sources have largely been drawn upon.

BRACHIOPODA INARTICULATA.

GENUS LINGULA. BRUGUIÈRE.

[ETY.: *Lingula*, a little tongue.]

(1789: Hist. Natur. des Vers Testacés. 1892: Pal. N. Y., Vol. VIII., Pt. I., p. 2.)

Shell with the valves nearly equal, and varying in outline from elongate-ovate to sub-triangular, always longer than wide. Valves arched. Animal attached by a long, muscular pedicle, which protrudes from between the beaks of the two valves.

LINGULA (GLOSSINA) LEANA. Hall. (Fig. 79.) (Pal. N. Y., Vol. IV., p. 9, Pl. II.)

Distinguishing Characters.—Size; robust character; pointed posterior (beak) end, with sides gradually sloping outward for two-thirds the length; rounded anterior end; somewhat greater convexity near the beak than near the front; fine concentric growth lines and occasionally faint radiating lines.

FIG 79. *Lingula leana.* Ventral valve, natural size (from Hall).

This species was found at Section 7, between eight and fourteen feet, and at twenty feet, below the Encrinal limestone.

Measurements.—12 by 9 mm., also 13 mm. by 10 mm. in greatest length and width.

LINGULA DELIA. Hall. (Fig. 80.) (Pal. N. Y., Vol. IV., p. 12, Pl. II.)

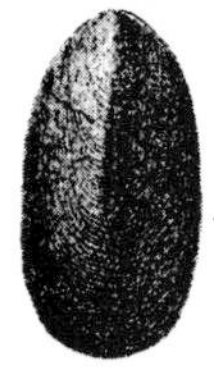

FIG. 80. *Lingula delia.* Natural size (from Hall).

Distinguishing Characters.—Length about twice the width; abruptly sloping cardinal margins; gently curving sides; rounded front; fine lines of growth, and occasionally coarser concentric lines; a median longitudinal depression appears in one valve, marking the position of a septum.

Found in the Demissa bed, at Section 5; ten feet below the Encrinal limestone, at Section 7; and twenty-five feet below the Encrinal limestone, in Idlewood Ravine.

LINGULA SPATULATA. Vanuxem. (Fig. 81.) (Pal. N. Y., Vol. IV., p. 13, Pl. I.)

Distinguishing Characters.—Small size, spatulate form; general form and proportions similar to preceding, but very much smaller; outline somewhat variable; occasionally acutely pointed; fine concentric growth-lines; occasional faint radiating striæ.

FIG. 81. *Lingula spatulata.* Enlarged, x 4. Genesee shale. (Original.)

Found in the Upper Naples (Gardeau) shales on the Lake Shore; in the Lower Naples

(Cashaqua) shales, at Section 1; in the Genesee shale, at Sections 1 and 2, and on the Lake Shore; in the Styliolina band, at Sections 1, 2, 3; in the Demissa bed, at Section 5; and between twelve and fourteen feet below the Encrinal limestone, at Section 7.

Measurements of a very large individual were 6 mm. long and 3.5 mm. wide. Usually they are much smaller.

GENUS ORBICULOIDEA. D'ORBIGNY.

[ETY.: *Orbicula*, a genus; *oides*, like.]

(1850: Prodr. de Paléont, T. I., p. 44. 1892: Pal. N. Y., Vol. VIII., Pt. I., p. 120.)

Shell varying from nearly circular to almost elliptical in outline, the valves unequal; apices eccentric; lower (pedicle) valve flat, or nearly so; a narrow pedicle furrow passes backward from just behind the beak, and ends near the margin in a short tubular sipho, which penetrates the shell and emerges on the inner sides, near the margin; upper (brachial) valve conical, apex directed backwards; surface marked by concentric lines of growth; shell substance partly corneous.

ORBICULOIDEA MEDIA. Hall. (Fig. 82.) (Pal. N. Y., Vol. IV., p. 20, Pl. II. *Discina media.*)

Distinguishing Characters.—Size; broadly elliptical or nearly circular outline; depressed brachial valve, with apex at one-third the distance from the posterior margin; pedicle furrow commonly in the longitudinal axis; fine regular surface striæ.

FIG. 82. *Orbiculoidea media.* Dorsal and ventral valves, natural size (from Hall).

Found in the upper Moscow shales (transition shales), at Section 3; in the middle Moscow (*O. media*) bed, at Sections 4 and 5; at ten feet below, and between fourteen and seventeen feet below the Encrinal limestone, at Section 7; and in the *Modiomorpha subalata* bed, on the Lake Shore.

ORBICULOIDEA DORIA. Hall. (Fig. 83.) (Pal. N. Y., Vol. IV., p. 19, Pl. II.)

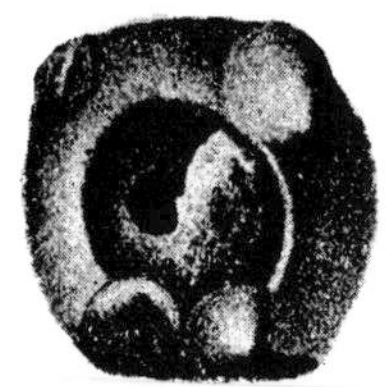

FIG. 83. *Orbiculoidea doria.* Several attached shells (from Hall).

Distinguishing Characters.—Sub-circular or oblate outline; greater transverse diameter; convex brachial valve, with apex near the margin; flat or concave pedicle valve with large oval pedicle groove; and fine concentric striæ, with occasionally coarser wrinkles.

Found in the middle Moscow (Orbiculoidea) bed, at Sections 4 and 5.

ORBICULOIDEA LODIENSIS. Vanuxem. (Fig. 84.) (Pal. N. Y., Vol. IV., p. 22, Pl. II.)

Distinguishing Characters.—Broadly oval-ovate outline; narrower posterior end; low brachial valve, with minute eccentric apex; linear pedicle groove extending more than half way from apex to margin in pedicle valve; concentric striæ, and faint radiating folds or undulations on the anterior half of the shell.

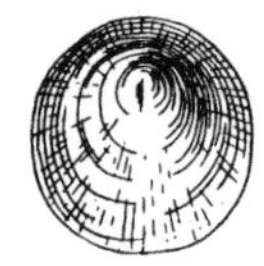

FIG. 84. *Orbiculoidea lodiensis.* Brachial valve, Demissa bed, x 2⅔. (Original.)

Found in the Demissa bed, at Section 5; the Pleurodictyum bed, at Wanakah Cliff; the Nautilus bed, in Avery's Ravine. It is rare in all.

Measurements: 6 mm. by 5 mm. in length and width.

GENUS SCHIZOBOLUS. ULRICH.

[ETY.: *Schiza*, a cleft; *obolus*, a genus.]

(1886: Contributions to American Palæontology, Vol. I., p. 25, Pl. III. Pal. N. Y., Vol. VIII., Pt. I., p. 87.)

Shell oval, valves slightly unequal, margins thickened; pedicle valve with a notch in the posterior margin; shell substance largely corneous. Muscular callosities of pedicle valve on each side of a median ridge with narrow curved lateral scars, brachial valve without the scars, but with thickened band just within posterior margin.

SCHIZOBOLUS TRUNCATUS. Hall. (Fig. 85.) (*Discina truncata.* Hall. Pal. N. Y., Vol. IV., p. 23, Pls. I. and II.)

Distinguishing Characters.—Abruptly rounded or truncate posterior margin; apices of both valves near posterior margin; marginal notch in pedicle (lower) valve; and concentric striæ.

FIG. 85. *Schizobolus truncatus.* Interiors of pedicle and brachial valves, showing median septum flanked by callosity in each; exterior of pedicle valve, x 2⅔, upper Moscow (transition) shales; eighteen Mile Creek. (Original.)

Found in the black Naples shales, at Sturgeon Point; in the upper Moscow shales (transition beds) and down to four feet from the top, at Sections 1, 2, 3, 4; and in the *Orbiculoidea media* bed of the middle Moscow shale, at Sections 4 and 5.

Measurements.—Length 6.2 mm.; width 5.7 mm. average.

GENUS CRANIA. RETZIUS.

[ETY.: *Kranion*, upper part of a skull.]

(1781: Schriften der Berliner Gesellschaft Naturforschender Freunde. Bd. II., p. 72. 1892: Pal. N. Y., Vol. VIII., Pt. I., p. 145.)

Shell with valves unequal, not articulated, and without perforation for the pedicle; attached by the apex or the entire surface of the lower valve; lower (attached) valve with apex slightly elevated if not conforming to surface to which it is attached; upper valve conical, with apex near the center; often strongly marked muscular impressions.

CRANIA CRENISTRIATA. Hall. (Fig. 86.) Pal. N. Y., Vol. IV., p. 28, Pl. III.)

Distinguishing Characters.—Nearly circular outline; low conical form; smooth apex; sharp, elevated and crenulated striæ, which radiate from the apex, and are increased in number by the appearance of new ones between the diverging older ones.

FIG. 86. *Crania crenistriata.* Lateral and top views of an elliptical dorsal valve (from Hall).

Found in the "Hamilton group, in Eighteen Mile Creek." (Hall, type.) The shell is attached to Cystiphyllum in the Demissa bed, at Section 5.

Genus CRANIELLA. Oehlert.

[Ety.: Diminutive of *crania.*]

(1888: Bull. de la Soc. d'Études Scientif. d'Angers, p. 37. 1892: Pal. N. Y., Vol. VIII., Pt. I., pp. 153, 170.)

Shell somewhat irregular, with an outline varying from nearly circular to almost quadrangular; no pedicle opening, but lower valve cemented, by its whole surface, to rocks or other shells; upper valve more or less elevated, apex behind the center; four large adductor muscle impressions, one pair near the center; outside of these lie S-shaped vascular impressions.

Craniella hamiltoniæ. Hall. (Fig. 87.) (Pal. N. Y., Vol. IV., p. 27, Pl. III.)

Distinguishing Characters.—Large size; adaptation to surface on which it is attached; irregularly rounded outline; and concentric lines of growth about an eccentric apex.

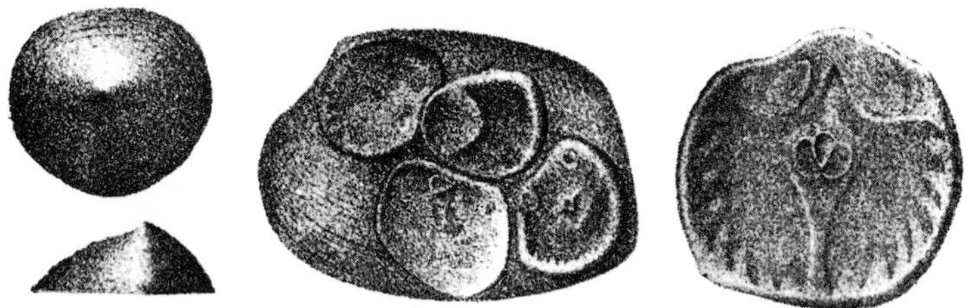

Fig. 87. *Craniella hamiltoniæ.* Top and lateral views of a dorsal valve; a group of ventral valves attached to a valve of *Cypricardella bellistriata;* enlargement of the interior of a ventral valve (from Hall).

Found in the coral layer of the Moscow shale, at Section 5 (?) and just above it; also in the Stictopora and Demissa beds, at Section 5; in the shale below the *A. spiriferoides* bed and two feet below the Trilobite beds, in Avery's Creek.

Genus PHOLIDOPS. Hall.

[Ety.: *Pholidos,* a scale.]

(1859: Pal. N. Y., Vol. III., p. 489. 1892: Pal. N. Y., Vol. VIII., Pt. I., p. 155.)

Shells small, with equal valves, patella-like in outline; they are inarticulate and unattached, without pedicle opening; position of apex variable; the edges of the valves are flattened where they join, and on the interior are elevated areas for the attachment of the muscles, etc. In molds of the interior, a strongly-marked impression of this callosity appears.

PHOLIDOPS HAMILTONIÆ. Hall. (Fig. 88.) (Pal. N. Y., Vol. IV., p. 32.)

Distinguishing Characters.—Small size; ovate outline; broader posterior end; eccentric, elevated apex, inclined backwards; lamellose lines of growth closely arranged.

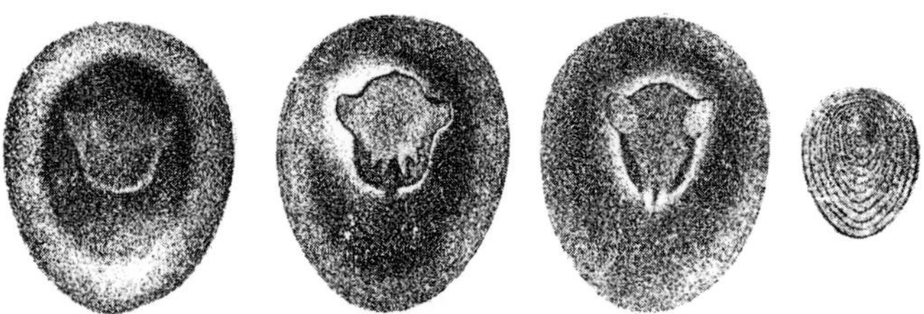

FIG. 88. *Pholidops hamiltoniæ.* Interior of ventral valve, x 8; impressions of interiors of ventral and dorsal valves, x 8; exterior of shell, x 4 (from Hall).

Found as single valves, molds, etc., and is common throughout the Hamilton shales, from the Trilobite beds upward. It occurs in the lower Moscow shale, at Sections 4 and 5.

Measurements.—Length, 4 mm.; width, 3 mm.

PHOLIDOPS LINGULOIDES. Hall. (Fig. 89.) (Pal. N. Y., Vol. IV., p. 414.)

Distinguishing Characters.—Linguloid outline; projecting apex, with flattened "area," striated by lines of growth.

Found in the Encrinal limestone and the Demissa bed, at Section 5.

Measurements.—Two specimens: length, 7 and 7.7 mm.; width, 5.2 and 6.9 mm.

FIG. 89. *Pholidops linguloides.* Interior and exterior of a ventral (?) valve, showing form, false area, and muscular callosities, Encrinal limestone, x 2⅔. (Original.)

PHOLIDOPS OBLATA. Hall. (Fig. 90.) (Pal. N. Y., Vol. IV., p. 414, Pl. III.)

Distinguishing Characters.—Nearly round outline; depressed convex form; small muscular areas, divided by longitudinal median septum.

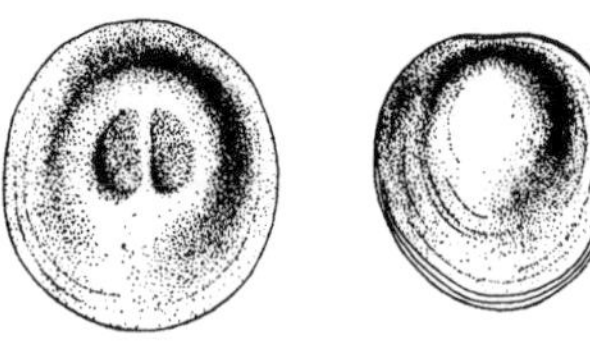

FIG. 90. *Pholidops oblata.* Impression of interior of valve in shale, showing double callosity; exterior of exfoliated specimen, showing submarginal beak, and a few lines of growth, Encrinal limestone, x 2⅔. (Original.)

Specimens referred to this species, showing the exterior with beak subterminal, and concentric striæ, are found in the Encrinal limestone, at Section 5.

Measurements. — Two specimens: length, 7 and 6.5 mm.; width, 6.6 and 6.3 mm.

BRACHIOPODA ARTICULATA.

GENUS RHIPIDOMELLA. OEHLERT.

[ETY.: *Ripid*, a fan; *ella*, diminutive.]
(Orthis in part.)

(1891: Journal de Conchyliologie, p. 372. 1892: Pal. N. Y., Vol. VIII., Pt. I., p. 209.)

Shell almost circular in outline; both valves convex, brachial valve more so than the pedicle valve. Hinge area narrow and short on the brachial valve, higher on the pedicle valve. A slight median depression in each valve. Surface covered with fine, rounded, hollow, tubular striæ, which frequently open upon the surface. On the interior of the pedicle valve appear two strong diverging teeth. Muscular area large, and deeply impressed, consisting of the large fluted diductor impressions, enclosing the small central adductors. The pedicle scar fills the cavity of the beak. Outside of the muscular area are commonly deeply-pitted ovarian markings. The interior of the brachial valve shows deep and narrow dental sockets, with prominent projecting crural plates. In the center is a strong cardinal process, below which is the indistinct small muscular area.

RHIPIDOMELLA VANUXEMI. Hall. (Fig. 91.) (Pal. N. Y., Vol. IV., p. 47, Pl. VI.)

Distinguishing Characters.—Sub-circular or transversely sub-oval outline; nearly flat or slightly-concave pedicle valve, becoming moderately convex near the beak; convex brachial valve; large muscular area in the pedicle valve.

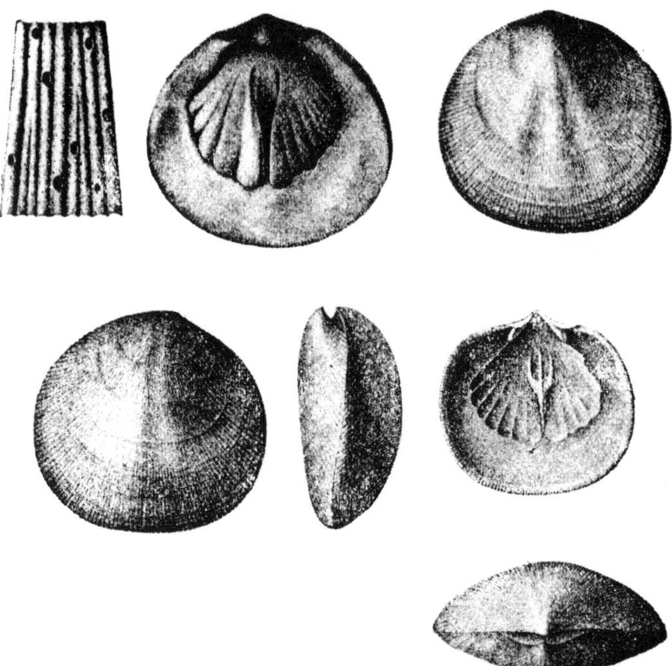

Fig. 91. *Rhipidomella vanuxemi.* Enlargement of surface striæ; mold of interior of pedicle valve; dorsal, ventral, lateral and cardinal views of a large and characteristic specimen; interior of pedicle valve (from Hall).

A series of specimens shows considerable variation in outline, convexity, and character of muscular impressions between the young and adult.

Found in the lower five feet of Moscow shales, at Sections 4 and 5; in the Encrinal limestone, at Section 5, etc.; in the Demissa bed and most of the beds below, at Sections 5, 6, 7, 8. It is rare in the Trilobite beds, at Section 8. It is found in the shales down to the Pleurodictyum beds, on the Lake Shore and in Avery's Creek.

Rhipidomella leucosia. Hall. (Fig. 92.) (Pal. N. Y., Vol. IV., p. 48, Pl. VII.)

Distinguishing Characters.—Broadly ovate outline, with greatest width below the middle; pointed beak; convex brachial and pedicle valves, the latter the less convex, and flattened toward the front; small areas; depression in the center of the brachial valve. Readily distinguished from *R. vanuxemi* by its more pointed posterior end.

FIG. 92. *Rhipidomella leucosia.* Lateral and cardinal view; pedicle valve of another specimen; impression and interior of pedicle valves; ventral view of first specimen (from Hall).

Found in the Encrinal limestone (rare), at Section 5; in the shale below the Trilobite beds, on the Lake Shore and in Avery's Ravine.

RHIPIDOMELLA PENELOPE. Hall. (Fig. 93.) (Pal. N. Y., Vol. IV., p. 50, Pl. VI.)

Distinguishing Characters.—Large size; width greater than length; plano-convex transverse section; regularly convex brachial valve; flat or slightly concave pedicle valve, which becomes somewhat convex near the beak; striæ strongly arched upwards on the cardinal margin; muscular area smaller and more rounded than *R. vanuxemi.*

Found in the Encrinal limestone (fairly common), at Section 5; Stictopora and Demissa beds (young?), at Section 5; in the shale below the Trilobite beds, in Avery's Ravine.

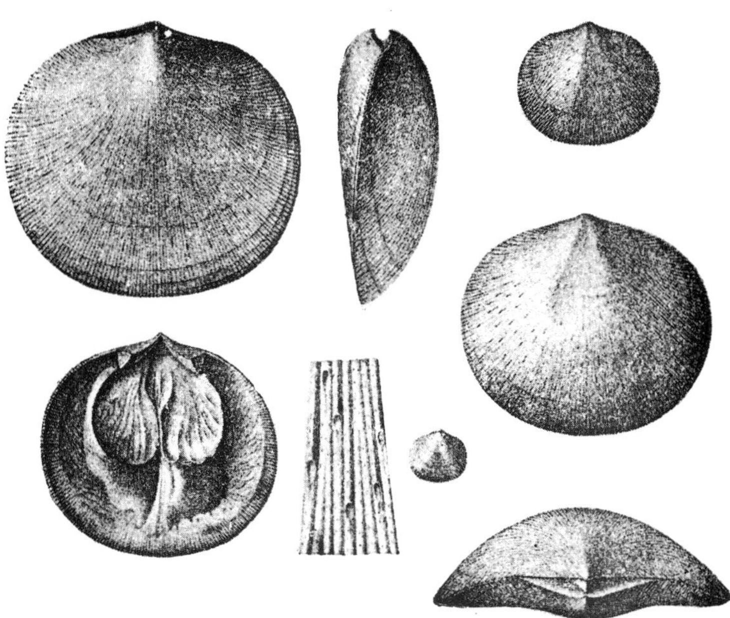

FIG. 93. *Rhipidomella penelope.* Dorsal, lateral and cardinal view of a large specimen; a small pedicle valve; a larger brachial valve; interior of pedicle valve; enlargement of striæ; a young specimen, dorsal view (from Hall).

Measurements.—Large specimen: length, one and seven-sixteenths inches (36 mm.); width, one and nine-sixteenths inches (40 mm.).

RHIPIDOMELLA IDONEA. Hall. (Fig. 94.) (Pal. N. Y., Vol. IV., p. 52, Pl. LXIII.)

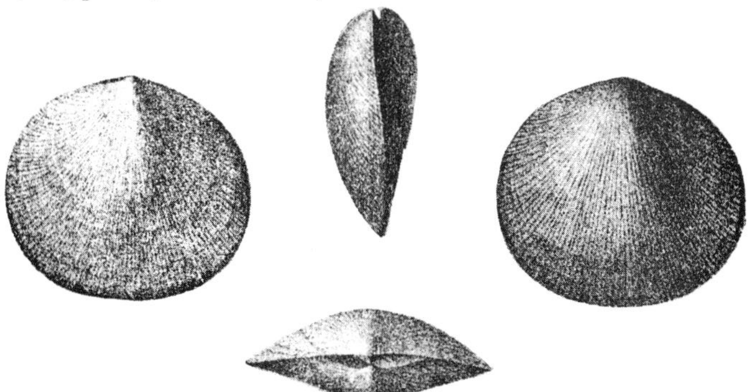

FIG. 94. *Rhipidomella idonea.* Ventral, lateral, cardinal and dorsal views of a characteristic specimen (from Hall).

Distinguishing Characters.—More nearly circular than *R. vanuxemi;* valves more nearly equal; pedicle valve flattened only near the front; brachial valve but slightly more convex.

Found rarely in the lower five feet of the Moscow shale, at Sections 4 and 5; in the Encrinal limestone, at Section 5, where it is also rare.

RHIPIDOMELLA CYCLAS. Hall. (Fig. 95.) (Pal. N. Y., Vol. IV., p. 52, Pl. VII.)

Distinguishing Characters.—Small size of adult; long cardinal line, equaling nearly half the width of the shell; appressed beaks; sharply prominent radiating striæ, which increase by bifurcation and implantation, and have a fasciculate appearance near the front.

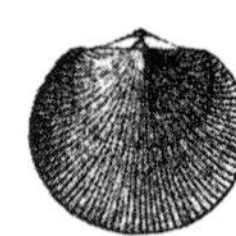

FIG. 95. *Rhipidomella cyclas.* Ventral and dorsal views, x 2 (from Hall).

Found in the Hamilton shales, about a foot below the Trilobite layers, in Avery's Ravine (one specimen).

Measurements.—Largest specimen (Hall): length, five-tenths of an inch +; width, six-tenths of an inch +; length of area, thirty-three hundredths of an inch (+).

GENUS ORTHOTHETES. FISCHER DE WALDHEIM.

[ETY.: *Orthos*, straighs; *theta*, the Greek letter θ.]

(1830: Bull. Soc. Imp. Naturl. d. Moscow. T. I., p. 375. 1892: Pal. N. Y., Vol. VIII., Pt. I., p. 253.)

Shell varying from plano-convex to bi-convex, sometimes becoming concavo-convex with age. Pedicle valve most convex about the beak, which often tends towards irregular growth; cardinal area well developed, with a thick, more or less convex deltidium covering the delthyrium. Teeth not supported by dental plates. Brachial valve most convex near the middle, with a narrow hinge area. Cardinal process quadrilobate as seen from above. Surface covered by slender radiating striæ, which are crenulated by concentric lines.

ORTHOTHETES ARCTOSTRIATUS. Hall. (Fig. 96.) (Pal. N. Y., Vol. IV., p. 71, Pl. IX.)

Distinguishing Characters.—Hinge line equal to or greater than the width of the shell, seldom less; sides of the shell rectangular to the hinge line, or curving inward from it; surface striæ closely arranged.

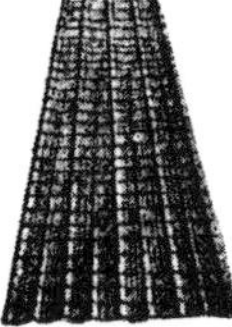
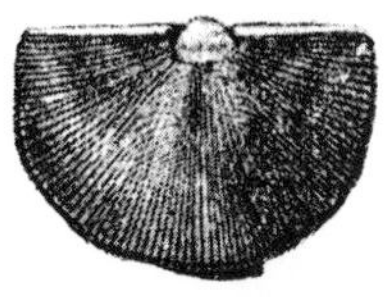

FIG. 96. *Orthothetes arctostriatus.* Two brachial valves and an enlargement of the surface striæ (from Hall).

Found in the upper part of the Moscow shales, Sections 2 and 3 (rare); in the lower Moscow shale, five feet above the Encrinal limestone. Stictopora and Demissa beds, at Section 5; between one and three feet below the Encrinal limestone, at Section 6 (common); below three feet, at Section 6 (sparingly); from seven to twelve feet below the Encrinal limestone, at Section 7 (common); below twelve feet, at Sections 7 and 8 (sparingly). Also found in the Trilobite beds, at Section 8 (rare); between the Trilobite and Strophalosia beds, on the Lake Shore and in Avery's Creek (common); in the Transition beds, on the Lake Shore (rare).

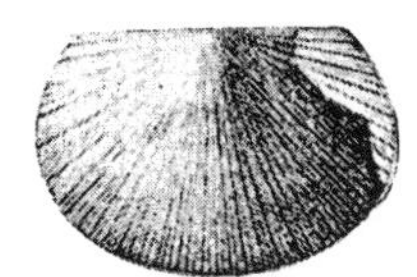

FIG. 97. *Orthothetes perversus.* Brachial valve; internal mold of large brachial valve; pedicle valve (from Hall).

ORTHOTHETES PERVERSUS. Hall. (Fig. 97.) (Pal. N.Y., Vol. IV., p. 72, Pl. IX.)

Distinguishing Characters.—Hinge line shorter than the greatest width of the shell; extremities rounded; length and width about as two to three; surface striæ distant.

Found in the Stictopora and Demissa beds, at Section 5 (rare); in the shale below the *Athyris spiriferoides* bed, at Section 7 (rare); and in the Pleurodictyum beds, in Avery's Ravine (rare).

Genus STROPHEODONTA. Hall.

[Ety.: *Stropheus*, hinge; *odous*, tooth.]

(1852: Pal. N. Y., Vol. II., p. 63. 1892: Pal. N. Y., Vol. VIII., Pt. I., p. 284.)

Shell concavo-convex, the convex valve being the pedicle valve. Outline varying from semi-circular to semi-elliptical, with the hinge line usually equal to or greater than the greatest width of the shell. Area of the pedicle valve higher than that of the brachial valve, both margins furnished with projecting denticulations, which interlock and form articulations. Muscular areas well marked and variously bounded. A strongly marked, commonly bifid, cardinal process occurs in the brachial valve.

A number of sub-genera are recognized.

Stropheodonta demissa. Conrad. (Fig. 98.) (Pal. N. Y., Vol. IV., p. 101, Pl. XVII.)

Distinguishing Characters.—Medium size; pedicle valve strongly convex; concavity of the brachial valve less; length and width nearly equal; surface striæ numerous, stronger and more elevated near the beak, increasing by intercalation and bifurcation towards the front; muscular impressions of the pedicle valve consist of large flabellate divaricators, separated towards the front and distinctly lobed, and small adductors lying between them separated from each other by a depression; in the brachial valve the adductor impressions are divided longitudinally by a narrow ridge, and often limited in front by elevated ridges.

Found in the Encrinal limestone, at Section 5 (one specimen); the Stictopora bed, at Sections 5 and 6 (rare); the

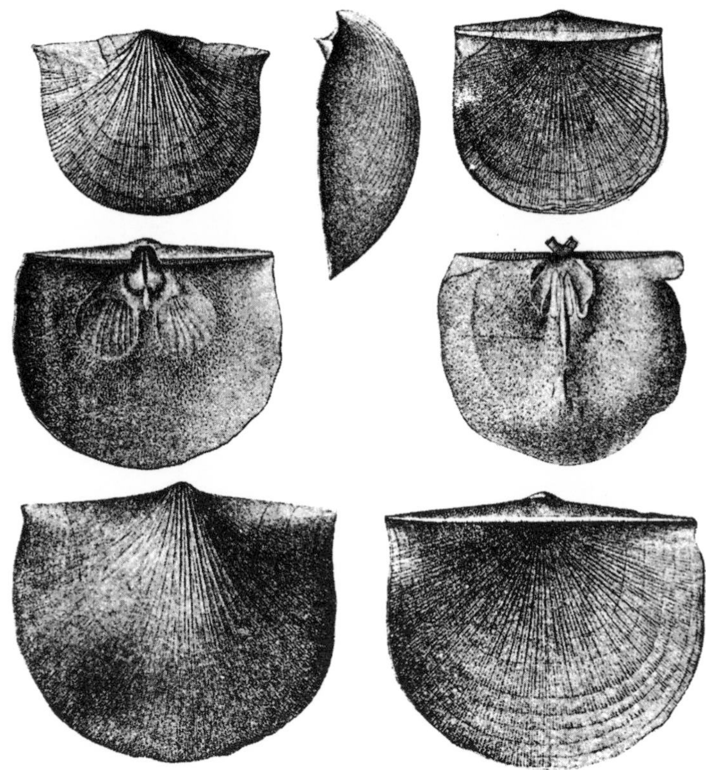

Fig 98. *Stropheodonta demissa.* Ventral and dorsal views; interior of pedicle and brachial valves; ventral, dorsal and lateral views of a large specimen (from Hall).

Demissa bed, Sections 5, 6, etc. (abundant); eighteen inches below the Encrinal limestone, at Section 6 (two specimens).

STROPHEODONTA CONCAVA. Hall. (Fig. 99.) (Pal. N. Y., Vol. IV., p. 96, Pl. XVI.)

Distinguishing Characters.—Large size; great convexity of pedicle valve; high areas almost at right angles to each other; surface of pedicle valve bearing coarse, sharp, crenulated striæ, with commonly one or two between, which are less elevated; surface of brachial valve bearing distant strong striæ, with a number of finer ones between, all crenulated by concentric striæ; large, spreading divaricator muscular impressions occur in the pedicle valve; in the brachial valve the adductor impressions are divided above by a rounded ridge, which supports the quadrilobed cardinal process.

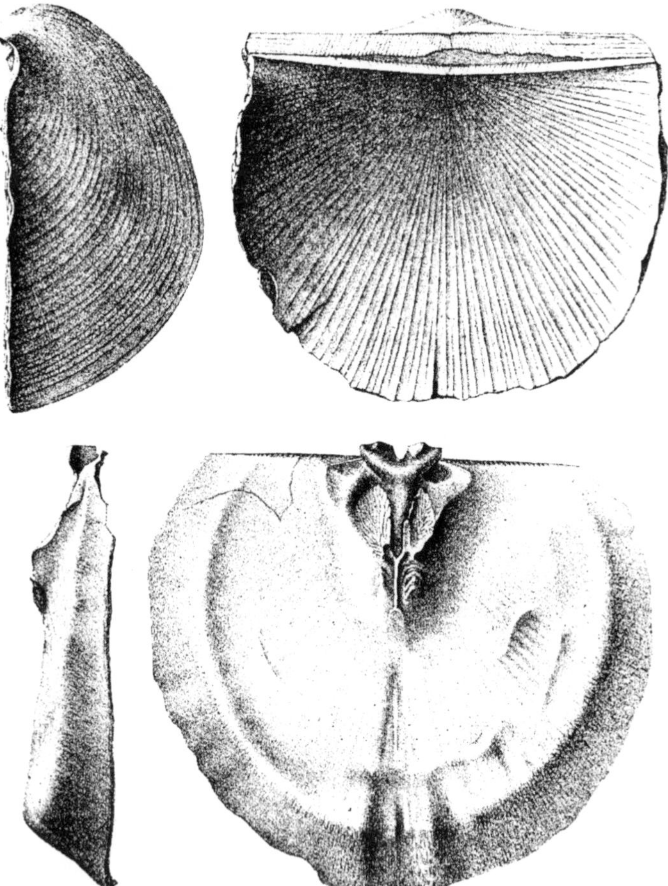

FIG. 99. *Stropheodonta concava.* Lateral and dorsal views of a complete specimen, showing depth of pedicle valve and hinge areas of both valves; side and front view of interior of brachial valve, showing depth, muscular impressions, and cardinal process; also the socket and the crenulations on the hinge area (from Hall).

Found in the Encrinal limestone, on the Lake Shore (rare); in the Demissa bed, at Section 5 (common); between the Trilobite and Pleurodictyum beds (common).

STROPHEODONTA (LEPTOSTROPHIA) PERPLANA. Conrad. (Fig. 100.) (Pal. N. Y., Vol. IV., p. 98, Pls., XI., XII., XVII., XIX.)

Distinguishing Characters.—Small to medium size; slightly convex, often almost flat; extremities of the hinge line usually prolonged; shells very thin; surface bearing fine, nearly equal striæ, increased by intercalation and bifurcation, and crenulated by fine concentric striæ; muscular

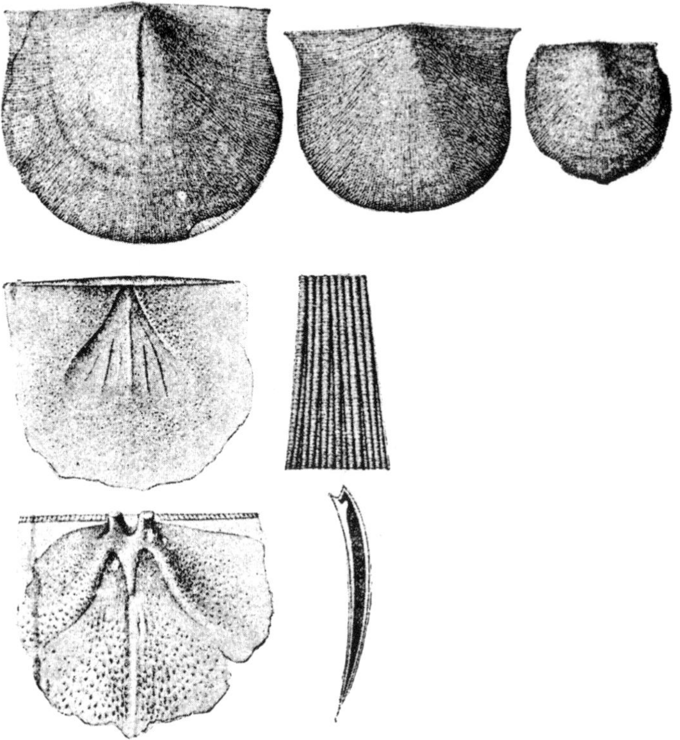

FIG. 100. *Stropheodonta perplana.* Three pedicle valves; interiors of pedicle and brachial valves, showing muscular impressions, crenulated hinge areas, and cardinal process; longitudinal section; enlargement of surface striæ (from Hall).

impressions of pedicle valve consist of large flabellate divaricators, spreading in front and extending more than half the length of the shell, and small adductors between; in the brachial valve strong, rounded ridges, curve forward and outward from the bifid cardinal process, limiting the muscular impressions, while a similar ridge divides them; interior strongly pustulose.

Found in the lower Moscow shales, at Sections 4 and 5 (common); Encrinal limestone, at Section 5 (common); Stictopora and Demissa beds, at Section 5 (common); shales between the Demissa and Trilobite beds, at Sections 6 and 7 (frequent); Trilobite beds, at Section 8, and in Avery's Creek (rare); shales below the Trilobite beds, on the Lake Shore and in Avery's Creek (occasionally); Pleurodictyum beds, in Avery's Ravine (rare); shale below the Nautilus bed (not uncommon).

STROPHEODONTA (DONVILLINA) INÆQUISTRIATA. (Conrad.) (Fig. 101.) (Pal. N. Y., Vol. IV., p. 106, Pl. XVIII.)

Distinguishing Characters.—Small size; considerable convexity of pedicle valve; extended hinge line with acute, sometimes auriculate, extremities; surface marked by distant

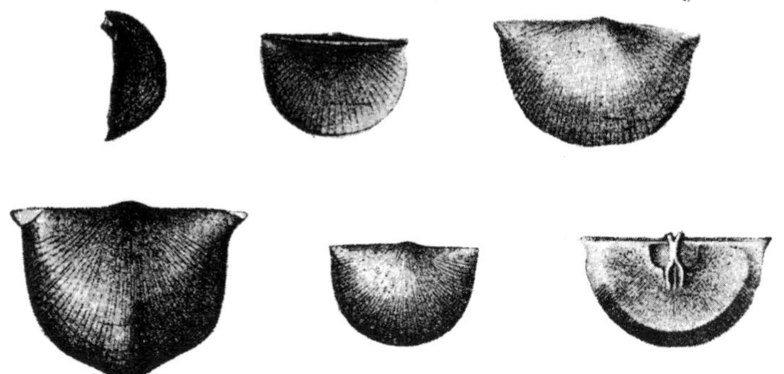

FIG. 101. *Stropheodonta inæquistriata.* Lateral and dorsal views of two specimens; three pedicle valves; interior of a brachial valve, showing cardinal process and muscular impressions (from Hall).

striæ, with finer, almost invisible, striæ between; in the brachial valve the bifid cardinal process is supported by a ridge, which divides anteriorly and encloses a muscular area, for the attachment of the anterior adductors.

Found in the Moscow shales, three to five feet above the base, at Sections 4 and 5 (common); Encrinal limestone, at Section 5 (rather rare); Stictopora bed, at Section 5 (frequent); Demissa bed, at Section 5 (very common); Trilobite beds, at Section 8, and on the Lake Shore (occasionally); shale and limestones between the Trilobite and Strophalosia beds, on the Lake Shore and in Avery's Creek (occasionally).

STROPHEODONTA (PHOLIDOSTROPHIA) NACREA. (Hall.) (Fig. 102.) (Pal. N. Y., Vol. IV., p. 104, Pl. XVIII.)

Distinguishing Characters.—Small size; convex character; smooth and nacreous surface; interior of the brachial valve with three diverging ridges in front of the muscular area.

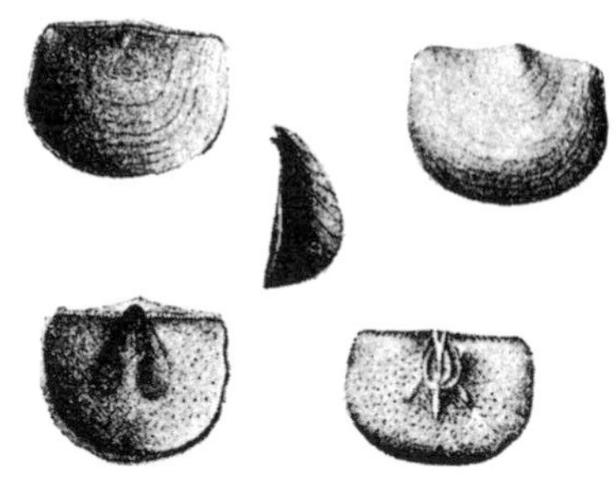

FIG. 102. *Stropheodonta nacrea.* Dorsal, profile and ventral views of a specimen; interiors of pedicle and brachial valves (from Hall).

Found in the Encrinal limestone, at Section 5 (common); in the *Modiomorpha subalata* bed (rare); Trilobite beds (especially the lower), at Section 8, on the Lake Shore and in Avery's Creek (frequent); shale below the Trilobite beds, in Avery's Creek (rare). Schuchert refers this species to *S.* (*P.*) *iowæensis.* (Owen.) (Bull. 87, U. S. G. S.)

STROPHEODONTA (LEPTOSTROPHIA) JUNIA. Hall. (Fig. 103.) (Pal. N. Y., Vol. IV., p. 108, Pl. XVIII., *S. textilis.*)

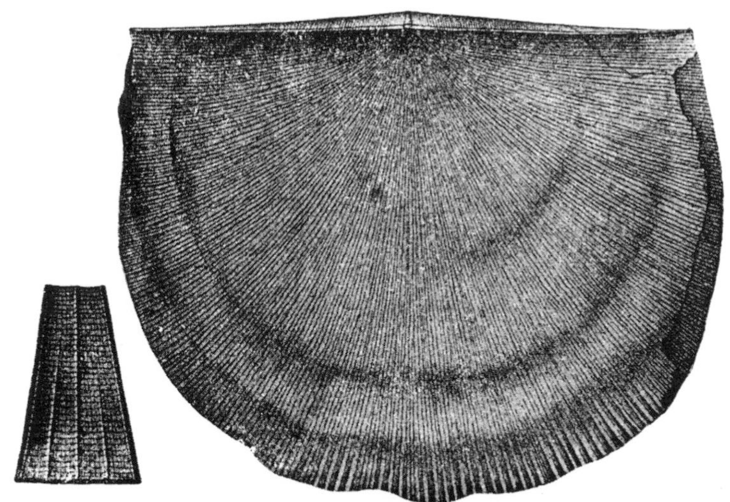

FIG. 103. *Stropheodonta junia.* Dorsal view of a large individual, showing the cardinal area of the ventral (pedicle) valve; enlargement of the surface striæ (from Hall).

Distinguishing Characters.—Medium to large size; slight convexity; surface striæ distant, increased by intercalation, and between these are very fine striæ, crossed by fine concentric striæ; muscular area in brachial valve defined by thickened rounded ridges, divided by central rounded ridge extending from the bifid cardinal process, and dividing anteriorly.

Found in the Demissa bed, at Section 5 (a few specimens only).

STROPHEODONTA PLICATA. Hall. (Fig. 104.) (13th Ann. Rep't N. Y. State Cab. Nat. Hist., p. 90. Pal. N. Y., Vol. IV., Pl. LXIII.)

FIG. 104. *Stropheodonta plicata.* Interior of brachial valve with the cardinal process broken away; slightly enlarged, from a gutta-percha cast. (Original.)

Distinguishing Characters.—Small size; strong rounded or sub-angular plications, which increase in number towards the front by implantation. These readily distinguish this species from *S. demissa*, its nearest ally.

Found only in the Demissa bed, at Section 5 (not common).

GENUS CHONETES. FISCHER DE WALDHEIM.

[ETY.: *Chone*, a funnel.]

(1837: Oryctographie du Gouv. de Moscow, Pt. II., p. 134. 1892: Pal. N. Y., Vol. VIII., Pt. I., p. 303.)

Shells concavo-convex (in our species), with the pedicle valve convex. Outline varying from semi-circular to semi-oval; hinge line straight, making the greatest diameter of the shell. Areas narrow; the triangular opening (delthyrium) in the area of the pedicle valve covered by a convex pedicle plate (deltidium). The upper margin of the area bears a single row of hollow spines. Area of brachial valve without spines. Cardinal process appearing quadrilobate. Interior of shell strongly papillose in the pallial region. A low median ridge divides the muscular area of the pedicle valve. A similar ridge occurs in the brachial valve. External surface usually covered by radiating striæ.

Chonetes mucronatus. Hall. (Fig. 105.) (Pal. N. Y., Vol. IV., p. 125, Pls. XX., XXI.)

Distinguishing Characters.—Small size; semi-oval outline; moderately convex character; rather distant and strong, radiating, rounded or sub-angular striæ, which are not as

Fig. 105. *Chonetes mucronatus.* Pedicle valve, natural size and enlarged, with profile of same; enlargement of another specimen, dorsal view (from Hall).

wide as the spaces between them (or are more or less closely crowded); abruptly outward-curving cardinal spines, of which there are two, or rarely three, on each side.

Found rarely in the upper Moscow shale, below the transition beds; in the lower Moscow shale, at Sections 4 and 5 (not very common); Encrinal limestone (var. *laticosta*), at Section 5 (rare); shale below the Trilobite beds, in Avery's Creek (rare); Pleurodictyum beds (rare); Transition shales, in Erie and Athol Springs Cliffs (rare); Marcellus shales, in Athol Springs and Bay View Cliffs (rare).

Chonetes vicinus. (Castelnau.) (Fig. 106.) (*Chonetes deflectus.* Hall. Pal. N. Y., Vol. IV., p. 126, Pl. XXI.)

Distinguishing Characters.—Semi-elliptical outline; strong convexity; deflected cardinal margins (as seen from the con-

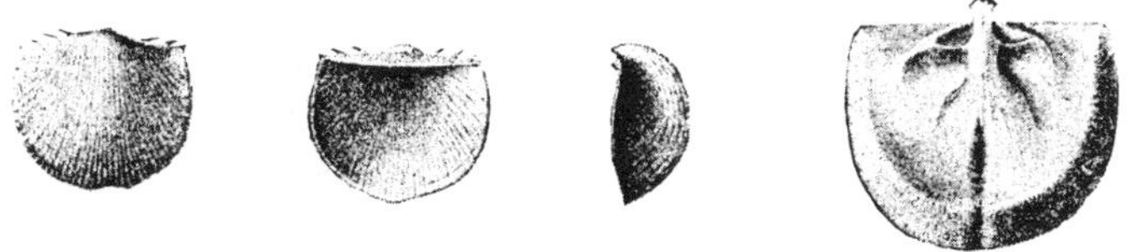

Fig. 106. *Chonetes vicinus (deflectus).* Ventral, dorsal and profile views of a characteristic specimen, natural size; enlargement of interior of a brachial valve, showing cardinal process and muscular impressions (from Hall).

vex side); abruptly outward-curving cardinal spines; finer, more numerous, and more closely crowded striæ than occur in *C. mucronatus.*

Found in the lower Moscow shale, at Sections 4 and 5 (common); Encrinal limestone, at Section 5 (rare); between the Trilobite and Strophalosia beds, in Avery's Creek, and on the Lake Shore (rare).

CHONETES SETIGERUS. (Hall.) (Fig. 107.) (Pal. N. Y., Vol. IV., p. 129, Pl. XXI.)

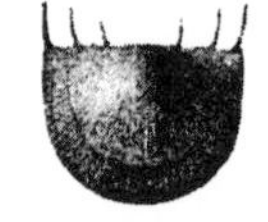

FIG. 107. *Chonetes setigerus.* Ventral valve, x 2 (from Hall).

Distinguishing Characters.—Semi-elliptical outline; moderate convexity; moderate number of rounded surface striæ and vertical cardinal spines, of which three occur on each side of the beak.

Found in the Hamilton shales, at Section 6, two to three feet below the Encrinal limestone (very rare); seventeen to twenty-one feet below the Encrinal, at Section 7 (rare); Pleurodictyum beds, in Avery's Creek (occasionally); Transition shales and Marcellus shales, in Lake Shore Cliffs (not very common).

CHONETES SCITULUS. Hall. (Fig. 108.) (Pal. N. Y., Vol. IV., p. 130, Pl. XXI.)

Distinguishing Characters.—Semi-oval outline; somewhat gibbous character; numerous surface striæ; numerous cardinal spines (as many as twelve or fourteen being sometimes

FIG. 108. *Chonetes scitulus.* Ventral (pedicle) and dorsal (brachial) views of a specimen, natural size; interior of pedicle and of brachial valves, enlarged (from Hall).

indicated), which pass obliquely outward; interior of brachial valve strongly pustulose, with a broad depression along the center, from which rises a slender median ridge; a similar median ridge occurs in the interior of the pedicle valve.

Found in the lower two feet of the Moscow shales, at Sections 4 and 5 (rare); in the Encrinal limestone (rare); throughout the Lower (Hamilton) shales, at Sections 5, 6, 7, 8, and on the Lake Shore, and in Avery's Creek (often abundant); Transition shales, on the Lake Shore (rare).

Measurements.—Large specimen: width, 11 mm.; height, 8 mm.

CHONETES LEPIDUS. Hall. (Fig. 109.) (Pal. N. Y., Vol. IV., p. 132, Pl. XXI.)

Distinguishing Characters.—Small size; semi-elliptical in outline; sub-hemispherical in convexity; slender, angular,

FIG. 109. *Chonetes lepidus.* Ventral and dorsal views of a specimen, natural size, and the former enlarged; enlargement of interior of brachial valve, with cardinal process broken away (from Hall).

bifurcating surface striæ, of which there are ten or twelve near the umbo, and twice as many, or more, near the front; sinus outlined by two stronger striæ near the center, with finer ones between them in a depressed area; cardinal spines, sometimes as many as ten.

Found in the Goniatite bed of the Naples shales, at Sections 1 and 2 (rare); Styliolina band, at Section 1 (rare); lower Moscow shales, at Sections 4 and 5 (rare); Hamilton shales, everywhere associated with the preceding, but usually more abundant; also in the Transition shales, on the Lake Shore.

CHONETES CORONATUS. (Conrad.) (Fig. 110.) (Pal. N. Y., Vol. IV., p. 133, Pl. XXI.)

Distinguishing Characters.—Large size; moderate convexity, with occasionally a shallow undefined sinus in the pedicle valve; numerous closely-arranged surface striæ; five or six oblique tubular spines on each side of the beak; interior of the pedicle valve shows diverging dental lamellæ, a narrow median ridge, and wide-spreading adductor impressions, outside of which the shell is strongly pustulose; in the brachial valve a median ridge runs forward from the cardinal process; the muscular impressions are faintly marked.

Found in the Encrinal limestone, at Section 5; Stictopora and Demissa beds, and immediately below, at Sections 5

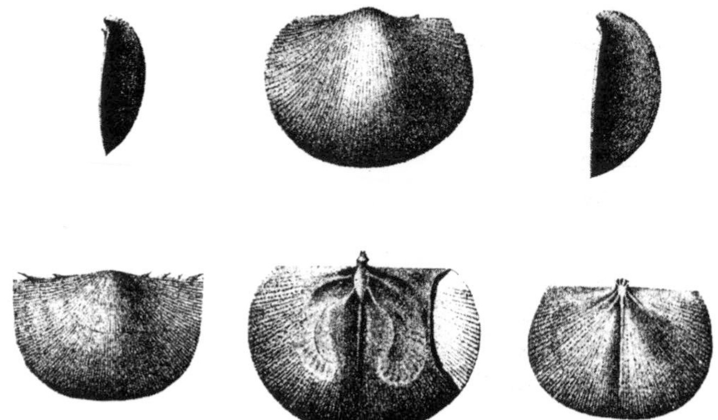

FIG. 110. *Chonetes coronatus* Profile of the pedicle valve, shown in full view below it; ventral and profile views of another specimen; two interiors of brachial valves, showing differences in cardinal process, strength of muscular impressions, etc. (from Hall).

and 6; Pleurodictyum beds and shale above, in Avery's Creek.

GENUS PRODUCTELLA. HALL.

[ETY.: Diminutive of Productus.]

(1867: Pal. N. Y., Vol. IV., p. 153. 1892: Pal. N. Y., Vol. VIII., Pt. I., p. 328.)

Shells small; concavo-convex, the pedicle valve strongly convex, and produced anteriorly. The beak of the pedicle valve is overarching, and the hinge line straight, with a narrow cardinal area, a deltidium and small teeth. Brachial valve small, concave operculiform, with a straight hinge line, dental sockets, and crural plates. Surface marked by radiating ridges, which bear spines at intervals.

PRODUCTELLA NAVICELLA. Hall. (Fig. 111.) (Pal. N.Y., Vol. IV., p. 156, Pl. XXIII.)

Distinguishing Characters.—Small size; great length, which exceeds the width; hinge line less than width of shell; pedicle valve very gibbous, with the beak very much incurved,

FIG. 111. *Productella navicella.* Dorsal, ventral and profile views of an elongated specimen of the variety occurring in the Encrinal limestone (from Hall).

and projecting below the hinge line, the shell extending about one-third its length above the hinge line; surface marked by fine spines above and coarse spine-bearing ridges below.

Found in the Encrinal limestone, at Section 5.

PRODUCTELLA SPINULICOSTA. Hall. (Fig. 112.) (Pal. N. Y., Vol. IV., p. 160, Pl. XXIII.)

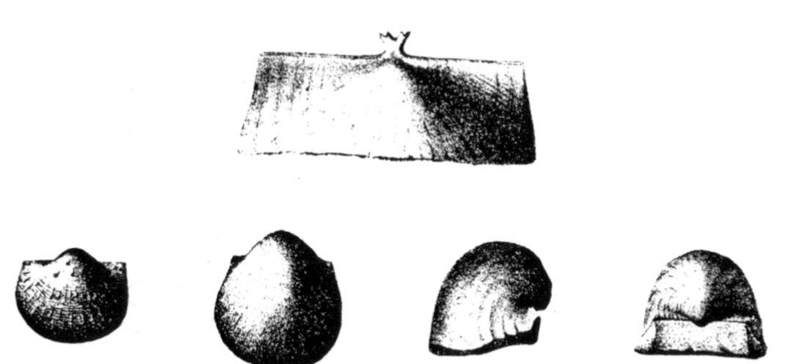

FIG. 112. *Productella spinulicosta.* Part of brachial valve enlarged, x 3, to show cardinal process; a small pedicle valve; ventral, lateral, and cardinal views of a gibbous pedicle valve, natural size (from Hall).

Distinguishing Characters.—Broad, semi-elliptical, or somewhat orbicular, outline; strongly incurved beak of pedicle valve, which does not project below the hinge line; strongly-wrinkled ears, bearing spines; several rows of interrupted spine bases, and concentric striæ or wrinkles.

FIG. 112A. A fragment of shale with crushed specimens of *Productella spinulicosta*, preserving the slender spines (from Hall). (Specimens of this character are found near the anticline, at Section 3, upper Moscow shale.)

Found in the upper Moscow shales, at Section 3; the Encrinal limestone, Stictopora and Demissa beds and shales below, to the Strophalosia bed, at Sections 5, 6, 7, 8, in Eighteen Mile Creek and Lake Shore Sections; Transition and Marcellus shales, on the Lake Shore.

NOTE.—*Productella shumardiana*, Hall, described on p. 157, et seq., of Vol. IV., as occurring in the Marcellus and Hamilton beds on the Lake Shore, is probably identical with *P. spinulicosta.*

Genus STROPHALOSIA. King.

[Ety.: *Strophe*, bending; *alos*, a disk.]

(1844. Annals and Magazine of Natural History, Vol. XIV., p. 313.
1892: Pal. N. Y., Vol. VIII., Pt. I., p. 314.)

Shell similar in form to Productella. A hinge area is present in each valve, and the central opening is in each case covered by a plate; a scar or cicatrix marks the former place of attachment. Dental lamellæ are absent. The cardinal process of the brachial valve is erect, bifid on its anterior face and quadrifid on its posterior face, continued in front in a septum which extends for half the length of the shell, and supported on each side by short, arched crural plates. The surface of the pedicle valve is covered with spines, that of the brachial valve either spinous, lamellose, or smooth.

Strophalosia truncata. (Hall.) (Fig. 113.) (Pal. N. Y., Vol. IV., p. 160, *Productella truncata.*)

Distinguishing Characters.—Small size; gibbous and regularly arched pedicle valve, which is broadly truncated

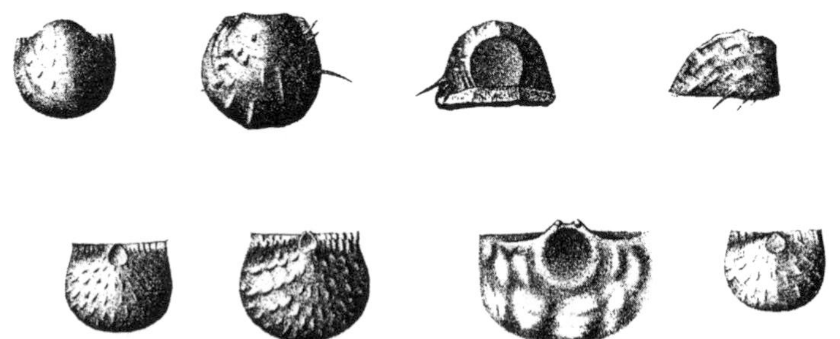

Fig. 113. *Strophalosia truncata.* Ventral valve, with beak slightly truncated; ventral, cardinal and profile views of a small specimen, from limestones of the Marcellus shales, x 3; four interiors of brachial valves, natural size, enlarged, x 2, much enlarged (portion only), and natural size (from Hall).

on the umbo; flattened auriculate cardinal extremities; minutely truncate, gently concave brachial valve; wrinkled cardinal margins, and scattered surface spines.

Found in the Nautilus bed on the Lake Shore (rare); Strophalosia bed on the Lake Shore (extremely abundant); Marcellus shale, in Bay View Cliff (rare).

Genus SPIRIFER. Sowerby.

[Ety.: *Spira*, spire; *fero*, to bear.]

(1815: Mineral Conchology, Vol. II., p. 42. 1893: Pal. N. Y., Vol. VIII., Pt. II., p. 1.)

Shell variously shaped, commonly very much wider than long, radially plicated or striated, crossed by concentric growth lines, which in some forms are lamellose or even marked by spines. Hinge line generally long and straight. Pedicle valve usually with moderately high area, with an open delthyrium, the margins of which are prolonged into stout simple teeth, supported by dental lamellæ. Area of the brachial valve lower. A calcareous brachidium in the form of a double spire, whose apices are directed towards the cardinal angles, nearly fills the cavity of the shell.

Spirifer mucronatus. (Conrad.) (Fig. 114.) (Pal. N. Y., Vol. IV., p. 216, Pl. XXXIV.)

Distinguishing Characters.—Medium size; low cardinal areas; much extended, often mucronate, hinge line, giving a

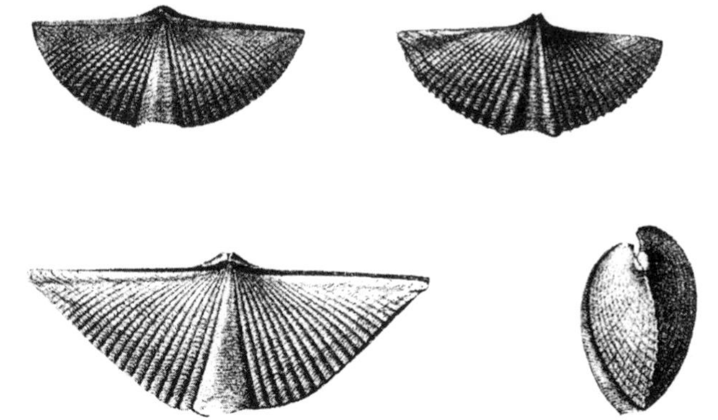

Fig. 114. *Spirifer mucronatus.* Dorsal (brachial) and ventral (pedicle) views of a medium-sized specimen; dorsal and lateral views of different individuals (from Hall).

width of from two to four times the height of the shell; well-marked sinus in the pedicle valve, and fold in the brachial valve, which is often flattened or grooved; radiating plications, the outer ones of which do not reach the beak, and lamellose lines of growth, often thickly crowded near the front; short dental plates, and striated muscular areas.

Found in the Moscow shales, at Sections 2, 3, 4 (rare); Encrinal limestone, at Section 5 (rare); Hamilton shales, at Sections 5 to 8, and on the Lake Shore (everywhere abundant); Strophalosia bed and Transition shales, on the Lake Shore (not uncommon); Marcellus shales, on the Lake Shore (rare).

Measurements.—A very much extended individual gave: width, 100 mm.; height, 15 mm.; average width is less.

SPIRIFER TULLIUS. Hall. (Fig. 115.) (Pal. N. Y., Vol. IV., p. 218, Pl. XXXV.)

Distinguishing Characters.—Small size (especially so in this region); gibbous character; sub-elliptical outline; well-defined sinus, which extends quite up to the beak; strongly

FIG. 115. *Spirifer tullius.* Ventral and cardinal views of pedicle valve and brachial valve of the normal form, as it occurs in the center of the State; the Eighteen Mile Creek specimens are much smaller (from Hall).

marked fold, which is wide at the bottom and narrow at top; comparatively high cardinal area of pedicle valve; low, round and rather flattened surface plications; and fine, uniform radiating striæ, which are especially well visible between the plications, on the fold and in the sinus; faint concentric striæ also occur.

Found in the Styliolina band, at Section 1; upper Moscow shales, between one and one-half and three feet below the Styliolina limestone, at Sections 2, 3, 4 (common).

Measurements.—Average specimen in this region: width, 8 mm.; height, 5 mm.

SPIRIFER (DELTHYRIS) SCULPTILIS. (Hall.) (Fig. 116.) (Pal. N. Y., Vol. IV., p. 221, Pl. XXXV.)

Distinguishing Characters.—Medium size; gibbous character; semi-elliptical to sub-triangular outline; extended hinge line; sub-angular sinus, and strongly elevated fold, with the summit flattened or grooved; small number of sharp and abrupt angular plications, and zigzag lamellose lines of growth.

FIG. 116. *Spirifer sculptilis.* Brachial and pedicle valves (from Hall).

Found in the Encrinal limestone, at Section 5, etc.

SPIRIFER (DELTHYRIS) CONSOBRINUS. D'Orbigny. (Fig. 117.) (Pal. N. Y., Vol. IV., p. 222, Pl. XXXV., *S. zigzag.*)

Distinguishing Characters.—General appearance like a short-winged, bulging and robust *S. mucronatus;* high concave cardinal area of pedicle valve; incurved beak; sharply defined sinus, bounded by strong plications; abruptly elevated mesial fold on the brachial valve, flattened or grooved along the top; few (sixteen to twenty-four on each valve) strong, elevated, angular plications, which are crossed by concentric zigzag lamellose lines of growth, with finer lines between; radiating striæ occasionally observed.

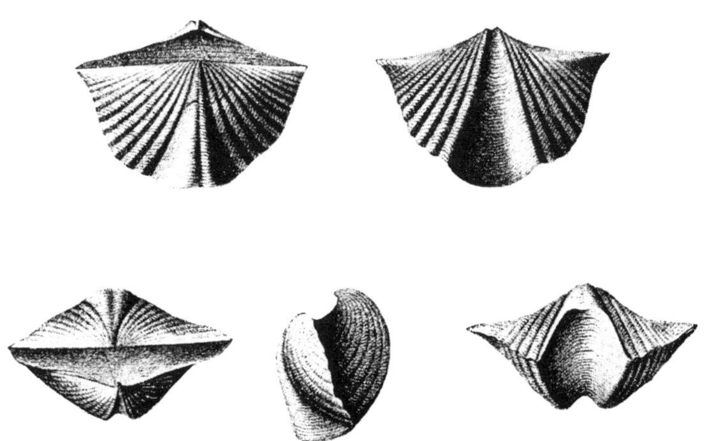

FIG. 117. *Spirifer consobrinus.* Dorsal, ventral, cardinal, profile, and front views of a large and well-preserved specimen (from Hall).

Found in the lower Moscow shales, two to five feet above the Encrinal limestone, at Sections 4, 5, etc.

S. clio, Hall (Pal. N. Y., Vol. IV., Pl. XXXV., Figs. 13, 14), is a variety of *S. consobrinus*, showing characters intermediate between that species and *S. sculptilis*.

SPIRIFER GRANULOSUS. (Conrad.) (Fig. 118.) (Pal. N. Y., Vol. IV., p. 223, Pls. XXXVI., XXXVII.)

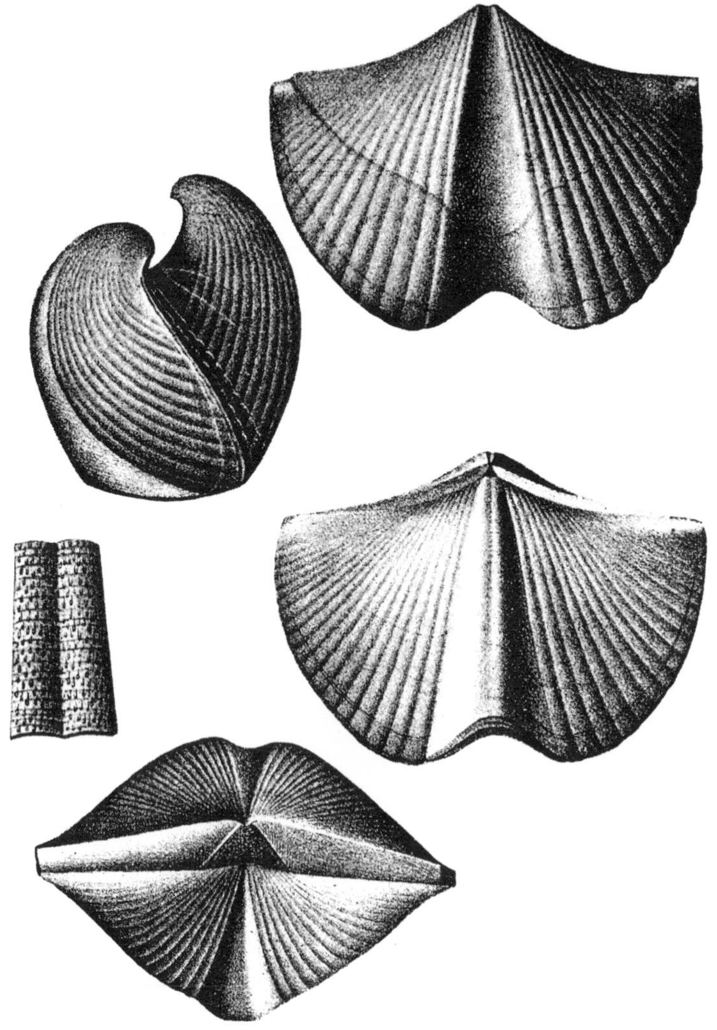

FIG. 118. *Spirifer granulosus.* Ventral, dorsal, profile, and cardinal views of a large and perfect specimen, and an enlargement of the surface plications to show the granulose character (from Hall).

Distinguishing Characters.—Large size; robust and bulging or gibbous character; moderately high, curved area of the pedicle valve, which extends to the extremity of the hinge line; similar, but lower, area of the brachial valve; mesial sinus, sub-angular above, broad rounded in front; prominent rounded fold, with medial depression; simple, low, rounded plications; strongly pustulose or granulose surface.

Found in the Encrinal limestone and the Demissa bed, at Section 5, etc. (common); two feet below the Encrinal limestone, at Section 6 (two specimens); shale below the Trilobite beds, in Avery's Ravine, and on the Lake Shore (rare); in the Calcareous bed, four feet below the Trilobite beds; and the Pleurodictyum beds, in Avery's Ravine, and on the Lake Shore (common); Nautilus bed, in Avery's Ravine and Erie Cliff (rare); Strophalosia bed, Erie Cliff (one specimen).

SPIRIFER GRANULOSUS, var. CLINTONI. Hall. (Fig. 118A.) (Pal. N. Y., Vol. IV., p. 225, Pl. XXXVII.)

FIG. 118A. *Spirifer granulosus*, var. *clintoni*. Dorsal, profile, and ventral views (from Hall).

Distinguishing Characters.—Sinus angular, cardinal extremities angular.

Found in the Encrinal limestone.

SPIRIFER AUDACULUS. (Conrad.) (Fig. 119.) (Pal. N. Y., Vol. IV., p. 227, Pl. XXXVIII., *S. medialis*.)

Distinguishing Characters.—Larger and more robust than *S. mucronatus*, smaller than *S. granulosus;* valves ventricose in old specimens; hinge line commonly extended beyond the width of the shell below; moderately, sometimes extremely, high concave area of pedicle valve; incurved beak;

linear area of brachial valve; slightly incurved beak; well-marked mesial fold and sinus; simple surface plications;

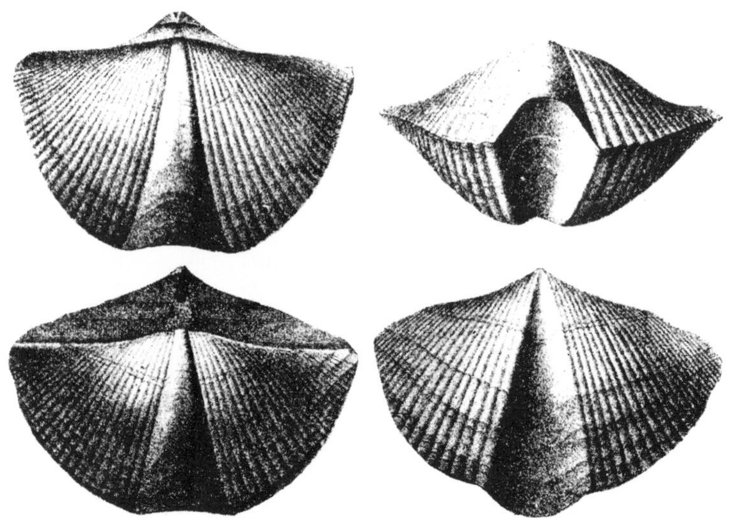

Fig. 119. *Spirifer audaculus.* Dorsal and front view of a specimen; dorsal and ventral views of another specimen, with a higher area and more projecting ventral beak (from Hall).

numerous, often imbricating, concentric lines, and fine radiating striæ.

Found in the lower Moscow shale, at Sections 4 and 5 (rare); also var. *eatoni;* Encrinal limestone, at Section 5 (common); Stictopora and Demissa beds, at Section 5 (abundant); four feet below the Encrinal limestone, at Section 6, etc. (rare); shales between the Trilobite beds, at Section 8, and on the Lake Shore; Pleurodictyum beds, in Avery's Creek, and on the Lake Shore.

Spirifer audaculus, var. eatoni. Hall. (Fig. 119A.) (Pal. N. Y., Vol. IV., p. 229, Pl. XXXVIII.)

Distinguishing Characters.—Robust, extremely convex and resembling a small *S. granulosus,* but without the granules.

Found in the lower Moscow shale, at Section 5, coral layer.

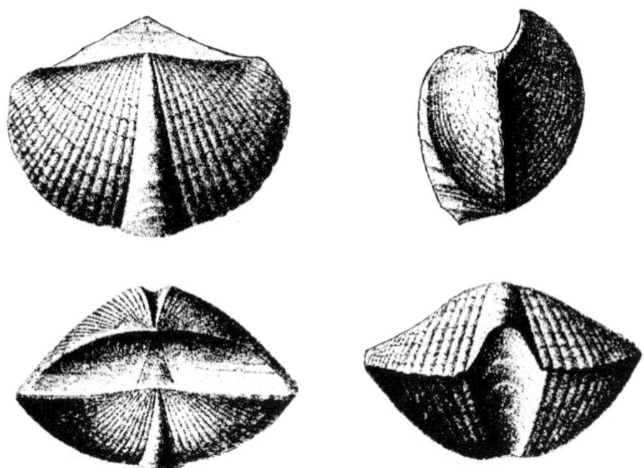

Fig. 119A. *Spirifer audaculus*, var. *eatoni*. Dorsal, profile, cardinal, and front views of a characteristic specimen (from Hall).

Spirifer angustus. Hall. (Fig. 120.) (Pal. N. Y., Vol. IV., p. 230, Pl. XXXVIII.A.)

Distinguishing Characters.—Depressed pyramidal outline; great lateral extension; pronounced inequality of valves; pedicle valve forming nearly the entire thickness of the shell,

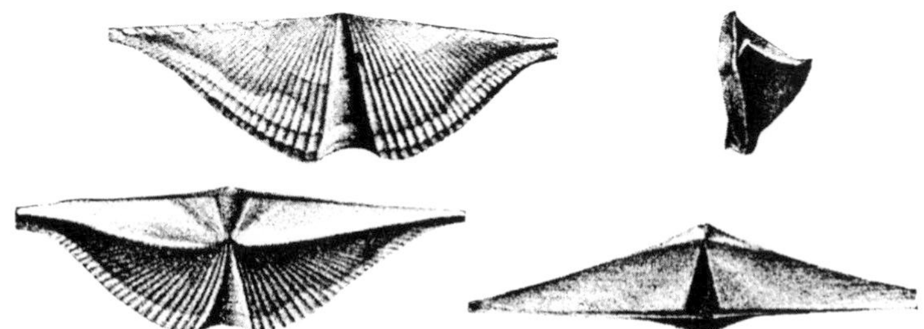

Fig. 120. *Spirifer angustus*. Dorsal, profile, ventral, and cardinal views of a large specimen, with extended cardinal extremities and a high cardinal area (from Hall).

with an area equaling in height the length of the shell; delthyrium about twice as high as wide, grooved on the sides; brachial valve flat, with a narrow area and low mesial fold; surface plications fine, simple and rounded, from forty-eight to fifty-six on each valve.

Found in the Demissa bed, at Section 5 (rare).

SPIRIFER MACRONOTUS. Hall. (Fig. 121.) (Pal. N. Y., Vol. IV., p. 231, Pl. XXXVIII.A.)

Distinguishing Characters.—General resemblance to *S. audaculus* (of which it may be only a variety), differing from that species mainly in the very high, flat, area, minute beak, comparatively shallow mesial sinus, which rapidly

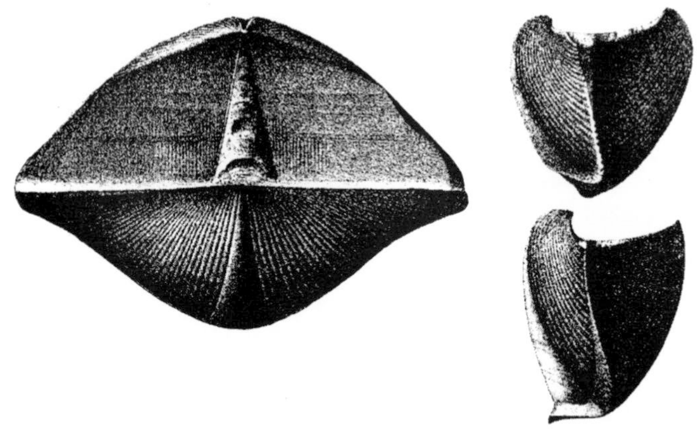

FIG 121. *Spirifer macronotus.* Cardinal view of a large individual; lateral views of two individuals, showing the character of the area (from Hall).

widens towards the front, and the number of plications, which varies from fifty to seventy on each valve, of which only three or four on each side of the fold and sinus reach the beak; the delthyrium is more than twice as high as wide, and the surface of the shell exhibits lamellose, imbricating growth lines.

Found in the Encrinal limestone, at Section 5 (common); Stictopora and Demissa beds, at Section 5 (common); one and one-half to three feet below the Encrinal limestone, at Section 6 (rare); shale below the Trilobite beds, in Avery's Ravine (rare).

SPIRIFER ASPER. Hall. (Fig. 122.) (Geol. Surv. of Iowa, 1858, Vol. I., Pt. II., p. 508, Pl. IV.)

Distinguishing Characters.—Small size; sub-pyramidal outline; high, flat cardinal area of pedicle valve; narrow and high delthyrium; broad, comparatively shallow sinus, rapidly narrowing towards the beak; low, rounded fold, broad below, narrowing rapidly towards the beak; fine, low and rounded surface plications and granulose character of the whole exterior of the shell.

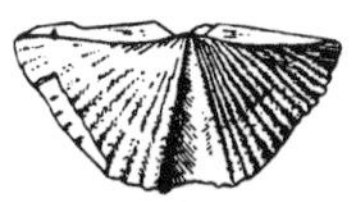

Fig. 122. *Spirifer asper*. Cardinal and ventral views of a characteristic pedicle valve, from the Demissa bed, at Section 5, natural size. (Original.)

Found in the Demissa bed, at Section 5.

Spirifer (Reticularia) fimbriatus. (Conrad.) (Fig. 123.) (Pal. N. Y., Vol. IV., p. 214, Pl. XXXIII.)

Distinguishing Characters.—Transversely sub-elliptical outline; hinge line less than width of shell; rounded cardinal extremities; gibbous and regularly convex valves; rounded sinus; well-marked fold, abruptly elevated in front, low near the beak; high and concave pedicle area; few (six to eighteen on each valve) low, rounded, often obscure, plications; concentric lamellose and imbricating growth lines, studded with elongated tubercles or spines (fimbriæ), which in perfect specimens show lateral fringes or spinules.

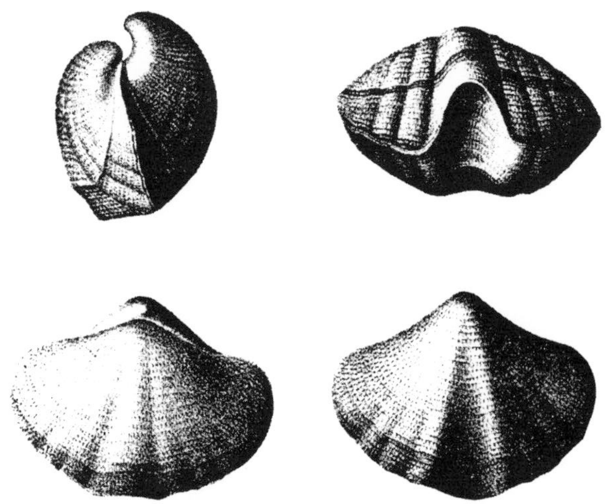

Fig. 123. *Spirifer fimbriatus.* Profile, front, dorsal, and ventral views of a large and well-preserved specimen (from Hall).

Found in the Encrinal limestone, at Section 5; the Stictopora and Demissa beds, at Section 5 (abundant); shales below the Trilobite beds, in Avery's Ravine (rather common); Pleurodictyum and Calcareous beds above (very rare).

SPIRIFER (MARTINIA) SUBUMBONUS. Hall. (Fig. 124.) (Pal. N. Y., Vol. IV., p. 234, Pl. XXXII.)

Distinguishing Characters.—Very small size (for a Spirifer); gibbous character; rounded cardinal extremities; smooth or concentrically-striated surface; high cardinal area in pedicle valve, with rounded margins; abruptly incurved beak of pedicle valve; narrow, almost obsolete, and never pronounced, sinus; absence of fold, an impressed line occasionally marking the center of the brachial valve; in well-preserved and partly exfoliated specimens numerous punctæ or pits appear, probably marking the former position of spines.

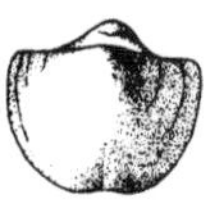

FIG. 124. *Spirifer subumbonus.* Dorsal and profile views of a specimen, enlarged; enlargement of the surface to show the pits (after Hall).

Found in the Styliolina band, at Section 1; Moscow shale (upper four feet), at Sections 2, 3, 4 (rare); Hamilton shales, about two feet below the Encrinal limestone, at Section 6 (one specimen); also in the shale between the Nautilus and Strophalosia beds, in Avery's Creek.

GENUS AMBOCŒLIA. HALL.

[ETY.: *Ambon*, umbo; *koilos*, belly.]

(1860: 13th Ann. Rep't N. Y. State Cab. Nat. Hist., p. 167.
1893: Pal. N. Y., Vol. VIII., Pt. II., p. 54.)

Shell of small size; plano-, concavo-, or gently bi-convex, the pedicle valve always deepest, and commonly extremely convex, with a strongly marked, arched and incurved umbo. A narrow median groove, more or less profound, is commonly present. The cardinal area is arched, its margins are well defined, and it is divided by an open delthyrium, with incomplete deltidial plates. Strong articulating teeth, and a well-marked muscular area occur. The brachial valve is always convex at the beak, below which it becomes flattened or slightly concave, or else continues with more or less uniform arcuation. Area narrow; cardinal process long and narrow, bifurcated at the free end. Brachidium consists of loosely coiled spirals, similar to Spirifer.

AMBOCŒLIA UMBONATA. (Conrad.) (Fig. 125.) (Pal. N. Y., Vol. IV., p. 259, Pl. XLIV.)

Distinguishing Characters.—Plano-convex, almost hemispherical contour; strong, distinct and continuous mesial

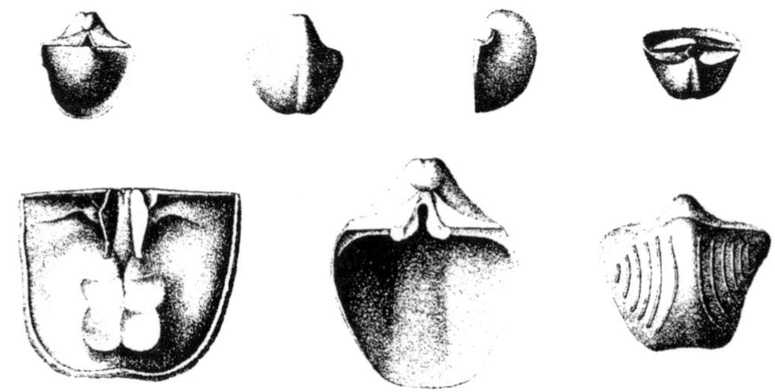

FIG. 125. *Ambocœlia umbonata.* Dorsal, ventral, profile, and cardinal views of a large and well-preserved specimen of normal form; interior of a brachial valve enlarged, showing muscular impressions, sockets, etc.; interior of pedicle valve enlarged, showing area, delthyrium, teeth, etc.; mold of interior, with spiral brachidium embedded in it, enlarged (from Hall).

sinus in the pedicle valve, which is very gibbous; semi-elliptical brachial valve, which is faintly convex at the umbo, and concave below the middle and at the sides; shell slightly wider than long.

Found in the Moscow shales (very rare in the upper, but common in the lower two or three feet, extremely abundant in the lower foot), at Sections 4 and 5; Encrinal limestone, at Section 5 (rare); Lower shales, at Sections 5 to 8, and on the Lake Shore (more or less abundant throughout); Transition shales, on the Lake Shore (frequent); Marcellus shale, in Bay View Cliff (not uncommon).

AMBOCŒLIA NANA. Grabau. (Fig. 126.) (1898: *Ambocœlia umbonata*, var. *nana*. Grabau. Report of N. Y. State

Geologist and Palæontologist for 1896. Faunas of the Hamilton Group, etc., p. 276.)

Distinguishing Characters.—Small size; transverse outline, the pedicle valve being much broader than long; convex brachial valve, usually bearing a shallow depression along the center; numerous elongated pits covering the surface, showing spine bases in well-preserved specimens.

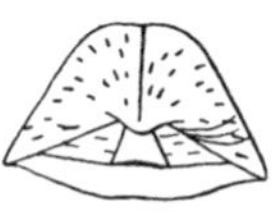

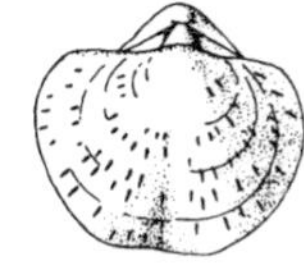

FIG. 126. *Ambocœlia nana.* Cardinal and dorsal views of a characteristic specimen, from the Nautilus bed, enlarged (after Grabau).

Found in the Nautilus bed at the base of the Hamilton shales, on the Lake Shore and in Avery's Creek (abundant); Strophalosia bed, on the Lake Shore (very rare).

AMBOCŒLIA PRÆUMBONA. Hall. (Fig. 127.) (Pal. N. Y., Vol. IV., p. 262, Pl. XLIV.)

Distinguishing Characters.—Large size; sub-globose character; short hinge line; length greater than width; ventricose pedicle valve, with narrow depression along center; moderately convex brachial valve, occasionally bearing a median depressed line.

FIG. 127. *Ambocœlia præumbona.* Two brachial valves; pedicle valve and profile of same (from Hall).

Found in the upper Moscow shale down to four feet from the top, at Sections 1 to 5 (abundant).

AMBOCŒLIA SPINOSA. Clarke. (Fig. 128.) (13th Ann. Rep't State Geol. N. Y., Vol. I., p. 177, Pl. IV.)

Distinguishing Characters.—Rather large size; hinge line equal to width of shell; brachial valve concave anteriorly, with upturned margins; low median elevation, indistinct and disappearing towards the front; elongate surface pits, probably marking positions of spinules.

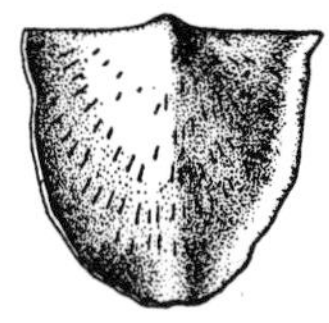

FIG. 128. *Ambocœlia spinosa.* Brachial valve of the type specimen, much enlarged (after Clarke).

Measurements.—Original specimen (Clarke): length, 7 mm.; width on the hinge line, 9 mm.

The original specimen comes from the Livonia Salt Shaft (Hamilton shales). Specimens showing the pits, but otherwise not differing much from *A. umbonata*, have been found at Eighteen Mile Creek, and are referred to this species. They were found in the following positions: Moscow shales, two feet below Styliolina band, at Section 3; Hamilton shales, nine to twenty-five feet below the Encrinal limestone, at Section 7.

GENUS CYRTINA. DAVIDSON.

[ETY.: *Kyrtia*, a fishing basket.]

(1858: Monogr. British Carbonif. Brachiopoda, p. 66. 1893: Pal. N. Y., Vol. VIII., Pt. II., p. 43.)

Shells Spirifer-like; usually small; valves very unequal; pedicle valve elevated, with a high cardinal area, the delthyrium of which is covered by an elongate, convex pseudodeltidium, which is perforated below the apex. Surface plicate. Dental lamellæ strong, converging rapidly, and meeting a median septum. Cardinal process a double apophysis. Brachidium an extroverted spire.

CYRTINA HAMILTONENSIS. Hall. (Fig. 129.) (Pal. N. Y., Vol. IV., p. 268, Pls. XXVII., XLIV.)

Distinguishing Characters.—Small size; pyramidal character of pedicle valve; slightly convex brachial valve; high, triangular, commonly arcuate, area; incurved, frequently distorted, beak; strong mesial sinus; broad fold; six to eight plications on each side of fold and sinus.

FIG. 129. *Cyrtina hamiltonensis.* Dorsal, ventral, cardinal, and profile views (from Hall).

Found in the lower Moscow shale (?); Stictopora and Demissa beds, at Section 5 (common); four to five feet below the Encrinal limestone, at Section 6 (very rare); nine to twelve feet below the Encrinal limestone, at Section 7 (very rare); shale below the Trilobite beds, in Avery's Creek (rare); Pleurodictyum beds and Calcareous bed above them, in Avery's Creek (rare).

CYRTINA HAMILTONENSIS, var. RECTA. Hall. (Fig. 130.) (Pal. N. Y., Vol. IV., p. 270, Pl. XLIX.)

FIG. 130. *Cyrtina hamiltonensis*, var. *recta*. Dorsal, ventral, and cardinal views (from Hall).

Distinguishing Characters.—Plane flat area; angular plications; beak not incurved.

Found in the upper Pleurodictyum bed (rare).

GENUS PARAZYGA. HALL AND CLARKE.

[ETY.: *Para*, beside; *zygos*, yoke.]

(1893: Pal. N. Y., Vol. VIII., Pt. II., p. 127.)

Shells transverse, biconvex; valves nearly equal, with median fold and sinus. Umbo of pedicle valve closely incurved. No hinge area. Surface covered with numerous fine, rounded, simple ribs, extending alike over median fold and sinus, and bearing short hair-like spines, which are commonly broken off, leaving only their bases. Brachidium a spire.

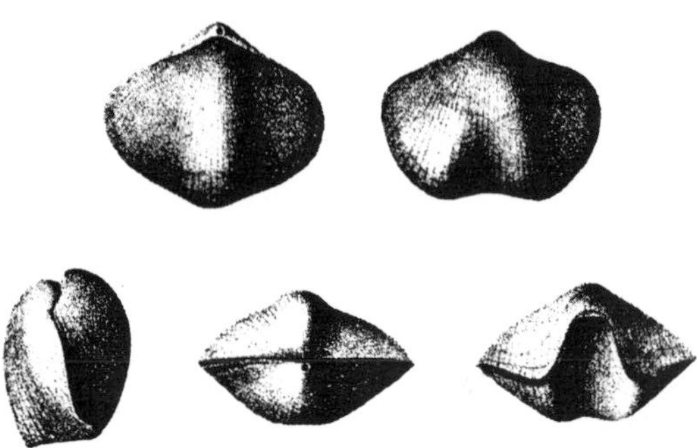

FIG. 131. *Parazyga hirsuta*. Dorsal, ventral, profile, cardinal, and front views (from Hall).

PARAZYGA HIRSUTA. Hall. (Fig. 131.) (Pal. N. Y., Vol. IV., p. 274.)

Distinguishing Characters.—Length and breadth as three to four; well-marked mesial fold and sinus, the sides of which are not strongly defined; granulose surface, from breaking off of spines.

Found at Eighteen Mile Creek, in the Hamilton shales (Hall), position not determined.

GENUS TREMATOSPIRA. HALL.

[ETY.: *Trema,* foramen; *spira,* spire.]

(1859: 12th Rep't N. Y. State Mus. Nat. Hist., p. 27. 1893: Pal. N. Y., Vol. VIII., Pt. II., p. 124.)

Shells transverse, with sub-equally convex valves. Surface radially plicate. Hinge line straight, cardinal extremities abruptly rounded. Anterior margin sinuate. Pedicle valve with a median sinus and an incurved beak, truncated by a circular foramen. Delthyrium covered by two short incurved plates, which are usually closely anchylosed, and appear continuous, with a narrow flattened false area on either side. Lower half of the delthyrium open, for the reception of the beak of the brachial valve. Teeth prominent, arising from the bottom of the valve; above the hinge line they curve backwards and towards each other, thus making a very firm articulation. Muscular area well defined. Brachial valve with median fold, and minute beak. Hinge plate greatly elevated, with a small chilidium resting against it; upper face of plate deeply divided by median longitudinal groove, and more faintly by transverse groove. Dental sockets small and deep, crura broad, thin and comparatively short. Brachidium of two spiral cones set base to base, as in Spirifer.

TREMATOSPIRA GIBBOSA. (Fig. 131A.) (Pal. N. Y., Vol. IV., p. 273, Pl. XLV.)

Distinguishing Characters.—Abrupt sinus and fold, especially in old shell; nine or ten angular plications on surface; three small plications on fold, and two small ones in mesial

Fig. 131A. *Trematospira gibbosa.* Dorsal, ventral, cardinal, profile, and front views of a characteristic individual (from Hall.)

sinus; zigzag lines, formed by concentric lamellæ of growth, in crossing plications; granulose character of surface.

Found in the Hamilton group, at Eighteen Mile Creek. (Coll. Am. Mus. Nat. Hist. New York.)

Genus NUCLEOSPIRA. Hall.

[Ety.: *Nucleus,* kernel; *spira,* spire.]

(1859: 12th Rep't N. Y. State Cab. Nat. Hist., p. 24. 1893: Pal. N. Y., Vol. VIII., Pt. II., p. 142.)

Shells usually small; sub-circular in outline; biconvex, with the valves nearly equal, often gibbous. A small area is present on the pedicle valve, but it is obscured by the incurvature of the beak. Strong teeth, and a median septum occur in the pedicle valve. Surface in perfect specimens covered with numerous long, slender spines, smooth in worn or macerated specimens. Brachidium a double spire.

Nucleospira concinna. Hall. (Fig. 132.) (Pal. N. Y., Vol. IV., p. 279, Pl. XIV.)

Distinguishing Characters.—Nearly circular outline; subequally convex valves; median septum (or its impression in the internal mold); surface spines.

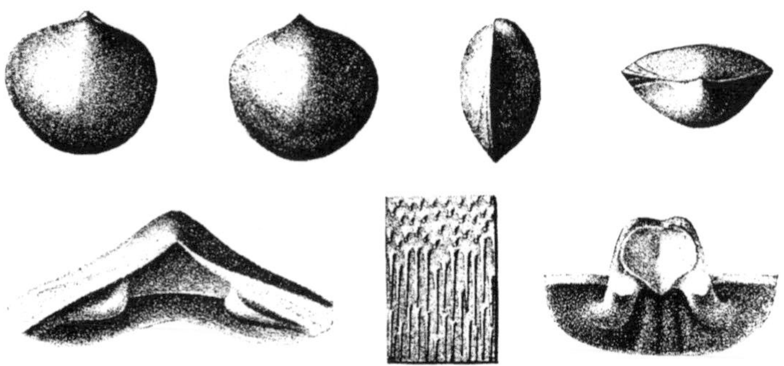

Fig. 132. *Nucleospira concinna.* Dorsal, ventral, profile, and cardinal views; beak of pedicle valve enlarged, showing teeth and false area; portion of surface enlarged, showing spines; cardinal process of brachial valve enlarged (from Hall).

Found in the lower Moscow shales, at Sections 4 and 5 (rare); Encrinal limestone (?), at Section 5; Stictopora and Demissa beds, at Section 5, etc. (abundant); Lower shales, occasionally down to the Nautilus bed, at Sections 5 to 8; and on the Lake Shore.

GENUS ATHYRIS. McCOY.

[ETY.: *A*, without; *thyris*, small door, i. e., absence of deltidial plates; erroneously applied.]

(1844: Synopsis Carbon. Foss. Ireland, p. 128. 1893: Pal. N. Y., Vol. VIII., Pt. II., p. 83.)

Shell biconvex, with the valves nearly equal; outline varying from sub-circular to transversely elliptical. Pedicle valve with the beak incurved, the pedicle opening and deltidial plates usually concealed. Teeth prominent, recurved at the tips, and supported by stout dental lamellæ. Strongly-marked muscular impressions. Brachial valve with the beak small, the dental sockets broad and deep, and the hinge plate strong, and perforated by a "visceral foramen." Brachidium consisting of spiral cones placed base to base. Surface lamellose, the pedicle valve marked by a shallow sinus, and the brachial by a corresponding gentle elevation.

ATHYRIS SPIRIFEROIDES. (Eaton.) (Fig. 133.) (Pal. N.Y., Vol. IV., p. 285, Pl. XLVI.)

FIG. 133. *Athyris spiriferoides*. Dorsal, ventral, cardinal, and front views of a characteristic specimen (from Hall).

Distinguishing Characters. — Robust character; size; "shouldered" expression; greater convexity of brachial valve; "nasute" front, caused by deep sinus; coarse surface lamellæ; outline of muscular impressions.

Found in the upper Moscow shale, two feet below the Styliolina band, at Section 3 (very rare); lower Moscow shale, at Sections 4 and 5 (common); Encrinal limestone, at Section 5 (common); Lower shales (fairly common below the Demissa bed, abundant nine feet below the Encrinal limestone—*A. spiriferoides* bed); also twenty feet below the Encrinal; also in the *Modiomorpha subalata* bed; it is again abundant in the shale between the lower and middle Trilobite layers; and occurs as low as the Nautilus bed, and the shales below it.

GENUS MERISTELLA. HALL.

[ETY.: Diminutive of *Merista; meros*, apartment (chamber).]

(1860: 13th Rep't N. Y. State Cab. Nat. Hist., p. 74. 1893: Pal. N. Y., Vol. VIII., Pt. II., p. 73.)

Shell unequally biconvex, often inflated, varying from transverse to elongate in outline; cardinal areas obscure. Anterior margin sinuate, caused by sinus and fold, which appear only near the front of the shell. Umbo of the pedicle valve incurved at maturity, concealing most, if not all, of the foramen. Teeth strong, supported by lamellæ; deep, sub-triangular muscular impression in pedicle cavity. In the brachial valve a median septum supports the hinge plate, and extends for somewhat more than one-third the length of the shell. Brachidium a spire.

FIG. 134. *Meristella haskinsi.* Dorsal, profile, and ventral views of a specimen (from Hall).

MERISTELLA HASKINSI. Hall. (Fig. 134.) (Pal. N. Y., Vol. IV., p. 306, Pl. XLIX.)

Distinguishing Characters.—Broadly ovate outline, with greatest width anterior to the middle; length and width about equal; slight sinuation in front; anchylosed deltidial plates; fine, thread-like, concentric surface striæ, and occasionally faint radiating striæ.

Found in the Encrinal limestone, at Section 5 (rather rare).

MERISTELLA ROSTRATA. Hall. (Fig. 135.)

(Pal. N. Y., Vol. IV., p. 307, Pls. L., LXIII.)

Distinguishing Characters.—Small size; greater length than width, rounded below and often subattenuate above; shallow, rounded sinus in pedicle valve; fine concentric striæ, and, in exfoliated specimens, slender, distant, radiating striæ.

Found in the Encrinal limestone, at Section 5 (rare).

FIG. 135. *Meristella rostrata.* Profile, dorsal, ventral, and front views of a specimen (from Hall).

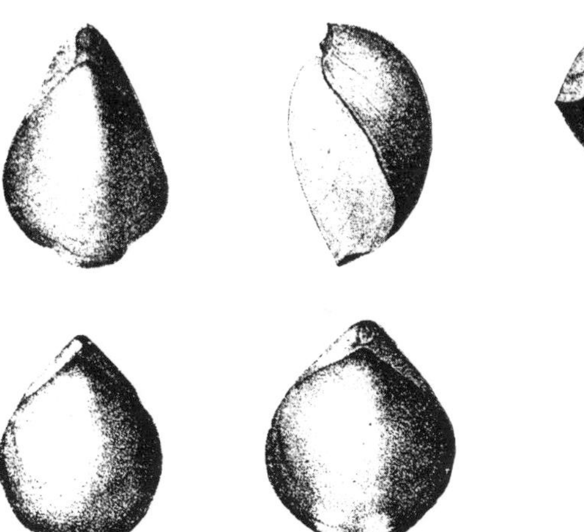

FIG. 135A. *Meristella barrisi.* Dorsal, lateral, and cardinal views of an elongated individual; dorsal views of two other individuals (from Hall).

Meristella barrisi. Hall. (Fig. 135A.) (Pal. N. Y., Vol. IV., p. 304, Pl. LXIX.)

Distinguishing Characters.—Gibbous form; rather closely incurved beak of pedicle valve, which overarches that of brachial valves; pedicle valve depressed in front, and in old shells produced into a short, linguiform extension: abrupt elevation near anterior margin of brachial valve; smooth or concentrically striate surface.

Found in the Hamilton group of Erie County. (Coll. Am. Mus. Nat. Hist. New York.)

Genus ATRYPA. Dalman.

[Ety.: *A*, without; *trypa*, foramen; erroneously applied.]

(1828: Kongl. Veteuskaps. Akad. Handlingar., p. 127. 1893: Pal. N. Y., Vol. VIII., Pt. II., p. 163.)

Shell varying in outline from nearly circular to longitudinally sub-oval. Valves very unequal, brachial valve being strongly convex or gibbous, while the pedicle valve is gently convex or almost flat or sometimes slightly concave, from the strongly-marked sinus. Beak of the pedicle valve small and incurved over that of the brachial. Large widely-separated and doubly-grooved teeth are present, unsupported by lamellæ. Strong muscular impressions. Spirals of the brachidium, with their bases parallel to the inner surface of the pedicle valve, and the apices directed towards the deepest point of the opposite valve. Surface radially plicate.

Atrypa reticularis. (Linnæus.) (Fig. 136.) (Pal. N. Y., Vol. IV., p. 316, Pls. LI.–LIII.A.)

Distinguishing Characters.—Great convexity of brachial and slight convexity of pedicle valve; rounded bifurcating surface plications, reticulated by concentric striations.

Found in the lower Moscow shale, especially in the coral layer, at Sections 4 and 5 (common); Stictopora and Demissa beds, at Section 5 (abundant); shale down to nine feet below the Encrinal limestone (rare).

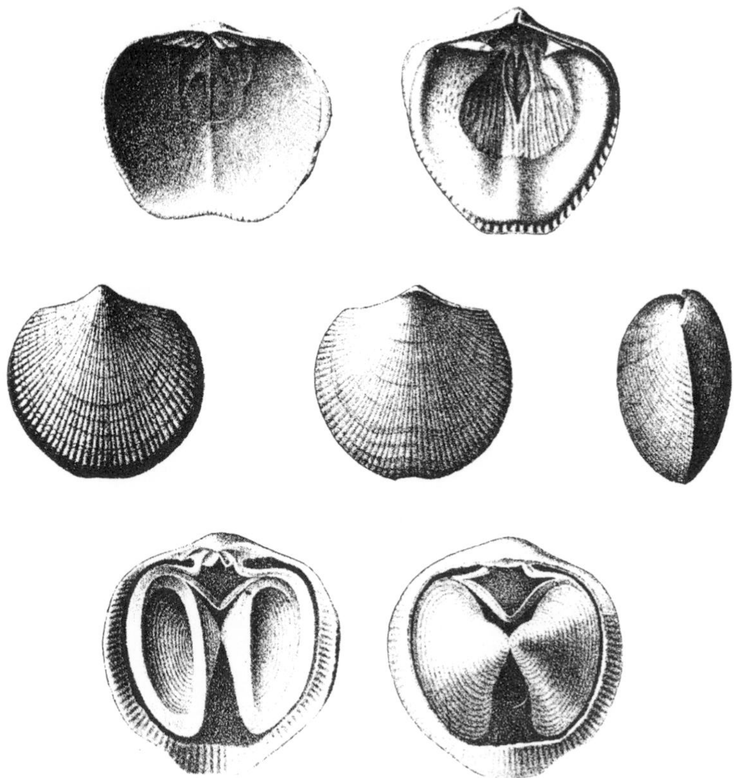

FIG. 136. *Atrypa reticularis.* Interior of brachial and pedicle valves; ventral (pedicle), dorsal (brachial), and lateral views of the exterior of a specimen; views of interior, with pedicle valve removed, with brachial valve removed, showing the position and characters of the spiral brachidia (from Hall).

ATRYPA SPINOSA. Hall. (Fig. 137.) (Pal. N. Y., Vol. IV., p. 322, Pl. LIII.A.) (= *A. aspera* of American authors.)

Distinguishing Characters.—Greater equality of valves, which are, in some specimens, almost equally convex; coarse

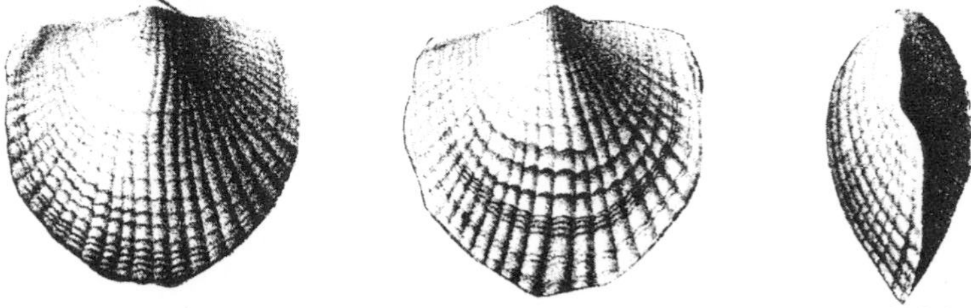

FIG. 137. *Atrypa spinosa.* Dorsal, ventral, and profile views of a specimen which has lost its spines (from Hall).

plications, which end roughly, or in perfect specimens are produced into spines projecting beyond the growth lines.

Found in the coral layer of the lower Moscow shale, at Section 5 (abundant; one specimen was found above this).

Genus VITULINA. Hall.

[Ety.: Mythological name.]

(1860: 13th Rep't N. Y. State Cab. Nat. Hist., p. 72. 1893: Pal. N. Y., Vol. VIII., Pt. II., p. 138.)

Shell rather small, plano-convex, transverse, the hinge line making the greatest diameter of the valve. Pedicle valve convex, with a well-developed cardinal area, divided in the center by an open delthyrium. Blunt, thick teeth, unsupported by lamellæ, are present. Brachial valve flat or very gently convex, with a narrow area divided as in the pedicle valve. Cardinal process straight and simple. Surface covered with a few coarse plications. Brachidium consists of loose spirals, the apices of which are directed towards the lateral margins of the shell.

Vitulina pustulosa. Hall. (Fig. 138.) (Pal. N. Y., Vol. IV., p. 410, Pl. LXII.)

Distinguishing Characters.—Size; rounded plications; elevated fold, with depression in the center on the pedicle valve; corresponding sinus with a simple or double low plication in

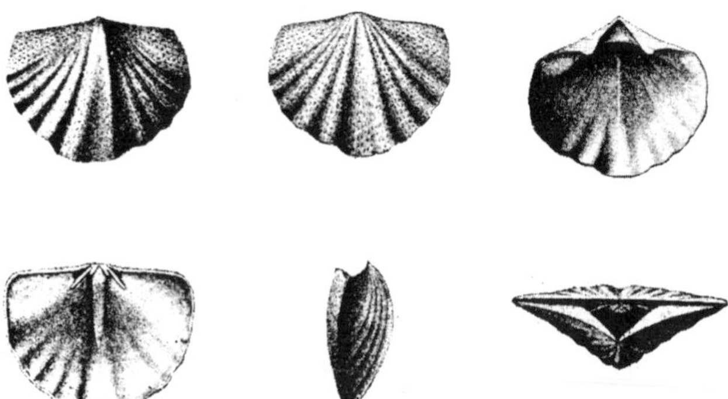

Fig. 138. ***Vitulina pustulosa.*** **Dorsal, ventral, profile, and cardinal views, and interiors of pedicle and brachial valves, enlarged, x 2 (from Hall).**

the center in the brachial valve; interrupted radiating lines, which form rows of elongated, lachrymiform pustules.

Found in the Encrinal limestone, at Section 5 (common).

Genus CAMAROTŒCHIA. Hall and Clarke.

[Ety.: *Kamara*, arched chamber.]

(1893: Pal. N. Y., Vol. VIII., Pt. II., p. 189.)

Shell rhynchonelloid, trihedral in contour, with shallow pedicle and convex brachial valve. No hinge area. Beak of pedicle valve projecting and incurved. Surface radially plicate, sinus and fold in pedicle and brachial valves respectively. Distinctive internal characters (separating this genus from other "Rhynchonellas") are: a median septum in the brachial valve, which divides posteriorly, so as to form an elongate cavity, which does not extend to the bottom of the valve. No cardinal process. In the pedicle valve slender vertical lamellæ support the teeth.

Camarotœchia horsfordi. Hall. (Fig. 139.) (Pal. N. Y., Vol. IV., p. 339, Pl. LIV.)

Distinguishing Characters. — Transversely sub-elliptical outline; nearly straight or broadly rounded front; length

Fig. 139. *Camarotœchia horsfordi.* Cardinal, front, dorsal, ventral, and profile views (from Hall).

and width about as five to six or seven; sinus of pedicle valve appearing first at about the middle of the shell, abruptly curved upwards in front; mesial elevation of brachial valve defined below the middle; fifteen to twenty-four angular plications on each valve, of which four to seven mark the fold or sinus; concentric undulating striæ.

Found in the lower Moscow shale, at Sections 4 and 5 (rare); Encrinal limestone, at Section 5 (rare); Stictopora bed, at Section 5 (rare); Nautilus bed, in Erie Cliff (?), (very rare).

CAMAROTŒCHIA SAPPHO. Hall. (Fig. 140.) (Pal. N. Y., Vol. IV., p. 340, Pl. LIV.)

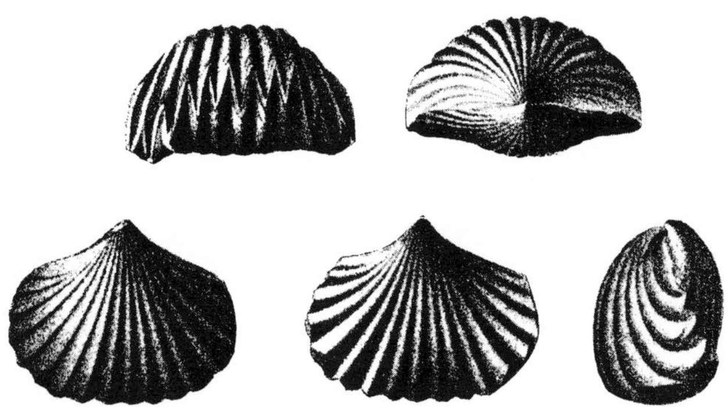

FIG. 140. *Camarotœchia sappho.* Front, cardinal, dorsal (brachial), ventral (pedicle), and lateral views of a characteristic specimen (from Hall).

Distinguishing Characters.—Rather large size; robust character; broader than long; shallow pedicle valve, which is prominently convex only at the umbo, and is depressed towards the front into a sinus, which first becomes perceptible near the middle of the length; more or less incurved beak of pedicle valve; gibbous brachial valve, with the fold conspicuous only near the front; coarse plications, twenty to twenty-four on each valve in mature specimens, all incised towards the front, for the reception of the opposite plication; sinus and fold with four to six plications each.

Found in the Encrinal limestone, at Section 5 (frequent); Lower shales, down to three feet below the Encrinal limestone, at Sections 5 and 6; seventeen to twenty-one feet below the Encrinal limestone, at Section 7 (common); middle Trilobite bed (very rare); also in the Pleurodictyum beds, in Avery's Creek.

CAMAROTŒCHIA DOTIS. Hall. (Fig. 141.) (Pal. N. Y., Vol. IV., p. 344, Pl. LIV.)

Distinguishing Characters.—Sub-triangularly ovate outline; rounded or semi-truncate front; shallow sinus and moderate fold; plications rounded or sub-angular, about eighteen in number (in full-grown specimens), those of the gibbous brachial valve abruptly curved down to the pedicle valve; plications, commonly three or four in the sinus and four or five on the fold.

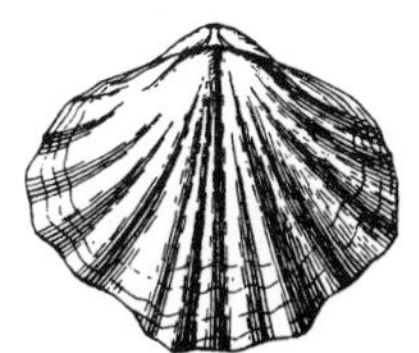

FIG. 141. *Camarotœchia dotis.* Dorsal view of a characteristic specimen, from the Nautilus bed, x 2. (Original.)

Found in the Encrinal limestone, at Section 5 (rare); Nautilus bed, in Avery's Creek and north shore sections (abundant); Strophalosia bed (?), in Erie Cliff.

CAMAROTŒCHIA CONGREGATA. (Conrad.) (Fig. 141A.) (Pal. N. Y., Vol. IV., p. 341, Pl. LIV.)

Distinguishing Characters.— Robust character; abrupt curvature of sides; moderate fold and sinus; conspicuous

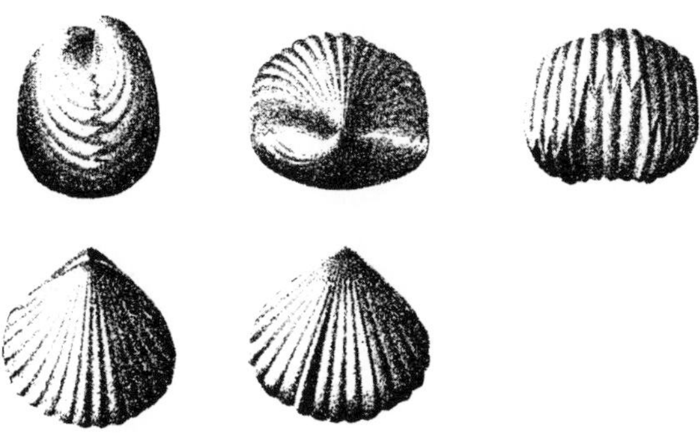

FIG. 141A. *Camarotœchia congregata.* Profile, cardinal, front, dorsal, and ventral views of an individual (from Hall.)

character of sinus at the front; three or four plications in sinus and four or five on mesial fold.

Found in a Calcareous band in the Hamilton group, at Alden, Erie Co. (Hall); and at Eighteen Mile Creek. (Coll. Am. Mus. Nat. Hist. New York.)

Genus LEIORHYNCHUS. Hall.

[Ety.: *Leios*, smooth; *rhynchos*, beak.]

(1860: 13th Ann. Rep't N. Y. State Cab. Nat. Hist., p. 75.
1893: Pal. N. Y., Vol. VIII., Pt. II., p. 193.)

Rhynchonelloid shells, with the plications on the median fold and sinus highly developed, but those on the lateral slopes usually slightly developed. Other external features as in Camarotœchia.

Leiorhynchus multicostus. Hall. (Fig. 142.) (Pal. N. Y., Vol. IV., p. 358, Pl. LVI.)

Distinguishing Characters.—Ovate outline; length and greatest width nearly equal (except in compressed speci-

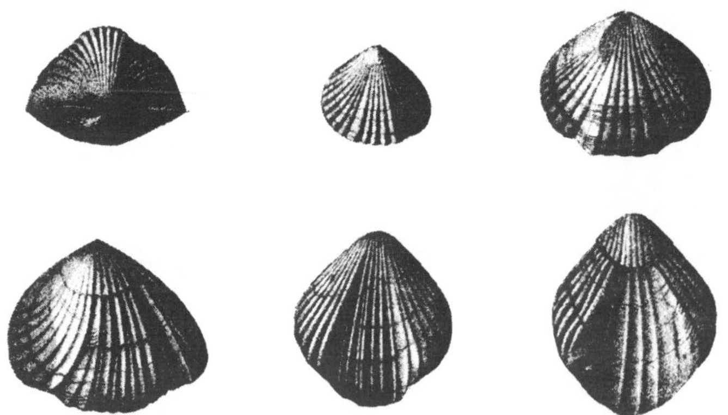

Fig. 142. *Leiorhynchus multicostus.* Cardinal view of a gibbous specimen; two brachial valves of different ages; three pedicle valves, one much distorted (from Hall).

mens); three to seven rounded plications in the sinus and on the fold, all bifurcating; obscurely bifurcating lateral plications, which become obsolete near the beak; concentric striæ. This species is considered identical with *L. laura* (Billings).

Found in the upper and lower Moscow shales, at Sections 1 to 8, and on the Lake Shore (especially abundant in the Schizobolus beds); Lower shales, five feet below, and from fourteen feet below the Encrinal limestone down, at Sections 7 and 8, and on the Lake Shore (often abundant).

LEIORHYNCHUS QUADRICOSTATUM. (Vanuxem.) (Fig. 143.) (Pal. N. Y., Vol. IV., p. 357, Pl. LVI.)

Distinguishing Characters.— Broadly ovate outline; almost smooth lateral slopes, the plications being very faint; small

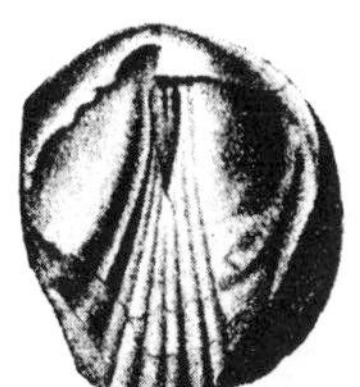

FIG. 143. *Leiorhynchus quadricostatum.* Two brachial valves and one pedicle valve, natural size, all much distorted (from Hall).

number (three to five) of rounded plications on the fold and sinus. This species is normal in the Genesee slate, but has not been found in it in the region under discussion. Specimens approaching it in character, if not identical with it, occur in the upper Moscow shale, at Section 1.

LEIORHYNCHUS LIMITARE. (Vanuxem.) (Fig. 144.) (Pal. N. Y., Vol. IV., p. 356, Pl. LVI.)

Distinguishing Characters.—Ovate to sub-orbicular outline; gibbous character of old uncompressed specimens; mesial fold and sinus become developed near the front; numerous angular or sub-angular plications, those of the fold and sinus bifurcating, those of the lateral slopes rarely dividing; fine concentric striæ.

FIG. 144. *Leiorhynchus limitare.* Dorsal, profile, and front views of a small specimen (from Hall).

Found in the lowest ten feet of the Transition shales, in the Lake Shore sections; upper Marcellus shales, in Bay View Cliff.

LEIORHYNCHUS DUBIUM. Hall. (Fig. 145.) (Pal. N. Y., Vol. IV., p. 364, Pl. LVII.)

Distinguishing Characters.—Ovate outline, rapidly expanding towards the front; moderate and almost equal convexity of valves; very faintly developed fold and sinus;

FIG. 145. *Leiorhynchus dubium.* A specimen without fold in brachial valve; dorsal, ventral, and profile views of a more strongly marked individual (from Hall).

twenty-four to twenty-six slender, rounded surface plications, of which about six are on the fold.

A specimen from Section 7, seventeen to twenty-one feet below the Encrinal limestone, appears to be of this species.

GENUS CENTRONELLA. BILLINGS.

[ETY.: A little point.]

(1859: Canadian Naturalist and Geologist, Vol. IV., p. 131. 1893: Pal. N. Y., Vol. VIII., Pt. II., p. 265.)

Shell plano-convex or concavo-convex, with a terebratuloid outline. The beak of the pedicle valve is acute and incurved, with a terminal foramen, which is continuous with a partially-closed delthyrium. The brachial valve bears a median sinus, while the center of the pedicle valve is angular, the sides sloping off rapidly. The brachidium consists of two branches, which unite medially to a triangular plate bearing a median ridge.

CENTRONELLA IMPRESSA. Hall. (Fig. 146.) (Pal. N. Y., Vol. IV., p. 402, Pl. LXI.)

Distinguishing Characters.—Sub-ovate outline; convex angular pedicle valve, the longitudinal outline of which is

FIG. 146. *Centronella impressa.* Dorsal, ventral, and profile views of a full-grown specimen of ordinary size; interior of a brachial valve, showing the cardinal process and the strong callosities to which the crura are attached.

slightly arched; beak truncated by the foramen; small brachial valve, flattened or sometimes sharply depressed along the center, with the front produced and curved downward to fill the sinuosity in the front of the pedicle valve; fine concentric surface striæ and almost obsolete faint radiating striæ.

Found in the upper layers of the Encrinal limestone, at Section 5, in Eighteen Mile Creek (rather common).

GENUS TRIGERIA. BAYLE.

(1875: Explic. Carte Géol. de France, Atlas, Pl. XIII. 1893: Pal. N. Y., Vol. VIII., Pt. II., p. 272.)

"Plicated centronellids with plano-convex valves. In the brachial valve the hinge plate is tripartite, the median division being perforated by a visceral foramen. Brachidium as in Centronella, though with a smaller anterior plate." (Hall and Clarke. Hand-book Brach., Pt. II., p. 108.)

TRIGERIA (?) LEPIDA. Hall. (Fig. 146A.) (Pal. N. Y., Vol. IV., p. 276, Pl. XLV.)

Distinguishing Characters.—Small size; sub-equally convex valves; much elevated beak of pedicle valve; elongate

FIG. 146A. *Trigeria lepida.* Ventral view of a specimen, natural size. Dorsal, ventral, and profile views of a specimen, enlarged, x 2. Dorsal view of an individual with unusually strongly marked sinus (from Hall).

oval opening, communicating with foramen above, and flanked below by two convex deltidial plates; simple regular surface plications, gradually enlarging towards the margins of the valves; shallow sinus on brachial valve, formed by depression of two or three central plications.

GENUS CRYPTONELLA. HALL.

[ETY.: Signifying a small cavity.]

(1861: 14th Annual Rep't, N. Y. State Cab. Nat. Hist., p. 102. 1893: Pal. N. Y., Vol. VIII., Pt. II., p. 286.)

Shell terebratuloid, with the valves of somewhat similar convexity. Beak of pedicle valve erect or slightly incurved and prominent; foramen limited below by well-developed deltidial plates. Brachidium consisting of a loop bent back upon itself, the juncture of the branches occurring a little below the plane of their origin.

CRYPTONELLA PLANIROSTRIS. Hall. (Fig. 147.) (Pal. N. Y., Vol. IV., p. 395, Pl. LXI.)

Distinguishing Characters.—Great convexity of valves; large size of adult; often truncate front and consequent sub-

FIG. 147. *Cryptonella planirostris.* Dorsal, ventral, and profile views of a large, strongly-marked individual; enlargement of beak of pedicle valve; dorsal, ventral, and profile views of a smaller and less strongly-marked individual (from Hall).

pentagonal outline of valves; angular umbonal margins of pedicle valve, with flat or concave faces on either side of the deltidial plates.

Found in the Encrinal limestone, at Section 5 (common). Doubtful specimens have been found in the shale between the Encrinal and Pleurodictyum beds.

CRYPTONELLA RECTIROSTRIS. Hall. (Fig. 148.) (Pal. N. Y., Vol. IV., p. 394, Pl. LXI.)

Distinguishing Characters.—Usually small size; sub-rhomboidal outline; frequently truncated front; erect beak, with inflected cardinal margins.

FIG. 148. *Cryptonella rectirostris.* Dorsal, ventral, and profile views of a specimen (from Hall).

Found in the Pleurodictyum beds, in Avery's Creek, and on the Lake Shore (common).

Genus DIELASMA. King.

[Ety.: *Di*, two; *elasma*, lamella.]

(1859: Proc. Dublin Univ. Bot. Zool. Assoc., Vol. I., p. 260. 1893: Pal. N. Y., Vol. VIII., p. 293.)

Terebratuloid shells, with frequently a median sinus in both valves. A large foramen and deltidial plates are present, though these latter may be obscured by the incurvature of the beak. A large hinge plate, raised but little above the bottom of the valve, and sometimes actually adhering to it, and a relatively short brachidium, with a rather short recurvature of the ascending lamellæ, are characteristic internal features.

The sub-genus Cranæna (Hall), was erected to receive such forms as *Terebratula romingeri* (Hall), in which the brachidium is that of a Dielasma, but the hinge plate resembles that of Cryptonella.

Dielasma (Cranæna) romingeri. Hall. (Fig. 149.) (Pal. N. Y., Vol. IV., p. 389, Pl. LX.)

Distinguishing Characters.—Small size; ovate outline; truncated or slightly sinuate front; rounded cardinal slopes; concentric striæ, which are often crowded into wrinkles near the front.

Fig. 149. *Dielasma romingeri.* Dorsal, ventral, and profile views (from Hall).

Found in the Pleurodictyum beds and the Calcareous bed above, on the Lake Shore, and in Avery's Ravine.

Genus TROPIDOLEPTUS. Hall.

[Ety.: *Tropis*, keel; *leptos*, slender.]

(1857: 10th Ann. Rep't N. Y. State Cab. Nat. Hist., p. 151. 1893: Pal. N. Y., Vol. VIII., Pt. II., p. 302.)

Shell concavo or plano-convex, with the hinge line much extended and straight, the whole aspect of the shell being "Strophomenoid" (compare Stropheodonta). In young shells the hinge line equals or exceeds in length the greatest width of the shell, but in mature shells it is shorter. Pedicle valve convex, with a moderately high area, divided by an open delthyrium. The teeth arise from the bottom of the valve as two erect divergent crests. Brachial valve slightly concave, or nearly flat, with a low area, a prominent convex chilidium, and a large cardinal process bilobed at the summit. The brachidium consists of two slender descending lamellæ, which unite near the middle of the valve with a sharp, thin median septum, which, towards the beak, passes into a low median ridge. Surface of both valves plicated.

TROPIDOLEPTUS CARINATUS. (Conrad.) (Fig. 150.) (Pal. N. Y., Vol. IV., p. 407, Pl. LXII.)

Distinguishing Characters.—Strophomenoid outline; broad, simple, rounded plications, wider than the interspaces; broadly sub-carinate center of pedicle valve, caused by the greater width and prominence of the central plication; longitudinally striated, convex chilidium of brachial valve; fine undulating concentric surface striæ, and occasional coarser imbricating lamellæ.

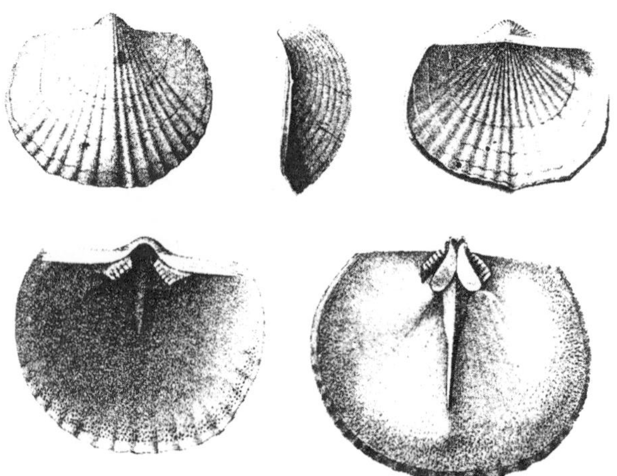

FIG. 150. *Tropidoleptus carinatus.* Ventral, profile, and dorsal views of a normal individual; enlargements of interiors of pedicle and brachial valves (from Hall).

Found in the Encrinal limestone, at Section 5 (common); four feet below the Encrinal limestone, at Section 6 (one specimen); seventeen to twenty-one feet below the Encrinal limestone, at Section 7; between the Trilobite beds and the Strophalosia bed, in Avery's Creek, and on the Lake Shore (not uncommon).

NOTE.—This species is, at Eighteen Mile Creek, almost entirely confined to the Encrinal limestone; but at Morse Creek, near Athol Springs, it is common in the shales below the limestone.

CLASS PELECYPODA. GOLDFUSS.

(*Lamellibranchiata.* Blainville.)

The Pelecypoda or Lamellibranchiata are marine or fresh-water molluscs, with a bivalve shell. The valves are complementary, and are in the majority of species of nearly similar outline and size. In each valve may be distinguished an initial point, or beak, around which the concentric *lines of growth* mark the successive additions of shelly matter.

The orientation of most shells is effected by holding them with the *hinge line* uppermost and the beaks pointing away from the observer. Thus placed, the upper border is the dorsal and the lower the ventral border. The end farthest away from the observer is the anterior end; that nearest, the posterior end. The valves are designated as the right and left valves, respectively. The articulation of the valves is commonly effected by the interlocking of *teeth* which are borne on the hinge or cardinal margin of the valves. They are very various, but they can usually be divided into the short, stout "cardinal teeth," which are situated under or near the beak, and the ridge-like lateral teeth. The opening of the valves is brought about by an elastic ligament stretched across the hinge from valve to valve, behind the beak, which acts whenever the tension of the *adductor muscles*, which close the valves, is relaxed. In many forms, an elastic, compressible cartilage, lodged in special grooves or pits, takes the place of the external ligament. The scars marking the attachment of the adductor or closing muscle, or muscles, vary greatly, and are frequently preserved in the fossil forms. When two are present they are designated, respectively, as the anterior and posterior adductor scars. The line of attachment of the fleshy mantle which builds the shells, i. e., the *pallial line,* is often visible. Near the posterior end it

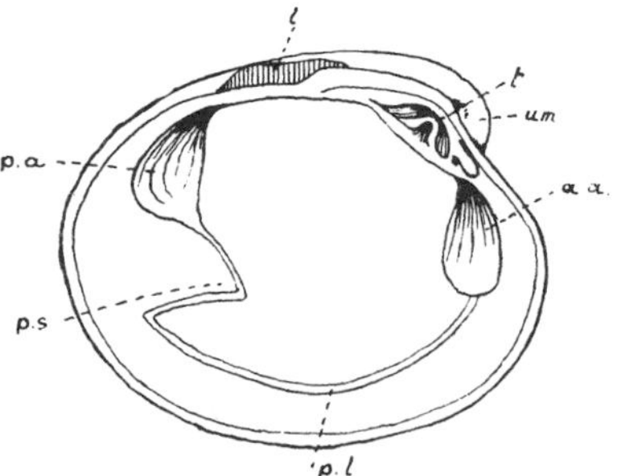

FIG. 151. Diagrammatic view of left valve of Cytherea; (*a. a.*) anterior adductor scar; (*p. a.*) posterior adductor scar; (*p. l.*) pallial line; (*p. s.*) pallial sinus; (*l.*) ligament; (*t.*) teeth; (*um.*) umbo (after Lang, adapted).

frequently makes a reëntrant curve — the *pallial sinus* — indicating that the animal had a retractile siphon. The various parts described are indicated in figure 151.

The principal soft parts of the animal comprise: the *mantle*, consisting of two fleshy folds, one lining each valve, and building it; the *abdomen*, with the anteriorly placed *mouth*, and the anterio-ventral *foot*; the *gills* or *branchiæ*, which consist of complicated lamellæ hanging on either side of the abdomen in the mantle cavity; and the *siphons* — present only in certain forms — posteriorly placed, often capable of great extension, and serving, the one for the entrance of the water and food particles, and the other for the exit of the water and waste products.

NOTE.—The numerous text-books and laboratory guides in zoölogy will furnish more detailed information on the anatomy of the animal, which should be verified by dissecting a clam, mussel, or other bivalve. Zittel's Text-book of Palæontology (Eastman's translation) contains the best comprehensive account of the fossil genera. The generic and specific description, of the forms here noted, may almost all be found in Vol. V., Pt. I., of the Palæontology of New York, to which reference is made in the text.

GENUS AVICULOPECTEN. McCOY.

[ETY.: From the Genera *Avicula* and *Pecten*.]

(1851: Annals and Magazine of Nat. Hist., 2d Ser., Vol. VII., p. 171.)

Shell with the valves unequal, the right valve usually smaller and flatter than the left valve, and having an anterior "byssal notch." The hinge line is straight and continued forward into the *ear*, and backward onto the *wing*, triangular, well-defined and somewhat flattened portions on either side of the beak. The cartilage lies in several shallow furrows, parallel to the hinge margin. The hinge line is shorter than the greatest antero-posterior diameter (length), and the surface is ornamented with rays.

AVICULOPECTEN PRINCEPS. (Conrad.) (Fig. 152.) (Pal. N. Y., Vol. V., Pt. I., Pls. I., V., VI., XXIV., LXXI.)

Distinguishing Characters.—Large size, obliquely broad-ovate outline with axis inclined more than sixty degrees to the hinge line; nearly equal length and height; straight posterior slope from the beak to the middle of the posterior end; large ear and wing; regular alternating rays, crossed by fine, sharp growth-lines.

Fig. 152. *Aviculopecten princeps.* A large left valve, much extended posteriorly (from Hall).

Found in the Encrinal limestone, at Section 5 (rare); in the shale down to and in the Trilobite beds, at Sections 6, 7, 8, and on the Lake Shore (rare); also in the shale below the Trilobite beds, in Avery's Creek.

Aviculopecten exacutus. Hall. (Fig. 153.) (Pal. N. Y., Vol. V., Pt. I., p. 8, Pl. III.)

Distinguishing Characters.—Beak more acute than in the preceding species; proportionally larger wing; concave posterior margin; sharp alternating rays, with broad concave interspaces, extending into the ear and wing.

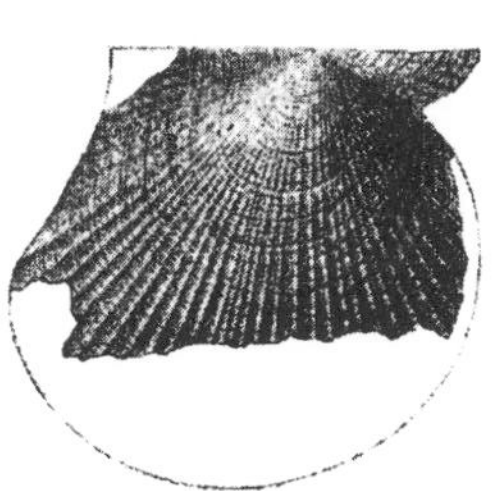

Fig. 153. *Aviculopecten exacutus.* Right and left valves, from Hamburg, Erie Co., N. Y.; the figure of the left valve does not show the concentric lamellæ, and the beak is represented as too acute (from Hall).

Found in the Stictopora and Demissa beds, at Section 5 (rare); in the shale nine to seventeen feet below the Encrinal limestone, at Section 7 (rare); and at "Hamburg, Erie County, N. Y." (Hall.)

AVICULOPECTEN INSIGNIS. Hall. (Fig. 154.) (Pal. N. Y., Vol. V., Pt. I., p. 34, Pls. I., III., LXXXI.)

Distinguishing Characters.—Small size; moderate ob-

FIG. 154. *Aviculopecten insignis.* A left valve; interior of a right valve, from Hamburg, Erie Co., N. Y., the specimen being embedded in shale shows the ornamentation on the interior (from Hall).

liquity; hinge nearly equal to the length of the shell; nearly central beak; strong radiating costæ.

Found at "Hamburg, Erie County, N. Y." (Hall.)

GENUS LYRIOPECTEN. HALL.

[ETY.: *Lyrion*, lyre — Pecten.]

(1884: Pal. N. Y., Vol. V., Pt. I., p. xii.)

Shell like Aviculopecten, but differing from that genus in its short hinge line and very small anterior ear.

FIG. 155. *Lyriopecten orbiculatus.* The type specimen from the Encrinal limestone, on the shore of Lake Erie, N. Y. (from Hall).

LYRIOPECTEN ORBICULATUS. Hall. (Fig. 155.) (Pal. N. Y., Vol. V., Pt. I., p. 42, Pls. IV., LXXXII.)

Distinguishing Characters.—Large size; orbicular outline; convex left valve; concave, flat, or slightly convex right valve; numerous strong, rounded radii crossed by concentric sharp lines, and separated by broader concave spaces.

Found in the "shale and Encrinal limestone, along Lake Erie Shore, Eighteen Mile Creek, Erie County, N. Y." (Hall.)

GENUS PTERINOPECTEN. HALL.

[ETY.: From Pterinea and Pecten.]

(1884: Pal. N. Y., Vol. V., Pt. I., p. xii.)

"Hinge line long; ears not well defined, being simple expansions or extensions of the upper lateral margins to the hinge line. Test ornamented with rays."

PTERINOPECTEN CONSPECTUS. Hall. (Fig. 156.) (Pal. N. Y., Vol. V., Pt. I., p. 66, Pl. XVII.)

Distinguishing Characters.—Length and height nearly equal; regularly rounded base; sharp constricted anterior ear; gently concave posterior margin of wing, with almost rectangular extremity; alternating radii of left valve, and sub-equal radii of right valve.

FIG. 156. *Pterinopecten conspectus.* An exfoliated left valve (from Hall).

Found in the lower Moscow shale, at Section 4 (rare); in the shales of the Demissa bed and down to seventeen feet below the Encrinal limestone, at Sections 6 and 7; also in the upper Pleurodictyum bed, and the shale below the Nautilus bed, in Avery's Ravine.

PTERINOPECTEN HERMES. Hall. (Fig. 157.) (Pal. N. Y., Vol. V., Pt. I., p. 64, Pl. XVII.)

Distinguishing Characters.—Longer than high; hinge line extended, forming acute angle with posterior slope; regular rounded surface striæ, with wider interspaces.

FIG. 157. *Pterinopecten hermes.* Two exterior views and one interior view of left valves — the ear of the first specimen is represented too acute (from Hall).

Found four feet below the base of the Trilobite beds, in Avery's Creek (rare); and very rarely in the shale between the Nautilus and Strophalosia beds.

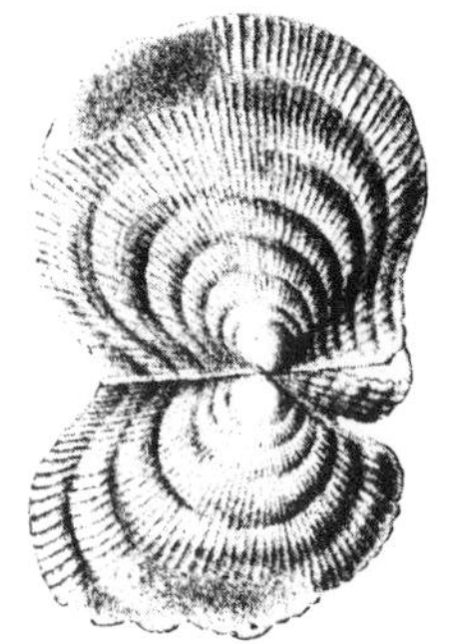

Fig. 158. *Pterinopecten undosus.* Small specimen, preserving both valves, and showing strong undulations (from Hall).

PTERINOPECTEN UNDOSUS. Hall. (Fig. 158.) (Pal. N. Y., Vol. V., Pt. I., p. 72, Pls. II., LXXXII.)

Distinguishing Characters.—Length greater than height; short hinge line; concave margins of ears and wing; sharp, crenulated striæ; concentric undulations; deep byssal notch of right valve.

Found (?) in the Demissa bed (rare).

GENUS PTERINEA. GOLDFUSS.

[ETY.: *Pteron*, a wing.]

(1826: Peterfact. Germ.)

Valves unequal, left valve most convex. The shell is very oblique, the wing large, and the ear small. Two or more cardinal teeth and linear oblique lateral teeth occur. The hinge line is straight, and has a linear flattened marginal cartilage facet, which is longitudinally striated. The surface of the shell is ornamented by rays.

Fig. 159. *Pterinea flabella.* Left valve (from Hall).

PTERINEA FLABELLA. (Conrad.) (Fig. 159.) (Pal. N. Y., Vol. V., Pt. I., p. 93, Pls. XIV., XV., LXXXIII.)

Distinguishing Characters.—Large size; convex left valve and flat or concave right valve; large, well-defined, triangular wing, with concave margin; small, rounded, well-defined ear; strong, rounded, distant rays, with smaller intermediate ones on the left valve; concentric striæ; and a few obsolete rays on the right valve.

Found in the Stictopora and Demissa beds (rather common); in the shale, down to twelve feet below the Encrinal limestone, at Sections 6 and 7 (rare); in the shale below the Nautilus bed, in Avery's Creek (rare); and at "Hamburg and elsewhere on Lake Erie Shore." (Hall.)

Genus ACTINOPTERIA. Hall.

[Ety.: *Aktin*, a ray; *pteron*, wing.]

(1884: Pal. N. Y., Vol. V., Pt. I., p. xii.)

"Characterized from Pterinea in the absence of a broad, striated ligamental area, and strong cardinal and lateral teeth. Right valve sub-convex; surface with fine rays."

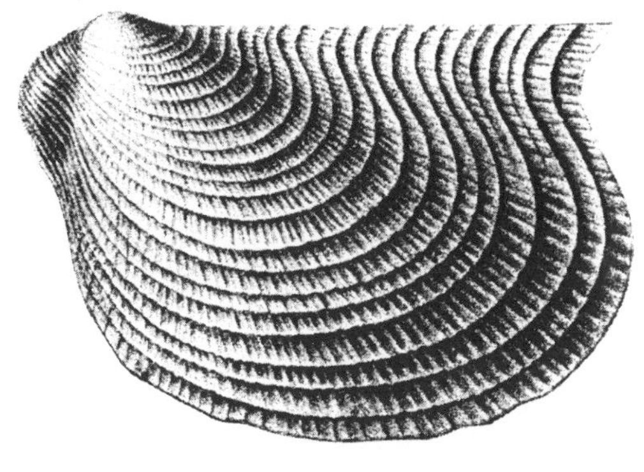

Fig. 160. *Actinopteria decussata.* Left valve, showing the strongly decussated radii; right valve not preserving the radii (from Hall).

Actinopteria decussata. Hall. (Fig. 160.) (Pal. N. Y., Vol. V., Pt. I., p. 111, Pls. XVII., XVIII., XX., LXXXIV.)

Distinguishing Characters.—Extreme obliquity; large size; long, well-defined wing; small ear, defined by a sulcus; regular rounded radii, with smaller ones between, regularly interrupted by concentric lamellæ; almost obsolete markings on right valve.

Found in the Encrinal limestone, at Sections 5 and 6; in the Stictopora and Demissa beds, at Section 5; and in the Pleurodictyum beds, and the Calcareous bed above them, in Avery's Ravine.

Actinopteria boydi. Hall. (Fig. 161.) (Pal. N. Y., Vol. V., Pt. I., p. 113, Pls. XIX., LXXXIV.)

Distinguishing Characters.—Less oblique than preceding; larger, less strongly defined wing; continuous surface striæ.

Fig. 161. *Actinopteria boydi.* Left and right valves (from Hall).

Found in the Pleurodictyum beds, and the Calcareous bed above; also in the shales below the Nautilus bed, in Avery's Creek and on the Lake Shore (rare).

Genus LEIOPTERIA. Hall

[Ety.: *Leios*, smooth; *pteria*, a genus.]

(1884: Pal. N. Y., Vol. V., Pt. I., p. xiii.)

Shell resembling Actinopteria in form, with a large wing, the extremity of which is produced. Rays absent. The ligamental area is external, and marked by fine, parallel, longitudinal striæ. Lateral teeth one or two, oblique, slender. Cavity of the beak partially separated from the anterior end by a short partition or diaphragm.

LEIOPTERIA RAFINESQUII. Hall. (Fig. 162.) (Pal. N. Y., Vol. V., Pt. I., p. 161, Pls. XV., XX., LXXXVIII.)

Distinguishing Characters.—Oblique, narrowly ovate body, with height equal to or greater than the length; flat wing, with concave margin and acute extremity; short, obtuse, convex ear.

Found in the Demissa bed (very rare).

FIG. 162. *Leiopteria rafinesquii.* A left valve (from Hall).

LEIOPTERIA CONRADI. Hall. (Fig. 162A.) (Pal. N. Y., Vol. V., Pt. I., p. 159, Pls. XX., LXXXVIII.)

Distinguishing Characters.—Strong obliquity; hinge line longer than length of valve, greatly extended posteriorly; acute extremity, and concave posterior margin of wing; small ear separated from shell by rounded sulcus; irregular, often crowded, concentric striæ. Readily distinguished from the species of Actinopteria occurring with it, by the absence of rays.

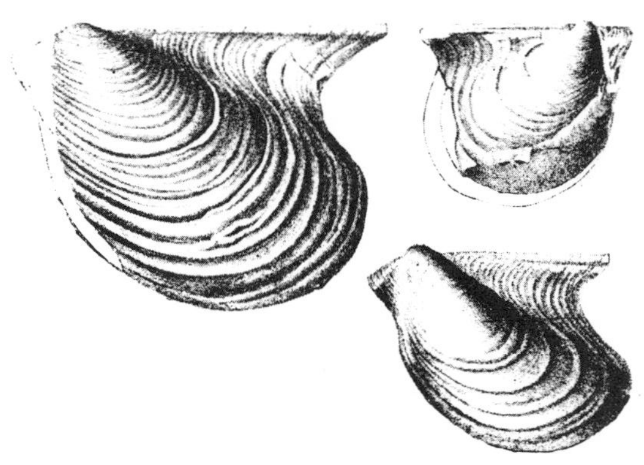

FIG. 162A. *Leiopteria conradi.* Two left valves and a right valve, of different sizes, showing variations (from Hall).

Found in the Hamilton group, at West Hamburg, Erie Co., N. Y. (Coll. Am. Mus. Nat. Hist. New York.)

Genus PLETHOMYTILUS. Hall.

[Ety.: *Pletho*, to be full; *mytilus*, a genus.]

(1884: Pal. N. Y., Vol. V., Pt. I., p. 14.)

Shell with equal gibbous valves, of an outline resembling Mytilus, and having a finely striated ligamental area, which extends across the shorter or transverse diameter of the valve. Height greatly exceeding the length. The posterior side is slightly winged. Small, oblique, lateral teeth are present, but no cardinal teeth have been observed. Test with concentric striæ.

Plethomytilus oviformis. (Conrad.) (Fig. 163.) (Pal. N. Y., Vol. V., Pt. I., p. 255, Pls. XXXI., LXXXVII.)

Distinguishing Characters.—Large size; ovate outline; beaks projecting above the cardinal line; truncate front,

Fig. 163. *Plethomytilus oviformis.* Left valve, showing striated hinge area; right valve, with attenuated beak (from Hall).

with small fissure for the passage of the byssus; wide ligamental area.

Found only in the upper part of the Encrinal limestone, at the lower end of Section 5 (common).

Genus GOSSELETTIA. Barrois.

[Ety.: Proper name.]

(1881: Ann. Soc. Geol. du Nord, Vol. VIII., p. 176.]

Shell sub-triangular, truncate on the anterior side, sub-alate on the posterior side. Ligamental area wide, longitudinally striate. Cardinal teeth strong, situated under the beak. Lateral teeth elongate. Surface marked by concentric striæ.

Gosselettia retusa. Hall. (Fig. 164.) (Pal. N. Y., Vol. V., Pt. I., p. 266, Pl. XXXIII.)

Distinguishing Characters.—Oblique rhomboidal outline; "anterior margin nearly straight for two-thirds of the length, inflated at the byssal opening, and concave below."

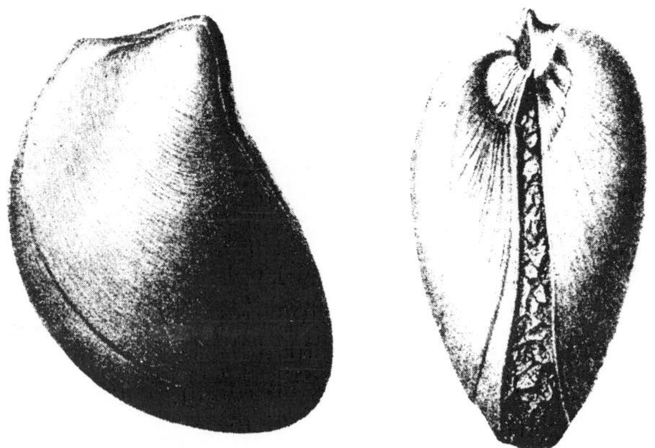

Fig. 164. *Gosselettia retusa.* Left and antero-cardinal view of the type specimen, from Eighteen Mile Creek (from Hall).

Found "in the Hamilton group, at Eighteen Mile Creek, Erie County, N. Y." (Hall, type.)

Genus MODIOMORPHA. Hall.

[Ety.: *Modiola*, a genus; *morphe*, form.]

(1870: Preliminary Notice Lamellibranchiata, 2, p. 72.)

Shells with equal but very inequilateral valves, which are sub-ovate in outline, largest posteriorly, and with a rounded, projecting anterior end. A depression, or "cincture," passes obliquely from beak to base, and the surface is marked by rugose, or undulating, concentric lines. The hinge bears a strong tooth in the left valve, which fits into a cavity in the right valve. The ligament is external and is attached to the thickened margin of the shell, which is often longitudinally grooved for its reception.

MODIOMORPHA CONCENTRICA. (Conrad.) (Fig. 165.) (Pal. N. Y., Vol. V., Pt. I., p. 275, Pls. XXXIV., XXXV., XXXVI.)

Distinguishing Characters.—Ovate outline; straight or slightly concave basal margin; arcuate to straight cardinal

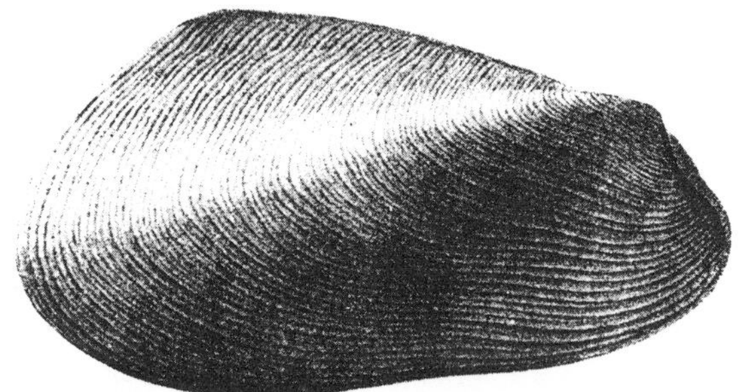

FIG. 165. *Modiomorpha concentrica.* Right side of a large individual, showing the arcuate form characteristic of old individuals (from Hall).

margin; rounded, projecting, well-defined, anterior end; strong, regular concentric lines.

Found in the Encrinal limestone, at Section 5 (common); in the shale, at twenty-five feet below the Encrinal and below the Trilobite beds, and in the Pleurodictyum beds, on the Lake Shore (rare).

MODIOMORPHA SUB-ALATA. (Conrad.) (Fig. 166.) (Pal. N. Y., Vol. V., Pt. I., p. 283, Pls. XXXV., XXXIX.)

Distinguishing Characters.—Sub-quadrangular to sub-ovate outline; sub-alate posterio-dorsal portion; well-marked umbonal ridge, passing from beak to base; large, but ill-defined, anterior end; sub-truncate posterior end.

Found in the shale below the Demissa bed and below the Athyris bed (rare); also in the Modiomorpha sub-alata bed, in Idlewood Ravine, and on the Lake Shore (in great

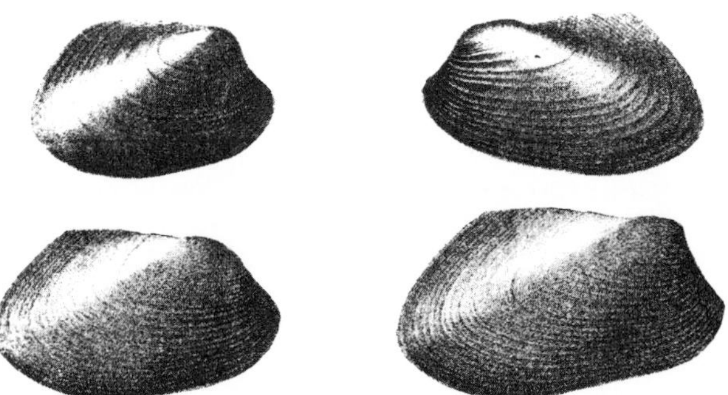

Fig. 166. *Modiomorpha sub-alata.* Three right valves and one left valve, showing variations (from Hall).

abundance); in the Trilobite beds and the shales above, at Section 8, and on the Lake Shore (common); and in the Pleurodictyum beds (rare).

Modiomorpha alta. (Conrad.) (Fig. 167.) (Pal. N. Y., Vol. V., Pt. I., p. 278, Pls. XXXVII., LXXX.)

Distinguishing Characters.—Broad rhomboid-ovate outline; curved posterior margin; elevated posterio-dorsal

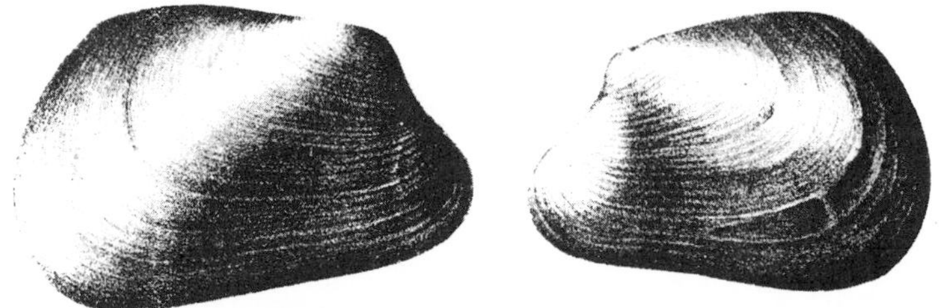

Fig. 167. *Modiomorpha alta.* Right and left valves of different individuals (from Hall).

portion; produced, rounded, but ill-defined, anterior portion; irregular surface striæ.

Found only in the middle Pleurodictyum bed, in Avery's Ravine (rare).

Genus GONIOPHORA. Phillips.

[Ety.: *Gonia*, an angle; *phoros*, bearing.]

(1848: Memoirs Geol. Surv. Gt. Britain, Vol. II., Pt. I., p. 264.)

Shells with equal, but very inequilateral, valves, rhomboidal or trapezoidal in outline, obliquely truncate behind, and rounded in front. Cardinal line usually straight, and not oblique. Umbonal slope a strong angular ridge, from the beak to the post-inferior margin. A broad, undefined cincture separates off the anterior portion. A strong cardinal tooth in the left valve fits into a depression in the right valve. Ligament external.

GONIOPHORA MODIOMORPHOIDES. Grabau. (Fig. 168.) (1898: Rep't N. Y. State Geol. 1896: Faun. Ham. Gr., p. 254.)

Distinguishing Characters.—Arcuate cardinal line; pronounced arcuate umbonal ridge, with the surface above the ridge flat or slightly concave; small anterior end, scarcely extending beyond the beaks; numerous strong, regular lines of growth.

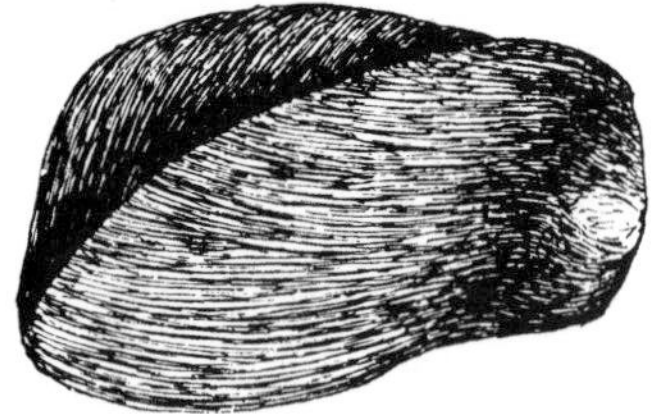

FIG. 168. *Goniophora modiomorphoides.* A characteristic right valve. (Original.)

Found in the Encrinal limestone, at Section 5 (where it is common).

GENUS CYPRICARDELLA. HALL.

[ETY.: Diminutive from *Cypricardia,* Cyprina and Cardium.]

(1856: Trans. Albany Inst., Vol. IV.)

Shells with equal, inequilateral valves, which are transversely sub-elliptical or sub-quadrate in outline. The cardinal line is straight or arcuate, the anterior end narrowed and rounded, and the posterior end broad and truncate. A more or less defined umbonal ridge extends from the small pointed beak to the posterior basal angle. Ligament external; cardinal teeth, one in each valve.

CYPRICARDELLA BELLISTRIATA. (Conrad.) (Fig. 169.) (Pal. N. Y., Vol. V., Pt. I., p. 308, Pls. XLII., LXXIII., LXXIV.)

Distinguishing Characters.—Projecting rounded anterior end, with a distinct depression, or lunule, below the beak;

almost vertically-truncate posterior end; well-marked angular umbonal ridge; strong, even, uniform, angular concentric striæ.

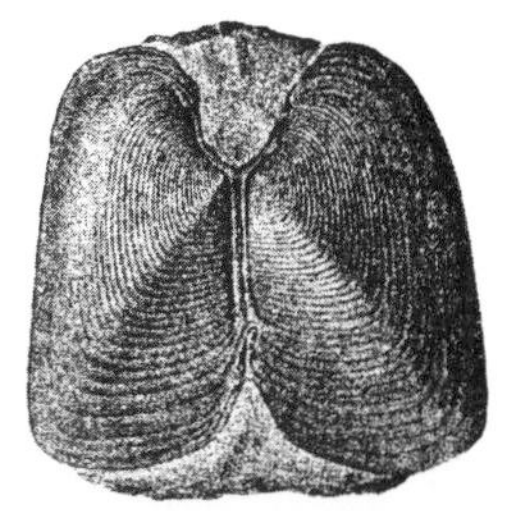

Fig. 169. *Cypricardella bellistriata.* A specimen retaining both valves in conjunction (from Hall).

Found in the Encrinal limestone, at Section 5 (very rare); nine to twelve feet below the Encrinal limestone, at Section 7; twenty-five feet below the Encrinal limestone, in Idlewood Ravine; and in the Pleurodictyum beds, and the shales just above, and down to and in the Strophalosia bed, in Avery's Creek, and on the Lake Shore.

Genus NUCULA. Lamarck.

[Ety.: *Nucula*, a little nut.]

(1801: Syst. An. Sans. Vert., p. 87.)

"Shell small, inequilateral, trigonal or transversely elliptical or sub-circular. Anterior or posterior extremity sometimes produced, usually rounded. Beaks anterior or posterior to the middle of the length, often sub-central. Cardinal line arcuate. Escutcheon marked. Surface marked by concentric striæ, which, in some species, are regular and rugose. Hinge furnished with a triangular, spoon-shaped cartilage-pit beneath the beaks, with a series of small transverse teeth on each side. There are two principal muscular impressions on each valve, with usually a smaller retractor scar adjacent, and also the cavity of the beaks often shows several pits for the attachment of umbonal muscles. Pallial line simple." (Hall, Pal. N. Y., Vol. V., Pt. I., p. xxvi.)

Nucula corbuliformis. Hall. (Fig. 169A.) (Pal. N. Y., Vol. V., Pt. I., p. 319, Pl. XLVI.)

Distinguishing Characters.—Broadly triangular, sub-ovate outline; length about one-fourth greater than height; longer, more pointed posterior end; broad and slightly incurved beaks, from which the cardinal line declines in both

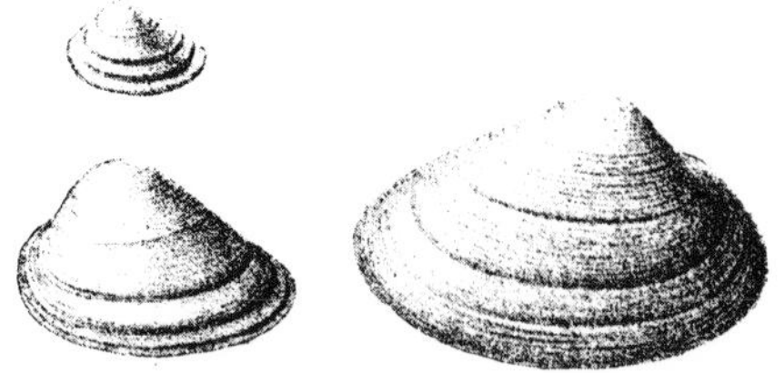

FIG. 169A. *Nucula corbuliformis.* Left valve, natural size and enlarged ; right valve enlarged (after Hall).

directions; not distinctly defined umbonal slope; fine concentric lines, and irregular concentric varices.

Found in the Hamilton group, on the shore of Lake Erie. (Coll. Am. Mus. Nat. Hist. New York.)

GENUS NUCULITES. CONRAD.

[ETY.: From *Nucula*, a genus; *nucula*, a little nut.]

(1841: Geol. Surv. N. Y. Ann. Rep't, p. 49.)

Shells with equal inequilateral valves, longer than high; with the anterior end rounded, and the posterior end sometimes obliquely truncate and pointed. The beaks are anterior, and the cardinal line arcuate. The hinge bears a row of transverse narrow teeth, which extend from the anterior to the posterior muscular scar. The ligament is external, a narrow groove serving as its receptacle. The anterior muscular scar is separated from the shell by a vertical, or slightly oblique, partition (clavicle). Surface concentrically striate.

NUCULITES OBLONGATUS. Conrad. (Fig. 170.) (Pal. N. Y., Vol. V., Pt. I., p. 324, Pl. XLVII.)

Distinguishing Characters.—Elongate ovate outline, widest at the anterior end; rounded umbonal ridge; strong vertical clavicle, or (in the internal mold) its impression.

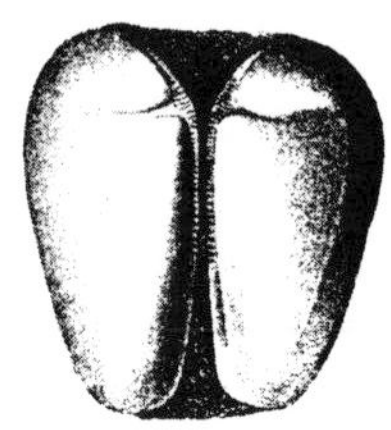

FIG. 170. *Nuculites oblongatus.* Three internal molds, showing the impression of the clavicle and the hinge crenulations (from Hall).

Found four feet below the Encrinal limestone, at Section 6 (rare), also in the Strophalosia bed, on the Lake Shore.

NUCULITES NYSSA. Hall. (Fig. 171.) (Pal. N. Y., Vol. V., Pt. I., p. 328, Pl. XLVII.)

Distinguishing Characters.—Broadly ovate outline, widest at the anterior end; oblique posterior margin, sub-truncate above and rounded below; narrow forward-curving clavicular ridge.

FIG. 171. *Nuculites nyssa.* Left and right valves, Eighteen Mile Creek (from Hall).

Found in the Strophalosia bed, on the Lake Shore; "in concretionary layers in the shales of the Hamilton group, on the shore of Lake Erie." (Hall, type).

NUCULITES TRIQUETER. Conrad. (Fig. 172.) (Pal. N. Y., Vol. V., Pt. I., p. 326, Pls. XLVII., XCIII.)

Distinguishing Characters.—Short trigonal outline; obliquely truncate posterior margin; arcuate cardinal margin; sub-angular, distinct umbonal ridge; strong, sharply-defined and curved clavicular ridge.

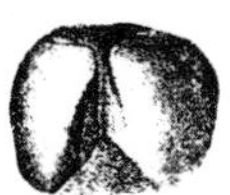

FIG. 172. *Nuculites triqueter.* A right valve; a left valve; both valves; the shell is exfoliated, showing impression of clavicle in internal mold (from Hall).

Found in Transition shales and the upper Marcellus shales, on the Lake Shore (rare).

GENUS SCHIZODUS. KING.

[ETY.: *Schizo*, split; *odous*, tooth.]

(1850: Monograph of the Permian Fossils of England, p. 185.)

Shell equivalve, inequilateral, with the posterior side the longest. Anterior outline rounded, posterior tapering. Right valve with two, left valve with three, cardinal teeth. Central tooth of left valve more or less bifid. Pallial line entire. Surface smooth or ornamented with fine raised concentric lines.

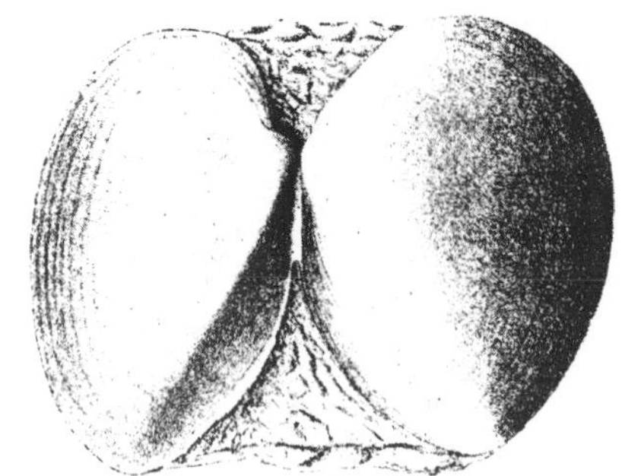

Fig. 172A. *Schizodus appressus.* Specimen with both valves conjoined (from Hall).

Schizodus appressus. (Conrad.) (Fig. 172A.) (Pal. N. Y., Vol. V., Pt. I., p. 449, Pl. LXXV.)

Distinguishing Characters.—Sub-rhomboidal-ovate outline; length greater than height; short cardinal line; obliquely truncate posterior extremity; sub-angular umbonal slope; fine concentric striæ.

Found in the Hamilton group of Eighteen Mile Creek. (Coll. Am. Mus. Nat. Hist. New York.)

Genus PALÆONEILO. Hall.

[Ety.: *Palaios*, ancient; *neilo*, a genus.]

(1870: Preliminary Notice Lamellibranchiata, 2, p. 6.)

Nucula-like shells, with equal, inequilateral valves, transversely ovate or sub-elliptical in outline; the posterior end extended, with a more or less well-defined sulcus along the umbonal slope. The cardinal line is arcuate, and the hinge furnished with a row of regular, small, transverse teeth, which change their direction under the beak, or are interrupted by several oblique teeth. Ligament external, lodged in a narrow and shallow groove.

Palæoneilo constricta. (Conrad.) (Fig. 173.) (Pal. N. Y., Vol. V., Pt. I., p. 333, Pls. XLVIII., LI.)

Distinguishing Characters.—Constricted and projecting posterior end; ovate-cuneate outline; abruptly declining

Fig. 173. *Palæoneilo constricta.* Two right valves and one left valve, showing variation (from Hall).

anterior portion of cardinal margin; fine, regular and even, thread-like striæ, which become obsolete in the furrow and on the post-cardinal slope.

Found in the Demissa bed, at Section 5 (rare); and in the shale below at three feet and twenty-one feet below the Encrinal limestone, at Section 7 (rare); also in the shale above the Pleurodictyum beds, in Avery's Ravine.

PALÆONEILO TENUISTRIATA. Hall. (Fig. 174.) (Pal. N. Y., Vol. V., Pt. I., p. 336, Pls. XLIX., XCIII.)

Distinguishing Characters.—Ovate elliptical outline; doubly-truncate posterior end; slight depression extending

FIG. 174. *Palæoneilo tenuistriata.* A specimen retaining both valves; a right valve (from Hall).

from posterior to the beak, to the post-inferior margin, where it causes a slight constriction in the margin; very fine concentric striæ, often crowded on the posterior portion of the shell.

Found in the lower Moscow shale, at Sections 4 and 5; in the Lower shale, down to and in the shale below the Trilobite beds, at Sections 5 to 8; and in the Strophalosia bed, on the Lake Shore (where it is very rare).

PALÆONEILO FECUNDA. Hall. (Fig. 175.) (Pal. N. Y., Vol. V., Pt. I., p. 336, Pl. XLIX.)

Distinguishing Characters.—Elongate ovate outline; length nearly twice the height; obtusely rounded, or doubly-truncate, posterior margin; fine concentric striæ, which become elevated into sharp lamellæ, alternating in size on the posterior slopes.

FIG. 175. *Palæoneilo fecunda*. Right and left valves of different individuals of the usual form (from Hall).

Found in the lower Moscow shale, at Sections 4 and 5 (rare); and in the Lower shale, down to twenty-one feet below the Encrinal limestone, at Sections 5 to 7.

PALÆONEILO MUTA. Hall. (Fig. 176.) (Pal. N. Y., Vol. V., Pt. I., p. 337, Pl. LXIX.)

Distinguishing Characters.—Like the preceding in outline and proportions, but entire surface marked by strong, regu-

FIG. 176. *Palæoneilo muta*. Two left valves and one right valve of different sizes (from Hall).

lar, lamellose, elevated striæ, with very fine intermediate striæ.

Found in the lowest two feet of the Moscow shale, at Sections 4 and 5; and in the shales down to and in the Strophalosia bed (very rare and at great intervals).

PALÆONEILO EMARGINATA. (Conrad.) (Fig. 177.) (Pal. N. Y., Vol. V., Pt. I., p. 338, Pl. L.)

FIG. 177. *Palæoneilo emarginata*. Two right and two left valves, showing variations (from Hall).

Distinguishing Characters.—Deeply sinuate or emarginate posterior margin; strong umbonal ridge, with depression above it; produced post-cardinal extremity; strong, elevated, distant, lamellose, concentric ridges, with finer striæ between.

Found in the Lower shales, down to twenty-five feet below the Encrinal limestone, at Sections 5 to 7 (common); also in the shale below the Nautilus bed, in Avery's Creek.

GENUS MACRODON. LYCETT.

[ETY.: *Macros*, long; *odous*, tooth.]

(1845: Murch. Geol. Chelt.)

Shells with equal inequilateral valves, which are transversely sub-elliptical, or sub-ovate, in outline. The anterior end is angular at the cardinal line and rounded below. The posterior end is rounded or obliquely sub-truncate. Beaks anterior to the middle; cardinal line long and straight. Ligament external. Cardinal teeth several; lateral teeth two to four, situated near the extremity of the cardinal line. Surface marked by concentric striæ, which are often lamellose, and in some species by fine radiating lines.

MACRODON HAMILTONIÆ. Hall. (Fig. 178.) (Pal. N. Y., Vol. V., Pt. I., p. 349, Pl. LI.)

Distinguishing Characters.—Obtusely sub-angular ends of hinge line; rounded post-inferior end; strong, distant

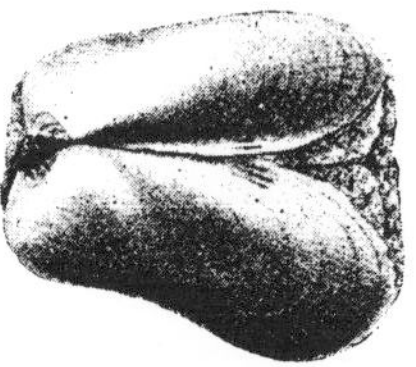

FIG. 178. *Macrodon hamiltoniæ.* A right valve; a specimen retaining both valves, the shell exfoliated (from Hall).

lamellose concentric lines; fine interrupted radii, strongest on the posterior part of the shell.

Found nine to twelve feet below the Encrinal limestone, at Section 7 (very rare).

GENUS GRAMMYSIA. DEVERNEUIL.

[ETY.: *Gramme*, a line of writing; *mys*, a mussel shell.]

(1847: Bull. Soc. Geo. France, 2d Ser., Tome IV., p. 696.)

Shell with equal inequilateral valves, which are transversely elliptical or sub-ovate. The beaks are prominent and incurved, and in front of them is a strong, heart-shaped depression, or "lunule," while behind them a similar, but somewhat elongate, impression, or "escutcheon," occurs. Usually an oblique cincture and fold traverse the shell from beak to base. The surface is marked by concentric striæ and frequently by concentric undulations. Ligament external.

GRAMMYSIA ARCUATA. (Conrad.) (Fig. 179.) (Pal. N. Y., Vol. V., Pt. I., p. 373, Pls. LXI., LXIII., XCIII.)

Distinguishing Characters.—Sub-anterior beaks; uniformly rounded anterior and posterior ends; strong, uniform concentric undulations, which pass around the shell from lunule

FIG. 179. *Grammysia arcuata.* Left and right valves (from Hall).

to escutcheon; fine, close, concentric striæ; cincture a mere flattening.

Found nine to twelve feet below the Encrinal limestone, at Section 7 (a fragment, the identification of which is questionable).

NOTE.—Although the genus Grammysia is well represented in the Hamilton group in central and eastern New York, it appears to be almost unrepresented in this portion of the State.

GENUS SPHENOTUS. HALL.

[ETY.: *Sphen*, wedge; *ous*, ear.]

(1884: Pal. N. Y., Vol. V., Pt. I., p. xxxiii.)

Shells with equal, very inequilateral, valves, elongate subtrapezoidal or cylindrical in outline. The anterior end is short, and the posterior end usually obliquely truncate. A long, straight hinge line; a well-marked umbonal ridge, with a secondary ridge usually occurring on the slope above it; a more or less defined oblique cincture; two short cardinal, and two slender lateral, teeth; external ligament, lodged in a slender groove, and concentric surface striæ, characterize this genus.

SPHENOTUS TRUNCATUS. (Conrad.) (Fig. 180.) (Pal. N. Y., Vol. V., Pt. I., p. 394, Pl. LXV.)

Distinguishing Characters.—Small size; straight base, slightly constricted anterior to the middle; angular umbonal

FIG. 180. *Sphenotus truncatus.* Specimen retaining both valves, x 2; left and right valves (from Hall).

ridge; obscure umbonal fold; shallow cincture; very fine radiating striæ.

Found in the Demissa bed, at Section 5 (very rare).

GENUS CONOCARDIUM. BRONN.

[ETY.: *Konos*, cone; *kardia*, heart.]

(1835: Lethæa Geognostica, Vol. I., p. 92.)

Shells with equal inequilateral valves of a trigonal or spindle-shaped outline. The anterior* end is obliquely truncated, and along the cardinal line it is produced into a tube, which is often broken away, leaving an opening. The

* I follow Zittel in regarding the truncated end as the anterior one.

posterior end is conical and gaping behind. A crenulated ventral margin; a straight cardinal line; prominent and strongly-incurved beaks; prominent umbonal ridge, ornamented with an expansion of the test in continuation of the truncated anterior end; external ligament; concentric striæ and strong radii,—are characteristic features of this genus.

CONOCARDIUM NORMALE. Hall. (Fig. 181.) (Pal. N. Y., Vol. VII., p. 411, Pl. LXVIII.)

FIG. 181. *Conocardium normale.* The left side of a large specimen (from Hall).

Distinguishing Characters.—Large size; trigonal outline; tapering posterior end; short, distant radii, with fine striæ in the interspaces; concentric, undulating striæ.

Found in the Encrinal limestone, at Section 5 (a fragment).

CONOCARDIUM EBORACEUM. Hall. (Fig. 182.) (Pal. N. Y., Vol. VII., p. 412, Pl. LXVIII.)

Distinguishing Characters.—Small size, sub-ovate outline; gently curving basal margin; slightly concave truncated

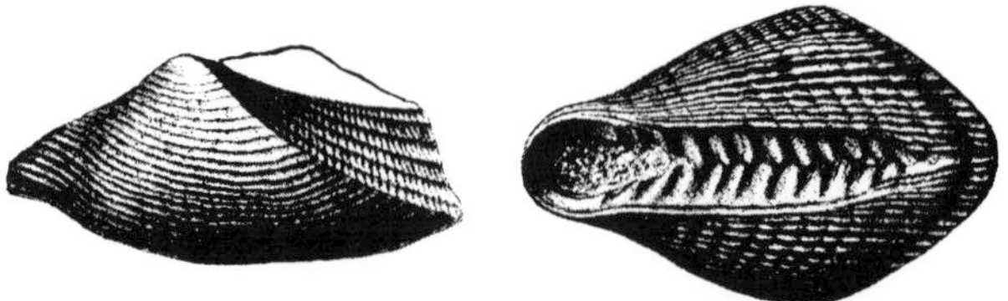

FIG. 182. *Conocardium eboraceum.* Right and ventral views of a small specimen enlarged, x 2 (from Hall).

end; abruptly-contracted and nasute tapering end; concentric lamellose striæ, and radiating plications, obscure on the perfect test; radii continued beyond the concentric laminæ at the margin as strong interlocking denticulations.

Found in the Encrinal limestone, at Section 5 (several fragments, probably of this species, though the characters are very much obliterated).

CONOCARDIUM CRASSIFRONS. (Conrad.) (Fig. 182A.) (*Pleurorhynchus crassifrons*. Conrad: Journ. Acad. Nat. Sci. Phil., Vol. VIII., Pt. I., p. 252, Pl. XIII., 1839.)

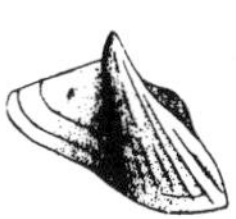

Distinguishing Characters.—Small size; short valves; broad truncated anterior end; narrow posterior (winged) end; elevated distant beaks; five or six convex radiating lines on each valve.

FIG. 182A. *Conocardium crassifrons.* Lateral and anterior views of a complete shell (after Conrad).

Found in the Hamilton group of Eighteen Mile Creek. (Am. Mus. Nat. Hist. New York.)

GENUS LUNULICARDIUM. MUNSTER.

[ETY.: *Lunula*, a little moon; *cardium*, a genus.]

(1840: Beiträge zur Petrefactenkunde, 3tes Heft., s. 69.)

Shells with equal inequilateral valves, transversely sub-elliptical, sub-circular, or trigonal in outline. From the terminal beaks a sharp angular ridge runs downward, delimiting a flattened, heart-shaped anterior area or lunule, which has a central byssal opening. Surface marked by concentric striæ, and often by strong radii.

LUNULICARDIUM FRAGILE. Hall. (Fig. 183.) (Pal. N. Y., Vol. V., Pt. I., p. 434, Pl. LXXI.)

Distinguishing Characters.—Small size; fragile condition; smooth surface, which shows only fine concentric lines, and rarely very fine radiating lines; lunule with a thin expansion

FIG. 183. *Lunulicardium fragile.* Four specimens, illustrating variations, enlarged x 2 (from Hall).

of the shell, visible only in the most perfectly preserved specimens.

Found in the black Naples (Gardeau) shales of the Lake Shore; in the gray Naples (Cashaqua) shales, at Section 1; in the Genesee shales (especially abundant in the lower black bands of Section 1, etc.); and on the Lake Shore; in the Styliolina layer (rare); in the lower Hamilton shales, between nine and twelve feet below the Encrinal limestone, at Section 7 (one specimen); also in the Transition shales, on the Lake Shore; and in the Marcellus shales, on the Lake Shore (where the species is common).

Fig. 184. *Lunulicardium ornatum.* A right valve, from the Chemung group (from Hall).

LUNULICARDIUM ORNATUM. Hall. (Fig. 184.) (Pal. N. Y., Vol. V., Pt. I., p. 437, Pl. LXXI.)

Distinguishing Characters.—Large size; broadly obovate outline; forty-five to sixty regular flattened radiating plications, with narrow interspaces, and crossed by closely-arranged, undulating, lamellose, concentric striæ.

Found (?) in the lower Genesee shale, at Section 1 (very rare).

LUNULICARDIUM CURTUM. Hall. (Fig. 185.) (Pal. N. Y., Vol. V., Pt. I., p. 437, Pl. LXXI.)

Distinguishing Characters.—Sub-trigonal outline; long truncated end, with a thickening along the margin; twenty-five to thirty narrow rounded, or sub-angular plications, with wider interspaces, crossed by fine lamellose concentric striæ.

Fig. 185. *Lunulicardium curtum.* Right valve, from the Marcellus shale of Alden, Erie Co., N. Y. (from Hall).

Found "in the Marcellus shale, at Alden, Erie County, N. Y., and in the Hamilton shales * * * at * * * Hamburg, N. Y." (Hall.)

GENUS PARACYCLAS. HALL.

[ETY.: *Para*, allied to; *cyclas*, a genus.]

(1843: Geol. Surv. N. Y., Report, 4th Dist., p. 171.)

Shells with equal, nearly equilateral, valves, sub-orbicular or broadly sub-elliptical. The anterior end is regularly rounded, the posterior end rounded or sub-truncate. Small low beaks, short hinge line, concentric striæ, and often concentric ridges, further characterize this genus.

PARACYCLAS LIRATA. (Conrad.) (Fig. 186.) (Pal. N. Y., Vol. V., Pt. I., p. 441, Pls. LXXII., XCV.)

Distinguishing Characters.—Nearly circular outline; medium size; strong concentric ridges.

Found in the hard layer of Marcellus age, ten feet above the base, at the northern end of Athol Springs Cliff (very rare).

FIG. 186. *Paracyclas lirata* (from Hall).

GENUS TELLINOPSIS. HALL.

[ETY.: Resembling a *Tellina.*]

(1880: Preliminary notice Lamellibranchiata, 2, p. 80.)

Shells with equal, nearly equilateral valves, sub-elliptical in outline. The anterior end is rounded and the posterior end sub-truncate or emarginate. Small beaks, gently curving cardinal line, prominent umbonal slopes, small external ligament, concentric striæ, and radiating striæ (sometimes obsolete), are other characteristic features.

TELLINOPSIS SUB-EMARGINATA. (Conrad.) (Fig. 187.) (Pal. N. Y., Vol. V., Pt. I., p. 464, Pl. LXXVI.)

Distinguishing Characters.—Sub-emarginate posterior end; large rounded anterior end; oblique depression extending from the beak to the posterior margin, or below; flattened space, limited on each side by a ridge and extending from the beak to the antero-basal margin; fine concentric and fine radiating striæ.

Fig. 187. *Tellinopsis sub-emarginata.* Two valves, showing variation in size and form (from Hall).

Found in the Strophalosia bed, in Avery's Creek, and the shale just above it (very rare).

Genus PHOLADELLA. Hall.

[Ety.: Diminutive of the modern genus *Pholas.*]

(1870: Preliminary Notice Lamellibranchiata, 2, p. 63.)

Shells with equal inequilateral valves, elongated, varying in outline. Anterior end rounded or obliquely truncate; posterior end truncate. Incurved anterior beaks; straight cardinal line; prominent rounded or sub-angular umbonal slopes; a deep, sharply-defined lunule; a well-marked escutcheon; concentric striæ and undulations, and distinct radii, covering all but the anterior and cardinal slopes,—mark this genus.

Pholadella radiata. (Conrad.) (Fig. 188.) (Pal. N. Y., Vol. V., Pt. I., p. 469, Pls. LXXVIII., XCVI.)

Distinguishing Characters.—Small size; cuneate outline; regularly rounded basal margin; obliquely to vertically

Fig. 188. *Pholadella radiata.* Two right and two left valves (from Hall).

truncate posterior end; anterior end obliquely truncate above, by the deep lunule; cincture extending from beak to base; fine concentric striæ, and strong radii.

Found ten feet below the Encrinal limestone, at Section 7; in the Modiomorpha sub-alata bed, in Idlewood Ravine, and on the Lake Shore.

Genus ORTHONOTA. Conrad.

[Ety.: *Orthos*, straight; *notos*, back.]

(1841: Annual Report Geol. Surv. N. Y., p. 50.)

Shells extremely elongate and inequilateral; anterior end rounded, posterior truncate. Beaks near the anterior end. Cardinal line straight, or sometimes slightly concave, extending nearly the entire length of the shell. Umbonal slopes rounded or angular, and defined by one or more distinct folds, which extend to the post-basal extremity. Surface marked by fine lines of growth, and often by strong undulations, which are least conspicuous on the anterior end. Two or more rounded or angular oblique folds extend from the beaks to the posterior and post-basal margins. Cardinal margin with a long linear fold embracing the ligament, which is apparently internal.

Orthonota (?) parvula. Hall. (Fig. 189.) (Pal. N. Y., Vol. V., Pt. II., p. 482, Pls. LXV., LXXVIII.)

Distinguishing Characters.—Elongate sub-trapezoidal form; straight ventral and dorsal margins; angular umbonal slope; flat or slightly concave post-cardinal slope; fine surface striæ, and absence of undulations.

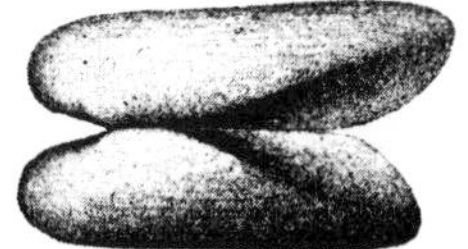

Fig. 189. *Orthonota* (?) *parvula*. Specimen retaining both valves in conjunction, x 2 (from Hall).

Found in the shale between the Nautilus and Strophalosia beds, in Avery's Creek (one specimen).

Genus CARDIOLA. Broderip.

[Ety.: *Kardia*, the heart.]

(1884: Trans. Geol. Soc.)

Shells with equal inequilateral valves, obliquely oval or sub-circular; with large prominent obliquely incurved beaks. Hinge line with a flattened cardinal area, which is widest between the beaks, and extends for its whole length. Surface radially plicated.

Cardiola retrostriata. von Buch. (Fig. 190.) (*Glyptocardia speciosa.* Hall: Pal. N. Y., Vol. V., Pt. I., p. 426, Pls. LXX., LXXX.)

Distinguishing Characters.—Small size, nearly circular outline; oblique truncation from beak to posterior extremity;

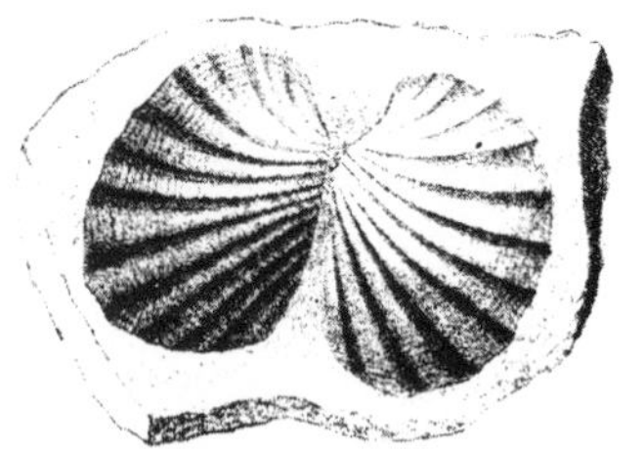

Fig. 190. *Cardiola retrostriata.* From the Genesee slate, enlarged to four diameters (from Hall).

broad, flat, rounded plications, with very narrow interspaces; arching lamellose concentric striæ.

Found in the lower gray Naples shales and Goniatite layer, at Sections 1 to 4 (common); also in the Strophalosia bed, on the Lake Shore (one fragment of a large specimen).

Genus CYPRICARDINIA. Hall.

[Ety.: Resembling the genus *Cypricardia.*]

(1859: Pal. N. Y., Vol. III., text, p. 266.)

Shells with unequal valves, the right valve more convex. Outline varying from obovate to trapezoidal, with a short rounded anterior end and a wider obliquely truncate posterior end. Sub-anterior incurved beaks; straight or arcuate cardinal line, which arises from the beak; external ligament; one long lateral tooth; concentric lamellose undulations and finer striæ, and in some specimens radiating striæ, characterize this genus.

Cypricardinia indenta. (Conrad.) (Fig. 191.) (Pal. N. Y., Vol. V., Pt. I., p. 485, Pl. LXXIX.)

Distinguishing Characters.—Slightly sinuate basal margin; straight cardinal line; distinct cincture on right valve, less

FIG. 191. *Cypricardinia indenta.* Left and right valves, enlarged to three diameters.

distinct on left valve; rounded umbonal slope of right valve, and sub-angular umbonal slope of left valve; strong, unequally distant concentric undulations and finer striæ; radiating striæ, and a second set of striæ vertical to the concentric lamellæ.

Found in the lower two feet of the Moscow shale, at Sections 4 and 5 (one specimen); in the Demissa bed, at Section 5 (abundant); also in the shale and limestone beds between the Trilobite and Strophalosia beds (fairly common).

GENUS ELYMELLA. HALL.

[ETY.: *Elymos,* a case.]

(1885: Pal. N. Y., Vol. V., Pt. I., p. l.)

Shells with equal inequilateral valves, ovate-elliptical in outline. The anterior end is short and rounded, the posterior end narrower and rounded at the extremity. Closely incurved beaks; prominent umbones; a short cardinal line; and concentric lines of growth, which are sometimes lamellose,—mark this genus.

ELYMELLA NUCULOIDES. Hall. (Fig. 192.) (Pal. N. Y., Vol. V., Pt. I., p. 503, Pl. XL.)

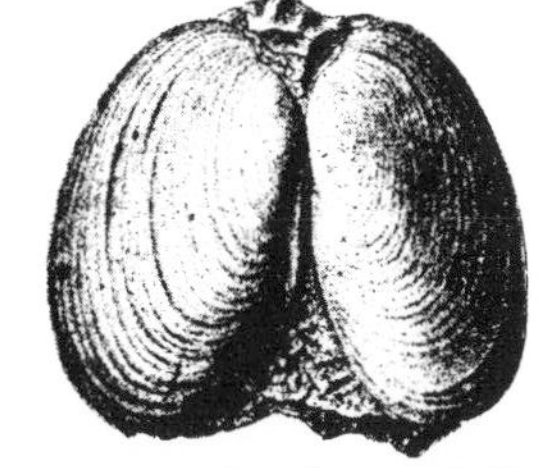

FIG. 192. *Elymella nuculoides.* Specimen, retaining both valves in conjunction, from Hamilton group (from Hall).

Distinguishing Characters.—Small size; obliquely ovate outline; regularly curving margins; hinge line straight, a little less than half the length of the shell; fine concentric striæ, fasciculate on the surface of the shell, giving rise to strong undulations.

Found "in the Hamilton shales, at Hamburg-on-the-Lake, Erie County, N. Y." (Hall, type.)

GENUS MODIELLA. HALL.

[ETY.: *Modus*, a measure; *ellus*, diminutive, dimin. of genus Modiola.]

(1870: Pal. N. Y., Vol. V., Pt. I., p. 54.)

Shells with equal, very inequilateral, valves, obovate in outline. Anterior end short, posterior broad and curved, or obliquely sub-truncate, at the extremity. Anterior beaks and arcuate cardinal line; hinge with elongate groove and fold; linear ligament; fine concentric striæ, and faint, curving, radiating striæ,—are characteristic of this genus.

MODIELLA PYGMÆA. (Conrad.) (Fig. 193.) (Pal. N. Y., Vol. V., Pt. I., p. 514. Pl. LXXVI.)

Distinguishing Characters.—Small size; obliquely obovate outline, resembling Modiola; broadly curved to obliquely truncate posterior margin; auriculate anterior margin, the ear defined by a distinct sulcus; curved radiating striæ.

FIG. 193. *Modiella pygmæa.* Two left valves, enlarged to two diameters (from Hall).

Found twenty-five feet below the Encrinal limestone, in Idlewood Ravine (very rare); also in the Strophalosia bed on the Lake Shore (rare).

CLASS GASTROPODA. CUVIER.

The gastropods, or snails, are molluscs, with a distinct head, a muscular foot, and a mantle consisting of a single lobe. They are terrestrial, marine, or fresh-water animals, and are commonly protected by a conical or spirally-coiled shell, which is secreted by the mantle. The apical portion of the shell usually consists of a simple coiled embryonic shell, or *protoconch.* Succeeding this is the shell proper, which, when coiled, comprises few or many *whorls,* the latter overlapping the earlier ones to a greater or less extent. The *suture* at the junction of the overlapping whorls may be faintly or strongly impressed. The whorls may coil closely, forming a compact central *columella;* or they may be loosely coiled, leaving a hollow columella, opening below in the *umbilicus.* The body-whorl opens in the aperture, the rim or *peristome* of which consists of an *outer*, and an *inner* or *columellar lip*. The peristome is *complete* when both inner and outer lip are present, and *incomplete* when the place of the inner lip is taken by the preceding whorl. In a great many species the peristome is notched anteriorly, or produced into a straight, or more or less flexed, canal. A posterior notch is also frequently found. The columellar lip, and in its absence the columella, may be smooth or furnished with one or more plications. Similarly, the outer lip may be smooth on its inner side or furnished with plications or *liræ*. Among the external features of importance are the transverse *lines of growth*, which mark the successive increments; *varices* or rows of spines, parallel to the lines of growth, and marking periodic resting stages during the growth of the shell; and revolving longitudinal lines or ridges, which may be uniform or alternating, or may show a gradation in size. When the varix is reduced to a single spine, this usually marks the angle between a *shoulder* and the body of the whorl. The shell will thus come to be ornamented by a revolving row of spines set at regular intervals on the shoulder-angle. In place of the spines, simple nodes may occur. When transverse and longitudinal lines cross each other, a reticulated surface ornamentation is produced; and when the shell is covered by an epidermis, or *periostracum*, hair-like spines not infrequently arise from the points of crossing. In Pleurotomaria and related gastropods, a siphonal notch occurs in the outer lip, and its progressive closure from behind leaves a marked revolving band, commonly visible only on the body-whorl.

Many species, especially of marine gastropods, secrete a horny or calcareous *operculum*, which is attached to the foot, and closes the aperture of the shell when the animal is withdrawn. This is seldom preserved in fossils.

NOTE.—The anatomy of gastropods is treated of in the text-books on zoölogy. The various manuals of conchology describe the recent as well as the fossil genera, with especial reference to the shells. For a modern classification, Zittel's text-book (Eastman's translation) should be consulted. The species described beyond are nearly all more fully described and illustrated in Vol. V., Pt. II., Pal. N. Y., to which reference is made in the text.

GENUS PLATYCERAS. CONRAD.

[ETY.: *Platys*, flat; *keras*, horn.]

(1840: Ann. Rep. N. Y., p. 205.)

Shell conical, irregular, with or without the apex inrolled. Aperture expanded, often reflexed; peristome entire, often sinuous. Surface variously striated, sometimes bearing spines.

Platyceras erectum. Hall. (Fig. 194.) (Pal. N. Y., Vol. V., Pt. II., p. 5, Pl. II.)

Distinguishing Characters.—Closely inrolled apex, for one and one-half volutions; rapidly expanding lower portion; outer surface regularly arcuate to the inrolled spire; concentric lamellose striæ, arched abruptly over narrow bands, marking former sinuosities in the peristome.

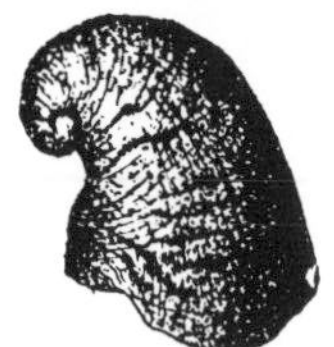

Fig. 194. *Platyceras erectum* (after Hall).

Found in the Demissa beds, at Section 5 (where small individuals, probably of this species, are common).

Platyceras carinatum. Hall. (Fig. 195.) (Pal. N. Y., Vol. V., Pt. II., p. 5, Pl. II.)

Distinguishing Characters.—Oblique, sub-conical or sub-pyramidal form; minute apex, making one or one and one-half volutions; rapid expansion below; strong carination on outside of body-whorl, with commonly a depression on either side; obscure plications; oblique aperture; sinuous peristome; undulating concentric striæ.

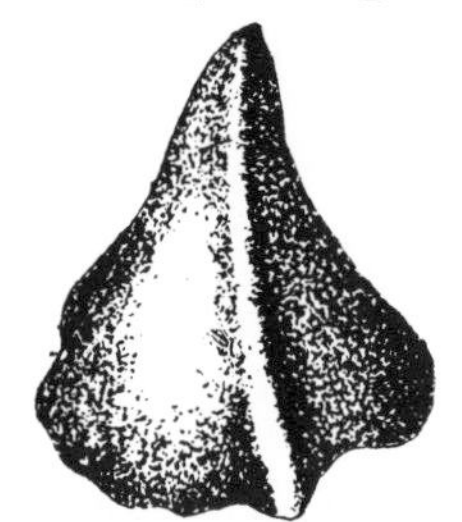

Fig. 195. *Platyceras carinatum* (after Hall).

Found in the Encrinal limestone, and in the Demissa bed, at Section 5 (rather rare); also, rarely, in the middle Trilobite bed.

Platyceras thetis. Hall. (Fig. 196.) (Pal. N. Y., Vol. V., Pt. II., p. 8, Pl. III.)

Distinguishing Characters.—Arcuate outer surface; closely inrolled apex, making one volution; gradually expanding lower portion; nearly round aperture; sinuous peristome; lateral longitudinal folds; closely arranged lamellose concentric striæ.

Fig. 196. *Platyceras thetis* (after Hall).

Found in the Demissa bed, at Section 5; and in the middle Pleurodictyum bed, in Avery's Creek.

Platyceras bucculentum. Hall. (Fig. 197.) (Pal. N. Y., Vol. V., Pt. II., p. 10, Pl. III.)

Distinguishing Characters.—Irregular form; closely inrolled spire, making one or two volutions; rapidly and unequally expanding lower portion; rounded longitudinal folds or semi-plications; faint revolving striæ.

Fig. 197. *Platyceras bucculentum* (after Hall).

Found in the Encrinal limestone, at Section 5 (doubtful).

Platyceras symmetricum. Hall. (Fig. 198.) (Pal. N. Y., Vol. V., Pt. II., p. 9, Pl. III.)

Distinguishing Characters.—Strongly arcuate and incurved form, with one or one and one-half volutions coiled in the same plane, last volution free; equally spreading lower portion; oblique, subquadrate to rhomboidal aperture; sinuate peristome; concentric striæ; and obscure longitudinal ridges.

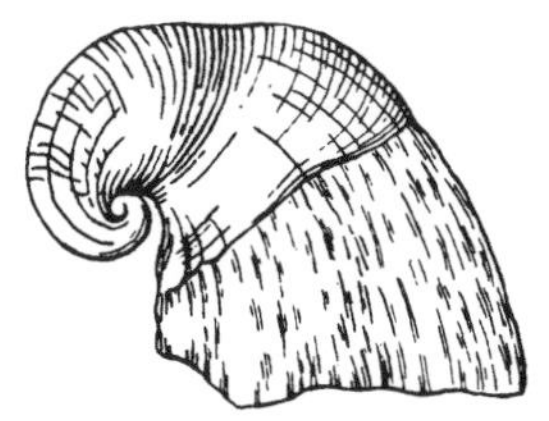

Fig. 198. *Platyceras symmetricum.* A characteristic specimen—the lower part is too strongly differentiated from the upper (from Hall).

Found in the middle Pleurodictyum bed, in Avery's Creek (rare).

Platyceras (Orthonychia) attenuatum. Hall. (Fig. 199.) (Pal. N. Y., Vol. V., Pt. II., p. 6, Pl. III.)

Distinguishing Characters.—Conical form; minute and slightly inrolled apex, making from one to one and one-half volutions; abrupt expansion of body-whorl; very oblique peristome; crowded, undulating concentric striæ; irregular, undefined longitudinal folds; sinuous peristome.

Fig. 199. *Platyceras attenuatum* (after Hall).

Found in the Encrinal limestone, and the Stictopora and Demissa beds, at Section 5; in the Trilobite beds, at Section 8 (rare).

GENUS PLATYOSTOMA. CONRAD.

[ETY.: *Platys*,* broad; *stoma*, mouth.]

(1842: Journ. Acad. Nat. Sci., Vol. VIII., p. 275.)

Shell with a short, depressed spire, a large, dilated aperture, and with the inner lip lying close against the body-whorl.

PLATYOSTOMA LINEATA. Conrad. (Fig. 200.) (Pal. N. Y., Vol. V., Pt. II., p. 21, Pl. X.)

Distinguishing Characters.—Volutions, four or five; large ventricose body-whorl, which is regularly convex, and a little depressed below the suture line; sub-orbicular peristome; thin outer lip, with sharp entire margin; thickened inner lip, folded and reflexed over the umbilicus, which in adult specimens is entirely covered; fine, nearly equidistant, thread-like revolving striæ, cancelled by similar concentric striæ.

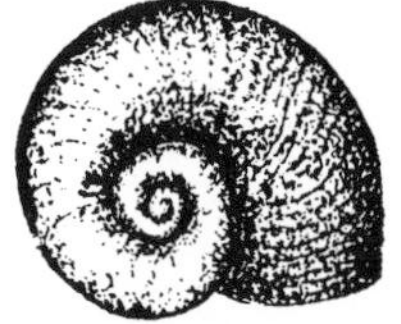

FIG. 200. *Platyostoma lineata.* Side and top views (after Hall).

Found in the lower Moscow shale, at Sections 4 and 5 (rare); in the Encrinal limestone, at Section 5 (common); in the Stictopora and Demissa beds, at Section 5 (common, but small); in the lower Trilobite bed, at Section 8 (rare); between the Trilobite and Strophalosia beds, in Avery's Creek (rather common).

Platyostoma lineata, var. *sinuosa*, Hall, has a deep sinus in the peristome, near the umbilicus.

Found at "Hamburg, on the shore of Lake Erie." (Hall.)

PLATYOSTOMA LINEATA, var. EMARGINATA n. var. (Fig. 200A.) (Compare Pal. N. Y., Vol. V., Pt. II., Pl. X., Fig. 7.)

Distinguishing Characters.—Spire and volutions similar to *P. lineata;* body-whorl less ventricose; the last whorl

* The correct orthography for this name is *Platystoma*, but this name was preoccupied for a shell by Klein, in 1753; for an insect by Meigen, in 1803; and for a fish by Agassiz, in 1829. Paul Fisher, in 1885, proposed the name *Diaphorostoma*, in his "Manuel de Conchyliologie." This has been adopted by some authors.

shows a distinct revolving band formed by the backward bending of the lines of growth near the suture, the lip thus having a deep emargination or sinus, as in Pleurotomaria; the early stages of the shell are typical of the species; surface reticulate by revolving striæ crossed by the lines of growth.

FIG. 200A. *Platyostoma lineata*, var. *emarginata*. Summit view. (Original.)

Found associated with Stictopora and Spirorbis, in the Demissa (?) bed (one specimen).

GENUS LOXONEMA. PHILLIPS.

[ETY.: *Loxos*, oblique ; *nema*, thread.]

(1841 : Pal. Foss. Cornwall, etc., p. 98.)

Shell elongate, with a tall spire composed of many whorls. The aperture is simple, narrow above, ample below. The lines of growth are doubly curved, and there is no umbilicus.

LOXONEMA HAMILTONIÆ. Hall. (Fig. 201.) (Pal. N. Y., Vol. V., Pt. II., p. 45, Pl. XIII.)

Distinguishing Characters.—Large number (about thirteen) of volutions, gradually increasing in size; ventricose body-whorl; ovate aperture, narrowing below; distant curving striæ, which bend gently backward from the suture, and forward from the base of the volution, with the greatest curve in the middle.

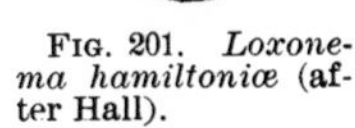

FIG. 201. *Loxonema hamiltoniæ* (after Hall).

Found * * * "at Eighteen Mile Creek" * * * (Hall), in the Strophalosia bed wherever exposed (common).

LOXONEMA DELPHICOLA. Hall. (Fig. 202.) (Pal. N. Y., Vol. V., Pt. II., p. 47, Pls. XIII., XIV.)

Distinguishing Characters.—Smaller number of volutions than preceding (about eight); flattening of whorls; strong striæ, bent slightly back for a short distance

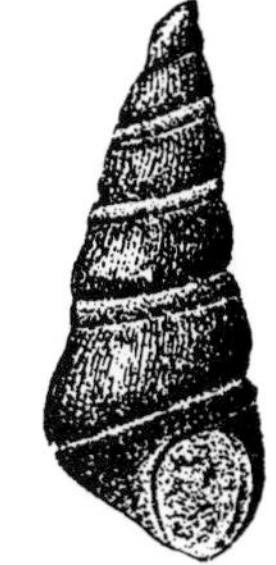

FIG. 202. *Loxonema delphicola* (after Hall).

below the suture, continuing in nearly a direct or slightly curving line almost to the base of the volution, and then bending forward to the suture; suture banded.

Found in the Strophalosia bed, in Avery's Creek.

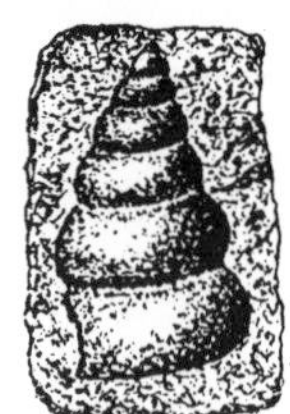

Fig. 203. *Loxonema* (?) *coapta*. An imperfect specimen in limestone, from Eighteen Mile Creek (after Hall).

Loxonema (?) coapta. Hall. (Fig. 203.) (Pal. N. Y., Vol. V., Pt. II., p. 44, Pl. XIII.)

Distinguishing Characters.—About six volutions to a fragment a little over three-fourths inch long; close, very gradually ascending and slightly convex volutions.

Found "in the Crinoidal* limestone of the Hamilton group, at Eighteen Mile Creek, Erie County, N. Y." (Hall, type.)

Loxonema breviculum. Hall. (Fig. 204.) (Pal. N. Y., Vol. V., Pt. II., p. 132, Pl. XXVIII.)

Distinguishing Characters.—Abruptly turriculate spire, with five or six moderately convex volutions; somewhat rapid expansion of spire below the apex; more gradual expansion below, the last volution scarcely more ventricose than the preceding; broadly sub-elliptical aperture.

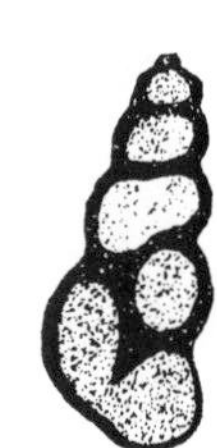

Fig. 204. *Loxonema breviculum*. Longitudinal section (after Hall).

Found "in calcareous concretions in the shales of the Hamilton group, at Hamburg, on the Shore of Lake Erie." (Hall, type.)

Genus ECCYLIOMPHALUS. Portloch.

[Ety.: *Eccyliomphalus*, unrolled umbilicus.]

(1843: Geol. Rep. Lond., p. 411.)

Shell consisting of a few tapering, widely-disconnected whorls, the upper surface of which is usually flattened in one plane, and the lower surface of the whorls round.

Eccyliomphalus laxus. (Hall.) (Fig. 205.) (Pal. N. Y., Vol. V., Pt. II., p. 60, Pl. XVI.)

* Encrinal.

Distinguishing Characters.—Four volutions, the inner ones rising moderately above the plane of the outer ones; gradually and regularly expanding whorls, with circular cross-section; crowded concentric striæ.

FIG. 205. *Eccyliomphalus laxus* (after Hall).

Found in the Encrinal limestone, at Section 5 (rare); in the Transition beds and the Upper Marcellus beds, on the Lake Shore (rare).

GENUS STRAPAROLLUS. MONTFORT.

[ETY.: *Strabos*, turned about.]

(1810: Conch. Syst., Vol. II., p. 174.)

Shell discoid, depressed conical, smooth or transversely striated. The whorls are rounded and closely joined. The umbilicus is very wide, exposing all the whorls. The thin, complete peristome is indented by the preceding whorl.

STRAPAROLLUS RUDIS. Hall. (Fig. 206.) (Pal. N. Y., Vol. V., Pt. II., p. 58, Pl. XVI.)

Distinguishing Characters.—About four volutions, rounded above and slightly flattened below; inner volutions rising above the plane of the outer one; fine surface striæ, often irregular and in fascicles.

Found in the Encrinal limestone, at Section 5 (very rare).

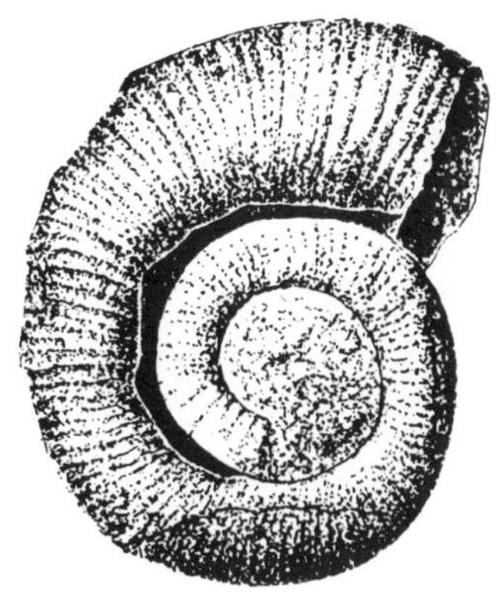

FIG. 206. *Straparollus rudis* (after Hall).

GENUS PLEUROTOMARIA. DE FRANCE.

[ETY.: *Pleura*, side; *tome*, cut or notch.]

(1824: Tableau d. corps Organises Fossiles, p. 114, and Dict. Sci. Nat., T. XLI., p. 381.)

Shell trochus shaped, more or less conical, with or without umbilicus. Volutions angular, flattened, or rounded, their surfaces variously ornamented. Aperture sub-quadrate to sub-orbicular, the inner lip thin. The outer lip bears a narrow, deep fissure, or sinus, which is the still unclosed continuation of a revolving band.

PLEUROTOMARIA LUCINA. Hall. (Fig. 207.) (Pal. N. Y., Vol. V., Pt. II., p. 67, Pl. XVIII.)

Distinguishing Characters.—Large size; sub-globose, or obliquely ovoid conical form; moderately elevated spire, with minute apex, and about four volutions; regularly and rapidly expanding body-whorl; expanded, nearly round, apertures, with shallow notch; neatly defined, slightly canaliculate suture; moderately wide revolving band, limited by revolving ridges on either side; revolving striæ, cancellated by concentric striæ of similar strength.

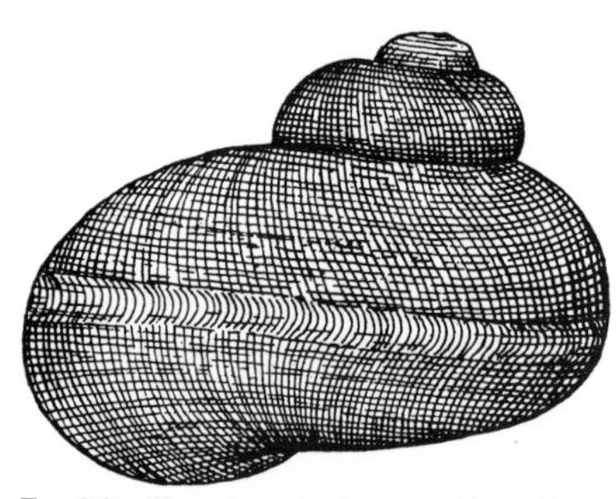

FIG. 207. *Pleurotomaria lucina.* View of a perfect specimen from the Onondaga limestone of Clarence Hollow; the specimens fr m the Hamilton group are commonly much distorted (after Hall).

Found in the Encrinal limestone, at Section 5 (very rare).

Pleurotomaria lucina, var. *perfasciata*, Hall, is distinguished by its coarser fasciculate striæ on the body-whorl, which give the shell a nodose appearance.

Found in the middle Pleurodictyum bed, in Avery's Ravine (one specimen).

PLEUROTOMARIA ITYS. Hall. (Fig. 208.) (Pal. N. Y., Vol. V., Pt. II., p. 76, Pl. XX.)

FIG. 208. *Pleurotomaria itys* (after Hall).

Distinguishing Characters. — Turbinate form, with ascending spire, higher than wide; four or five volutions, gradually expanding to the ventricose body-whorl; broadly oval aperture, somewhat higher than wide; strong revolving striæ, crossed and cancellated by fine concentric striæ; band limited by linear carina on either side, the concentric striæ making an abrupt retral curve within.

Found in the Pleurodictyum beds, chiefly as casts.

Pleurotomaria itys, var. *tenuispira,* Hall, differs in the greater number of volutions (seven or more); greater rotundity of the last two volutions; strong revolving striæ, coarser crenulations, and absence of revolving carina limiting the "band."

Found "in the shales of the Hamilton group, at Hamburg, shore of Lake Erie." (Hall, type.)

PLEUROTOMARIA CAPILLARIA. Conrad. (Fig. 209.) (Pal. N. Y., Vol. V., Pt. II., p. 77, Pl. XX.)

Distinguishing Characters.—Turreted spire, with four or more volutions, rapidly increasing in size; ventricose body-whorl, an angularity on its upper side caused by two or three prominent revolving carinæ; revolving and concentric striæ.

FIG. 209. *Pleurotomaria capillaria* (after Hall).

Found in the Strophalosia bed, on the Lake Shore (rare).

PLEUROTOMARIA PLANIDÓRSALIS. Hall. (Fig. 210.) (Pal. N. Y., Vol. V., Pt. II., p. 82, Pl. XXI.)

Distinguishing Characters.—Depressed trochiform, sub-discoidal spire; sub-angular volutions, rounded below; aperture straight on upper side, somewhat rounded below; strong revolving carina, two-thirds distant from suture to peripheral band; similar carina on the lower side; simple band; strong concentric striæ.

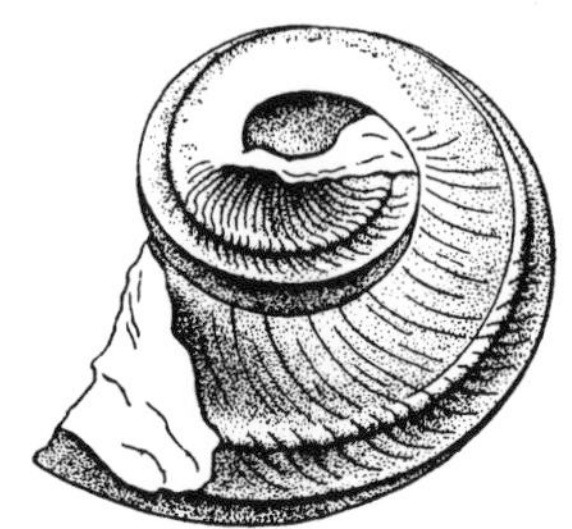

FIG. 210. *Pleurotomaria planidorsalis.* An obliquely compressed specimen, with spiral band nearly obliterated (after Hall).

Found "in the Calcareous shales of the Hamilton group, at Hamburg, on the Shore of Lake Erie." (Hall.)

PLEUROTOMARIA RUGULATA. Hall. (Fig. 210A.) (Pal. N. Y., Vol. V., Pt. II., p. 75, Pl. XX.)

Distinguishing Characters.—Low spire, rapidly expanding volutions, the body-whorl forming almost the entire bulk of the shell; broadly banded periphery; very convex lower side, abruptly compressed to the umbilical area; fine surface striæ. Usually occurs as internal molds.

FIG. 210A. *Pleurotomaria rugulata* (after Hall).

Found in the Hamilton group of Eighteen Mile Creek. (Coll. Am. Mus. Nat. Hist. New York.)

GENUS BELLEROPHON. MONTFORT.

[ETY.: Mythological name.]

(1808: Conch. Syst., Vol. I., p. 50.)

Shell symmetrically coiled in a single plane, with a flaring mouth, which bears a notch or sinus in the center of the outer lip. This notch is continued backwards in a revolving band, of varying strength, while the concentric growth-lines make a sharp reëntrant. The inner lip is thickened and expanded on the inrolled spire.

BELLEROPHON PATULUS. Hall. (Fig. 211.) (Pal. N. Y., Vol. V., Pt. II., p. 100, Pls. XXII., XXIV.)

Distinguishing Characters.—Sub-globose, ventricose form; small umbilicus, closed before reaching center; abruptly and widely dilated aperture, semi-circular in outline; flattened, broadly sinuate lip; reflexed inner lip, which extends over and partly covers the preceding volutions, forming a thickened pustulose "callus"; concentric striæ; strong concentric costæ on the inrolled portion of the shell.

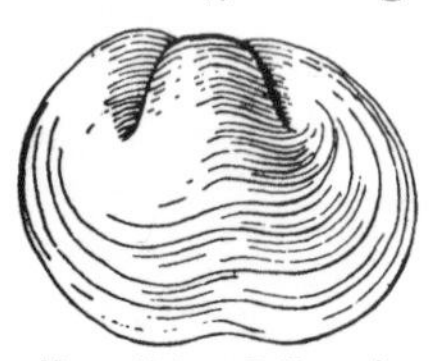

FIG. 211. *Bellerophon patulus.* Dorsal view, reduced (after Hall).

Found "* * * in the soft Calcareous shales, on the Shore of Lake Erie, at Eighteen Mile Creek." (Hall.)

BELLEROPHON LEDA. Hall. (Fig. 212.) (Pal. N. Y., Vol. V., Pt. II., p. 110, Pl. XXIII.)

Distinguishing Characters.—Sub-globose outline, slightly flattened on back; rapidly expanding body-whorl; wide aperture; abruptly spreading peristome, broadly sinuate and notched in front; reflexed inner lip, extending in a callus over the preceding whorl; strong revolving striæ, alternating in size; finer, sub-equal, thread-like, cancellating, concentric striæ; narrow, flattened, or slightly concave revolving band, usually marked by several fine revolving striæ.

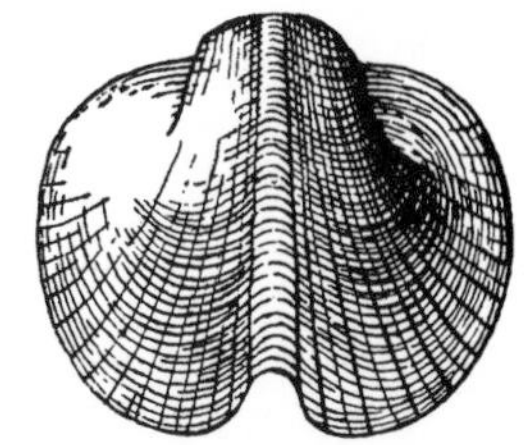

FIG. 212. *Bellerophon leda* (after Hall).

Found in the shales below the Trilobite beds, and in the Pleurodictyum beds (rare); Strophalosia bed, in Avery's Creek, and on the Lake Shore (common, though usually compressed); also in the Transition shales, twenty feet below the Strophalosia bed, in Erie Cliff (rare).

CLASS PTEROPODA. CUVIER.

The pteropods, or sea butterflies, are pelagic animals, often found in vast numbers swimming near the surface of the water after dark. Though frequently naked, a large number bear more or less transparent shells, which are very variable in outline. The shells are often found in vast quantities on the ocean floor, constituting "pteropod oozes."

The head of the pteropod is indistinctly defined, the eyes are rudimentary, and the foot is represented by two lateral fin-like or wing-like appendages, near the head; the body is straight or variously inrolled. Fig. 213 shows a modern pteropod with shell.

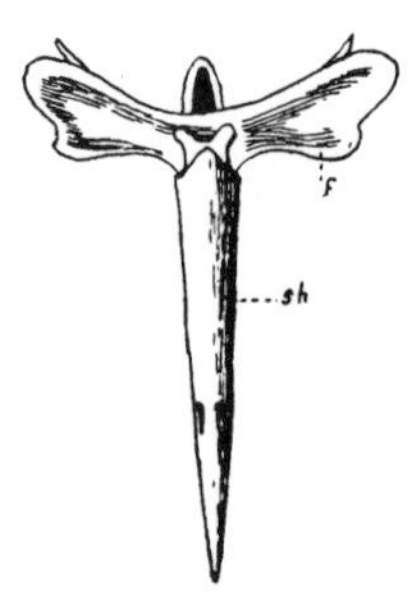

FIG. 213. *Styliola recta*. Lesueur. Recent (after Adams, from Zittel). This is a modern form, closely related to the most abundant fossil species of our rocks, i.e., *Styliolina fissurella*. Hall. (*sh*) Shell; (*f*) modified foot.

Genus STYLIOLINA. Karpinsky.

[Ety.: Diminutive of the recent genus Styliola.]

(1884: Die fossilen Pteropoden am Ostabhange des Urals. Mem. de l'Acad. St. Petersburg, 7th Ser., T. XXXII., No. 1.)

Shells small, needle-shaped, with a circular transverse section. The apex is solid and usually bulbiform, and the surface is smooth, with only fine lines of growth.

Styliolina fissurella. (Hall.) (Fig. 214.) (Pal. N. Y., Vol. V., Pt. II., p. 178, Pl. XXXI.)

Fig. 214. *Styliolina fissurella.* A fragment of slate with numerous individuals, x 3, and a specimen much enlarged (after Hall).

Distinguishing Characters.—Small size; needle-like form; minute, often bulbiferous, apex; transverse and sometimes longitudinal striæ; sharply depressed central fracture line in all the compressed specimens.

Found everywhere in the rocks of this region; especially abundant in the lower Genesee, where these shells make up the Styliolina limestone; also abundant in the Marcellus shale, on the Lake Shore (not observed in the Encrinal limestone).

Styliolina spica. (Hall.) (Fig. 214A.) (Pal. N. Y., Vol. V., Pt. II.; supplement, Vol. VII., p. 7, Pl. CXIV.)

Fig. 214A. *Styliolina spica*, x 2 (after Hall).

Distinguishing Characters.— Greater size and more robust form than *S. fissurella;* absence of indications of annulations or apical node.

Found in the Hamilton shales, at "Hamburg, Erie County." (Hall.)

Genus TENTACULITES. Schlotheim.

[Ety.: *Tentaculum,* feeler; *lithos,* stone.]

(1820: Schlotheim Petrefactenkunde, p. 337.)

Shells straight, elongate, attenuately conical tubes, their surfaces marked by strong rings or annulations, which are closely arranged near the apex, and more distant and stronger near the mouth. Fine transverse and rarely longitudinal striæ are present.

TENTACULITES BELLULUS. Hall. (Fig. 215.) (Pal. N. Y., Vol. V., Pt. II., p. 169, Pls. XXXI., XXXI.A.)

Distinguishing Characters. — Elongate conical form, becoming cylindrical towards the mouth; apex attenuate, with close acute annulations, the extreme portion apparently smooth; annulations acute, interspace rounded, with concentric striæ.

Found in the upper Moscow shales, at Section 2 (?); in the Stictopora and Demissa beds, at Section 5 (rare); five to fourteen feet below the Encrinal limestone, at Section 7.

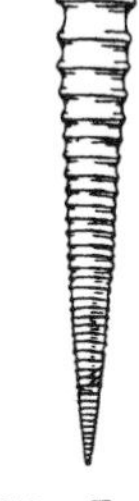

FIG. 215. *Tentaculites bellulus.* Enlarged (after Hall).

TENTACULITES GRACILISTRIATUS. Hall. (Fig. 216.) (Pal. N. Y., Vol. V., Pt. II., p. 173, Pls. XXXI., XXXI.A.)

Distinguishing Characters.—Small size; general resemblance to *S. fissurella;* sub-equidistant annulations, with wider interspaces; smooth apical portion; continuous fine longitudinal striæ, invisible to the unaided eye.

Found in the upper Moscow shale; especially abundant two feet below the Styliolina, at Section 3; rarely in the Demissa bed four feet below Styliolina, at Section 6; in the upper Trilobite beds and associate shales (rare); in the Transition and upper Marcellus beds, on the Lake Shore (common).

FIG. 216. *Tentaculites gracilistriatus.* Much enlarged (after Hall).

GENUS COLEOLUS. HALL.

[ETY.: *Koleos*, sheath.]

(1879: Pal. N. Y., Vol. V., Pt. II., p. 184.)

"Shell tubiform, extremely elongate conical, straight or slightly curved, comparatively thick; inner walls smooth.

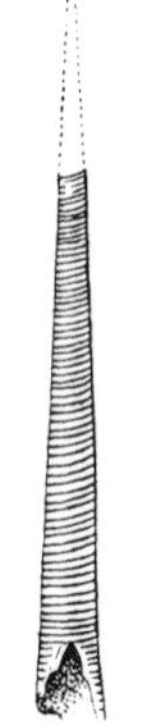
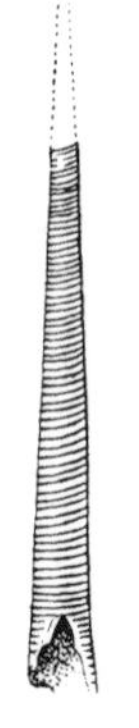

FIG. 217. *Coleolus tenuicinctum* (after Hall).

Surface marked by annulating striæ or rings, which are more or less oblique, or sometimes rectangular to the axis; sometimes longitudinally striated."

COLEOLUS TENUICINCTUM. Hall. (Fig. 217.) (Pal. N. Y., Vol. V., Pt. II., p. 185, Pls. XXXII., XXXII.A.)

Distinguishing Characters.—Long, tapering, conical outline, with the diameter of mouth 6 mm. in a specimen 75 mm. long; concentric or oblique striæ, sinuate on one side; interrupted longitudinal striæ.

Found in the Nautilus bed, on the Lake Shore (rare).

FIG. 218. *Coleolus (?) gracilis.* A specimen from the Demissa bed, natural size. (Original.)

COLEOLUS (?) GRACILIS. Hall. (Fig. 218.) (Pal. N. Y., Vol. V., Pt. II., p. 190, Pl. XXXII.A.)

Distinguishing Characters.—"Form extremely attenuate, slightly curving, elongate, cylindro-conical, tubular; shell comparatively thick; surface unknown, but apparently transversely striate."

A specimen agreeing with this description was found in the Demissa bed, at Section 5.

GENUS CONULARIA. MILLER.

[ETY.: *Conulus*, little cone.]

(1821: Sowerby's Mineral Conchology, Vol. III., p. 107.)

Shell elongated pyramidal, with the transverse section varying from quadrangular to octagonal. Angles indented by longitudinal grooves. The surface is variously ornamented by transverse or reticulating striæ. Near the apex the shell is furnished with a transverse septum.

CONULARIA UNDULATA. Conrad. (Fig. 219.) (Pal. N. Y., Vol. V., Pt. II., p. 208, Pls. XXXIII., XXXIV.)

Distinguishing Characters.—Quadrangular basal section; shallow groove in the center of each face; fine transverse surface striæ, slightly deflected at the median groove, and crossing the angles: pustulose or crenulate character of striæ; smooth interstriate spaces, which are about twice as wide as the striæ. In external molds the striæ will be represented by narrow grooves, in which the pustulose or crenulate character appears, separated by wide flat ridges, which represent the wider smooth interstriate spaces.

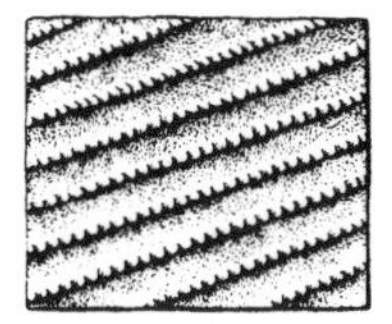

FIG. 219A. Enlargement of part of surface of *Conularia undulata*, showing crenulate character of striæ, x 6 (after Hall).

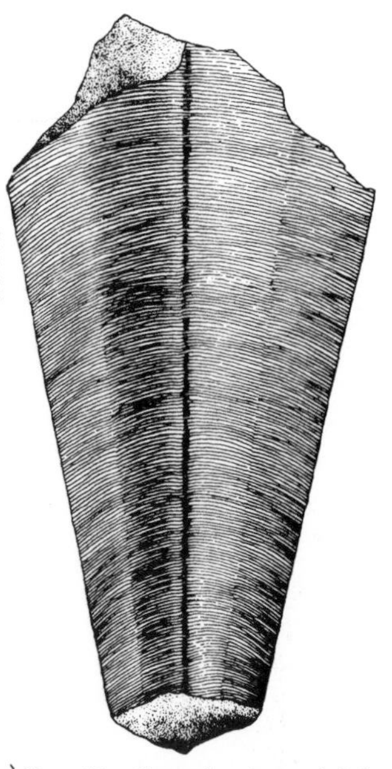

FIG. 219. *Conularia undulata.* Natural size (after Hall).

A fragment of an external mold was found between fourteen and twenty-three feet below the Encrinal limestone, at Section 7.

CLASS CEPHALOPODA. CUVIER.

The cephalopods are the most highly developed molluscs, possessing a distinct, well-defined head, a circle of eight or more arms surrounding the mouth and generally furnished with suckers or hooks, a funnel-like "*hyponome*" or swimming organ, and a highly-developed nervous system. The majority of modern genera are naked, or with only a rudimentary internal shell (squids, cuttle-fish, etc.). Nautilus is the only modern genus with a typical external shell.

The shells of cephalopods are chambered, i. e., divided, by a series of transverse floors or *septa,* into *air chambers.* The last or *living chamber* lodges the animal. The septa are pierced by a corresponding series of holes, which are often prolonged backwards or forwards into *siphonal funnels,* the whole constituting the *siphuncle.* The line of junction between the septum and the shell (the *suture*) is either simple or complex, and is best shown when the shell has been removed, after the chambers have been filled up by foreign material, a condition commonly realized in fossil forms.

In the NAUTILOIDEA, the sutures are, as a rule, simple or but slightly lobed, and the siphuncle is commonly central or excentric, but seldom marginal, with the funnels generally directed backwards. The embryonic shell, or protoconch, is rarely retained.

In the AMMONOIDEA, the sutures are lobate to highly complex, with forward-bending *saddles* and backward-bending *lobes*, both often highly compound, usually with a *ventral* or *siphonal lobe* marking the position of the marginal siphuncle. The siphonal funnels are commonly directed forwards. A globular or egg-shaped embryonic chamber, or protoconch, is generally retained. The position of the hyponome variously influences the form of the aperture and the character of the ornamentation in the Ammonoids as well as in the Nautiloids.

The shells of cephalopods are either straight (more or less conical) or variously curved and coiled to close involution.

NOTE.—The anatomy of modern cephalopods is treated of in text-books of zoölogy. A detailed description of fossil genera will be found in Hyatt's "Genera of Fossil Cephalopods" (Proc. Bost. Soc. Nat. Hist., Vol. XXII., 1883). A detailed classification and synopsis of families is given in Hyatt's article on Cephalopods, in Zittel's "Handbook of Palæontology" (Eastman's translation). All the Ammonoids noted below are described in great detail, and with especial reference to their stages of development, in Clarke's "Naples Fauna" (16th Ann. Rep't N. Y. State Geol., 1898). References to the Palæontology of New York are made in the text.

NAUTILOIDEA.

GENUS ORTHOCERAS. BREYNIUS.

[ETY.: *Orthos*, straight; *keras*, horn.]

(1732: Dissertatio Physica de Polythalamiis.)

Shell a straight conical tube, with a large body chamber and numerous air chambers, separated by convex septa. Sutures simple, at right angles to the long axis of the shell; siphuncle central, sub-central, or excentric, cylindrical or sometimes widening in the chambers. Surface smooth or variously ornamented by transverse or longitudinal striæ, or by annulations.

ORTHOCERAS ERIENSE. Hall. (Fig. 220.) (Pal. N. Y., Vol. V., Pt. II., p. 274, Pl. XL.)

Distinguishing Characters.—Large size; straight, robust form, regularly enlarging to the slightly contracted aperture: circular cross section; apical angle, eight degrees;

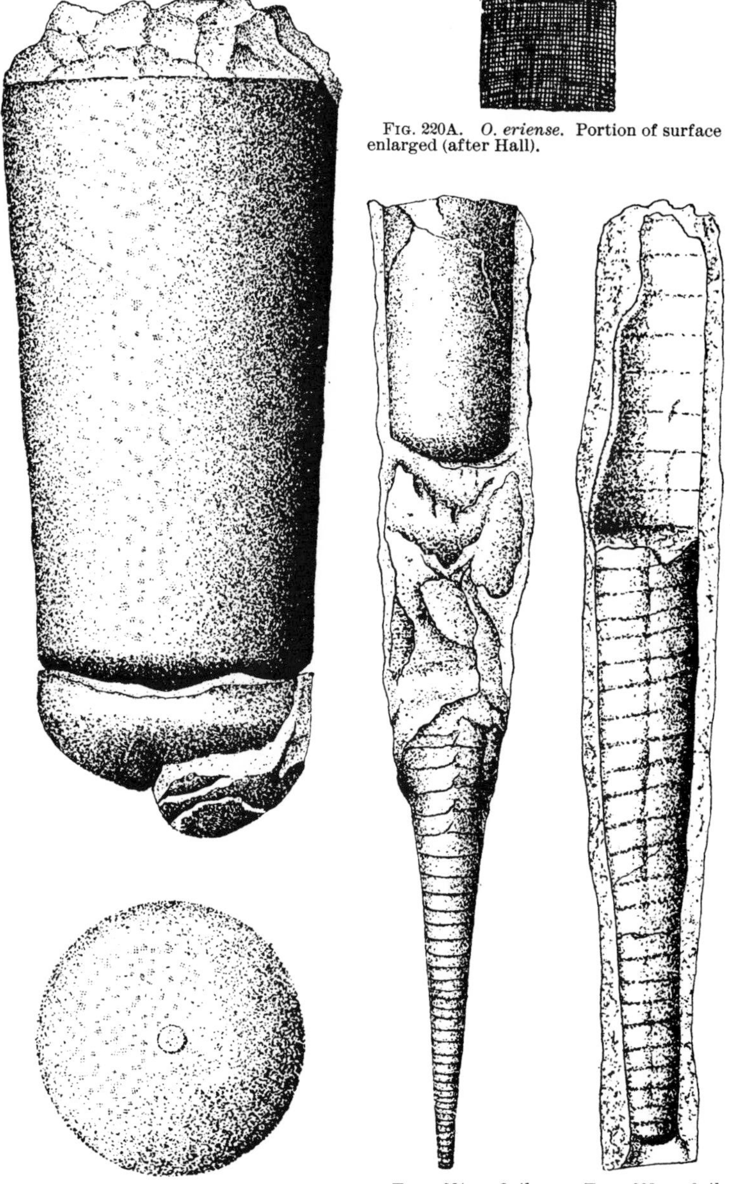

FIG. 220A. *O. eriense.* Portion of surface enlarged (after Hall).

FIG. 220. *Orthoceras eriense*, x ½. The living chamber and septa, and a basal view, showing position of siphuncle (after Hall).

FIG. 221. *Orthoceras subulatum.* A specimen with crushed living chamber (after Hall).

FIG. 222. *Orthoceras exile.* Portion of a specimen (after Hall).

living chamber twice as long as its median diameter: numerous regular air chambers; thin, smooth septa, concavity equal to an arc of 116 degrees; large straight central cylindrical siphuncle; concentric and longitudinal striæ.

Found "in the Hamilton group, on Lake Erie Shore * *." (Hall, type.)

ORTHOCERAS SUBULATUM. Hall. (Fig. 221.) (Pal. N. Y., Vol. V., Pt. II., p. 283, Pls. XXXVIII., LXXXIV., LXXXVI.)

Distinguishing Characters.—Straight, regularly expanding subulate form: circular cross-section; sub-central siphuncle; living chamber three times as long as its basal diameter; thin, smooth septa, with concavity equal to an arc of about 125 degrees.

Found in the upper Moscow shale, two feet from the top, at Section 2 (rare); in the Encrinal limestone, at Section 5 (rare); three feet below the Encrinal limestone, at Section 6 (rare); and in the Strophalosia bed, in Avery's Creek (common).

FIG. 223. *Orthoceras telamon.* The living chamber, with one air chamber attached, and basal view of same, showing position of siphuncle (after Hall).

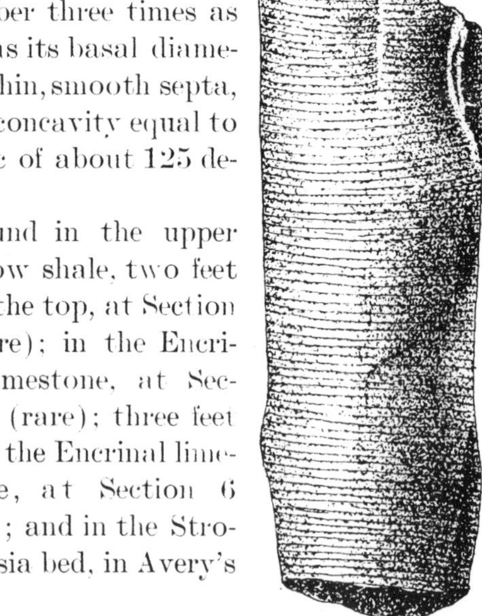

FIG. 224. *Orthoceras aulax.* A fragmentary specimen, from Hamburg-on-the-Lake (after Hall).

ORTHOCERAS EXILE. Hall. (Fig. 222.) (Pal. N. Y., Vol. V., Pt. II., p. 290, Pls. XXXIX., LXXXIV., LXXXV.)

Distinguishing Characters.—Straight, slender, regularly enlarging form, with circular cross-section, and apical angle of five degrees; concavity of septa equal to depth of chamber; living chamber more than three times as long as its basal diameter; siphuncle one-third the diameter of the shell from the margin.

Found in the "Hamilton group, on the south Shore of Lake Erie" (Hall); doubtfully in and above the Modiomorpha bed.

ORTHOCERAS TELAMON. Hall. (Fig. 223.) (Pal. N. Y., Vol. V., Pt. II., p. 291, Pl. LXXXV.)

Distinguishing Characters.—Regularly and gradually enlarging tube; circular cross-section; apical angle four degrees; cylindrical living chamber about three times as long as its basal diameter; depth of air chambers 5 mm., where diameter of shell is 9 mm.; concavity of septa equal to an arc of about 110 degrees; large excentric siphuncle, less than one-third diameter from the margin.

Found in the Encrinal limestone, at Section 5 (rare, and somewhat doubtful).

FIG. 225. *Orthoceras nuntium.* Natural size, and a portion of the surface enlarged (after Hall).

ORTHOCERAS AULAX. Hall. (Fig. 224.) (Pal. N. Y., Vol. V., Pt. II., p. 293, Pl. LXXXIV.)

Distinguishing Characters.—Slender, very gradually enlarging tube; numerous regular, low, rounded, transverse surface ridges, about twelve in the space of 10 mm., with regularly concave interspaces, equal in width to the ridges; fine, sharp longitudinal striæ.

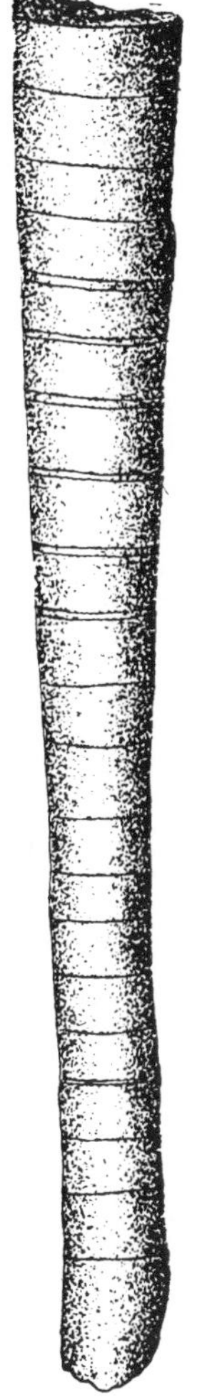

FIG 225A. *Orthoceras emaceratum.* The type species from Lake Erie (after Hall).

Founded upon a compressed fragment "from the shales of the Hamilton group, at Hamburg, Erie County, N. Y." (Hall.)

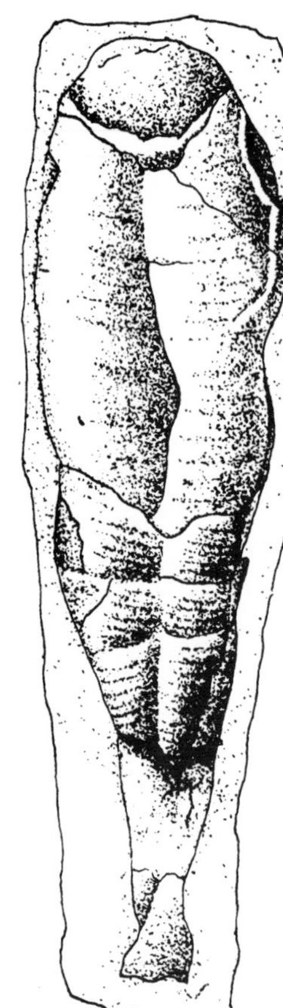

Fig. 225B. *Orthoceras sp.* Eighteen Mile Creek (after Hall).

ORTHOCERAS NUNTIUM. Hall. (Fig. 225.) (Pal. N. Y., Vol. V., Pt. II., p. 299, Pls. XLIII., LXXXII.)

Distinguishing Characters.—Regularly and rapidly enlarging tube; sub-circular transverse section; apical angle about nine degrees; numerous regular air chambers, 2 mm. deep, where diameter is 10 mm.; septal concavity greater than depth of chambers; sub-central siphuncle; numerous regular horizontal annulations; regular longitudinal striæ, and concentric lines of growth.

Found in the Trilobite beds, at Section 8, on the Lake Shore, and in Avery's Creek; also in the shales, two to four feet below the Trilobite beds, in Avery's Creek (very rare).

Fig. 225C. *Orthoceras constrictum.* Living chamber, showing constriction, and several air chambers (after Hall).

ORTHOCERAS EMACERATUM. Hall. (Fig. 225A.) (Pal. N. Y., Vol. V., Pt. II., p. 292, Pl. XXXIX.)

Distinguishing Characters.—Sub-circular transverse section; apical angle four and one-half degrees; regular air chambers, gradually increasing in depth towards the living chamber; straight and horizontal sutures.

Found in the Hamilton shales, on the south Shore of Lake Erie. (Hall.)

ORTHOCERAS SP. (Fig. 225B.) (Pal. N. Y., Vol. V., Pl. LXXXVII.)

A macerated specimen of an undetermined species, from Eighteen Mile Creek, Lake Erie Shore, showing the effect of compression in the soft shales.

The figure is reproduced from Hall.

ORTHOCERAS CONSTRICTUM. Vanuxem. (Fig. 225C.) (Pal. N. Y., Vol. V., Pt. II., p. 288, Pls. LXXXIV., LXXXV.)

Distinguishing Characters.—Straight, regularly enlarging shell, with apical angle six degrees; circular transverse section; living chamber broadly constricted anterior to the middle; numerous regular air chambers with a depth of from 2 to 3 mm.; smooth, thin septa; central siphuncle. Distinguished from *O. exile* by its more closely placed septa, and its central siphuncle.

Found in the Hamilton group of Eighteen Mile Creek. (Coll. Am. Mus. Nat. Hist. New York.)

GENUS GOMPHOCERAS. SOWERBY.

[ETY.: *Gomphos*, club; *keras*, horn.]

(1839: Murch. Sil. Syst., p. 620.)

Shell straight or curved, pear-shaped, greatest diameter in front of the middle; cross-section circular. Mouth contracted, opening by a T-shaped aperture. Siphuncle central or excentric, sub-cylindrical or expanding between the septa (moniliform).

GOMPHOCERAS MANES. Hall. (Fig. 226.) (Pal. N. Y., Vol. V., Pt. II., p. 339, Pl. CXXIII. Supplement.)

Distinguishing Characters.—Large size; fusiform outline; greatest gibbosity at last septum; regularly tapering towards both ends; large aperture, with entire margins; nearly smooth surface.

Found * * "in the dark Carbonaceous beds of the Genesee slate, south of Alden, Erie County, N. Y." (Hall, type.)

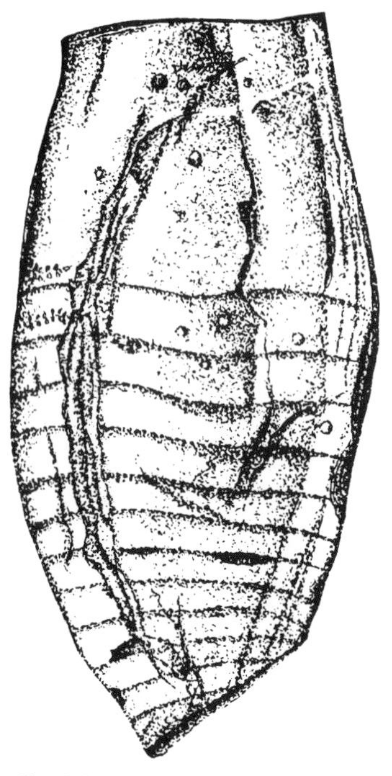

Fig. 226. *Gomphoceras manes*, x ½ (after Hall).

Gomphoceras lunatum. Hall. (Fig. 227.) (Pal. N. Y., Vol. V., Pt. II., p. 341, Pl. XCV.)

Distinguishing Characters.—Large size; regularly arcuate form; broadly oval cross-section, the lateral diameter longest; one side (dorsal) is concave, and the others are convex, the longitudinal section being lunate; large living chamber, with the greatest expansion anterior to the last septum; siphuncle expanded between the septa; lamellose lines of growth, and distinct longitudinal striæ.

Found in the shales of the Hamilton group, at Hamburg, Erie County, N. Y. (Hall.)

Genus NAUTILUS. Breynius.

[Ety.: *Nautilos*, sailor or navigator.]

(1732: Dissert. Polyth., p. 11.)

Shell with numerous volutions, coiled in a single plane, the volutions contiguous, the later ones indented by the preceding ones. The septa are simple, concave upwards, with simple, arched or waved sutures. Siphuncle central or subcentral; lips sinuous; surface smooth or variously ornamented.

Nautilus magister. Hall. (Pl. XXVIII.) (Pal. N. Y., Vol. V., Pt. II., p. 422, Pls. LXII., CVII., CVIII.)

Distinguishing Characters.—Large size; transverse and ventro-dorsal diameter about as eleven to twelve; volutions embracing to one-third the diameter of the inner contiguous

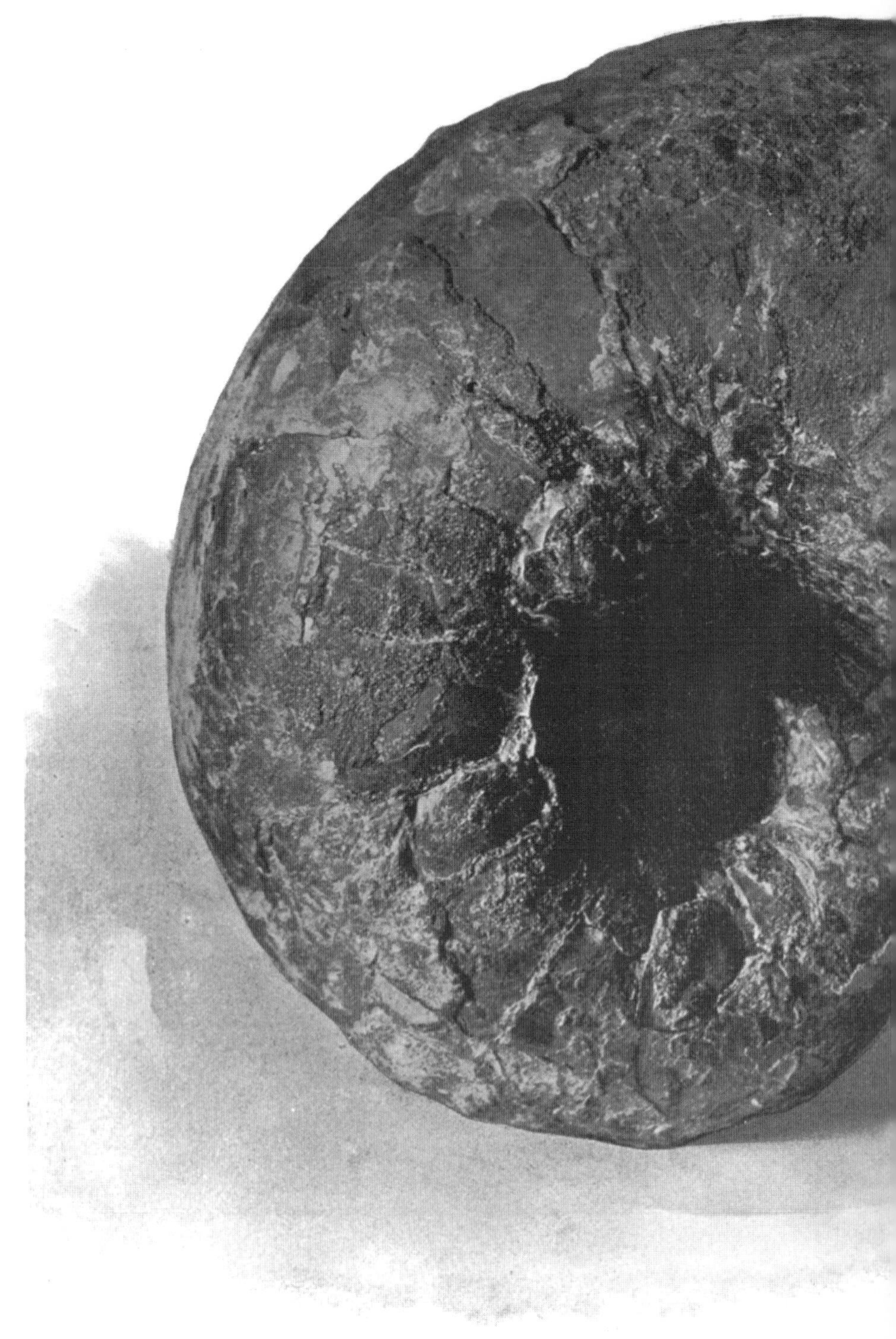

NAUTILUS MAGISTER

HAMBURGH-ON-THE-LAKE, ERIE CO., N. Y.

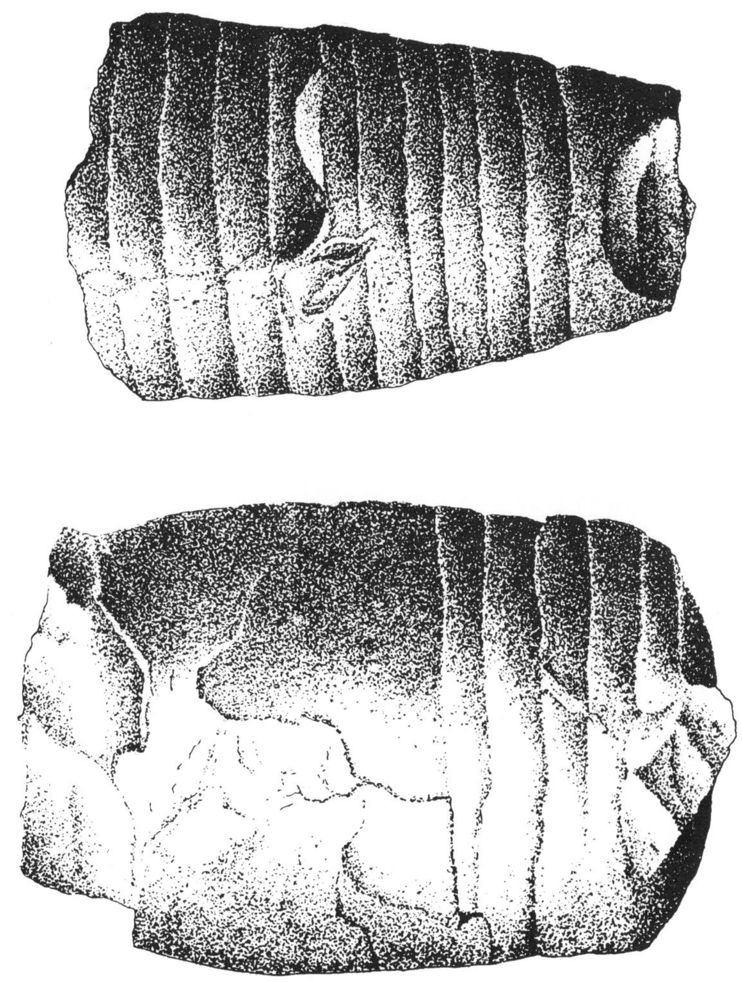

Fig. 227. *Gomphoceras lunatum.* Two portions of a specimen, showing septa and living chamber (after Hall).

volution; narrow and profound umbilicus; large ventricose living chamber; very concave septa; large, abruptly expanding siphuncle; concentric and radiating lines, and obscure low rounded nodes.

Found only in the Nautilus bed, near the base of the Hamilton group, in Avery's Creek, and in Erie Cliff.

NAUTILUS (CENTROCERAS*) MARCELLENSIS. (Vanuxem.) (Fig. 228.) (Pal. N. Y., Vol. V., Pt. II., p. 428, Pls. LXV., CIX.)

Distinguishing Characters.—Discoid, somewhat compressed, form; contiguous, but not embracing, volutions; wide and deep umbilicus, exposing entire lateral faces of the inner volutions; angularity of margins of volutions giving a sub-quadrangular cross-section; septal sutures forming a distinct angular saddle on the umbilical margin, a broad shallow lobe on the lateral face of the volution, a distinct angular saddle on the outer margin, and a rounded lobe on the outer face of the volution; siphuncle near the outer margin of the volutions.

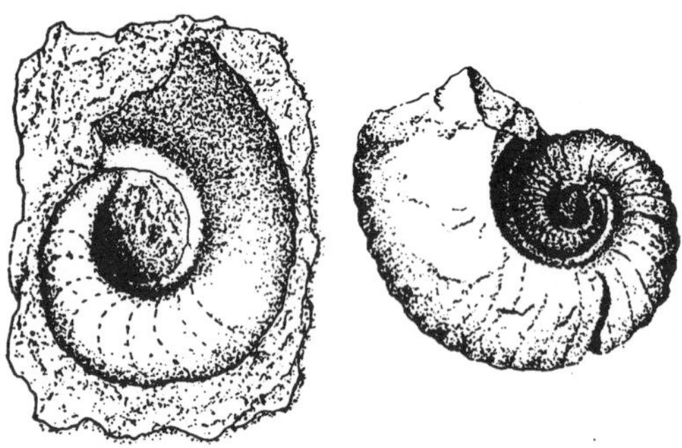

FIG. 228. *Nautilus marcellensis.* A young specimen on stone natural size (original); adult (after Hall) reduced to one-fourth natural size.

Found in the impure limestone band, which forms the dividing line between the upper Marcellus and the Transition shales in Erie Cliff.

NOTE.—This species has heretofore been recorded only from the Goniatite limestone, which forms the dividing line

* Centroceras, Hyatt, "includes Devonian species, with much compressed whorls, abdomen often hollow, sometimes narrow, with one row of tubercles along the edge of the abdomen on either side; the sutures have deep V-shaped ventral lobes, deep lateral and dorsal lobes; no annular lobes in species observed. The dorsum is frequently gibbous, and has an impressed zone only in the more compressed and more involute species." Type, *C. Marcellense.* (Gen. Foss. Ceph., p. 283.)

between the lower and upper Marcellus shales in Central New York. The present specimen measures a little over an inch in greatest diameter.

AMMONOIDEA.

GENUS BACTRITES. SANDBERGER.

[ETY.: *Baktron,* a staff.]

(1841: Leonh. und Bronn's Jahrbuch, p. 240.)

Shell long, straight, slender, gradually tapering, round or elliptical in cross-section. The siphuncle is thin and near the margin. The sutures have very gentle lateral curves and a funnel-shaped siphonal lobe. The protoconch is egg-shaped and erect.

BACTRITES GRACILIOR. Clarke. (Fig. 229.) (1898: Naples Fauna, p. 124, Pl. IX.)

Distinguishing Characters.—Section of uncompressed specimen sub-circular; depth of air chambers decreases *relatively* from the older to the newer parts; septa quite regularly concave, considerably oblique, sloping toward the dorsum; fine, concentric, oblique, closely crowded surface lines on the young, and obscure, broad, and low oblique ribs on the adult shell, all sloping backward to the dorsum; fine vertical sub-equal lines on the body chamber, seen only on well-preserved specimens.

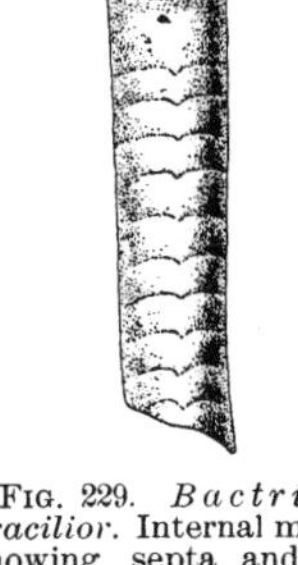

FIG. 229. *Bactrites gracilior.* Internal mold, showing septa and siphonal lobe, enlarged (after Clarke).

For discussion of the development and relations of this species, see Clarke's monograph, referred to.

This species occurs in the black shale of the Styliolina band, at Section 1 (replaced by iron pyrites).

BACTRITES ACICULUM. (Hall.) (Fig. 230.) (*Coleolus aciculum.* Hall. Pal. N. Y., Vol. V., Pt. II., p. 187, Pl. XXXII.A.)

FIG. 230. *Bactrites aciculum.* A crushed and flattened specimen, reduced (after Hall).

Distinguishing Characters.—"Fossil extremely elongate cylindro-conical, having in the larger specimens a diameter at the base (in its flattened condition) of about 7 mm., with a length of more than three inches, becoming extremely slender and attenuate towards the apex."

Found in the Goniatite limestone of the lower Naples shale, usually in a compressed condition, at Sections 1 to 3 (rare); lower Genesee shale, at Section 1 (rare).

The section of this species is more elliptical than in the preceding species, and the protoconch is smaller.

GENUS GONIATITES. DE HAAN.

[ETY.: *Gonia*, an angle; *lithos*, stone.]

(1825: Monographiæ Ammoniteorum et Goniatiteorum, p. 159.)

Shell coiled in a single plane, the whorls embracing, and sometimes closing, the umbilicus; sutures zigzag, with forward-bending *saddles* and backward-bending *lobes*. Living chamber long, never expanded; siphuncle on the outer side of the volutions (venter) marked by siphonal lobes and sometimes saddles in the suture.

GONIATITES (TORNOCERAS*) UNIANGULARIS. Conrad. (Fig. 231.) (Pal. N. Y., Vol. V., Pt. II., p. 444, Pls. LXXI., LXXII., LXXIV. Clarke: Naples Fauna, p. 111, et seq.)

Distinguishing Characters.—Closed umbilicus; sutures with a prominent saddle occupying the inner half of the disc, thence abruptly recurving, and describing a somewhat semi-elliptical curve, which limits the deep lateral lobe; in the ventral curve, upon the peripheral margin,

*Tornoceras (Hyatt) "includes species which * * * have compressed whorls, and annular lobes; the sutures have rounded saddles on the venter, and rounded lateral lobes with the typical magno-sellarian saddles of the family. The first pair of saddles have no corresponding saddles on the dorsum, and the annular lobes are situated immediately between the large dorsal saddles, corresponding to the magnosellarian saddles. The ventral lobes and sutures in the larval stages are similar to the adults of Anarcestes. The stage at which the ventral saddles are in a primitive condition has close resemblance to the older stages of Parodiceras." (Genera of Foss. Cephalopods, p. 320.)

is included a distinct saddle of semi-elliptical form, sometimes with a sub-acute apex; ventral lobe narrowly triangular, penetrating about one-third the depth of the preceding air chamber.

Found in the Pleurodictyum beds of Wanakah Cliff (rare).

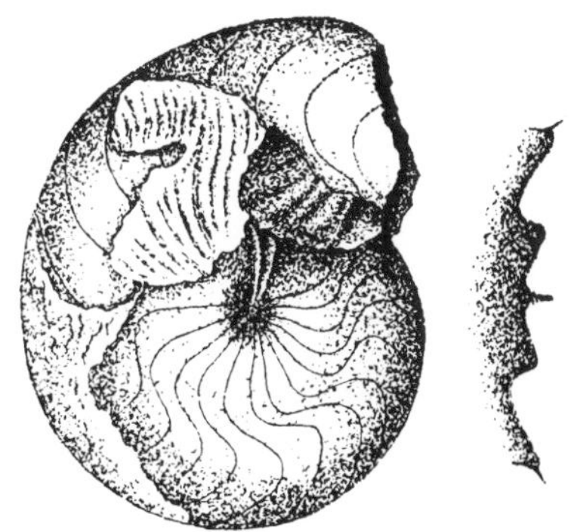

FIG. 231. *Goniatites uniangularis*, and suture (after Hall).

The variety *obesum*, Clarke, characterized by "much greater thickness and tumidity of the whorls," and the variety *compressum*, Clarke, "laterally compressed shells, with a sub-angular periphery," are cited by Clarke from Erie County. (Naples Fauna, p. 116.)

The former occurs on the Lake Shore, and the latter in the Hamilton shales, at Wende Station. (See C. E. Beecher, Am. Journ. Sci., Vol. XL., pp. 71-75, Pl. I., 1890.)

GONIATITES (TORNOCERAS) BICOSTATUS. Hall. (Fig. 232.) (Pal. N. Y., Vol. V., Pt. II., p. 450, Pls. LXXII., LXXIV. Clarke: Naples Fauna, p. 118.)

Distinguishing Characters.—Discoidal form of adult; broadly convex or flat venter; closed umbilicus (only in last volution); "about the ventral periphery runs a pair of low revolving grooves, one on either side, without which are rather low hyponomic ridges"; surface ornamentation of concentric lines, curving broadly backward over the lateral slopes, sharply forward on the hyponomic grooves, and backward, "in a deep linguiform festoon," on the venter; lateral lobe of suture more prominent and more isolated than in preceding

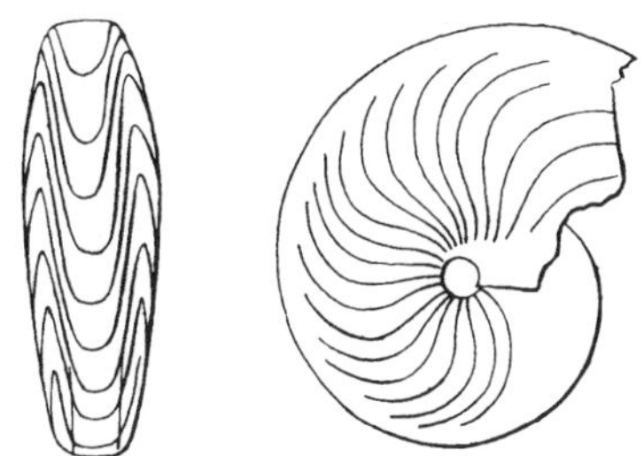

FIG. 232. *Goniatites bicostatus*. Ventral and lateral views of immature individuals, Naples shales, Erie County, N. Y. (after Clarke).

species. (For discussion of the immature stages, see Clarke's Naples Fauna.)

Found in the Naples shales of Big Sister and Farnum creeks; and on the Lake Shore, near Angola. (Clarke.)

GONIATITES (PROBELOCERAS*) LUTHERI. Clarke. (Fig. 233.) (Bull. 16th U. S. Geol. Surv., p. 50, Pl. II. Clarke: Naples Fauna, pp. 90–102.)

Distinguishing Characters.—"Shell widely umbilicated, more so than any species with which it is associated * * *. Septa numerous and closely appressed * *; the sutures are characterized by their acute lobes and saddles; ventral saddle very small, short, and very slightly rounded, the two lateral lobes strong and acute; the lateral saddle very strong and acute, with its sides somewhat rounding; the dorsal saddle well defined and rounded, with a slight, sharp carinal lobe * * *; the septa are so closely crowded together that they are very nearly parallel to each other except at the apices of the lateral saddles, where the distance between them is somewhat greater than elsewhere; surface markings * * * finely incised, equidistant lines, curving gently forward as they near the dorsal surface * *." (For a discussion of the immature stages, etc., see Clarke's Naples Fauna.)

FIG. 233. *Goniatites lutheri.* Showing sutures (after Clarke).

Found in the Goniatite concretions of the lower Naples shale, at Sections 1 to 4.

GONIATITES COMPLANATUS. Hall. (Fig. 234.) (Pal. N. Y., Vol. V., Pt. II., p. 455, Pl. LXX.)

This species was originally described in the Report on the Fourth Geological District, from a compressed specimen from the Naples shales of Cashaqua Creek. (*Clymenia* (?)

---

*Probeloceras, Clarke, 1898, Naples Fauna, p. 90, has the following diagnostic characters, differentiating it from other Goniatites: "Discoidal, laterally compressed, umbilicated shells, with a narrow peripheral band, concave and with raised edges in immature stages, convex in the adult. Suture with a single large and acutely-angled lateral saddle, and two acute lobes; ventral and sub-lateral lobes rounded. Early stages show a gradual derivation of the suture from a manticoceran outline by the sharpening of the principal saddle and sub-lateral lobe."

complanata.) No sutures were shown in the original specimen, which was lost. Subsequently the species was redescribed in Vol. V. of the Palæontology of N. Y., and a number of specimens, which Clarke has since shown to belong to different species, were referred to it. The general characteristics of these specimens were discoidal form, wide umbilication and fine concentric surface striation, features characteristic, according to Clarke, of the exterior of at least three well-defined species in these shales. The specimen from the "Portage Group, Eighteen Mile Creek, Lake Erie Shore, N. Y.," figured on Pl. LXX., Fig. 10, Vol. V., Pal. N. Y., and here reproduced, probably represents a *G. lutheri.*

FIG. 234. *Goniatites complanatus — G. lutheri* (?) — (after Hall).

GONIATITES (MANTICOCERAS*) INTUMESCENS. Beyrich. (Figs. 235, 236.) *G. patersoni.* Hall. (Pal. N. Y., Vol. V., Pt. II., p. 464, Pls. LXXII., LXXIV. Clarke: Naples Fauna, p. 42.)

Distinguishing Characters.—About four volutions, the outer embracing the inner to one-half or more of their dorsoventral diameter; moderately large umbilicus, exposing all the inner volutions; suture forming a narrow acute lobe near the inner margin, then a broad, oblique semi-elliptical saddle, a second narrow, elongate acute lobe, near the outer margin, and a narrow obtuse saddle on the periphery, with one side extremely elongate, and the other very short, forming

* Manticoceras, Hyatt, "includes species with compressed and often very involute whorls, which are, however, directly traceable by the closest gradations into forms with broad whorls, open umbilici, and an aspect similar to that of Anarcestes. The young are invariably less discoidal than in Gephyroceras, the abdomens rounded, and the sides divergent outwardly. * * The adult sutures have the same general aspect as those of Gephyroceras, but the septa in the compressed involute forms become more decidedly convex. The lobes remain rounded until later stages of the growth, the funnel lobes are generally smaller, the larger lateral saddles are also more persistent and retain their forms unchanged even in the extreme old age of the largest specimens." (Genera of Fossil Cephalopods, p. 317.)

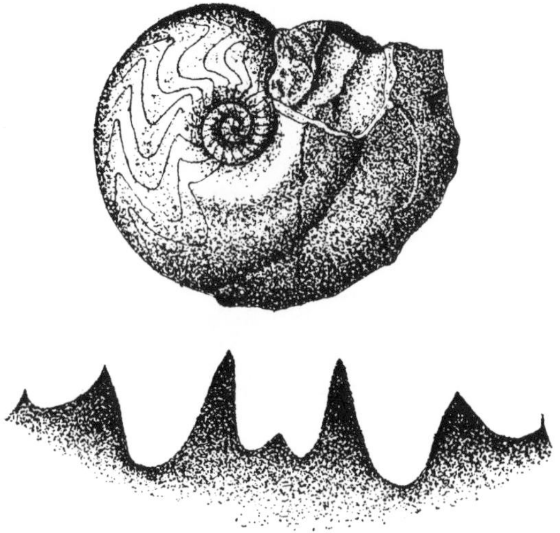

FIG. 235. *Goniatites intumescens* (*patersoni*), and suture enlarged (after Hall).

with its mate from the opposite side a short acute siphonal lobe. (For development and detailed discussion, see Clarke's Naples Fauna.)

Found in the Goniatite concretions of the lower Naples shale. (The identification is not without doubt.)

FIG. 237. *Goniatites* (*Manticoceras*) *rhynchostoma*. Outline of the type specimen from Big Sister Creek, one-third natural size (after Clarke).

GONIATITES (MANTICOCERAS) RHYNCHOSTOMA. Clarke. (Figs. 237, 238.) (Clarke: Naples Fauna, 16th Ann. Rep't N. Y. State Geol., 1898, pp. 65, 69, Pls. IV., V.)

Distinguishing Characters.—Greater size than in preceding species at any corresponding stage in development; lateral slopes more convex, venter sharper at its periphery. Sutures as in *G. intumescens.*

NOTE.—The following figures (236, 238, 240), reproduced from Professor Clarke's monograph, and representing

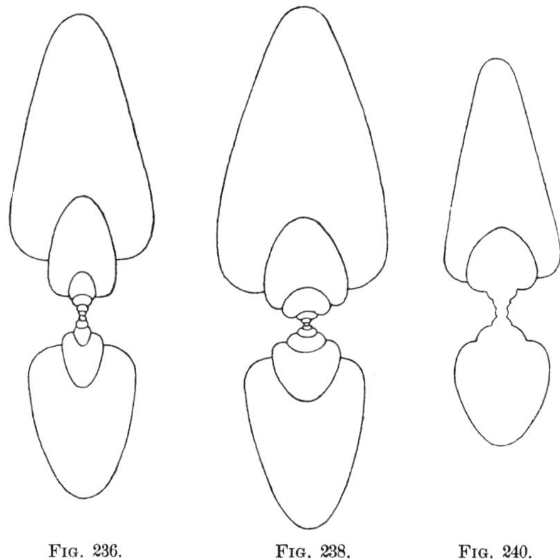

FIGS. 236, 238, 240. Vertical sections through shells of *M. intumescens*, *M. rhynchostoma* and *M. sororium* (after Clarke).

vertical sections through adult shells, will show the characteristic differences in outline between this species and that preceding and that following it.

The remarkable specimen figured by Clarke on Plate V. of his Naples Fauna, and an outline of which is here reproduced, was found with others (depicted on Plate IV.) in the Naples shales of Big Sister Creek, near Angola, N. Y.

GONIATITES (MANTICOCERAS) SORORIUM. Clarke. (Figs. 239, 240.) (Clarke: Naples Fauna, 16th Ann. Rep't N. Y. State Geol., 1898, pp. 75, 76, Pl. IV.)

Distinguishing Characters.—Ornamental lines; these begin in the young shell as strong simple varices, retaining their strength through the third and part of the fourth volution, and becoming obsolescent on the latter part of the fourth volution; on the ventral side they form a deep and narrow backward loop, curving forward on the hyponomic ridges, and backward with a broad curve on the lateral slopes; the difference in whorl-section is shown by a comparison of the cross-sections (Figs. 240, 238, 236); suture and umbilication as in *M. intumescens.*

FIG. 239. *Goniatites sororium.* Young specimen from the Naples shales of Big Sister Creek, Erie Co., N. Y. (after Clarke).

This species * * "has been found only in the vicinity of Angola, on the Lake Erie Shore, and along Big Sister and Farnham creeks, Erie County." (Clarke.) The species occurs in the Naples shales.

FIG. 241. *Goniatites holzapfeli.* Copy of Clarke's figure of the type specimen, from the Naples shales of Eighteen Mile Creek; suture of one side enlarged (after Clarke).

GONIATITES (GEPHYROCERAS*) HOLZAPFELI. Clarke. (Fig. 241.) (Naples Fauna, 16th Ann. Rep't N. Y. State Geol., p. 87, Pl. VII.)

Distinguishing Characters.—Resembles *P. lutheri* in its compressed, discoidal whorls and flattened, grooved periphery; differs from it in being more widely umbilicated, and in having the lateral saddles and sublateral lobes obtuse, a condition characteristic of the younger stages of *P. lutheri.*

* Gephyroceras, Hyatt, " * * includes species with discoidal young whorls, with broad and more or less flattened abdomens in the adolescent stages, and the side divergent as in Manticoceras. * * The adult whorls become compressed and sub-acute in several species, but retain their open umbilici, except in the most involute species. * * The depth of the ventral lobes causes the septa to assume a convex aspect, but the median line remains concave until a late stage of growth. The large lateral saddles when first formed, and until a comparatively late stage in radical species, have no corresponding dorsal saddles; these arise later as two minute saddles in the dorsal lobe, on either side of the annular lobe." (Hyatt: The Genera of Fossil Cephalopods, p. 316.)

A single specimen was found by Dr. D. F. Lincoln, at Section 1, Eighteen Mile Creek. It probably came from the lower Naples shales.

CLASS CRUSTACEA. LAMARCK.

ORDER OSTRACODA. LATR.

The ostracods are small crustacea, with a bivalve calcareous or horny shell covering the entire body. The valves are joined dorsally by a membrane, and open along the ventral side. The body is indistinctly segmented, and bears seven pairs of appendages, two pairs of which represent the trunk limbs. The shell corresponds to the carapace of the higher crustaceans. These organisms are minute and will ordinarily be overlooked, unless search is made for them, with a lens, on the surfaces of the shale laminæ. They are especially abundant in the finer-grained shales.

NOTE.—The anatomy of modern Ostracoda should be studied with the aid of the current text-books of zoölogy or anatomy.

GENUS PRIMITIA. JONES AND HALL.

[ETY.: *Primitia*, first of the kind.]

(1865: Ann. and Mag. Nat. Hist., 3d Ser., Vol. XVI., p. 415.)

Carapace minute with the valves equal, convex and oblong; hinge line straight; surface of each valve impressed dorsally, either at or anterior to the middle, by a vertical sulcus of variable size.

PRIMITIA SEMINULUM. Jones. (Fig. 242.) (Ann. and Mag. Nat. Hist., Ser. V., Vol. XVII., p. 413, Pl. XIV.)

Distinguishing Characters.—Convex, almost symmetrically semi-circular outline; dorsal sulcus almost central, extending across one-third the width of the valve, or more; surface clearly and elegantly reticulated.

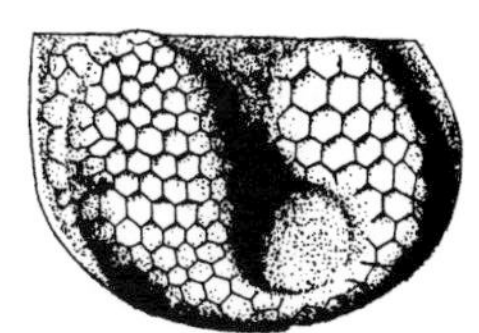

FIG. 242. *Primitia seminulum.* Left valve, broken in the middle, x 25 (after Jones).

Found in the Encrinal limestone, at Eighteen Mile Creek, Lake Erie Shore. (Jones: Quart. Journ. Geol. Soc., Vol. XLVI., p. 5.)

Genus PRIMITIOPSIS. Jones.

[Ety.: Derived from Primitia.]

(1887: Notes on some Silurian Ostracoda, from Gothland, p. 5.)

Carapace bivalved, resembling Primitia externally, except that the anterior end has a specially smooth area corresponding to an internal portion, which is partitioned off from the rest of the cavity by a cross-wall.

Primitiopsis punctulifera. (Hall.) (Fig. 243.) (*Leperditia punctulifera.* Hall: 13th Ann. Rep't N. Y. State Mus. Nat. Hist., p. 92.)

Distinguishing Characters.—Sub-cylindrical outline; sub-equal rounded extremities; surface with three small smooth tubercles, and a reticulated mesh-work, which gives the appearance of minute pits, and dies out at the ends; meshes more distinct around central tubercle.

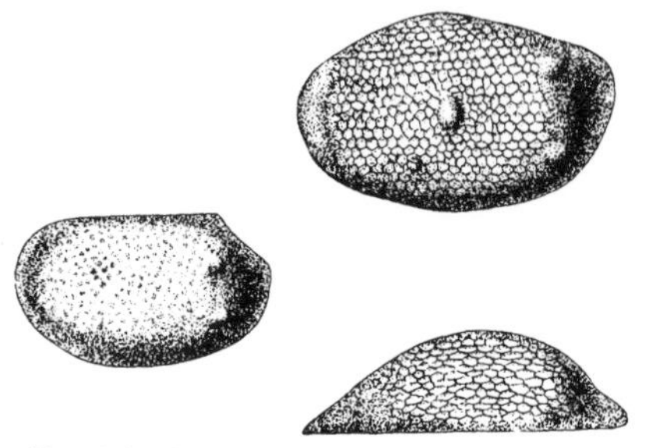

Fig. 243. *Primitiopsis punctulifera.* A young left valve; lateral and edge views of a left valve, x 25 (after Jones).

Found commonly in the Lower shales, at Sections 5 to 8; and on the Lake Shore.

Genus ENTOMIS. Jones.

[Ety.: *Entoma*, cut in two.]

(1873: Ann. and Mag. Nat. Hist., Ser. IV., Vol. XI., p. 413.)

Carapace ovato-oblong, bean shaped, rounded at both ends. Valves equal, indented by a vertical sulcus, which begins at about one-third the length of the valve from the front, and extends about half way across the valve. There is often a spine or tubercle in front of the furrow.

Entomis rhomboidea. Jones. (Fig. 244.) (Quart. Journ. Geol. Soc., Vol. XLVI., p. 10, 1890.)

Distinguishing Characters.—Rhomboidal outline; straight upper and lower margin; obliquely rounded ends; flattish surface; numerous strong, longitudinal, inosculating, raised striæ, or thin wrinkles with a tendency to become concentric.

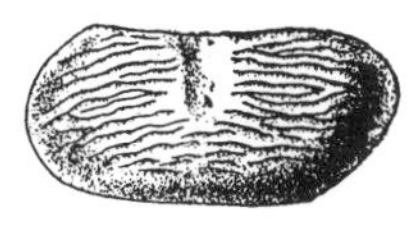

FIG. 244. *Entomis rhomboidea.* Lateral and edge views of a left valve, x 25 (after Jones).

Found at "Eighteen Mile Creek, Lake Erie Shore, N. Y." (Jones.)

GENUS STREPULA. JONES AND HOLL.

[ETY.: Dimin. of *Strepa*, a stirrup, loop-like pattern of ridges.]

(1886: Ann. and Mag. Nat. Hist., Ser. V., Vol. XVII., p. 403.)

Carapace with slightly convex valves, sub-oblong with rounded unequally curved ends. Surface with narrow concentric or irregular ridges running into the slightly thickened dorsal margin. The intervening furrows form broad valleys, and a sub-central tubercle, or even a lobular swelling, is sometimes present. The chief ridge is a free supra-marginal lamina, standing outwards and downwards, and hiding the real marginal edge in a side view. Edge view narrow ovate, cross-barred at the sides into straight and parallel, and oblique and divergent ridges.

STREPULA SIGMOIDALIS. Jones. (Fig. 245.) (1890: Quart. Journ. Geol. Soc., Vol. XLVI., p. 11.)

Distinguishing Characters.—Acute, sub-ovate outline, with straight hinge line; sharp anterior and rounded posterior end; sharp ridge bifurcating forward, the upper branch forming a sigmoid flexure.

FIG. 245. *Strepula sigmoidalis.* Left valve, x 25 (after Jones).

Found in the "Hamilton group, at Eighteen Mile Creek, Lake Erie Shore, N. Y." (Jones.)

STREPULA PLANTARIS. Jones. (Fig. 246.) (Quart. Journ. Geol. Soc., Vol. XLVI., p. 540, Pl. XV.)

FIG. 246. *Strepula plantaris.* Interior and exterior of a left valve, x 25 (after Jones).

Distinguishing Characters.—Somewhat sole-shaped outline; semi-circular in front, obliquely rounded behind; broad hinder end, with thin flat lip-like margin, bearing about ten obscure shallow pits; narrow front end, with six strong outstanding marginal denticles; surface with tortuous branching ridge.

Found in the "Hamilton group, at Eighteen Mile Creek, Lake Erie, N. Y." (Jones.)

GENUS BEYRICHIA. McCOY.

[ETY.: Proper name.]

(1844: Synop. Sil. Foss. Ireland, p. 57.)

Carapace with equal oblong convex valves, their extremities rounded, their ventral border semi-circular, and dorsal border straight. Valves wider posteriorly than anteriorly, and impressed with transverse sulci, with raised lobes between.

BEYRICHIA HAMILTONENSIS. Jones. (Fig. 247.) (1890: Quart. Journ. Geol. Soc., Vol. XLVI., p. 19.)

Distinguishing Characters.—Multi-lobed with middle lobe isolated and oblique; anterior lobe forked by vertical sulcus; posterior lobe similarly, but less deeply, furcate, continuing downward and forward to a swollen portion just at the middle of the ventral region; granulose surface, with some of the granules sharp and prickly at the dorsal region.

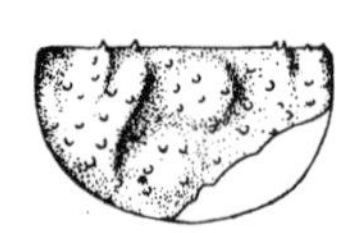

FIG. 247. *Beyrichia hamiltonensis.* A left valve, x 15 (after Jones).

Found in the Hamilton group, Eighteen Mile Creek, Lake Erie Shore. (Jones.)

BEYRICHIA TRICOLLINA. Ulrich. (Fig. 248.) (Journ. Cin. Soc. Nat. Hist., Vol. XIII., p. 189, Pl. XII.)

Distinguishing Characters.—Sub-oblong, semi-ovate, moderately convex valves, with a long straight hinge line, and wide marginal frill; surface with three rounded tubercles, one near the posterio-cardinal angle, another, perhaps twice as large, near the center of the dorsal margin, the third, smaller than either, between and a little beneath them; additional slight swellings in the posterio-ventral fourth; moderate depression between largest and smallest tubercles.

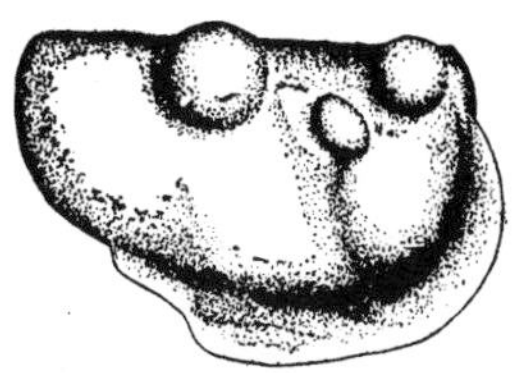

FIG. 248. *Beyrichia tricollina.* A left valve, with the frill broken away at the anterior end, x 20 (after Ulrich).

Found in the "shales of the Hamilton group, in Eighteen Mile Creek, N. Y." (Ulrich, type.)

GENUS ISOCHILINA. JONES.

[ETY.: *Isos*, equal; *cheilos*, lip.]

(1858: Can. Org. Remains, Decade 3, p. 197.)

Carapace with equal valves, whose margins meet uniformly and do not overlap. Greatest convexity central, or towards the anterior end; anterior tubercle present.

ISOCHILINA (?) FABACEA. Jones. (Fig. 249.) (Quart. Journ. Geol. Soc., Vol. XLVI., p. 22, Pl. II.)

Distinguishing Characters.—"Narrow, oblong, bean-shaped, straight above, gently curved below, semi-circular in front, obliquely rounded behind; faintly impressed in the middle of the dorsal region; sloping gently dorsally, and more abruptly on the free margins; surface apparently punctate, but in reality delicately reticulate, all over."

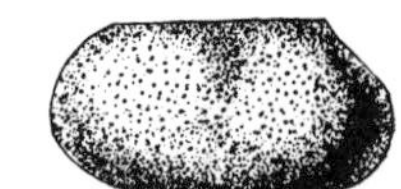

FIG. 249. *Isochilina (?) fabacea.* Left valve, x 25 (after Jones).

Found in the "Hamilton group, Eighteen Mile Creek, Lake Erie Shore, N. Y." (Jones.)

GENUS LEPERDITIA. RONAULT.

[ETY.: *Lepis*, scale; *dittos*, double.]

(1851: Bull. Soc. Geol. France, 2d Ser., T. VIII., p. 377.)

Carapace with unequal valves, the right valve the larger and overlapping the left valve, along the ventral and, to some extent, along the anterior and posterior ends. Valves smooth, oblong, and horny.

LEPERDITIA HUDSONICA. Hall. (Fig. 250.) (Pal. N. Y., Vol. III., 1859, p. 375.)

FIG. 250. *Leperditia hudsonica.* Lateral edge and end views of a right valve, x 25 (after Jones).

Distinguishing Characters.—Symmetrical, very convex (sub-globular) form, almost as thick as high; straight dorsal border, with the anterior cardinal angle more developed than the posterior; well-rounded free margins, with anterior extremity less truly rounded than the posterior.

Found in the Encrinal limestone (?), at "Eighteen Mile Creek, Lake Erie Shore, New York State." (Jones.)

GENUS ÆCHIMINA. JONES AND HOLL.

[ETY.: *Aichme,* a sharp point.]

(Ann. and Mag. Nat. Hist., Ser. IV., Vol. III., p. 217.)

Carapace with thick valves, straight at hinge line, rounded at the ends, and convex at the ventral border. Surface drawn out into a broad-based and sharp-pointed hollow cone, which either involves the whole surface, or rises from the posterio-dorsal or centro-dorsal region.

ÆCHIMINA MARGINATA. Ulrich. (Fig. 251.) (Journ. Cin. Soc. Nat. Hist., Vol. XIII., p. 184, Pl. XVI.)

FIG. 251. *Æchimina marginata.* Left valve, x 20 (after Ulrich).

Distinguishing Characters.—Small size; elongate form; narrowed anteriorly; straight and long dorsal margin, with obtuse angles; nearly semi-circular free margin, with a slightly elevated marginal rim; very long and slender spine.

Found in the "shales of the Hamilton group, in Eighteen Mile Creek, N. Y." (Ulrich.)

Genus CTENOBOLBINA. Ulrich.

[Ety.: *Ktenos*, comb; *bolbos*, bulb.]

(1890: Journ. Cin. Soc. Nat. Hist., Vol. XIII., p. 108.)

Carapace small, elongate, sub-oval, strongly convex. The posterior two-fifths more or less decidedly bulbous, or sub-globular, and separated from the remainder by a deep narrow sulcus, extending in a gentle curve from the dorsal margin more than half the distance across the valves towards the posterio-ventral border. The anterior three-fifths, often with another oblique, but less impressed, sulcus. Valves equal, the dorsal margin straight, hingement simple, the ventral edge thick, and the true contact margins generally with a row of small spines on each side; in a lateral view both are concealed by a "frill" or flattened border, usually mistaken for the true contact edges. Surface generally granulose.

Ctenobolbina minima. Ulrich. (Fig. 252.) (Journ. Cin. Soc. Nat. Hist., Vol. XIII., p. 188, Pl. XV.)

Distinguishing Characters.—Small size; strong oblique sulcus; ventral spine posteriorly; dorsal spine wanting, or represented by a minute tubercle on the posterior side of the sulcus; smooth, moderately convex, surface.

Fig. 252. *Ctenobolbina minima.* A right valve, x 20 (after Ulrich).

Found in the "Hamilton shales, at Eighteen Mile Creek, near Buffalo, N. Y." (Ulrich, type.)

Genus MOOREA. Jones and Kirby.

[Ety.: Proper name.]

(1869: Ann. and Mag. Nat. Hist., Ser. IV., Vol. III., p. 225.)

Carapace with simple, thick, flattened valves, longer on the dorsal than the ventral margin, without any sub-central pit, and ornamented with narrow, rounded ridges, following more or less closely and completely the marginal contour.

Moorea bicornuta. Ulrich. (Fig. 253.) (Journ. Cin. Soc. Nat. Hist., Vol. XIII., p. 191, Pl. XVI.)

Fig. 253. *Moorea bicornuta.* Side, end, and ventral views of a right valve, x 20 (after Ulrich).

Distinguishing Characters.—Sub-oblong, elliptical, rather strongly convex valves; strongly rounded, nearly equal ends; straight hinge line occupying the two central fourths of the length; gently convex ventral edge; two blunt spines near anterior margin; prominent posterior crescentic ridge.

Found in the "Hamilton group, at Eighteen Mile Creek, N. Y." (Ulrich, type.)

Genus BAIRDIA. McCoy.

[Ety.: Proper name.]

(1846: Synop. Carb. Foss. Ireland, p. 164.)

Carapace varying in form from broadly triangular to narrowly elongate sub-triangular; extremities more or less acute; surface smooth, finely punctate or setiferous. Left valve overlapping the right. Interior of marginal borders, except on the dorsal edge, cased with a narrow lamelliform plate, as in Cypris, except frequently for a slight fold or notch at the angles of the hinge line.

Bairdia leguminoides. Ulrich. (Fig. 254.) (Journ. Cin. Soc. Nat. Hist., Vol. XIII., p. 197, Pl. XVII.)

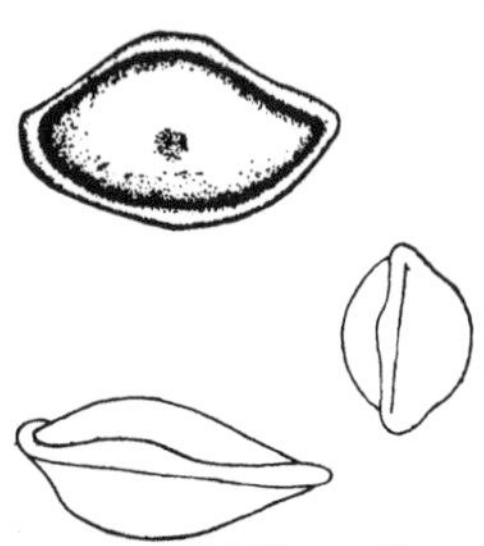

Fig. 254. *Bairdia leguminoides.* Right side, ventral, and anterior views of a perfect carapace, x 20 (after Ulrich).

Distinguishing Characters.— Acuminate sub-equal ends, the posterior a little more blunt; dorsal edge arched in the middle, concave on the sides; regularly curving ventral border; thick overlapping edge of left valve; faintly marked central spot of right valve.

Found in the "shales of the Hamilton group, at Eighteen Mile Creek, N. Y." (Ulrich, type.)

Order Trilobitæ. Burmeister.

The trilobites are extinct crustacea, wholly confined to the Palæozoic sea. The body was covered with a carapace, longitudinally divisible into three parts. The anterior portion comprises the head-shield or *cephalon*, which is usually semi-circular, with a straight posterior border. The central of the three cephalic lobes is the *glabella*, which is the most prominent part of the cephalon. It is of varying outline, and more or less divided by transverse furrows or pairs of furrows. The last furrow is the *occipital furrow*, and delimits the *occipital ring*, which is just anterior to the first segment of the thorax. On either side of the glabella is a pair of *cheeks*, divided by the *facial suture* into *fixed cheeks* (those next to the glabella) and *free cheeks* (the outermost portion). The latter are often prolonged into *genal spines*. The compound eyes are situated on the free cheeks, and they are overshadowed by more or less prominent eyelids or *palpebral lobes*, which are lateral lobes from the fixed cheeks. The facial suture thus passes between the eyes and the palpebral lobes, and when, as is often the case, the free cheeks become separated after the death of the animal, only the palpebral lobes remain on the central portion of the cephalon. The border of the cephalon is often distinctly marked, and is spoken of as the *cephalic limb*. At the margin it is folded down and back, making the *doublure*, which, continued backwards, often produces hollow or solid genal spines. To the anterior lower portion of the doublure is attached the lower lip, or *hypostoma*, which is often found separate.

The *thorax* consists of a varying number of segments or rings, articulated with each other, and commonly permitting enrollment. They consist of a central *annulus* and lateral *pleuræ*.

The tail, or *pygidium*, consists of a single piece, comprising a central *axis* and lateral *lobes*. The axis and the lobes commonly show transverse furrows, corresponding to the divisions of the thorax, and they are often so strongly marked that a line of division between thorax and pygidium is difficult to determine.

Great advances have recently been made in our knowledge of the ventral side of Trilobites. Probably all of them had jointed appendages, which included antennæ, mouth parts, and legs, comparable in a general way to those of modern crustacea.

Note.—For a fuller account, and for a bibliography, the student is referred to Zittel's Text-book of Palæontology. Of special interest are the recent papers by Walcott, Beecher, Matthew, and others, on the appendages and development of Trilobites, published in the American Journal of Science, the American Geologist, and other periodicals.

GENUS HOMALONOTUS. KŒNIG.

[ETY.: *Homalos*, on the same level; *notos*, back.]

(1825: Icones Foss. Sectiles, p. 4.)

Body usually large, depressed above, with abruptly sloping sides. The axial furrows are indistinct or obsolete. Cephalon depressed-convex, wider than long, with rounded genal angles, and somewhat produced anterior margin. Glabella almost rectangular, smooth, or with faint lateral furrows. Small eyes situated behind the middle, and converging facial sutures are characteristic. Thorax of thirteen deeply grooved segments. Pygidium smaller than the cephalon, elongate-triangular, rounded or produced posteriorly. Axis with ten to fourteen annulations; lateral lobes smooth or with posteriorly sloping ribs.

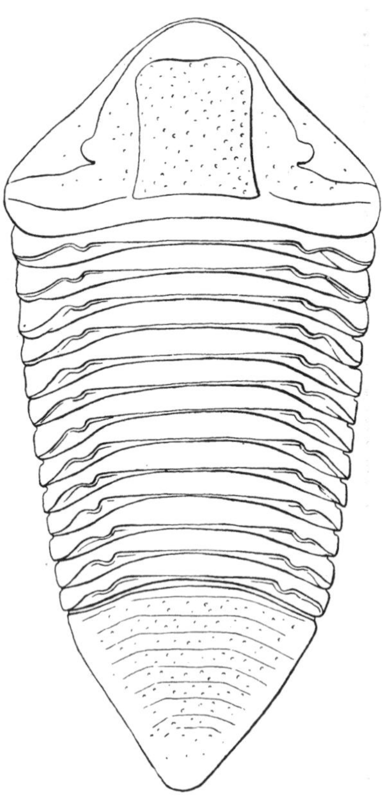

FIG. 255. *Homalonotus dekayi* (after Hall and Clarke—reduced).

HOMALONOTUS DEKAYI. (Green.) (Fig. 255.) (Pal. N. Y., Vol. VII., p. 7, Pls. II., III., IV., V.)

Distinguishing Characters.—Elongate linguiform outline; sub-triangular cephalon, nearly equilateral in perfect specimens; flattened, abruptly deflected movable cheeks; broad thorax, width equal to length; surface scarcely trilobate and axis very broad; pleuræ narrow, deflected along their median line; sub-triangular, faintly trilobate pygidium, the annulations of which become obsolescent at maturity; surface pitted.

Found at "Hamburg and Eighteen Mile Creek, Erie County." (Hall and Clarke.) It occurs in the lowest Trilobite bed, and in the shale below it, down to and in the Pleurodictyum beds of Avery's Ravine. It is a rare form, and no perfect specimens have so far been obtained from this region.

GENUS PHACOPS. EMMRICH.

[ETY.: *Phakos*, lens; *ops*, eye.]

(1839: Emmrich.—De Trilob. Dissert.)

"Body oval. Cephalon parabolic; genal angles obtuse, or produced into minute spines. Glabella tumid, prominent, widest anteriorly; the two anterior pairs of lateral furrows indistinct. Eyes very large, conspicuous, bearing numerous corneal lenses. Thorax sub-quadrate; segments eleven; pleuræ arched, and rounded at their extremities. Pygidium moderately large, composed of few annulations; margin entire and not prolonged into a terminal spine." (Pal. N. Y., Vol. VII., p. xxix.)

PHACOPS RANA. (Green.) (Fig. 256.) (Pal. N. Y., Vol. VII., p. 19, Pls. VII., VIII., VIII.A.)

Distinguishing Characters.—Sub-semi-circular outline of cephalon; sub-pentagonal outline of glabella, the posterior furrow alone distinguishable; prominent, grooved doublure; eyes with forty to fifty lenses; axis of thorax widest about

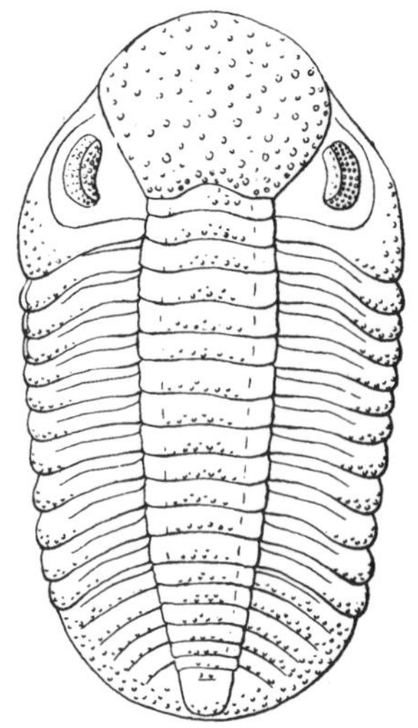

FIG. 256. *Phacops rana.* A perfect specimen (after Hall and Clarke).

one-third the length from the front, tapering towards both ends; flat, furrowed, abruptly deflected pleuræ; regularly and evenly rounded margin of pygidium; pustulose surface.

Found in almost all the beds, from near the top of the Moscow shales to the Marcellus shales (often abundant). Especially common in the Trilobite beds of Section 8, on the Lake Shore and in Avery's Creek.

GENUS DALMANITES. BARRANDE.

SUB-GENUS CRYPHÆUS. GREEN.

[ETY.: *Kryphæus*, hidden.]

(1837: Journ. Acad. Nat. Sci., Vol. VII., p. 217.)

"Genal angles produced into long, often laterally compressed and narrow spines. Posterior thoracic segments produced and acute. Pygidium with five annulations and five pairs of marginal lobes or spines. Terminal lobe more or less developed." (Hall: Pal. N. Y., Vol. VII., p. xxxiii.)

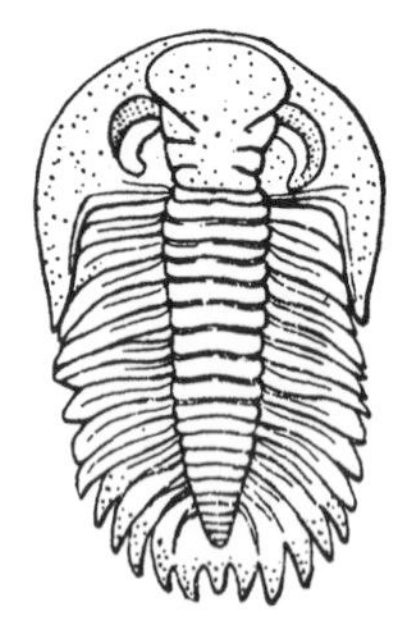

FIG. 257. *Cryphæus boothi.* Outline of an average adult specimen (after Hall and Clarke).

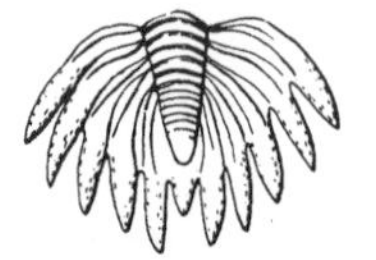

FIG. 257A. *Cryphæus boothi.* Pygidium enlarged (after Hall and Clarke).

CRYPHÆUS BOOTHI. Green. (Fig. 257.) (Pal. N. Y., Vol. VII., p. 42, Pls. XVI., XVI.A.)

Distinguishing Characters.—Large cephalon, with broad, thin, blunt genal spines, which normally reach the sixth thoracic segment; large pear-shaped or sub-pentagonal glabella; pygidium with eleven fimbriæ or spines, which are stout, flat and pustulose.

Found in the lower three or four feet of the Moscow shales, at Sections 4 and 5 (rare); in the Encrinal limestone at Section 5 (rare); in the Lower shales of Sections 5 to 8, and on the Lake Shore, it is sparingly represented, occurring usually with *Phacops rana*; in the Trilobite beds of Section 8, etc., it is common, and it occurs in the shales below the Trilobite beds in Avery's Creek.

CRYPHÆUS BOOTHI, var. CALLITELES. Green. (Fig. 258.) (Pal. N. Y., Vol. VII., p. 45, Pls. XVI., XVI.A.)

Distinguishing Characters.—Long, flat, tapering genal spines, their acute extremity reaching to the eighth thoracic segment, their flattened end grooved by the occipital furrow; wide occipital ring, with central spiniform node; thorax annulations with spiniform nodes, increasing in size backwards; distant, narrow, lanceolate pygidial spines; faintly granulose surface, with glabella and pygidial lobes usually quite smooth.

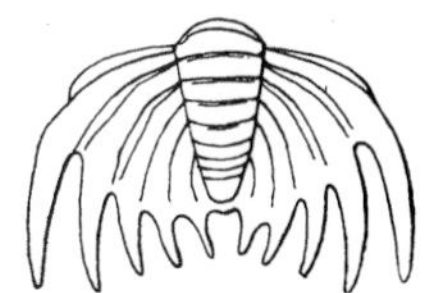

FIG. 258. *Cryphæus boothi*, var. *calliteles*. Pygidium (after Hall and Clarke).

Found in the Encrinal limestone, at Section 5 (rare); also in the Trilobite beds of Section 8, etc., associated with the preceding.

GENUS PROËTUS. STEININGER.

[ETY.: Mythological name.]

(1831: Mem. Soc. Geol. de France.)

Cephalon semi-circular, with thickened margins. Glabella very convex, parabolic, rounded anteriorly, with few lateral furrows. Eyes prominent, smooth, close to the glabella. Thoracic segments ten, pleuræ with oblique furrow. Pygidium trilobed, semi-circular; axis short and convex.

PROËTUS MACROCEPHALUS. Hall. (Fig. 259.) (Pal. N. Y., Vol. VII., p. 116, Pls. XXI., XXIII.)

Distinguishing Characters.—Sub-semi-circular or lunate cephalon; thin acute genal spines; sub-conate, pustulose glabella, with sides broadly tapering to the anterior extremity, its width three-fourths the length; single

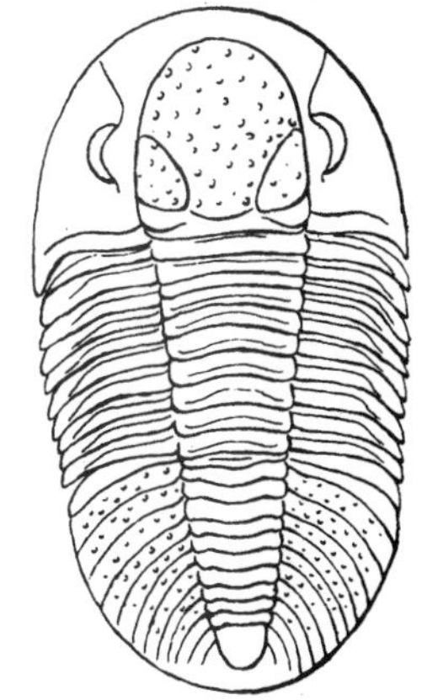

FIG. 259. *Proëtus macrocephalus*. Outline of a specimen (after Hall and Clarke).

pair of oblique furrows (occasionally others indistinctly visible); strong, bifurcating occipital furrow; lunate eyes; granulose thorax; abruptly deflected pleuræ; semi-elliptical, well-grooved pygidium, with strong border.

Found in the Encrinal limestone, at Section 5 (very rare).

PROËTUS ROWI. (Green.) (Fig. 260.) (Pal. N. Y., Vol. VII., p. 119, Pls. XXI., XXIII.)

Distinguishing Characters.—Semi-elliptical to semi-circular cephalon; broad flat border; genal spines reaching to fourth thoracic segment; simple, elongate sub-conate glabella, sloping to a broadly rounded anterior extremity; lateral furrows absent; large lunate eyes; axis occupying more than one-third the width of the thorax; pleuræ with grooves; pygidium with nine or ten low, flattened annulations in the axis, and six in the lateral lobes, with indications of a seventh; conspicuously thickened border; smooth or faintly pustulose surfaces.

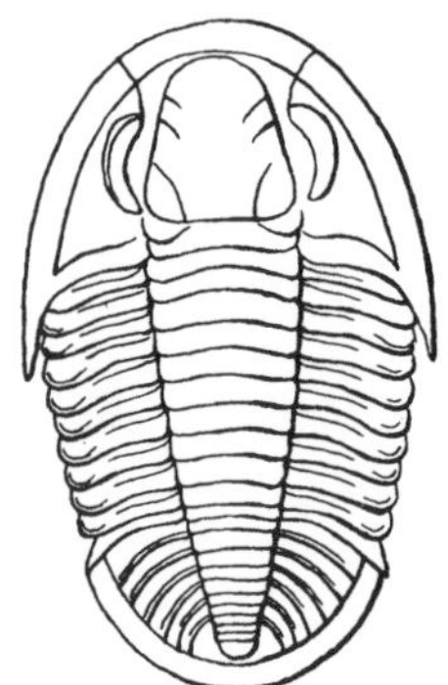

FIG. 260. *Proëtus rowi.* Outline of a small individual, enlarged to two diameters (after Hall and Clarke).

Found at "Hamburg and Eighteen Mile Creek, Erie County" (Hall). Found in the Trilobite (?) beds, at Section 8 (R. P. Johnson).

PROËTUS CURVIMARGINATUS. Hall. (?) (Fig. 261.) (*Proëtus sp.* Grabau: Faunas Ham. Group, p. 242. Compare Pal. N. Y., Vol. VII., p. 94, Pl. XXII.)

Distinguishing Characters.—Sub-triangular glabella, rounded anteriorly; three pair glabellar furrows, the last pair curving strongly backwards and reaching the occipital furrow, the two anterior pair somewhat less curving, and shorter. Surface strongly pustulose. The specimen here described and figured retains only the glabella, which has the outline and pustulose character of *P. curvimarginatus* from Pendleton, Indiana.

FIG. 261. *Proëtus curvimarginatus.* (?) The glabella, x 1⅛. Pleurodictyum beds, Wanakah Cliff. (Original.)

Found six feet below the lowest Trilobite bed, at Wanakah Cliff.

GENUS PHÆTHONIDES. ANGELIN.

[ETY.: *Phæthon*, radiant.]

(1878: Palæontologia Scandinavica, p. 21.)

Cephalon semi-circular, with genal spines. Glabella strongly arched, short and narrow, with strong and generally duplicate lateral furrows, and two small pyriform basal lobes. Thorax of seven, or probably more, narrow segments, with a wide axis. Pygidium proëtoid, relatively large, bearing from eight to twelve annulations upon the axis, and eight or nine upon the pleuræ. These annulations extend to the margin, and are conspicuously duplicate their entire length. Surface tubercled or smooth.

PHÆTHONIDES GEMMÆUS. Hall and Clarke. (Fig. 262.) (Pal. N. Y., Vol. VII., p. 136, Pl. XXIV.)

Distinguishing Characters.—Strong broad arched axis, being nearly one-half the width of the body on the anterior margin; width increasing backward for a short distance, and thence tapering rapidly toward the pygidium, bearing from three to five longitudinal rows of pustules; convex, sulcate and pustulate pleuræ; semi-circular pygidium; axis with five rows of tubercles, the middle one the strongest; lateral lobes, with four, five, or six tubercles on each segment.

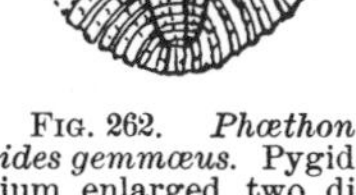

FIG. 262. *Phæthonides gemmæus.* Pygidium enlarged two diameters; from Eighteen Mile Creek (after Hall).

Found in the "Hamilton group * *, Eighteen Mile Creek, Erie County." (Hall.)

GENUS CYPHASPIS. BURMEISTER.

[ETY.: *Cyphos*, convex; *aspis*, shield.]

(1843: Burmeister: Organisation der Trilobiten, p. 103.)

"Cephalon semi-circular; genal angles produced into long spines. Glabella strongly arched, short and narrow, with two small pyriform basal lobes, bounded on all sides by deeply-impressed furrows. Anterior lateral furrows obsolete. Cheeks broad, granulose; eyes small, semi-lunate. Facial sutures beginning near the genal angles, and in front of the eyes diverging to the frontal margin. Thorax composed of from ten to seventeen segments, which are rounded at their extremities. Pygidium semi-circular, bearing from two to eight annulations upon the axis." (Hall: Pal. N. Y., Vol. VII., p. xlviii.)

CYPHASPIS ORNATA. (Hall.) (Fig. 263.) (Pal. N. Y., Vol. VII., p. 145, Pls. XXI., XXIV.)

Distinguishing Characters.—Sub-ovoid glabella, about one-half the length of the cephalon, slightly elevated along the axial line; two isolated pyriform lobes, cut off by baso-lateral furrows; faint pustules on glabella; numerous sharp tubercles on frontal area; frontal border with a single row of bead-like tubercles.

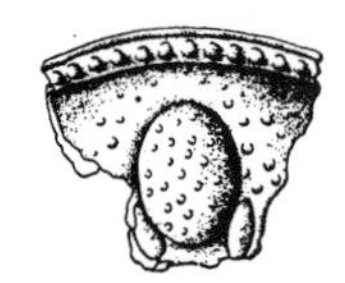

FIG. 263. *Cyphaspis ornata.* Portion of cephalic shield, with glabella, x 3 (after Hall).

Found in the Hamilton group of Eighteen Mile Creek. (Hall.) (Coll. Am. Mus. Nat. Hist. New York.)

CHAPTER III.

THE RELATION OF MARINE BIONOMY TO STRATIGRAPHY.

Marine Bionomy is that division of thalassography or oceanography which deals with the nature and distribution of marine organisms, and their relation to the environment. It is a strictly geological study, for thalassography itself is a branch of physiography, which in turn is that branch of geology which deals with the present surface features of the earth, and the causes which have produced them. Marine bionomy is, in fact, the study of the palæontology of the present geologic epoch in its marine aspect, carried on under the most favorable circumstances, by contemporary observers.

In studying the laws of the distribution of animal and plant life in the sea, we must consider two distinct phases of our subject: first, the physical conditions of the sea, and, secondly, the nature and habits of the organisms, i. e., their bionomic characteristics. If the two are harmonious in a given case, it is evident that the locality considered can be inhabited by the organism in question. Under physical conditions we must include the presence of suitable food in sufficient quantity, and the absence or paucity of competing organisms.

We may consider the physical conditions of the sea in three aspects: climatic, topographic, and organic. The climate of the sea is much more uniform than that of the land. It is true, that in the very shallow parts of the sea the water is often heated to such a degree as to make these regions uninhabitable for most animals. Ordinarily, however, the continual change of water, due to tidal and other currents, is sufficient to keep the temperature at a moderately low, and more or less uniform, degree. The daily range of temperature in the sea is of less importance to organisms than the total amount of heat received; for daily changes affect chiefly the upper strata of the water, which are directly influenced by the heat of the sun. At a moderate depth below the surface, the stratum of mean temperature is reached, this, where not affected by oceanic currents, varying mainly with the change in latitude.

A combination of the climatic and topographic factors is the chief cause of ocean currents, which are of great importance in the geographic distribution of marine organisms, not only affecting the temperature of the regions through which they pass, and, consequently, their faunas and floras,* but also to a large extent determining the directions of migrations.

Next to the climate of the sea the topography of the sea bottom, and that of the adjacent land, is the most powerful factor in determining the distribution of marine organisms. The facies of the ocean floor, or the material of which it is composed, is perhaps the most significant part of sea-bottom topography, though submarine ridges and barriers are of great importance, especially when such barriers cut off marginal bodies of water, the inhabitants of which may be prevented from intermingling. The separation thus produced may lead to the development of local faunas and floras. The importance of the greater inequalities of the sea bottom, and the submarine continental shelves and deep oceanic basins, due to them, as well as the conformation of the coast-line, with its varying facies, will be considered later.

Of all the topographical features which influence the distribution of marine organisms, northward and southward stretching bodies of land, like the continents of North and South America, are perhaps the most important. For since they form a continuous barrier across the warmer portions of the ocean, extending into the cold regions, the migration of the warmer-water species from one side to the

---

* Differences of faunas and floras due to oceanic currents are well illustrated by the marine life north and south of Cape Cod.

other is prevented. Thus the marine faunas on opposite sides of North or South America differ widely.

The organic conditions of the sea likewise exert an important influence in the distribution of marine life. By organic conditions of the sea is meant, the nature and abundance of food supply, and the relative importance of competing organisms. Since plants primarily furnish the food supply of animals, those portions of the sea rich in plant life are, in general, well adapted to the existence of animal life. Yet even in regions where plant life is wholly absent, as in the deep sea, an abundant fauna exists, the food supply of which is however derived from regions where plants grow.

Closely related to the food supply, is the struggle for a living among species and individuals. It is a well known fact, that most animals have such an enormous offspring that, supposing none were destroyed, in a short time all the space in a given region would be occupied by the progeny of a single pair, and that the number would be such as to enormously exceed that determined by the food supply. Migration to new regions is, therefore, a necessity, and emigrants are continually sent out in all directions from the mother country. If no other occupants were in the region, an intraspecific struggle for existence would characterize every locality settled by these migrants, members of the same species fighting among themselves for a living. Such struggle would, of course, result in the destruction of vast numbers and the emigration of others. When, however, the newly opened area is entered simultaneously by several species, or if the area is already occupied by other species, an interspecific struggle will occur, the outcome of which will depend on the relative ability of the contending species to hold their ground. The resident species may be driven out by the newcomer, or it may hold its own and prevent the intruder from settling; or, again, what is perhaps more common, the two species may enter into a compromise and jointly occupy the area.

Bionomic Districts.

For bionomic purposes, the inhabitable portion of the earth may be divided into a number of life districts; the character and limitation of each being determined by the interrelation of three primary factors, viz: the character of the medium in which the organism lives, the degree of illumination, and the absence or presence of a substratum. The medium may be either air or water, and determines the method of respiration of the organism. The medium water is naturally divided into salt water and fresh water, each distinct from the other and containing its own types of organisms, though an intermingling occurs near the junction of the two.

Thus three great organic realms may be recognized: the marine, or *halobiotic;* the fluvial, or *limnobiotic;* and the terrestrial, or *geobiotic*. Each of these realms is again divisible into a light and a dark region, the latter being of chief moment in the marine realm, where it is characteristic of the abyssal districts. The deeper parts of great lakes, and perpetually lightless cave districts, represent the dark regions of the fluvial and terrestrial realms respectively. Where light is absent, assimilating plant life is absent; and hence, animals occupying such regions are dependent for food on organic matter brought to them from the light regions, where food material is produced through the influence of the sun's rays.*

The final division into life-districts depends on the absence or presence of a substratum, and this division can be equally well carried out in the marine, fluvial, and terrestrial realms. The absence of the substratum compels the organism to float or swim in the medium, and for this purpose special organs and a specially modified body-form commonly exist. The substratum may be visited for food or other purposes, but the organism is perfectly at home in the medium.

---

* Schimper ('98) makes a more precise division with reference to the distribution of plant life in the sea. He distinguishes: first, a light or *photic* region, where the intensity of the light is sufficient for the normal development of macrophytes; secondly, a dusk or *dysphotic* region, where macrophytes exist but scantily or not at all, while certain moderately assimilating microphytes, especially diatoms, still exist; and, thirdly, a dark or *aphotic* region, where only the non-assimilating vegetable organisms can exist. The depths at which these regions pass into one another vary with the locality and the purity of the water.

The marine realm may, then, be divided into the following life-districts, the medium in all cases being salt water:*

1. *Littoral district:* Light; substratum present.
2. *Pelagic district:* Light; substratum absent.
3. *Abyssal district:* Dark; substratum present.
4. *Abysso-pelagic district:* Dark; substratum absent.

The littoral district extends from the shore at high-water mark to the edge of the continental shelf, where it quickly merges into the abyssal district. Around oceanic islands and young continents the littoral district is very narrow, the ocean floor soon falling off to deep water. The origin of the littoral district is to be sought in the activities of various geologic agencies, chief among which are the inland cutting of waves and currents, thus extending the sea landward, and the deposition of the land-derived detritus on the edge of the continental shelf, thus pushing this edge seaward and widening the submarine platform. Subsidence of the land permits the advance of the sea over the low country, and broad Epicontinental seas, as Chamberlin has called them, are formed by the "creeping out upon the low parts of the land of a film of the sea, as it were."†

The conditions become more favorable for the development of littoral life as the continent grows older, provided, of course, no important oscillatory movements occur. As time progresses, the breadth of the submerged continental shelf increases,—both by landward cutting and by seaward building,—and the surface of the land becomes more and more reduced, thus bringing about a decrease in the amount of detrital material, which is carried into the sea, and a concomitant increase in the purity of the water. When peneplenation, or the reduction of the land to base level, has been accomplished, the amount of detritus carried into the sea is practically nil, and organisms, like corals, adapted only

* Ortmann ('95) makes the terrestrial and fluvial realms each coördinate in rank with the littoral, pelagic, and abyssal districts of the marine realm, treating them as districts. It seems more natural, however, to divide his terrestrial and fluvial "districts" into districts comparable to the three marine districts, though, of course, the resulting divisions will not always be of uniform quantitative value.

† Chamberlin, '98, p. 603.

to pure water can flourish close to the continental shore, and deposits of a purely organic nature, such as the extensive deposit of pteropod shells constituting the Styliolina limestone in Western New York, may form in comparatively shallow water.

The epicontinental seas are especially adapted for the development of local or provincial faunas. Such provincializing of faunas is most marked if, by some oscillatory movement of the land or some other physical change, the basin of the epicontinental sea should become separated from the extra-continental portion of the littoral district sufficiently to prevent intercommunication between the organisms of the two provinces. A barrier is thus formed, which need not necessarily be a land barrier, and a great diversity of faunas may result. Such diversity of fauna existed in early Tertiary time between the Mississippi embayment and the Atlantic coast; and in Palæozoic time, between the Bay of New York and the Central Interior sea. Recent provincial faunas are frequently met with. It requires only a comparatively slight elevation of the sea floor, or a moderate deepening of the abyssal oceanic basins, to draw off the water from the shallower regions, and lay large portions of the littoral district dry. Such a change would, of course, result in an extinction of the whole of the littoral flora and fauna thus exposed, and force the survivors to accommodate themselves to a narrower field. Revival of stream activities, consequent upon elevation of the land, would result in carrying a large amount of debris into the sea, and thus produce conditions unfavorable to the existence of many organisms. Such an elevation of the land and extinction of faunas occurred at the close of Ordovicic time* in the area of the central and eastern interior Palæozoic sea. A few survivors only, of the Ordovician fauna, occur in some of the lower detrital beds of the next succeeding formation, in certain localities. In the Siluric era a new fauna developed, as conditions again became favorable.

---

* Weller, '98, p. 693.

Landwards, the littoral district interlocks with the corresponding districts of the terrestrial and fluvial realms, the faunas and floras of all more or less intermingling. It is in this portion of the littoral district that an important subdivision must be considered, namely, the shore. The shore is that part of the littoral district which lies between the highest water mark (often considered as even including the highest point of the wave mark) and the lowest line drawn during the lowest ebb. In the greater part of this division of the littoral district there is a change of medium twice every twenty-four hours, and a change of the consequent physical conditions attendant upon the character of the medium. Organisms living in this portion of the littoral zone must be capable of withstanding the effects of the partial or complete removal of their normal medium for a greater or less time. It is here that the interlocking of the marine and terrestrial faunas and floras becomes most marked, and an intermingling, and a migration from one district to the other, occurs. Migration from the land to the sea is seen in the whales, seals, and other aquatic mammals, which have become marine in so far as their mode of locomotion is concerned. Owing, however, to the inability of air-breathing animals to adapt themselves to a water-breathing habit, all terrestrial animals passing into the sea must assume a pelagic life, where they can retain their normal method of breathing.

Among other animals which have exchanged their normal terrestrial habit for a prevailingly marine one, may be mentioned, several birds, such as the Penguin and the Albatross, certain snakes, turtles, and crocodiles, and a number of insects. The birds and insects here considered represent a passage from the aërial to the marine pelagic; while the reptiles, like the mammals, illustrate a passage from the land to the pelagic district of the sea.

While thus the land fauna, in advancing into the sea, naturally takes to a pelagic life, the land flora can adapt itself to the conditions of the littoral district. This is well shown by the eight species of phanerogams, which have acquired a wholly marine habit, and are now known as sea-grasses. In the case of these plants, the adaptation is so pronounced that they cannot live out of their adopted habitat. The mangrove plants, on the other hand, are only partially accommodated to the conditions of the marine littoral district, for it is necessary that their crowns of leaves should be above water.

Marine animals and plants likewise attempt migrating from the sea to the land. In their adaptation to the new habitat, the animals are the most successful, just as the plants are the most successful in migrating the other way. Thus two genera of fish, Periophthalmus and Boleophthalmus, are able to pass the greater part of their lives out of water. They "skip along close to the water-line on the sea shore, where they hunt for molluscs (Onchidium) and insects." (Semper, '81, p. 189.) The large branchial cavity of these fishes is not completely filled by the gills, but serves in part as an air cavity or primitive lung. In certain fishes, such as *Anabas scandens* of the Philippines, this gill-cavity is further modified into a "labyrinthine organ," or much prolonged cavity, the mucous membrane of which is thrown into complicated folds, thus greatly increasing the surface. These fish are able to exist for days out of water, and can make long overland excursions. Semper holds that these fish may be regarded "as Amphibians with quite as much reason as toads and frogs, or even better, since they are capable of changing the nature of their respiration—of air, that is, or of water—at will, and suddenly without any interruption." Several of our littoral gastropods, e. g., Littorina, Ilyanassa, etc., are capable of existing out of water for a considerable time, commonly crawling out of the vessels in which they are kept. In Brazil, Littorina climbs the trees of the mangrove high above water, and oysters and other bivalves are attached to the roots of these trees, and laid bare at low tide. Ampullaria forms a connecting link between marine and land snails, for it not only breathes by means of gills, but also has a lung-cavity like that of the land snails, into which air is carried by means of a long breathing-siphon.

Among Crustacea there are several species of crabs (e. g., *Birgus latro*, etc.) which live in damp woods far from all water, and whose respiration is carried on chiefly without the intermediation of their normal medium.

The advent of marine vegetation on the land has only occurred up to the limit of the salt spray on exposed shores, and here the number of species is small. But at or just below high-tide limit, a number of algæ find a congenial abode, and grow there in luxuriant masses. Chief of these in our northern latitudes are the Fuci, with *Fucus vesiculosus* and *Ascophyllum nodosum* predominating. At low tide these hang like a wet fringe over the exposed rocks and give shelter to numerous species of the smaller littoral animals beneath them.*

The littoral districts of the marine and fluvial realms likewise interlock along the shores, where streams mouth into the sea, or expand into broad estuaries. Here marine animals will venture up into the fresh-water littoral district; while, similarly, fresh-water animals pass into the littoral district of the marine realm. The common meeting-ground of the two approaching faunas and floras is in the estuarine or brackish water facies of the littoral districts.

In an ideal cross-section of a shore supplied only with terrigenous deposits we may distinguish a variety of facies of the material composing it, which progressively decreases in coarseness of texture seaward. These various facies may be classed as follows:

1. Rocky-cliff facies.
2. Bouldery facies.
3. Gravelly facies.
4. Sandy facies.
5. Muddy facies.

---

* A similar interrelation between the littoral districts of the terrestrial and fluvial realms occurs, with a passage of the fauna and flora of the one to the other.

Beyond the reach of the terrigenous sediments, the floor of the sea may exhibit chiefly an organic facies, and this will also be true of the immediate continental or island shore, wherever sediments of a purely detrital character are absent. It is comparatively rare that this gradation of facies is observed in nature. One or more facies are generally wanting, while not infrequently two or more interlock. Thus a rocky cliff may descend into the sea without a beach at its base; or there may be simply a bouldery beach, or only a sandy or gravelly one. The landward boundary of the shore may be a sand, gravel, or boulder beach, and extensive mud-flats may stretch seaward from a shore formed mainly of vegetable accumulations, such as salt marshes. It will thus be seen that the shore presents the greatest variety of physical features, and that hence the physical conditions, and the organisms existing under them, must be most varied.

The shallow sea, or "Flachsee," is that portion of the littoral district which is never uncovered. It is separated as a distinct district by Walther, who restricts the term littoral to the shore zone. It is, however, so intimately connected with the shore zone, in all its physical and bionomic characteristics, that a separation is not natural. The bottom of the shallow-sea zone of the littoral district is less diversified than that of the shore zone. In its upper portion and in its shoals it may partake of the character of the shore zone; but in its deeper portions the character of the bottom is usually more uniform, being either rocky or, what is more common, composed of fine detrital material mingled with organic matter in various stages of dissolution. According to the character of the bottom, plant life will vary, and with it, to a greater or less extent, animal life.

Taken as a whole, the littoral district is the most important portion of the sea, both from a bionomic point of view and from its bearing on palæontology. "The littoral region," says Lovèn,* "comprises the favoured zones of the

* Swen Lovèn . . On Pourtalasia, a genus of Echinoidèa.—Stockholm, 1883, p. 86.

sea, where light and shade, a genial temperature, currents changeable in power and direction, a rich vegetation spread over extensive areas, abundance of food, of prey to allure, of enemies to withstand or evade, represent an infinitude of agents competent to call into play the tendencies to vary which are embodied in each species, and always ready, by modifying its parts, to respond to the influences of external conditions." This district may perhaps be regarded as the cradle of organic life, from which, on the one hand, were peopled the abyssal and pelagic districts, and, on the other, the terrestrial and fluvial realms and their various districts.

The marine pelagic, or halo-pelagic district, or more briefly, the pelagic district, is the common meeting-ground of most of the life districts. It touches all shores and communicates with the corresponding districts of both terrestrial and fluvial realms. It has direct communication with the littoral district, many inhabitants of which leave the bottom at times to lead a temporary existence in the pelagic district; while, in turn, many pelagic animals visit the bottom or shores for food. Occasionally, inhabitants of the pelagic district enter for a time the corresponding district of the terrestrial realm, i. e., the aërial, as, for example, the so-called flying fish; and, in turn, as already noted, many aërial animals spend a part of their lives in the marine pelagic district, or, at least, show a decided preference for a pelagic life. The passage of land animals to the halo-pelagic district has already been noted. Similar intermingling of fresh water, or limno-pelagic, and salt water pelagic types occurs in the estuaries and stream mouths, and it is well known that halo-pelagic fish will enter the limno-pelagic district in breeding time. It is quite probable, as Sir William Flower suggests, that the Cetacea, in their transition from a terrestrial to a marine life, passed through a stage in which they lived in fresh water. A similar transition for the sea-grasses is not improbable, though they can no longer live in fresh water. Intercommunication between the abysso-pelagic and pelagic districts also occurs, as well as between the abysso-pelagic and abyssal.

The marine abyssal districts comprise the lightless depths, or generally those depths exceeding one hundred fathoms. As assimilating plant life is absent in these districts, the food supply of the organisms existing in them must be wholly derived from the districts in which such assimilating vegetation exists. A large proportion of the food of the abyssal animals is contained in the organic oozes and sediments which constantly settle down in a more or less decomposed state from the lighted districts. The abysso-pelagic district is frequently invaded by organisms from the pelagic district, which descend into the dark regions during the day.

Bionomic Characteristics of Marine Organisms.

Having now considered the life-districts, we will next turn to a study of the organisms inhabiting them. A bionomic classification of animals and plants cannot strictly agree with a classification based on purely anatomical characteristics. It is a more primitive classification; but from the point of view here adopted, it is the most convenient. The following five groups, based on the habits and mode of locomotion of the organisms, will be found to be a convenient, and, from the bionomic point of view, a natural classification: Plankton, Nekton, Benthos, Mero-plankton, and Pseudo-plankton.

The term plankton was first introduced by Victor Hensen in 1887. It was derived from the Greek πλαγκτος—meaning to drift about aimlessly. In the marine realm it comprises those organisms which spend their lives in the sea, drifting about from place to place, without sufficient power to direct their own course.* It comprises organisms ranging from microscopic dimensions to medusæ 50 cm. in diameter. (Walther, '97, p. 211.) While some of the larger animals of

*I follow Walther rather than Ortmann in the definition of the term plankton. The latter employs it in a sense which I consider synonymous with pelagic as here defined. The distinction between Plankton and Nekton seems an important one, even though intermediate types are common.

this group have power to propel themselves through the water, they nevertheless are subject to the force of strong waves or currents, which will render them helpless. The marine, or halo-planktonic organisms, are wholly pelagic, and are characterized by a more or less transparent body, and by the absence of opaque skeletal structures, only a few forms retaining delicate calcareous shells inherited from their benthonic ancestors. In their horizontal distribution the halo-planktonic organisms are dependent chiefly upon the marine currents, as they are practically unable to undertake independent migrations, though many of them can dart about in quiet water. They hence fall an easy prey to actively predaceous animals. The occurrence of these animals in swarms is also accounted for by their lack of independent locomotion, for the eggs, liberated by the floating parent, commonly develop without separating far from the parent, with whom they are carried along by the currents of the sea. These animals have, however, the power to rise and descend in the water, and during the hours of the day many of them live at a depth of from fifty to one hundred and fifty fathoms, coming to the surface only on quiet nights. The animals of this class also occur in the abysso-pelagic district.*

The halo-plankton forms one of the chief sources of food for many marine animals, and is commonly devoured in vast quantities. The dead organisms which sink to the sea floor in an incomplete state of decomposition form the chief element of the organic oozes, which furnish food to many littoral, as well as abyssal, animals. The skeletal portions of the dead plankton will often accumulate in vast quantities on the bottom; and in the greater depths, where terrigenous sediments are absent, they commonly form diatomaceous, radiolarian, globigerina, pteropod and other oozes. The purity of such oozes, i. e., their freedom from clastic sediment, is usually an index of the purity of the water in which they were deposited, but from this we cannot always decide

* Fresh-water plankton, or limno-plankton, is to be met with in almost all waters. Probably no permanent aërial or geo-plankton exists, though bacteria and other micro-organisms may float about in the atmosphere for an indefinite period of time.

that such oozes, when found in a fossil state,* indicate deep sea. The absence of clastic sediment may be due to the low relief of the land, which may have been worn down to base level, thus allowing water of moderate depth near shore to be free from detrital material.

The term nekton, derived from the Greek νηχω, to swim, was introduced by Hæckel in 1890,† for those animals which lead an actively swimming life. The group is typified by the class of fishes.‡ A torpedo-like form, terminating anteriorly in a head, and perfect bilateral symmetry, are the chief characteristics of these animals. A strong musculature for propulsion is commonly situated in the posterior portion of the body, while appendages for balancing and steering are usually present. The body is non-transparent, and a calcareous supporting skeleton is ordinarily developed. Typical nektonic animals of the modern sea are: the squids, the fish, and the degenerate mammals, i. e., whales, porpoises, etc.

The term benthos, from βένθος, the depths of the sea, was likewise introduced by Hæckel in 1890. It covers those organisms which inhabit the sea-bottom.§

We may divide the benthos into sedentary and vagrant (vagile) benthos, the former attached to the bottom, the latter moving over it. Living in such intimate relation to the sea bottom, halo-benthonic organisms are to a high degree dependent upon its facies, and their remains, moreover, are generally entombed in the region where they have lived, instead of being deposited anywhere, as is the case with planktonic and nektonic organisms. The sedentary benthos

---

*Styliolina limestone of the Genesee.

†Planktonstudien — τὸ νεκτὸν, that which swims.

‡Fish are typical halo nektonic and limno-nektonic animals. Geo-nektonic animals are represented by flying insects, reptiles, birds, and mammals. None of these lead a permanently nektonic life in the air, for all return more or less frequently to the substratum. Nevertheless, during their period of flight — which often is very long — they must be considered as nekton of the air.

§To speak of fluvial or limno-benthos, and terrestrial or geo-benthos, is certainly a stretching of the word beyond its original significance, but the value of the term in that connection more than counterbalances the etymological defects. The limno-benthos contains comparatively few sedentary animals, of the classes of Protozoa, sponges, Hydrozoa, and Bryozoa, but a much larger number of plants. The geo-benthos is pretty sharply divided into vagrant geo-benthos, or animals, and sedentary geo-benthos, or plants, excepting some of the lowest of the latter.

is to a large degree dependent for food on those organisms which are swept within its reach by the currents, while the vagrant benthos becomes more actively engaged in seeking out its food. A large number of sedentary benthonic animals have assumed a radial structure—especially well typified in corals and crinoids, and also shown in the corona of the barnacle; while others, such as brachiopods, have a bilateral symmetry of high degree. Some of the lower vagrant benthonic animals, e. g., echinoderms, are also built on the radial plan, but the majority of free benthonic animals are bilaterally symmetrical. Among the vagrant benthos the struggle for existence is most intense, and, as a result, the variety of adaptations and the wealth of form and color is almost unlimited. Transitions from the vagrant benthos to the nekton are numerous, and it becomes sometimes difficult to decide if an animal belongs to the vagrant benthonic or to the neytonic type. The gradation is just as complete as between nekton and plankton. In general a radial form may be said to be characteristic of the sedentary benthos, while a bilaterally symmetrical form is as characteristic of the vagrant benthos. Examples of change of form with change of habit occur in many classes.

The term mero-plankton, from μερος, a part, was also introduced by Hæckel, and is applicable to the larvæ of benthonic animals which lead, during the larval stages, a truly planktonic existence, and which occur with, and suffer the same vicissitudes as, the true or holo-plankton. The upper strata of the ocean are commonly crowded with such mero-planktonic organisms, and to them is due the horizontal distribution of benthonic species. Floating about in the sea, in perfect clouds or swarms, these mero-planktonic organisms pass their short existence, a sport of the waves and currents. Sooner or later, however, they will sink to the bottom, a veritable rain of seedling organisms, and if they fall upon a fertile soil, in other words, if they reach the proper facies of the substratum, they will develop into the benthonic adult; but if they fall upon an unfavorable bottom, or if food supply is scarce, they will perish. Thus, other things being favorable, wherever the facies of sea bottom normal to a particular species of benthonic organism exists, that bottom may be peopled with that species by the larvæ which reach it from the upper waters, where they are carried by waves and currents during their mero-planktonic wanderings. As Walther says, should unfavorable circumstances temporarily destroy a whole fauna, its depopulated home will at once be surrounded by swarms of delicate larvæ, and as soon as the old conditions are reëstablished, this fauna will again appear with countless individuals. This explains the sudden reappearance, in later strata, of the fauna of an earlier bed, even though absent from the intervening strata.*

From a geological point of view, the mero-plankton is of vast importance, for to it are due the wide dispersal and migration of the benthonic organisms, which of all marine organisms are the best indices of the physical conditions of the sea bottom. It is during the larval period that benthonic marine invertebrates undertake their wanderings, and that migration to distant regions occurs.†

The term pseudo-plankton was introduced by Schütt‡ for such organisms, which, like the Sargassum, are normally, or in early life, benthonic, but continue their later existence as planktonic organisms. Walther has extended the meaning of the term so as to include those organisms which are carried about by floating objects, to which they are either attached as sedentary benthos or which serves them as a substratum on which they lead a vagrant benthonic existence. Such organisms are the algæ, hydroids, and

* An example of this in the Hamilton group of Eighteen Mile Creek is the fauna of the Demissa bed, near the top of the Hamilton shales, which is in many respects the fauna of the Pleurodictyum beds and associated shales near the base of the Hamilton shales, the modifications being chiefly in the form of additions. (See the author's paper on Faunas of the Hamilton Group, etc., p. 312.) Other examples are the frequent recurrence of beds crowded with *Liorhynchus multicostus*, and others crowded with *Ambocœlia umbonata*, at intervals separated by thicknesses of greater or less extent, in which they are rare or wanting.

† The mero-plankton of the fluvial realm belongs in general to the same classes as that of the marine realm. In the terrestrial realm, the mero-plankton is typically represented by the spores and seeds of plants, and perhaps by the spores or larval stages of some lowly aquatic or parasitic animals.

‡ Das Pflanzenleben der Hochsee — Plankton expedition, I.

bryozoans attached to the floating Sargassum and other algæ, and the Crustacea, molluscs and other animals living among their branches.

A large number of algæ, especially the shallow-water forms, have attached to them sedentary animals as well as other species of algæ. Among the animals hydroids and bryozoans are the most common, though other sedentary animals, such as Spirorbis, are frequently very abundant. Animals belonging to the vagrant type of the benthos are by no means rare. The large fronds of the Laminaria, cast up on our northern shores during every storm, are frequently veritable menageries of invertebrate life,—which under favorable conditions may float about for days. These fronds, for example, are commonly covered with a dense growth of the delicate littoral hydroid *Obelia geniculata*, while Bugula and other Bryozoa, and Spirorbis are usually common. The hollow stem is commonly surrounded by an extensive growth of Membranipora, while not infrequently tubularian and other hydroids find this a suitable resting place. The root-like base of the stem not uncommonly embraces a shell of Modiola or Cyprina, which, in turn, is overgrown with coralline algæ. Sponges are also common among the "roots" of the Laminaria, and Acmea, Chiton, Crepidula, Anomia, and other molluscs are attached to the shell, or the stone, which frequently takes its place. Finally, worms and crustaceans are not uncommon inhabitants of the sheltering space between the branches of the "roots"; and sea-anemones, small star-fish, brittle stars, and sea-urchins also occur, both on the basal portion of the stem and on the frond itself. Such floating menageries may be carried far out to sea, or, what is perhaps more frequent, they are driven on shore. Not infrequently they are carried far up into estuaries, and, becoming stranded, are buried in the mud; or else they are thrown upon mud-flats, behind some sheltering bar or ledge.

While these cases illustrate a pseudo-planktonic existence due to accident, the cirriped Lepas illustrates an habitually pseudo-planktonic existence, this barnacle rarely occurring except as attached to floating objects. Many of the animals found on the Sargassum seem to be characteristic of it in its floating condition, not occurring on it in its native haunts. (Ortmann.) Walther has adduced evidence which goes to show conclusively that many of the larger fossil Pentacrini, and perhaps other crinoids, occurred with their stems wound around floating timbers, and he explains the occurrence of these marine animals in fresh-water coal strata as due to stranding in estuaries of species leading a pseudo-planktonic existence.

Bionomic Characteristics of the Classes of Marine Invertebrates Important from a Palæontological Point of View.

Foraminifera.—The Foraminifera are typically marine organisms, though a considerable number of species have become adapted to brackish water, living in estuaries and near the mouths of streams, while a number of species, commonly placed in this class, live entirely in fresh water. Their distribution is so great that scarcely any marine sediments are wholly free from the shells of these animals. Most Foraminifera belong to the vagrant benthos, though sedentary benthonic forms also occur. Only something over twenty living planktonic species are known, these belonging chiefly to the genera Globigerina, Orbulina, and Pulvinulina (Hæckel), the first predominating. The small number of species is, however, counterbalanced by the enormous number of individuals. The benthonic Foraminifera are confined chiefly to the littoral district, where the character of the bottom and the temperature of the water exerts important influences on the distribution of these organisms. A muddy facies of the sea bottom seems to be conducive to the existence of a large number of species, but the rocky bottoms are not without their types; while algæ and sea-grasses commonly form the home of vast numbers of these organisms. The coarse, sandy and gravelly bottoms are not generally inhabited by these animals, though their dead shells are not uncommon in the sands along our beaches; while along some shores they are so abundant as to constitute the greater portion, if not the whole, of the deposit.* The vertical range of the benthonic Foraminifera is very great, species sometimes passing through a range of several thousand fathoms. In such cases there is often a change in the size or thickness of the shell with the change in depth. Although the planktonic Foraminifera comprise so few species, the number of their individuals is enormous. From their shells the Globigerina oozes form in deep water, where no sediment is carried; but it is evident that in a region where the land is reduced to near base level, so that little or no sediment is carried into the sea, pure accumulations of such shells will occur near shore, thus forming a foraminiferal ooze in shallow water. But not only planktonic shells but the benthonic species as well would form a pure accumulation of foraminiferal shells, as has been the case in the chalk, in which the planktonic species are practically wanting. (Walther, '97, p. 215.) Reproduction of the Foraminifera is carried on by fission, budding, and spore formation. In the first two cases, the resulting part and the buds have the characteristics of the parent, except its size, and there are no special structures which serve for the greater distribution of the species. When spores are formed, these may be provided with a flagellum, when the organisms pass through a mero-planktonic stage.

While the geographical distribution of the benthonic species is very restricted, and influenced by the facies of the sea bottom, the geographical distribution of the pelagic species is prevented from being world wide only by the changes in the temperature of the water and by the ocean currents. The pelagic species are extremely abundant in tropical regions, and their shells form vast accumulations on the sea

* Dana states, that in the great barrier-reef region the shells of Orbitolites are so abundant that * * "they seemed in some places to make up the whole sand of the beaches, both of the coral islets and of the neighboring Australian shore."

bottoms over which they live. In the great depths these shells are absent, for they may be completely dissolved while they sink to the bottom, or shortly after reaching it.

Radiolaria.—The Radiolaria are marine planktonic Protozoa. They inhabit principally the open sea, where they occur at the surface or at various depths below it. In regions of terrigenous sedimentation or where an influx of fresh water occurs, these animals are seldom met with. Hence their siliceous shells occur in abundance only in the deposits found at a distance from shore, and in deep water, where they may constitute as high as seventy per cent of the mass. The greatest abundance of radiolarian skeletons was found by the "Challenger" expedition at a depth between 2,000 and 4,475 fathoms—the greatest depth sounded. In many places in the Pacific the bottom ooze is almost entirely composed of radiolarian shells with some intermixture of sponge spicules. The celebrated Barbados earth, a Tertiary deposit, is likewise composed of radiolarian remains, to the exclusion of almost every other substance. Fission, budding, and spore formation constitute the methods of reproduction in Radiolaria. The spores may be provided with flagella, constituting "swarm spores," which, like their progenitors, lead a planktonic existence.

Spongiæ.—The sponges are marine or fresh-water animals, of a sedentary benthonic habit. In general only such species as secrete a calcareous or siliceous skeleton—either continuous or consisting of separate spicules—are capable of preservation in a fossil state. The vertical distribution of marine species ranges from the shore zone down to the greater depths of the sea. Not infrequently species are found which regularly undergo an exposure of several hours between tides, though most littoral species occur below low-water mark, or in tide pools from which the water is never drained. Sponges will grow wherever a suitable surface for attachment is found, the most usual substratum chosen being cliffs, boulders, or the stems and "roots" of the larger algæ. In deeper and quieter water, the sandy and gravelly bottoms are inhabited by sponges, and in the great depths they occur on the oozes and other soft deposits. A pseudo-vagrant benthonic habit is assumed by a number of species which attach themselves to the carapaces of Crustacea. Certain sponges bore into shells and other calcareous substances, forming extensive galleries and commonly destroying the shell. *Clione sulphurea*, common on our Atlantic coast, completely riddles shells, and then forms large irregularly rounded masses of a sulphur yellow color, often entirely enveloping the shell.

The reproduction of the sponges is either asexual or sexual. In the former case buds are formed, which, growing larger, without detaching themselves put out buds of their own, thus forming a colonial aggregation. Sponges torn into several pieces will frequently form as many new individuals, and sponges which were placed in close juxtaposition, by Bowerbank, in a relatively short time united into one. A method of internal gemmation occurs, in which groups of cells, or gemmulæ, become detached and after a time develop into complete sponges. Sexual reproduction, from either hermaphrodite or sexually distinct parents, leads to a free swimming blastula. This develops into a gastrula, which attaches itself and develops into the adult. Thus a meroplanktonic stage occurs in sponges, which serves as a means of extensive distribution.

Hydrozoa.—The Hydrozoa are typically marine Cœlenterates, though a few species occur in fresh water.* Some Scyphomedusæ (Aurelia, Cyanea), according to Moseley, seem to prefer to float near the mouths of fresh-water streams; while in New South Wales these medusæ were observed swimming in shoals where the water was pure enough to be drinkable. The majority of species have a sedentary benthonic stage, the hydriform stage, which is generally

* To the three fresh-water species of hydroids — *Hydra viridis*, *H. fusca* (*vulgaris*), and *Cordilophora lacustris* — none of which possess a medusiform stage, has recently been added the remarkable fresh-water medusa of Lake Tanganyika: *Limnocnida tanganyikæ* Günther, which, together with a peculiar molluscan and fish fauna, seems to indicate that Lake Tanganyika is a "cut-off" from the Mesozoic sea, with a fauna which has gradually become adapted to lacustrine conditions.

colonial, the compound polype stock being attached to rocks, algæ, shells, timbers, or other objects of support, by means of a thread like branching rootstock or hydrorhyza, which spreads out over the object of support and from which the individual polyparia arise, each with a distinct stem or hydrocaulus. A few forms, like *Hydractinia polyclina* and some Podocoryne, lead a pseudo-vagrant benthonic life, being attached to the shells of gastropods carried about by hermit crabs. Some species, like *Bougainvillia fruticosa*, prefer a pseudo-planktonic habit, becoming attached to floating timbers, a similar habit being assumed by the hydroids which live attached to the floating Sargassum. A pseudo-nektonic manner of life may perhaps be considered the habit of Hydrichthys, which lives parasitic upon a fish. *Corymorpha pendula*, though not attached, lives partly buried in the mud of the shallow sea; while Hydra leads, at times at least, a kind of vagrant benthonic life, though its journeyings are perhaps never very great.

A large number of Hydrozoa have a distinct medusiform person, which, when perfect, is perhaps the best type of a holoplanktonic organism. In a few Hydrozoa—Hydra, Sertularia (?)—the medusiform stage is wanting, in others it is degenerate, never becoming free (Clava); but in a large number of species it is a free individual. Again, in the Narco- and Tracho-Medusæ, as well as in some others, only the medusa occurs, the hydroid being suppressed. Compound medusæ occur as well as compound hydroids. The former are the Siphonophora, in which, by budding from the parent medusa, a compound colony is formed which leads a holoplanktonic existence. Lucernaria is an example of an attached medusa. The medusæ, whether free or attached, produce the sexual products which give rise to new hydroid colonies or directly to new medusæ. The egg develops into a ciliated planula which leads a mero-planktonic existence before it settles down to become a benthonic hydroid, or before it develops into the medusa. A number of hydroids grow attached to rocks and seaweeds, or to bridge piles, in such a position as to become regularly exposed for several hours each day during ebb tide. Even the delicate and unprotected Clava of our northern shores delights to live under such conditions, and is rarely found in deeper water or in tide pools. Most hydroids, however, can not withstand such exposure, and hence they are found only in the deeper waters or the deeper tide pools.

The majority of hydroids are inhabitants of the littoral district, and they usually occur in the more moderate depths. The tubularian hydroids probably never extend to any considerable depths, the deep-water forms belonging chiefly to the Plumularidæ.* One of the abyssal Plumularians was obtained by the "Blake" at a depth of 1,240 fathoms, which exceeded by more than 300 fathoms that at which Plumularians were obtained by the "Challenger."†

The Palæozoic class of graptolites is the most important group of the Hydrozoa from a stratigraphist's point of view, for it constitutes one of the most important classes of index fossils known. The bionomic characters of this class have been most thoroughly discussed by Professor Lapworth, a synopsis of whose views will here be given.‡

Two distinct groups of Graptolites are generally recognized, viz: *Cladophora*, or dendroid graptolites, in which the polyparium is more or less tree-like with a distinct hydrocaulus, and *Rhabdophora*, or virgulate graptolites, without a hydrocaulus, but with a horny axis, the virgula, which is prolonged beyond the end of the colony. To the former group belongs Dyctyonema, to the latter the true graptolites (Monograptus, Diplograptus, etc.). The majority of the dendroid graptolites undoubtedly grew attached to sea-weeds, rocks, or other supports, in the manner of most modern hydroids, but some were attached to floating algæ, leading a pseudo-planktonic existence. Cases of such attachment have actually been observed among these fossils.

---

* Agassiz, '88, II., 35.
† Agassiz, loc. cit.
‡ Walther, '97.

The true graptolite colony (Rhabdophora) begins with a small conical cup or hydrotheca, which is known as the sicula.

The base of this cup is prolonged into a slender thread, the *nema*, which in many forms serves as an organ for attachment. In the earlier genera, the second and succeeding hydrothecæ continue to grow in the same direction as the sicula, so that if the colony was attached to floating objects by the nema, the openings of the hydrothecæ all pointed downwards. In later genera the second and succeeding hydrothecæ open in the opposite direction from the sicula, having attained this condition through intermediate stages, and as a result of the permanent attachment of the colony to floating objects. The nema in these graptolites becomes prolonged, and constitutes the virgula or axial supporting rod, the tip end of which is fastened to the supporting object. Thus, the new hydrothecæ come in, successively, between the sicula and the attached end of the prolonged nema, ranging themselves along this prolonged nema for support.

Some graptolites appear to have led a holo-planktonic existence, the nema being attached to a central organ or disk, which probably served as a float. This was long ago demonstrated in a number of species by Professor Hall, and lately has been shown in great detail in Diplograptus by Ruedemann. Whether holo-planktonic or pseudo-planktonic, either method of life accounts for the wide distribution of the graptolites. The fact that they are almost universally found in carbonaceous shales suggests that floating algæ may have been the principal carriers of these organisms, the decaying vegetable furnishing the carbon for coloring the muds in which the organisms were buried. On the other hand, it is not improbable that much of the carbonaceous material was derived from the graptolites themselves. The general slight thickness of these beds, and the fact that in successive beds the species change, indicate a slow accumulation of the deposits in relatively quiet water.

According to Ruedemann's* observations the young Diplograptus upon leaving the gonophore has already advanced into the sicula stage, so that a free-swimming planula stage appears not to exist. It is probable that this is true of most, if not all, graptolites, and that hence the distribution of these animals is such as will be accounted for by the vicissitudes which they met with while a floating colony.

Anthozoa.—The Anthozoa are typically marine sedentary benthonic animals, inhabiting chiefly the warmer waters of the oceans. A large number are without hard supporting parts, and, consequently, leave no remains; while others, probably the majority of Anthozoa, secrete a calcareous or horny corallum, which is capable of preservation. Among the Actinaria, or fleshy polyps, a certain amount of locomotion of a creeping or gliding nature is often observable (Metridium, etc.), the individuals possessing this ability thus passing from a normal sedentary to a vagrant benthonic life. A few forms are also met with among the plankton. Occasionally, pseudo-planktonic individuals are met with attached to floating algæ or timbers, and pseudo-vagrant benthonic individuals attached to moving crustaceans are not unknown.

The Madreporaria, or stone corals, are normally sedentary forms, though they are not necessarily attached, but may rest upon the sands. (Fungia, some Porites.) Though the normal medium of the Anthozoa is salt water, a few are known in brackish and even in tolerably fresh water. *Cilicia rubeola* is reported by the "Challenger"† in the river Thames in New Zealand; and Dana‡ states that "* * * upon the reefs enclosing the harbor of Rewa (Viti Lebu), where a large river, three hundred yards wide, empties, which during freshets enables vessels at anchor two and a half miles off its mouth to dip up fresh water alongside, there is a single porous species of Madrepora (*M. cribripora*), growing here

* Ruedemann, R., Development and Mode of Growth of Diplograptus. McCoy. 14th Ann. Rep. N. Y. State Geol., 1895, pp. 219-249, Pls. I.-V.

† Report, Vol. XVI., II., p. 36.

‡ Corals and Coral Islands, 1872, p. 120.

and there in patches over a surface of dead coral rock or sand. In similar places about other regions species of Porites are most common." Several species of corals grow at the mouth of the Rio della Plata.

Porites limosa flourishes in muddy water and *Astræa bowerbanki* does not seem to mind mud or sediment, or even muddy brackish water, growing on, and incrusting the stones at the mouth of the Mangrove Creek, Australia, these stones being covered with mud and slime, and washed over twice in the twenty-four hours by muddy, brackish water. (Tenison-Woods.) A common Red Sea coral, *Stylophora pistillata*, is recorded by Milne Edwards and Haime from the intensely salt and dense waters of the Dead Sea.

The simple corals (Caryophyllia, etc.) are chiefly found on muddy bottoms, often attached to a shell or other object resting on the mud. The bathymetric distribution varies from shallow water to a thousand fathoms or more. This method of life corresponds well with what is known of the Palæozoic Tetracoralla, which commonly lived on a muddy bottom, with their bases not infrequently showing signs of attachment to shells or other foreign objects. The compound corals build heads or stocks often of great size and weight. They are commonly attached to stones, shells, or to the rock bottom, and through rapid increase, by budding or division, masses of great size may be formed over a small object of support. Even on muddy bottoms a small object of support may serve as the nucleus around which a coral mass will grow, which, as it increases in size and weight, will sink more or less deeply into the mud on which it rests.

The typical compound or reef-corals are very restricted in their bathymetrical distribution. They do not normally occur below fifty fathoms, and the majority live in less than twenty fathoms of water. Very many, indeed, live so close to the surface as to be exposed at the lowest tides. A minimum annual temperature of twenty degrees Centigrade marks the regions in which most reef-building corals occur, though in a few cases colder regions are known to be inhabited by true reef-builders. In all seas, however, which are subject to freezing, or are regularly invaded by floating ice, reef-building corals cannot thrive, and hence the occurrence of modern or ancient coral reefs is a reliable indication of a minimum winter temperature above freezing.

The reproduction of the Anthozoa is both asexual and sexual. The asexual method is carried on by fission and budding, the new-formed corallites commonly remaining united with their parents, thus producing colonial forms. In some cases, however, the buds will become free and begin an independent life. (Fungia, Balanophyllia, etc.) New colonies, however, are chiefly begun by sexually generated individuals. From the fertilized egg develops a meroplanktonic ciliated embryo, not unlike in appearance to the planula of the Hydrozoa. After attachment, this develops into the polyp, which early begins to secrete its horny or calcareous corallum.

Crinoidea.—The crinoids are without exception marine organisms, though *Antedon rosacea* has been taken in water containing only 2.5 per cent. of salts, or nearly a third less than in normal sea water. The majority of crinoids belong to the sedentary benthos, being anchored or attached to the sea bottom either by a stem or by the base of the calyx. Antedon must be classed with the vagrant benthos, for although it ordinarily rests on the sea bottom or other stationary objects of support, it is able to walk about on the bottom by means of its arms; and also to swim with graceful movements through the water. Planktonic crinoids appear to have existed in the Mesozoic seas (Saccocoma, Uintacrinus), and, as already noted, Walther has furnished evidence which indicates that some of the stemmed Pentacrini of the Lias lead a pseudo-planktonic life, growing attached to floating timbers with which they were carried about, calyx downward. The bathymetrical distribution of the modern crinoids ranges from shallow water to 2,000 fathoms, rarely more. One species of Antedon (*A. abyssicola* Carp.) has been obtained at a depth of 2,900 fathoms, but most of the species of this genus live in shallow water, *A. loveni* Beel occurring in three to four fathoms. This genus is perhaps the most cosmopolitan of modern crinoids, its geographic range being between eighty degrees northern and fifty-two degrees southern latitude. The following modern stalked crinoids have been obtained in less than ninety fathoms of water:*

Eudiocrinus indivisus Semp., 30 fathoms.
Metacrinus rotundus Carp., 70 fathoms.
Pentacrinus asterius L., 80 fathoms.
P. decorus Wy. Th., 84 fathoms.
P. mülleri Oerst, 84 fathoms.
Promachocrinus kerguelensis Carp., 28 fathoms.
Rhizocrinus lofotensis Sars, 80 fathoms.
R. rawsoni Pourt., 73 fathoms.

The egg of Antedon develops into an egg-shaped meroplanktonic larva, which has a tuft of long flagella on the anterior end, and five ciliated rings surrounding it. No mouth or anus is present. The embryo swims about for a length of time, varying from a few hours to several days, and, on settling down to a benthonic life, attaches itself at a point on the ventral side between the first and second ciliated rings. The whole anterior part, as far as the third ciliated ring, becomes the stalk, the posterior part developing into the calyx. In Antedon the stem is retained only during the earlier stages of development, the adult animal being free.

Asteroidea, Ophiuroidea.—These belong to the marine vagrant benthos, living mainly in shallow water or in moderate depths, though some species descend to depths of 2,000 fathoms or over. Some littoral starfish can undergo an exposure for several hours in regions laid bare by the tide. A sandy or muddy bottom seems to be the most characteristic facies for these animals, and from such bottoms thousands are often brought up in a single haul of the dredge. Their relative scarcity in beds in which they are

* From list given by Walther in '94, pp. 298—300.

known to occur is probably due to the fact that after the death of the animal the skeleton quickly falls apart into its component plates, which become separately embedded in the sediments. In the majority of the Asterozoa mero-planktonic, bilaterally symmetric, ciliated larvæ occur, which in the Asteroidea are known as Bipinnaria and Brachiolaria, and in the Ophiuroidea as Pluteus. These are often found in great numbers in the pelagic fauna.

Echinoidea.—The Echinoids, or Sea Urchins, are without exception marine vagrant benthonic animals, living usually in large numbers in moderate depths. A few species descend to depths between 2,000 and 3,000 fathoms, but the majority prefer the shallow portions of the littoral districts. On the coast of Maine thousands of *Strongylocentrotus drobachiensis* are exposed at very low tides, lying among stones and covered with fragments of shells and with small pebbles. The Echinoidea delight in a sandy bottom, from which they are brought up in vast numbers at each haul of the dredge. Some species prefer fine mud, in which they are often buried to some extent. When living on rocks, they commonly bore holes for themselves, and even the solid granite has been known to be thus attacked by the animal. If corners and crannies are available, these are often occupied by the animal in preference to a drilled hole.

The larva of Echinoidea is known as a Pluteus, and is a mero-planktonic, bilaterally symmetrical, commonly more or less ciliated organism, with a number of processes or arms. It is often carried by marine currents to great distances, remaining in some cases afloat for several weeks before settling down.

Holothuroidea.—The Holothurians are, like the Echinoidea, marine benthonic organisms, but their habit of life is often more sedentary than vagrant, the animals being buried in the sand and mud, though never attached. Their bathymetric range is from the shore zone, where they may be dug out of the sand at low tide, to the depths of the abyssal district. Sandy or muddy bottom is usually preferred by these animals, though many live among coarse blocks, and vast numbers occur among the coral masses of every coral reef. The ciliated larva, or Auricularia, of the Holothurians is a mero-planktonic organism, with definite mouth and anal opening.

From the fact that only isolated plates occur in the skin of the Holothurians, they do not constitute any important part of marine deposits.

Nemathelminthes, Gephyrea, Annelida.—These worms are marine, fresh-water, or terrestrial animals, with the exception of the Gephyrea, which are wholly marine. They belong chiefly to the benthos, though some marine forms lead a partially nektonic existence, while others are typically planktonic. Among the benthonic species all grades of a sedentary life are observable, from the tube-building orders, which live permanently in attached tubes, to those which only temporarily occupy a given area. Tubicolar worms, which, like Spirorbis, attach their tubes chiefly to algæ, may often lead a pseudo-planktonic existence when such algæ are torn from their anchorage and drifted away by currents.

Muddy bottom seems to be the favorite haunt of the littoral species, except such forms as build attached tubes (e. g., Serpulidæ, etc.), which occupy stony and shelly bottoms. These latter often build extensive reefs of interwoven calcareous tubes.

Besides calcareous tubes, many worms build tubes of agglutinated sand grains or shell particles, and worms living in the shells of dead mollusca are frequently met with. These agglutinated sand tubes are often very resistant, sometimes, with the castings, covering the mud flats and beaches in great numbers, and not infrequently being heaped together in windrows. The dredge often brings large numbers of these tubes, together with numerous castings, from the deeper water. The bathymetric distribution of the worms is varied. The majority are undoubtedly littoral species, but deep-sea forms are also common. Beyond the hundred fathom line, the tubicolar Annelids are the most characteristic, specimens having been obtained from a depth of 4,000 fathoms off Teneriffe. ("Challenger.") Other worms also occur. Even species of the same genus have a widely varying distribution in depth. Thus, the tubicoloid genus Spirorbis has its littoral species growing within the shore zone; while another species, *S. nautiloides*, has been dredged at a depth of 700 fathoms. Similarly, the Gephyrean Phascolosoma is represented along our northern shores by a species living in the mud and sand above low tide, while the "Blake" brought up a species in a Dentalium shell from a depth of 1,568 fathoms.*

Among the Annelids the family Eunicidæ is of particular interest, in that its several members are characteristic of different bathymetric zones, thus furnishing, in a measure, an index to the bathymetric position of the fauna which they characterize. This family is well represented in the lithographic shales of Bavaria. (Ehlers.) Among the worms, regeneration of lost parts, and generation of new individuals from fragments of old ones, is not uncommon. Thus in one of our common pelagic worms—Autolytus—swimming buds carrying the sexual products are periodically constricted off, each regenerating a new head, with highly developed eyes, at the anterior end. The earth worm—Lumbriusc—falls into pieces in autumn, all of which are able to regenerate into complete animals.†

A mero-planktonic ciliated larva, the Trochophore, is characteristic of worms, this being the product of a sexual mode of reproduction. These larvæ are often obtained in vast numbers in the tow-net, together with other mero-planktonic and many holo-planktonic forms.

Bryozoa.—The Bryozoa are marine or fresh water, chiefly colonial, benthonic animals. A few occur parasitic on a living substratum, but the majority of species are epiphytically attached to organic or inorganic objects, either basally or in an encrusting manner. The majority of species

---

* Agassiz, '88, II., 53.

† Lang, A.—Text book of Comparative Anatomy.

are marine, and their bathymetric distribution ranges from the shore zone, where they are exposed at low tide, to the abyssal depths, a species of Bifaxia having been obtained below 3,000 fathoms. The majority of species, however, live in moderate depths. While the Bryozoa normally lead a strictly sedentary benthonic life, a few species may drift about with the seaweed to which they are attached, thus assuming a pseudo-planktonic habit.

The egg of the bryozoan develops into a mero-planktonic, ciliated larva, which later on settles down, becomes attached, and develops into a full-grown individual, which, by budding, produces the colony.

Brachiopoda.—The Brachiopoda are marine benthonic organisms, of exceptional stratigraphic importance, since they are to a high degree dependent on the facies of the sea bottom. While typically marine, some species can become adapted to brackish and even fresh water. Thus Davidson* states that at Trias Cove whole colonies of *Terebratulina septentrionalis* were discovered on stony bottom in clear fresh water. Some species of Terebratula and Lingula can withstand a considerable exposure, the former having been noted out of water for hours together at low tide. Lingula is buried, by means of its long fleshy peduncle, in the sand near shore; Crania is attached to rocks and shells by its shell; while the majority of bachiopods are attached by their fleshy pedicles to rocks, shells, corals, or to one another. They seldom live on muddy or sandy bottoms, but are readily embedded in these, by becoming detached after death from the rocks or other objects to which they adhered.

The bathymetric distribution of the Brachiopoda ranges from shallow water to 2,900 fathoms (in one case), the majority of species occurring above the hundred fathom line, while quite a number have been obtained in depths of ten fathoms or less. A number of species have an individual range of several hundred fathoms, this range in one or two cases being nearly 800 fathoms.

* Mon. Rec. Brach., I., p. 28.

The mero-planktonic larva of brachiopods is known as the Cephalula, and consists of a ciliated umbrella-like anterior end, carrying four eyes, a middle portion carrying the mantle lobes, and a posterior portion. When the larva becomes attached by the posterior end, which develops into the pedicle of the adult, the anterior end becomes enveloped by the forward turning mantle lobes and develops into the body of the brachiopod.

Pelecypoda.—The pelecypods are marine or fluvial benthonic molluscs, which lead either a sedentary or a vagrant life. The majority of species live in the sea, but of these some can adapt themselves to brackish or even fresh water. Thus, species of Cardium, Solen, Mya, and other marine pelecypods have been obtained in fresh, or nearly fresh, water.

A number of pelecypods inhabit the shore-zone, but the majority of these live buried in the sands and muds, and so are protected from dessication at low tide. *Mytilus edulis,* however, is a good example of a shore pelecypod, for it habitually grows in positions where it will be periodically exposed at low tide. The closely related *Modiola modiolus,* which occurs on our northern shores associated with the preceding, is, however, seldom exposed, growing either in deep water or in tide pools which are never drained.

Ostrea arborea is another striking shore mollusc, growing in vast quantities on the free roots of the mangrove, and withstanding a periodic exposure under a tropical sun. *Ostrea borealis,* on the other hand, is at home only in water of several fathoms depth.

The bathymetric range of the Pelecypoda is very great, and even a single species may have a range of considerable magnitude. Thus, while *Mytilus edulis* does not occur below fifty fathoms, another species, *M. phascolinus,* ranges from the shore to a depth of 3,000 fathoms. In the greater depths, the pelecypods are commonly characterized by exceeding delicacy of shell and sculpture, the shell being often quite transparent. Some deep-water species show bright colors, but the majority are pale. Altogether there are to be found among these deep-water forms "innumerable illustrations of beauty, adaptation, or unusual characteristics. . . ." (Agassiz.) In the littoral district, on the other hand, the thick-shelled pelecypôds predominate, and this is especially true of the shore zone.

Pelecypods, like brachiopods, are excellent facies indicators, for, though they live on all kinds of sea bottom, the species, or at least the faunal combinations, are dependent on, and characteristic of, the particular facies on which they live. The majority of pelecypods are free animals, a few, such as the oyster, mussel, and the like, being attached to foreign objects—either by direct cementation or by a byssus. The free pelecypods have frequently the power of locomotion, Unio Mactra and others traveling occasionally for considerable distances. Generally, however, these molluscs lie buried wholly or partially in the sand, and never change their location except when disturbed by storm waves. Some few pelecypods (Pecten, Lima) have the power of swimming short distances by the opening and closing, in rapid succession, of their valves, and the forcible ejection of water. Even Solen, though normally a burrowing animal, will swim for some distances in search of the proper bottom, and it may often be seen circling around in an aquarium, by a series of jerks, due to the periodic ejection of the water from the siphons. A number of pelecypods bore into wood or stone (Teredo, Lithodomus, Saxicava, etc.), leading a sedentary life within the habitation thus formed.

The bivalve molluscs have many enemies which prey upon them. Not the least of these are the carnivorous gastropods, whose depredations are usually marked by the vast number of shells with round holes bored into them which are scattered along our beaches. Boring sponges will riddle the shells of littoral species, and corallines, Bryozoa, worms, and hydroids will attach themselves to the shells. There is abundant evidence in the riddled and punctured shells, that the Palæozoic molluscs were subject to similar attacks of boring sponges and carnivorous gastropods. When the animals die, their valves commonly fall apart, and from their position, and the character and direction of the waves and currents, one valve may be carried shoreward, the other seaward. This explains the frequent predominance, along the shore and in certain local portions of fossiliferous beds, of one valve, the other being often entirely absent or at least very rare.

The marine pelecypod normally passes through a meroplanktonic larval stage—the Trochophore—in which the young is provided with a velum, furnished with vibratory ciliæ (veliger stage). At certain seasons of the year these ciliated embryos swarm in the pelagic district, especially in the neighborhood of the shores, where they become the sport of the currents, which distribute them far and wide. When they finally settle down on the sea bottom, upon the loss of the velum, they will develop further if they reach the proper substratum, other conditions being favorable. Vast numbers of the larvæ are destroyed before they reach the bottom, serving as food for all kinds of animals, or succumbing to unfavorable conditions, and vast numbers of others die from falling on an unfavorable bottom. That most species, nevertheless, develop to the fullest extent is due to the enormous fecundity of most pelecypods. As an extreme example, may perhaps be mentioned our common northern oyster, *Ostrea virginiana*, which, according to Brooks,* produces nine millions of eggs. In fresh-water pelecypods the meroplanktonic veliger larva exists in one species only (*Dreissensia polymorpha*), which is said to have migrated from salt to fresh water in recent geologic times. (Lang.) In the other fresh-water pelecypods the development proceeds in a different manner—special adaptations to special modes of life being met with. In some cases (Pidium, Cyclas) the eggs develop in special brood-capsules in the gills of the mother, leaving these with shell fully formed, as young bivalves. In these genera the velum remains rudimentary, the animal

* Arch. Zoöl. Experim., IX., p. 28.

passing through the Trochophore stage within the gills of the mother. In the Unionidæ the embryo passes through its several stages in the gill of the mother, leaving it with a bivalve shell, which is, however, furnished with a triangular process on the ventral border of each valve, by means of which the embryo attaches itself to the fins (Anodonta) or gills (Unio) of fishes. In this manner the animal leads a pseudo-nektonic existence, becoming enclosed by the rapid growth of the epithelium of the part where the embryo is attached, and leading thus a truly endo-parasitic life. After several weeks the embryo has become transformed into a young mussel, which, breaking through the enclosing tissue of its nest, falls to the bottom of the water, there to develop into the adult.

Scaphopoda and *Amphineura.*—The first of these classes is represented by the Dentalidæ, the second by the Chitonidæ, which alone are important palæontologically. Both are marine, being of a sedentary benthonic habit, though not permanently attached. Dentalium lies buried in the mud and sands usually at great depths, while Chiton and its allies cling to stones, shells, etc., and are rare in deep water, where only their more archaic representatives occur. A few species of Dentalium occur in moderately shallow water, but most of them live below the hundred-fathom line, some reaching a depth of 2,000 fathoms or more. Chiton seldom extends below 500 fathoms. In both groups a mero-planktonic larva occurs.

Gastropoda.—The gastropods are typical benthonic animals, inhabiting the sea, fresh water, and the land. They almost invariably belong to the vagrant benthos, though the degree of locomotion varies greatly among different species. Among the exceptions to the general vagrant habit, are Vermetus and some other genera, which live a truly sedentary benthonic life, being attached to rocks or shells. Some genera, like Capulus, adhere continually to shells and the tests of Echinoderms and Crustacea; while the limpets, though adhering powerfully to rocks and shells by the muscular foot, are, nevertheless, in the habit of crawling about in search of food. Swimming and floating gastropods are also known, the latter (Janthina, Glaucus, etc.) belonging to the true plankton.

The number of species living on land and in fresh water is relatively small, though the individuals often occur in great numbers. The sea, however, is the home of most gastropods, though some marine forms can live in fresh water as well.

The variety of form and coloration is exceedingly great among the gastropods, a fact which can easily be correlated with their high degree of cephalization and actively vagrant life. They occupy all parts of the sea, being much less dependent on the facies of the sea bottom than the pelecypods are. The division into carnivorous and herbivorous forms is also much more strongly emphasized than in the pelecypods, which live largely upon the plankton.

The shore zone is occupied by a number of species which can withstand periodic exposure. Many of them require this exposure, and will invariably crawl to the surface if kept in confinement, even if the water is kept cool and well aërated. Others live in shallow water, even if stagnant, and will not stand a long exposure.

The majority of gastropods are shallow-water forms, though a number of them range to depths of between 1,000 and 2,000 fathoms. The deep-sea gastropods are characterized by faint colors, though often this is counterbalanced by the brilliancy and beauty of the iridescence, and even the non-iridescent abyssal species give out "a sort of sheen which is wanting in their shallow-water allies." (Agassiz, '88, II., p. 63.) The coarse ornamentation by knobs, spines, etc., so common in shallow-water species, does not occur in the deep-sea forms, where the ornamentation is more delicate, though often of exquisite richness and beauty. Gastropods feeding on vegetable matter are wanting in the deep sea, where no vegetable matter occurs, except what is brought down as sediment. The food of deep-sea molluscs is largely confined to soft-tissued animals, since thick shells and other hard armors are generally absent in these depths. Agassiz states that the Pleurotomidæ outnumber any other group of molluscs in the abyssal fauna. These gastropods are characterized by a notch in the outer lip near the suture, this serving for the discharge of the refuse, thus preventing fouling of the water used for respiration. Some of these are provided with hollow barbed teeth and poison fangs, which they use to kill their prey. This apparatus "is even more fully and generally developed in the related group of the Conidæ, few of which reach any great depth."* A few gastropods are viviparous (*Paludina vivipara*, *Littorina rudis*), producing their young in an advanced state of development.

In nearly all the marine gastropods a veliger larva occurs, the velum being commonly large, wing-like, and fringed with cilia. This velum may be retained until the shell is long past the protoconch stage. While in most marine gastropods the veliger larva leads a mero-planktonic existence, some marine forms (Fulgur, Sycotypus) and the oviparous land and fresh-water gastropods pass through their veliger stage within the egg capsule, losing the velum and other larval organs before passing from the capsule, which they leave as young gastropods with well-developed shells.

In the case of the marine forms cited, the velum, though of no use as a locomotor organ to the animal, is very large, and is lost only just before the embryo leaves the egg-capsule. In terrestrial and fresh-water forms, on the other hand, the velum is reduced to a single ring of cilia or to two lateral ciliated streaks (Lang, II., p. 257); while in some terrestrial species it is wanting entirely. It is obvious that the distribution of species thus deprived of a temporary pelagic life must be more restricted, other things being equal, than that of species having a free veliger stage of greater or less duration.

* Agassiz, '88, II., p. 66.

Pteropoda.—The pteropods are marine planktonic molluscs, which live in vast numbers in the pelagic district, usually at some distance from shore. While able to swim about in the water, they are nevertheless at the mercy of waves and currents. Their food consists of pelagic organisms, and not uncommonly one species of pteropod will prey upon another. They shun the light, descending during the day to the regions of perpetual twilight or even darkness, some descending as low as 700 fathoms. Nearly all the shelled pteropods of the present time are confined to the warmer waters, and they are especially abundant in the warm ocean currents. A veliger larva similar to that of gastropods occurs.

Cephalopoda.—The cephalopods are marine nektonic or benthonic molluscs, inhabiting water of moderate depths. Swimming is accomplished by the forcible ejection of water from the hyponome, and probably also by the use of the arms. Among the Dibranchiata the majority of Decapoda (Squids, Calamaries) are active swimmers, usually inhabiting the open sea, but appearing periodically on the coasts in great shoals. They live mostly on small fish. The Octopoda are less adapted to active swimming, lying usually in wait for their prey on the sea bottom or in crevices and hollows. The Argonauta is, however, a partial exception to this, for though it crawls about on the sea bottom, like other octopods, it is often met with swimming near or at the surface, by the ejection of the water from its hyponome. Argonauta is, therefore, like other cephalopods, at times a vagrant benthos, at others a nekton—inclining perhaps more to the latter, as do most of the decapods; while other octopods are more commonly benthonic. Among the less active decapods, Sepia may be mentioned as more normally a vagrant benthonic form, crawling about on the sea bottom, though able to swim as well. A sedentary benthonic cephalopod is also known. This is Spirula, which attaches itself to rocks like an Actinia (Agassiz, Walther), or lies partly buried in the mud with its beautiful coiled and chambered shell wholly concealed by the fleshy parts. A perfect specimen was dredged off Grenada in the Caribbean by the "Blake," from a depth of 950 fathoms.*

Spirula would seem to be a widely distributed form, judging from the occurrence of its shell in almost all parts of the tropical and temperate seas. The animal, however, is very rare, only one specimen with soft tissues preserved having been obtained by the "Challenger" expedition, this being taken close to the island of Banda, in 360 fathoms ("Challenger" Narrative). Altogether, perhaps, only about half a dozen animals with the soft parts preserved have been obtained. The wide distribution of the shell of Spirula is due to the fact, that after the death of the animal the shell ascends to the surface, owing to the air-filled chambers, and then becomes a part of the plankton. It is carried hither and thither by the currents and waves, and finally may reach the sea bottom in regions remote from its original home, and be buried in sediments of every description, and under conditions under which the animal never existed. Thus the shell of Spirula will become an excellent index-fossil, being widely distributed and buried in all kinds of sediment.

To a more restricted degree this method of distribution of the shell, after the death of the animal, occurs also in Nautilus, the only modern representative of the tetrabranchiate cephalopods. The animal belongs to the benthos, living in shallow water in the tropics. Occasionally, it swims near the surface, but before long it returns to the bottom, where it crawls about with its shell uppermost, feeding on Crustacea and other animals. On the death of the animal, the shell may float for a considerable time on the surface, buoyed up by the air in the chambers, and thus it will be carried to a greater or less distance before it settles to the bottom, where it will be buried in all kinds of sediment.

What is true of the shells of Nautilus and Spirula is true of the shell of Sepia, and was undoubtedly true of the shells of

* Agassiz, '88, II., p. 61.

Ammonites as well.* In fact, we may even believe that the shells of the Ammonites were better floaters than either those of Spirula or Nautilus, for these two genera are retrosiphonate, the siphonal funnels passing backward and thus giving more easy access to the water; while the shells of the Ammonites were prosiphonate, their siphonal funnels bending forward like the neck of a bottle, and thus making the entrance of water more difficult. This conception of the planktonic wanderings of the shells of cephalopods after the death of the animal furnishes a satisfactory explanation of many anomalies observed in the occurrence of these animals in the geologic series. It accounts especially for the sudden appearance and disappearance of the same species in widely separated localities, irrespective of the character of the rock, or its normal faunal contents. This wide-spread distribution of these shells makes them excellent index-fossils, so that even small formations can readily be correlated by their species of Ammonites, even though widely separated.

It does not follow, of course, that Ammonoid shells must always be regarded as strangers which have drifted to their present position. In fact, it is often easy to see that such has not been the case in any particular locality, from an examination of the shells themselves, as well as from extraneous evidence. Thus Clarke† says that the Ammonoids of the Naples beds of Western New York " * * bear sufficient demonstration in themselves that they have lived and died in these sediments." Many of the most delicate shells retain their apertures unbroken, and their surface ornamentation uninjured, a fact which is not consistent with wave and current transportation. The presence of the young in all stages of development further argues for an indigenous occurrence. "On the other hand," says Clarke, "there are excellent reasons for regarding the prenuncial Intumescens fauna, that of the Styliola (Styliolina) limestone, as due to transportation from some adjoining

* Walther, '94, p. 509; '97, p. 258, et seq.

† Naples Fauna, p. 135, et seq.

province not yet known to us." The Goniatites of this fauna are associated with the millions of planktonic Styliolina, with floated logs, and probably other pelagic organisms, and the sediment in which they were embedded was such as probably was not conducive to the well-being of such animals, so that their occurrence is best explained by the hypothesis of flotation.

Of the embryology of Nautilus, and hence the whole group of Tetrabranchiata, nothing is known. The Dibranchiata develop directly within the egg capsule, no veliger stage occurring.

Cirripedia.—The cirripeds, or barnacles, are marine sedentary benthonic Crustacea which have degenerated much from the true type of crustacean, owing no doubt to their attached mode of life. The body is covered with calcareous plates variously arranged, which fall apart after the death of the animal, after which, from single pieces, it becomes quite impossible to determine the species, owing to the great variation of the skeletal parts (Darwin). Balanus and its congeners are sessile, being attached to the rocks and other solid supports along the shore, seldom venturing into water of great depths. Some species are exposed periodically at low tide for many hours at a time, some, in fact, being never covered more than one or two hours at flood tide, so high up on the shore do they attach themselves. Balanus has been found at a depth of 500 fathoms, but it usually lives in lesser depths. *Balanus improvisus* occurs also in brackish water. *Coronula diadema* leads a pseudo-nektonic life, attaching itself to the body of whales. *Verruca incerta*, a common West Indian type, occurs in the Globigerina ooze. Lepas and its congeners are pedunculate, attaching themselves by a fleshy peduncle, which represents the elongated head end. The majority of the Lepadidæ are pelagic, leading a pseudo-planktonic existence, attached to floating logs, pumice, or other objects. Three species of Lepas were found by the "Challenger" attached to the Sargassum. Some members of this family descend into deep water, *Scalpellum* *regium*, having been dredged by the "Challenger" from nearly 3,000 fathoms. These abyssal cirripeds are usually attached to nodules, dead or living shells, corals, large Crustacea, to spines of sea-urchins and other objects.* The cirripeds, upon hatching from the egg, pass through several larval stages, the first of which is the Nauplius stage. In this the body is unsegmented with median frontal eye, dorsal shield, frontal sensory organs, and three pairs of limbs. After a series of moults the Cypris stage is reached, in which the larva is enclosed in a bivalve shell, like that of the Ostracoda. During these stages the larva belongs to the mero-plankton. When it settles down and becomes attached, it passes through a pupa stage, during which the transformation of the larva into the cirriped takes place.

Ostracoda.—The ostracods are marine or fresh-water planktonic or vagrant benthonic Crustacea, whose imperfectly segmented body is enclosed in a bivalve shell. The majority of the marine forms are planktonic, living in shallow water or moderate depths, though a few species were found by the "Challenger" at depths exceeding 2,000 fathoms. Some species are cosmopolitan, and the order is represented in nearly all waters. Their shells occur in nearly all the bottom deposits. The animals are also abundant on algæ, over which they crawl slowly. The fresh-water Cypris swims about, subject, however, to the influences to which other members of the plankton are subject, or crawls about over the vegetation. Cypris is also represented in brackish and salt-water. The larva of Ostracoda is a pelagic Nauplius.

Xiphosura.—The xiphosurans are represented by the single living genus Limulus, which is a marine vagrant benthonic animal, though often swimming on the back when young. The usual habitat of this animal is in shallow water, where it is often partly buried in the mud or sand. Portions of the coast are often strewn with the cast-off exoskeletons of Limulus, which commonly lie on their back,

* Agassiz, '88, II., p. 50.

a position which these structures will naturally take on sinking to the bottom.

The young Limulus on hatching is a trilobiti-form, free swimming, commonly mero-planktonic organism, without a caudal spine. (J. S. Kingsley.)

Gigantostraca.—These Crustacea are entirely extinct, being represented by Eurypterus and Pterygotus. They were undoubtedly marine, and probably belonged to both nekton and vagrant benthos.

Trilobitæ.—The trilobites are extinct Palæozoic Crustacea of an undoubted marine habitat, probably able to swim as well as crawl, and so belonging at one time to the nekton, at another to the vagrant benthos. Whether or not a mero-planktonic larva existed is not known, but this might be assumed from the wide distribution of some species. As trilobites cast off their exoskeleton like Limulus, some of these may have been floated for some distances, coming to lodge where trilobites never lived. It is certain that from the number of fossil trilobites we can not judge the number of individuals existing at a given place, since a number of specimens may represent the cast-off exoskeletons of one individual.

Decapoda.—The decapods belong chiefly to the benthos, inhabiting either fresh or salt water, rarely the land. Pelagic species also occur, some of which are good swimmers. They commonly feed on living or dead animal matter. The bathymetric distribution varies greatly, though the majority of species are confined to comparatively shallow water, generally not exceeding fifty fathoms. The range of individual species is often great, *Alpheus avarus*, for example, ranging on the Australian coast, from less than ten to about 2,500 fathoms. Among the hermit crabs occur some forms which have left their native element, and have taken to the land. The "Challenger" found some of them in the mountains of the Antilles, up to 300 meters. They sometimes inhabit the shells of land snails and have been observed climbing trees. Among the true crabs, or Brachyura, shallow-water species predominate, comparatively few occurring below 400 fathoms. A number of species live in fresh water or on land. The majority of decapods leave the egg in the Zoëa stage, in which the abdominal region is perfectly segmented, though still without appendages, except perhaps the rudiments of the sixth pair. The compound eyes are stalked. Other larval stages follow until the adult is reached. These larvæ often occur in vast quantities in the plankton.

Migration of Marine Invertebrates.

Whatever the present distribution of animal life in the sea, it is clear that it has not always been so. Even the most cosmopolitan species had its circumscribed center of origin, it being extremely unlikely that the same species originated in more than one locality. From this locality the species dispersed to occupy whatever territory was available.

"The species," says Wagner,* "which originate in isolated areas, seek every opportunity to occupy new regions, and migrate from their place of origin to other localities." However, as Ortmann insists, species can only occupy areas the facies of which correspond to those of regions where they originated, in the degree in which the species is dependent upon the facies. Thus, while emigration from the original home of the species may take place on a large scale, immigration and settlement of this species in other regions is only possible under certain circumstances.

It must not be forgotten in this connection, that, as already pointed out, the organic factor is of foremost importance in determining whether or not an area is to be permanently occupied by a new immigrant. If the food supply is insufficient, or if contending species hold the ground, the new arrivals may be prevented from occupying the territory, even though the facies is well adapted to their needs.

Continuity of the conditions of existence, in space, favors dispersion, for in a continuous area there are no barriers to surmount. On the other hand, discontinuity of the

* Ortmann, '95, p. 33.

conditions of existence hinders or prevents dispersion, for the barriers separating the localities with similar, or but slightly different, conditions may be insurmountable. Under barriers to migration we may place topographical barriers first, especially the northward and southward stretching continents, as already pointed out. But topographical barriers are not the only ones, nor in many cases the most important. Differences in temperature, character and direction of ocean currents, improper facies of the sea bottom and insufficient food supply, as well as hostile species, constitute some of the chief barriers to emigration. If by some means or other a barrier is surmounted, and a new colony established, this new colony may become more or less isolated, the barrier proving too effective for all but a few individuals. "Migration," says Ortmann ('96, II., p. 186), "is often slow or only possible under peculiar circumstances, often it is accidental, and only a few individuals can transgress the original limits on rare occasions; then even migration acts as a means of separation. The few individuals occupying a new locality are afterwards practically separated from the original stock remaining in their native country, and thus they may develop separately into a different species, even in the case that immigration from the original stock is not altogether impossible, since any rare individuals of the latter reaching the new colony from time to time are soon absorbed by the new form and their characters disappear by the continuous crossing with the modified individuals and by the transforming power of the external conditions."

The fauna of any area may be considered as belonging to one or more of the following groups: endemic species, immigrants, or relicts. Endemic species are those which originated in the locality in which they are found. Immigrants have invaded the region, and established themselves in it. Relicts are remnants, in favored places, of a once widely distributed fauna, which, by the breaking up of the area which they occupied, became resolved into a number of local remnants, which remain separated.

The following are the marine zoögeographical areas of the present geologic epoch, as given by Ortmann ('96, I., p. 66):

I. Littoral life-district.
   1. Arctic region. 2. Indo-Pacific region. 3. West American region. 4. East American region. 5. West African region. 6. Antarctic region.

II. Pelagic life-district.
   1. Arctic region. 2. Indo-Pacific region. 3. Atlantic region. 4. Antarctic region.

III., IV. Abyssal life-districts.
   No regions distinguishable.

LITERATURE.

Agassiz, A., '88.—Three Cruises of the "Blake." 2 Vols. (Bull. Mus. Comp. Zoöl., Vols. XIV., XV.)

Chamberlin, T. C., '98.—A Systematic Source of Evolution of Provincial Faunas. (Journ. Geol., Vol. VI., p. 597.)

Chun, Carl, '86.—Ueber die geographische Verbreitung der pelagisch lebenden Seethiere. (Zoolog. Anzeiger, Nr. 214, 215.)

Chun, Carl, '88.—Die pelagische Thierwelt in grösseren Meerestiefen und ihre Beziehungen zu der Oberflächen-Fauna. (Bibliotheca Zoologica, Heft I.)

Chun, Carl, '90.—Die pelagische Thierwelt in grossen Tiefen. (Verhandl. d. Gesellschaft deutsch. Naturfr. und Aerzte. Bremen, 1890.)

Conn, H. W., '85.—Marine Larvæ and Their Relation to Adults. (Stud. Biol. Lab., Johns Hopkins Univ., Vol. III., pp. 165–192, Pls. VIII. and IX.)

Dall, William H., '90.—Deep Sea Molluscs and the Condition Under Which They Live. (Pres. Addr. Biol. Soc., Wash. Proceed., Vol. V., pp. 1–27.)

Fuchs, Th., '82.—Ueber die pelagische Flora und Fauna. (Verhandl. d. k. k. Geolog. Reichsanstalt in Wien, 4 Febr., 1882, pp. 49–55.)

Hæckel, Ernst, '90.—Planktonstudien. Vergleichende Untersuchungen über die Bedeutung und Zusammensetzung der pelagischen Fauna und Flora. (Jena, 1890.)

Hæckel, Ernst, '93.—Planktonic Studies. Translated from the German by George W. Field. (Rept. U.S. Fish Com., 1889–1891, pp. 565-641.)

Heilprin, A., '87.—The Geographical and Geological Distribution of Animals. (International Scientific Series, Vol. LVII.)

Hensen, Victor, '87.—Ueber die Bestimmung des Planktons, oder des im Meere treibenden Materials an Pflanzen und Thieren. (V. Bericht der Commission zur Wissenschaftlichen Untersuchung der deutschen Meere.)

Hensen, Victor, '90.—Einige Ergebnisse der Plankton-Expedition der Humboldt Stiftung. (Sitzungsberichte der Berliner Akademie der Wissenschaften. vom 13 März, 1890, pp. 243–253.)

Kirchhoff, Alfred, '99.—Pflanzen und Tierverbreitung. (Hann, Hochstetter u. Pokony, Algemeine Erdkunde, 5th ed., Vol. III. Leipzig.)

Moseley, H. N., '82.—Pelagic Life. Address at the Southampton Meeting Brit. Assoc. (Nature, Vol. XXVI., No. 675, p. 559.)

Moseley, H. N., '85.—The Fauna of the Sea Shore. (Nature, Vol. XXXII., p. 417.)

Murray, John, '85.—Narrative of Cruise of H. M. S. "Challenger," with a General Account of the Scientific Results of the Expedition. ("Challenger" Report, Vols. I., II.)

Ortman, Arnold E., '95.—Grundzüge der Marinen Tiergeographie. (Jena, G. Fischer.)

Ortman, Arnold E., '96, 1.—On Separation and its Bearing on Geology and Zoögeography. (Am. Journ. Sci. IV., Vol. II., pp. 63–69.)

Ortman, Arnold E., '96, 2.—On Natural Selection and Separation. (Proc. Am. Phil. Soc., Vol. XXXV, pp. 175–192.)

Schimper, A. F. W., '98.—Pflanzengeographie auf physiologischer Grundlage. (Jena, G. Fischer.)

Semper, Karl, '81.—Animal Life as Affected by the Natural Conditions of Existence. (Intern. Scientific Series, Vol. XXX.)

Smith, J. P., '95.—Geologic Study of Migration of Marine Invertebrates. (Journ. Geol., Vol. III., 1895, pp. 481-495.)

Thompson, Wyville, '73.—The Depths of the Sea. An Account of the General Results of the Dredging Cruises of H. M. S. S. "Porcupine" and "Lightning."

Wallace, Alfred Russell, '76.—The Geographical Distribution of Animals. (London, 1876.)

Walther, Johannes, '94.—Einleitung in die Geologie als historische Wissenschaft. I. Bionomie des Meeres. II. Die Lebensweise der Meeresthiere. III. Lithogenesis der Gegenwart. (Jena, Gustav Fischer, 1893–1894.)

Walther, Johannes, '97.—Ueber die Lebensweise fossiler Meeresthiere. (Zeitschrift d. Deutschen Geol. Gesellsch. Bd. XLIX, Heft II., pp. 209-273.)

Weller, Stuart, '95.—A Circum-insular Palæozoic Fauna. (Journ. Geol., Vol. III., pp. 903-927.)

Weller, Stuart, '98.—The Silurian Fauna Interpreted on the Epicontinental Basis. (Journ. Geol., Vol. VI., pp. 692–703.)

White, Charles A., '84.—The Application of Biology to Geological History. Presidential Address. (Proc. Biol. Soc., Washington, Vol. III., 1884–1886, pp. 1–20.)

CHAPTER IV.

Glossary of Palæontological Terms.

Aberrant—differing from the type.

Acanthopores—hollow spines occurring between the apertures, on the frond of a Bryozoan.

Adductor muscles—the closing muscles in bivalve shells.

Agglutinate—firmly united.

Air-chambers—the chambers below the living chamber in the shells of Cephalopods.

Alar—pertaining to wings; the lateral primary septa of the Tetracoralla.

Alate—having wing-like expansions.

Ambulacral areas—the perforated areas in the test of an Echinoderm, through which the tubed feet project.

Anastomosing—uniting so as to form a net work.

Anchylosed—firmly united; grown together.

Annulus—a ring; a segment of the thorax of a Trilobite.

Anterior—front.

Apophysis—a calcareous process (in interior of shells, etc.).

Appressed—pressed closely against.

Arcuate—arched; bent like a bow.

Articulated—joined by interlocking processes, or by teeth and sockets.

Auricle—the ear, or anterior projection of the hinge of many Pelecypods.

Auriculate—eared.

Azygous—unpaired; the azygous side of the calyx of a crinoid has plates differing from those of the regular sides.

Axial furrows—the furrows or depressions delimiting the axis in Trilobites.

Axis—the central longitudinal division of the body of a Trilobite.

Basals—the lowest cycle or cycles (in forms with dicyclic base) of plates in the Crinoidea.

Beak—the area of the apex or initial point of a shell.

Biconvex—both valves convex, as in most Brachiopods.

Bifid—split in two.

Bifurcating—dividing in two,—forking.

Biserial—with double series or rows.

Brachial—pertaining to the brachia or arms of Brachiopods or Crinoids; one of the arm plates of Crinoids.

Brachidium—the calcareous support of the arms in Brachiopods.

Branchiæ—gills.

Bryozoum—the whole compound colony of the Bryozoa.

Bulbiform—bulb-shaped.

Byssal notch—the notch or opening for the emission of the byssus (supporting-threads spun by the foot) in the Pelecypoda.

Callus—the thickened portion of the inner lip of Gastropods, which usually covers portions of the preceding volutions.

Calyx—(1) the cup of corals, limited below by the septa; (2) the body, exclusive of the arms, of Crinoids, Cystoids, and Blastoids.

Carapace—the hard shield or shell of Crustacea.

Cardinal—pertaining to the area of the beak in Brachiopods and Pelecypods.

Cardinal process—the process from under the beak of the brachial valve of Brachiopods, to which the diductor (opening) muscles are attached.

Cardinal quadrants—the two quadrants of a Tetracorallum which bound the main, or cardinal, septum.

Cardinal septum—the first or main of the four primary septa of a Tetracorallum; the cardinal septum has the pinnate arrangement of the secondary septa on both sides.

Cardinal teeth—the teeth under the beak in the Pelecypods; the teeth in the pedicle valve of the Brachiopods.

Carina—a projecting ridge running down the center of the branches in some Fenestelloid and other Bryozoa; the projecting ridges on the septa of Heliophyllum and other corals.

Cartilage—the compressible, elastic substance between the hinge-margins of the valves of Pelecypods. The *cartilage* is the internal, the *ligament* the external, medium for opening the valves.

Cast—the impression taken from a mold.

Celluliferous—cell bearing. (Bryozoa commonly have a *celluliferous* and a *non-celluliferous* side.)

Cephalic limb—the anterior border of the cephalon of a Trilobite.

Cephalon—the head-shield of Trilobites.

Cheeks—the lateral portions of the cephalon of a Trilobite; it is divided into fixed and free cheeks.

Cheilyrium—the triangular opening under the beak of the brachial valve in those Brachiopods in which that valve is furnished with a hinge area.

Chilidium—the covering for the cheilyrium.

Cicatrix—a scar.

Cincture—a depression anterior to the beak in the shell of some Pelecypoda.

Cirri—root-like appendages to the stems of Crinoids.

Clavicle—a heavy internal ridge running downward from the beak in some Pelecypods.

Columella—a central or axillary rod.

Composite corallum—a compound corallum with cœnenchyma or extrathecal calcareous tissue connecting the corallites. (Ex. Galaxia and many other recent forms.)

Compound corallum—made up of corallites, either separate or closely joined by their walls (Ex. Favosites).

Concavo-convex—the shells of Brachiopods are normally concavo-convex, when the brachial valve is concave and the pedicle valve convex; reversed or *resupinate*, when the reverse condition obtains.

Confluent—blended so that the line of demarcation is not visible.

Corallites—the individual tubes of a compound corallum.

Corallum—the calcareous skeleton of a single, or of a colonial, coral stock.

Corneous—horny.

Costæ—the extrathecal extensions of the septa of the corals.

Costals—the first brachial or arm-plates of the Crinoids lying between the radials and the first bifurcation of the arms.

Counter quadrants—the quadrants bounding the counter septum of a Tetracorallum.

Counter septum—the front primary septum of the Tetracoralla, opposite the cardinal septum; the secondary septa are parallel to it.

Crenulated—notched, so as to produce series of teeth.

Crura—the apophyses to which the brachidium of the Brachiopods is attached.

Cuneate—wedge-shaped.

Cyathophylloid—in form like Cyathophyllum; one of the Tetracoralla.

Cyst—a closed cavity.

Delthyrium—the triangular fissure under the beak of the pedicle valve of the Brachiopoda.

Deltidial plates—the two plates which close the delthyrium in the higher Brachiopoda (Telotremata).

Deltidium—the single covering plate of the Delthyrium (also called pedicle plate).

Dendroid—branching after the manner of a tree.

Denticulate—toothed.

Denticulation—set of denticles or small teeth.

Dicyclic—with two cycles of basals; applied to Crinoids.

Diductor muscles—opening muscles of the Brachiopoda.

Discinoid—resembling Discina.

Discoid—disk-like.

Dissepiments—partitions; the intrathecal connecting plates between the septa of the corals; the connecting bars between the branches of a Fenestelloid bryozoum.

Distal—situated away from the center of the body.

Distichals—the second series of arm-plates or brachials of Crinoids, situated above the axillary costals.

Divaricators—the opening muscles of Brachiopoda; also called diductors.

Dorsal—pertaining to the back.

Doublure—the infolded margin of the cephalon of a Trilobite.

Ear—the anterior cardinal expansion of the Pelecypod shell. It is usually smaller and more distinctly defined than the posterior expansion or wing.

Ectoderm—the outer cellular body layer.

Emarginate—with a notched margin.

Endoderm—the inner cellular body layer.

Endothecal—within the theca; intrathecal; used for corals.

Epitheca—the extrathecal sheath or covering, usually wrinkled, found in most Tetracoralla and many Hexacoralla.

Escutcheon—the depression behind the beak of the Pelecypod shell.

Exfoliate—peeling off.

Exothecal—same as extrathecal.

Extrathecal—outside of the theca of corals.

Extroverted—turned base to base; applied to spirals of Brachiopods.

Fasciculate—clustered.

Fenestrule—the open spaces between the branches and dissepiments of a Fenestella frond.

Filiform—thread-like.

Fimbriœ—the spines or lateral prolongations of the pleuræ in Trilobites.

Flabellate—fan-shaped.

Fold—an elevation on the surface of a shell (Brachiopoda).

Foramen—an opening or pore; specifically the opening for the pedicle in the pedicle valve of the Brachiopoda.

Fossula—a groove in the calyx of a coral, usually due to the abortion of a septum.

Frond—the foliaceous or leaf-like expansion of the skeleton of Bryozoa and other organisms.

Genal spines—the posterior prolongations, or spines, of the free cheeks of Trilobites.

Gibbous—swollen or humped.

Glabella—the central, most prominent, portion of the Trilobite cephalon, bounded by the fixed cheeks.

Gonopolyp—the reproductive polyp of Hydrozoa.

Hexacoralla—a class of corals built on the plan of six.

Hinge area—the flat area bordering the hinge line of many Brachiopods.

Hinge line—the line of articulation.

Hydrotheca—the cup enclosing the nutritive polyp in thecaphore Hydrozoa.

Hyponome—the water tube, or squirting organ, of squids, cuttlefish, and other Cephalopods.

Hypostoma—the underlip of the Trilobites, usually found detached.

Imbricate—overlapping serially.

Implantation—planting between, as a new plication suddenly appearing between two older ones.

Inarticulate—not articulating by teeth and sockets; of Brachiopoda.

Incised—cut into.

Infrabasals—the lower cycle of basal plates in the Crinoids with dicyclic base.

Infundibuliform—funnel-shaped.

Inosculating—connecting, so as to have intercommunication.

Interambulacral—between the ambulacra.

Interapertural—between the apertures.

Interbrachials—the plates in the calyx of a Crinoid, lying between the brachials.

Intercalation—irregular interposition.

Intercellular—between the cells or meshes.

Interdistichals—the plates in the calyx of a Crinoid, lying between the distichals.

Interradials—the plates in the calyx of a Crinoid, lying between the radials.

Interstitial—pertaining to an intervening space; between lines, plications, etc.

Intrathecal—within the theca; endo-thecal.

Introverted—turned apex to apex; applied to the spirals of Brachiopods.

Keel—a strong central carina or ridge (Tæniopora).

Lacrymiform—tear-form; drop-shaped—pear-shaped in form, but without the lateral contractions.

Lamellose—made up of lamellæ.

Lateral gemmation—a budding from the sides, as in some corals.

Ligament—the external structure for opening the valves in the Pelecypoda.

Limb—the lateral area or marginal band of the cephalon of Trilobites on either side of the glabella, corresponding to a pleuron of the thoracic region.

Linguiform—tongue-shaped.

Linguloid—tongue-shaped; like Lingula.

Lip—the margins of the aperture of univalve shells.

Listrium—the depressed area surrounding the pedicle opening in the pedicle valve of Orbiculoidea and other discinoid Brachiopods.

Lobes—the backward bending portions of the suture of Cephalopod shells.

Lophophore—the ciliated, or tentaculated oval disk of Bryozoa; the oval disk and brachia of Brachiopods.

Lunarium—a more or less thickened portion of the posterior wall of the cell in many Palæozoic Bryozoa, which is lunate or curved to a shorter radius, and usually projects above the plane of the cell aperture.

Lunule—the depression in front of the beak of Pelecypod shells.

Macerate—softening and disintegrating by immersion in water.

Maculæ—irregular, usually depressed, areas on the celluliferous face of a Bryozoan frond, which are free from cells, or otherwise differentiated.

Mesial—central.

Mesoglœa—the central, non-cellular layer in the body of Cœlenterates.

Meso-pores—irregular meshes, or cysts, on the intercellular spaces of certain Bryozoa.

Mesotheca—a median wall separating opposed cells in certain Bryozoan fronds.

Mold—Any impression of a fossil, in rock matrix, whether external or internal.

Moniliform—resembling a necklace or string of beads.

Monticules—elevated areas on the surface of certain coral and Bryozoan colonies, commonly carrying larger apertures.

Mucronate—produced into a long pointed extension.

Mural pores—the pores in the walls of the corallites of the Favositidæ.

Nacreous—pearly; the nacreous layer of shells is the inner smooth pearly layer.

Nasute—projecting, nose-like.

Node—a knob; usually considered as ornamental.

Nodose—bearing nodes or tubercles.

Obconical—inversely conical.

Occipital—applied to the posterior part of the cephalon of a Trilobite.

Occipital furrow—the transverse groove on the cephalon of Trilobites, which separates the last, or occipital, ring from the rest of the cephalon.

Occipital ring—the posterior division of the glabella of a Trilobite cephalon.

Operculiform—resembling an operculum.

Operculum—a lid or cover.

Pallial line—the line on the interior of the shell of molluscs, marking the attachment of the mantle.

Pallial sinus—the reëntrant angle in the pallial line, usually at the posterior end of the shell of Pelecypods; it marks the attachment of the siphon muscles.

Palmars—the third series of brachial plates of the Crinoidea, lying above the axillary distichals.

Palmate—palm-shaped.

Palpebral lobes—the supra-orbital extensions from the fixed cheeks of Trilobites.

Papillose—covered with papillæ or fine projections.

Parabasals—the second cycle of basal plates in Crinoids.

Pedicle—the fleshy peduncle or stem used for attachment in the Brachiopoda.

Periderm—the outer chitinous covering of Hydrozoa.

Periostracum—the epidermis or outer organic coating of shells.

Peristome—the margin of an aperture, *i. e.*, the mouth of a univalve molluscan shell, the mouth of a Bryozoan cell, etc.

Peritheca—the epithecal covering which surrounds a colony of Corallites, *i. e.*, a compound corallum.

Pinules—the finest divisions of the arms of Crinoids.

Plano-convex—normally in Brachiopods, with the pedicle valve convex and the brachial valve flat.

Pleuræ—the lateral portions of the thoracic rings of Trilobites.

Polyp—the animal of a simple Cœlenterate or Bryozoan.

Polypite—the individual polyp of a colony.

Post-palmars—all the plates superior to the axillary palmars in the arms of Crinoids.

Proliferous—reproducing buds from the calyx.

Protoconch—the embryonic shell of a cephalous molluscan.

Pseudo-columella—false columella in corals, formed by a twisting of the septa.

Pseudo-deltidium—false deltidium (*Spirifer*), formed by union of the two deltidial plates.

Pseudo-septa—septa-like ridges of Chætedes, etc.; the projecting ends of the lunaria in the cells of certain Bryozoa.

Pustulose—bearing pustules or projections.

Pygidium—the posterior or tail-portion of the carapace of Trilobites.

Pyriform—pear-shaped.

Quadrifid—cut into four points.

Quadrilobate—bearing four lobes.

Rachis—the central stem of a frond in Bryozoa, etc.

Radials—the main plates of the calyx of a Crinoid, resting on the para-basals, and alternating with them.

Radii—the ribs or striations diverging from the beak of a shell.

Ramose—branching.

Reticulated—like a network.

Retral—backward.

Rhynchonelloid—resembling Rhynchonella.

Rugosa—an old name for the Tetracoralla.

Saddles—the forward bending portions of the suture in the shells of Cephalopods.

Scalæ—small transverse plates in the genus Unitrypa of the Bryozoa (which see).

Scalariform—stair or ladder-shaped.

Sclerenchyma—the calcareous tissue deposited by the coral polyps.

Septum—a partition; in corals, the radiating calcareous plates; in Cephalopods, the transverse partition between the chambers.

Setiferous—bristle-bearing.

Sigmoid—curved like the Greek letter ς (sigma).

Sinuate—wavy, winding.

Sinus—an impression in the surface or margin of a shell.

Siphonal funnel—the siphonal projection from the septum of a Cephalopod shell.

Siphonal lobe—the lobe, in the suture of an Ammonoid shell, corresponding in position to the siphuncle.

Siphuncle—the tubular canal, passing through the air-chambers in the shells of Cephalopods.

Spatulate—shaped like a spatula; spoon-shaped.

Spinulose—spine bearing.

Sub—in composition indicates a low degree: sub-angular—rather angular; sub-carinate—somewhat toothed, etc.

Sulcus—a furrow.

Suture—in Cephalopods—the line of juncture between shell and septum, seen on breaking away the former; in Gastropods—the external line of juncture between the several whorls; in Trilobites—the dividing line between fixed and free cheeks, commonly called *facial suture;* in Crinoids—the line of juncture between adjacent plates.

Tabulæ—the transverse, continuous partitions or floors in corals, etc.

Tegmen—the vault or cover of the calyx in Crinoids.

Terebratuloid—like the recent genus Terebratula.

Test—shell.

Tetrameral—on the plan of four.

Theca—the proper wall of the individual corals.

Thorax—the central part of the body of the Trilobites.

Trabeculæ—projecting bars.

Trigonal—three-angled.

Trihedral—with three equal faces.

Tripartite—divided into three parts.

Turbinate—top-shaped.

Umbilicus—the external opening of the hollow axis of a loose coiled shell.

Umbo—the area about and including the beak in Pelecypods and Brachiopods.

Varix—a row of spines, a ridge or other mark, denoting the former position of the lip on the shell of a gastropod (Pl. *varices*).

Ventral—pertaining to the lower side, or venter.

Ventricose—strongly swollen, or bulging.

Vesicular—bearing vesicles, or hollow cavities.

Vestibular area—the area surrounding the cell apertures of some Bryozoa; often depressed.

Whorl—a single volution of a coiled shell.

Wing—the posterior larger expansion along the hinge line of a Pelecypod.

Zoarium—the aggregates of the polypites of a Bryozoan colony.

Zoœcium—the Bryozoan cell.

Zoöid—one of the "persons" or individuals of a zoarium.

APPENDIX.

A List of Reference Works.

(Additional papers have been cited in foot-notes.)

A.— Text Books.

ELEMENTARY.

W. O. Crosby.—Common Minerals and Rocks. D. C. Heath & Co.

Joseph LeConte.—Elements of Geology. D. Appleton & Co.

ADVANCED.

James D. Dana.—Manual of Geology, 4th edition. American Book Co.

Archibald Geikie.—Text Book of Geology, 3d edition. Macmillan & Co.

H. Alleyne Nicholson and Richard Lydekker.—Manual of Palæontology, 3d edition. William Blackwood & Sons, Edinburgh and London.

Karl A. von Zittel.—Text Book of Palæontology. Translated by Charles R. Eastman, Ph. D. Macmillan & Co.

B — Books of a General Character.

G. F. Wright.—The Ice Age in North America. D. Appleton & Co.

H. S. Williams.—Geological Biology. An introduction to the Geological History of Organisms. Henry Holt & Co., 1895.

J. W. Dawson.—The Geological History of Plants, Vol. LXI., International Scientific Series. D. Appleton & Co.

Geo. P. Merrill.—Rocks, Rockweathering and Soils. The Macmillan Co., N. Y.

C.— Government Reports, Etc.

New York State Geological Survey.

James Hall.— Geology of New York, Part IV., comprising the survey of the Fourth Geological District. Albany, 1843. (Natural History of New York Series.)

James Hall.— Annual Reports of the State Geologist (1 to 16). Special papers referred to below.

James Hall.— Palæontology of New York, Vol. IV., Brachiopoda of the Upper Helderberg, Hamilton, Portage, and Chemung Groups. 1867.

James Hall.— Palæontology of New York. Illustrations of Devonian Fossils. 1876. (Partly republished in later volumes.)

James Hall.— Palæontology of New York, Vol. V., Part I. (in two volumes). Lamellibranchiata of the Upper Helderberg, Hamilton, Portage, and Chemung Groups. 1885.

Vol. V., Part II. (in two volumes). Gasteropoda, Pteropoda, and Cephalopoda of the Upper Helderberg, Hamilton, Portage, and Chemung Groups. 1879.

James Hall and Geo. B. Simpson.— Palæontology of New York, Vol. VI. Corals and Bryozoa of the Lower Helderberg, Upper Helderberg, and Hamilton Groups. 1887.

James Hall and John M. Clarke.— Palæontology of New York, Vol. VII. Trilobites and other Crustacea of the Oriskany, Upper Helderberg, Hamilton, Portage, Chemung, and Catskill Groups. 1888.

James Hall and John M. Clarke.— Palæontology of New York, Vol. VIII. (in two volumes). An Introduction to the Study of the Genera of Palæozoic Brachiopoda. 1892 and 1894.

UNITED STATES GEOLOGICAL SURVEY.

MONOGRAPHS.

J. S. Newberry.—The Palæozoic Fishes of North America, Mon. XVI. 1889.

BULLETINS.

Henry S. Williams.—On the Fossil Faunas of the Upper Devonian, along the meridian of 76° 30′, from Tompkins County, N. Y., to Bradford County, Pa. Bull. 3, 1884.

John M. Clarke.—On the Higher Devonian Faunas of Ontario County, N. Y. Bull. 16, 1885.

Henry S. Williams.—On the Fossil Faunas of the Upper Devonian—the Genesee Section, N. Y. Bull. 41, 1887.

Henry S. Williams.—Correlation Papers—Devonian and Carboniferous. Bull. 80, 1891.

Charles S. Prosser.—The Devonian System of Eastern Pennsylvania and New York. Bull. 120, 1894.

D.—Special Papers in Serial Publications, Etc.

Ashburner, C. A.—Petroleum and Natural Gas in New York State. (Trans. Am. Inst. Min. Eng., Vol. XVI., pp. 1-54, 1888.)

Ashburner, C. A.—The Geology of Buffalo, as related to Natural Gas Explorations along the Niagara River. (Trans. Am. Inst. Min. Eng., 1889, pp. 1–9.)

Beecher, C. E.—On the Development of the Shell in the Genus Tornoceras. Hyatt. (From Hamilton strata of Wende, Erie County, N. Y.) (Am. Journ. Sci., 3d Ser., Vol. XL., pp. 71-75, Pl. I., 1890.)

Beecher, C. E.—North American Species of Strophalosia. (Amer. Journ. Science, Vol. XL., pp. 240–246, Pl. IX., 1890.)

Bishop, I. P.—Salt Wells of Western New York. (5th Ann. Rep't State Geologist, pp. 12-47.)

Bishop, I. P.—The Structural and Economic Geology of Erie County, N. Y. (15th Ann. Rep't State Geologist, pp. 305-392, Pls. I.–XVI., 3 maps.)

Clarke, J. M.—A Brief Outline of the Geological Succession in Ontario County, N. Y. (Ann. Rep't State Geol. for 1884, pp. 2–22, map.)

Clarke, J. M.—Devonian Spores. (Amer. Journ. Science, Vol. XXX., pp. 284–290, 1885.)

Clarke, J. M.—Annelid Teeth, from the lower part of the Hamilton Group and from the Naples Shales of Ontario County, N. Y. (6th Ann. Rep't State Geol., pp. 30-32, Pl. I., 1887.)

Clarke, J. M.—The Fauna with Goniatites intumescens, Beyrich. (Amer. Geol., Vol. VIII., pp. 86-105, 1891.)

Clarke, J. M.—Die Fauna mit Goniatites intumescens im Westlichen New York. (Neues Jahrb. für Min., Bnd. I., pp. 161-186.)

Clarke, J. M.—Discovery of Clymenia in the Fauna of the Intumescens Zone (Naples beds) of Western New York, and its Geological Significance (Amer. Journ. Science, Vol. XLIII., pp. 57-64, 1892.)

Clarke, J. M.—American Species of Autodetus and some Paramorphic Shells, from the Devonian. (Amer. Geol., Vol. XIII., pp. 327-335, 1894.)

Clarke, J. M.—The Succession of the Fossil Faunas in the Section of the Livonia Salt Shaft. (13th Ann. Rep't, N. Y. State Geol., p. 131, 1894.)

Clarke, J. M.—New or Rare Species of Fossils, from the Horizon of the Livonia Salt Shaft. (13th Ann. Rep't, N. Y. State Geol., p. 159, 1894.)

Clarke, J. M.—The Stratigraphic and Faunal Relations of the Oneonta Sandstones and Shales, the Ithaca and Portage Groups in Central New York. (15th Ann. Rep't, N. Y. State Geol., 1895, 1897, pp. 27–82.)

Clarke, J. M.—The Naples Fauna (Fauna with *Manticoceras intumescens*) in Western New York. (16th Ann. Rep't, N. Y. State Geologist, 1898.)

Clarke, J. M.—(See Hall and Clarke).

Claypole, E. W.—On the Vertical Range of Certain Fossil Species in Pennsylvania and New York. (Amer. Naturalist, Vol. XIX., pp. 644-654.)

Claypole, E. W.—Buffalo and Chicago; or, "What might have been." (Amer. Naturalist, Vol. XX., pp. 856–862.)

Claypole, E. W.—Same. (Proc. Amer. Ass. Adv. Sci., Vol. XXXV., p. 224, 1887.)

Claypole, E. W.—The Ancestry of the Upper Devonian Placoderms of Ohio. (Am. Geol., Vol. XVII., pp. 349-360, 1896.)

Coleman, Arthur P.—Lake Iroquois and its Predecessors at Toronto. (Bull. Geol. Soc. Am., Vol. X., pp. 165–176.)

Crosby, W. O.—The Origin of Parallel and Intersecting Joints. (Am. Geol., Vol. XII., pp. 368–375. Abstract Tech. Quart., Vol. VI., pp. 230–236.)

Dawson, J. W.—Recent Discoveries in the Erian (Devonian) Flora of the United States. (Amer. Journ. Science, Vol. XXIV., pp. 338-345, 1882.)

Dawson, J. W.—On Rhizocarps in the Palæozoic Period. (Proc. Amer. Ass. Adv. Sci., Vol. XXXII., pp. 260–264, 1884.)

Dawson, J. W. and Penhallow, D. P.—Notes on Specimens of Fossil Wood from the Erian (Devonian) of New York and Kentucky. (Canad. Record of Science, Vol. IV., Jan., 1891, pp. 242-247, Pl. I.)

Fairchild, H. L.—Glacial Waters in the Finger Lakes Region of New York. (Bull. Geol. Soc. Am., Vol. X., pp. 27-68, Pls. III.-IX.; also other papers on Glacial Geology of Western New York, in same bulletin.)

Gilbert, G. K.—Glacial Sculpture in Western New York. (Bull. Geol. Soc. Am., Vol. X., pp. 121–130.)

Gilbert, G. K.—Dislocation at Thirty Mile Point, New York. (Bull. Geol. Soc. Am., Vol. X., pp. 131–134, Pl. XII.)

Gilbert, G. K.—Ripple Marks and Cross-bedding. (Bull. Geol. Soc. Am., Vol. X., pp. 135–140, Pl. XIII.)

Girty, G. H.—Description of a Fauna found in the Devonian Black Shale of Eastern Kentucky. (Am. Journ. Sci., 4th ser., Vol. VI., pp. 384–395, 1898.)

Grabau, A. W.—The Faunas of the Hamilton Group of Eighteen Mile Creek and Vicinity, in Western New York. (16th Ann. Rep't N. Y. State Geol. for 1896, 1898, pp. 279–339, Pls. I.–V.)

Grabau, A. W.—Moniloporidæ, a new Family of Palæozoic Corals. (Proc. Bost. Soc. Nat. Hist., Vol. XXVIII., pp. 409–424, Pls. I.–IV., 1899.)

Hall, James.—Bryozoa (Fenestellidæ) of the Hamilton Group. (36th Ann. Rep't N. Y. State Mus. Nat. Hist., pp. 57–72.)

Hall, James.—Discussion upon the Manner of Growth, Variation of Form and Characters of the Genus Fenestella, and Its Relations to Hemitrypa, Polypora, Retepora, Cryptopora, etc. (Ann. Rep't State Geol., 1882, pp. 5–16.)

Hall, James.—Descriptions of the Bryozoans of the Hamilton Group. (Ann. Rep't State Geol. for 1883, pp. 5–61.)

Hall, James.—On the Mode of Growth and Relations of the Fenestellidæ. (Ann. Rep't State Geol., 1884, pp. 35–45, Pls. I., II.)

Hall, James.—Note on the Intimate Relations of the Chemung Group and Waverly Sandstone, in Northwestern Pennsylvania and Southwestern New York. (Proc. Amer. Ass. Adv. Sci., Vol. XXXIII., pp. 416–419.)

Hall, James.—Descriptions of Fenestellidæ of the Hamilton Group of New York. (6th Ann. Rep't State Geol., pp. 41–70, Pls. I.–VII., 1887.)

Hall, James.—Description of New Species of Fenestellidæ of the Lower Helderberg Group, with Explanations of Plates Illustrating Species of the Hamilton Group, described in the Report of the State Geologist for 1886. (Ann. Rep't State Geol., 1887, pp. 391, 392 [41st Mus. Rep't], Pls. VII.–XV.)

Hall, James, and Clarke, J. M.—Handbook of the Brachiopoda, Pt. I. (11th Ann. Rep't N. Y. State Geol. for 1891, pp. 133-300, Pls. I.–XXII., 1892.)

Hall, James, and Clarke, J. M.—Handbook of the Brachiopoda, Pt. II. (13th Ann. Rep't N. Y. State Geol. for 1893, pp. 749–943, Pls. XXIII.–LIV., 1894.)

Harris, G. D.—Notes on the Geology of Southwestern New York. (Amer. Geol., Vol. VII., pp. 164–178, Pl. IV., 1891.)

Hinde, G. J.—On Conodonts from the Chazy and Cincinnati Groups of the Cambro-Silurian, and from the Hamilton and Genesee Shale Divisions of the Devonian, in Canada and the United States. (Quart. Journ. Geol. Soc., London, Vol. XXXV., pp. 351–369, Pls. XV.–XVII., 1879.)

Johnson, Laurence.—The Parallel Drift Hills of Western New York. (Annals N. Y. Acad. Sci., Vol. II., pp. 249–266, Pl. XVIII.)

Johnson, Laurence.—Same. (Trans. N. Y. Acad. Sci., Vol. I., pp. 77–80.)

Jones, T. Rupert.—On some Devonian and Silurian Ostracoda from North America, France, and the Bosporus. (Quart. Journ. Geol. Soc., London, Vol. XLVI., pp. 534–556, Pls. XX., XXI., 1890.)

Jones, T. Rupert.—On some Palæozoic Ostracoda from North America, Wales, and Ireland. (Quart. Journ. Geol. Soc., London, Vol. XLVI., pp. 1–31, Pls. I.–IV., 1890.)

Kindle, Edward M.—The Relation of the Fauna of the Ithaca Group to the Faunas of the Portage and Chemung. (Bull. of Am. Pal., No. VI.)

Kindle, Edward M.—The Devonian and Lower Carboniferous Faunas of Southern Indiana and Central Kentucky. (Bull. Am. Pal., No. XII., 1899.)

Leverett, Frank.—On the Correlation of New York Moraines with Raised Beaches of Lake Erie. (Amer. Journ. Sci., Vol. L., pp. 1–20, 1895.)

Lewis, H. C.—Report on the Terminal Moraine in Pennsylvania and Western New York. (Report Z, 2d Geol. Surv. Penn., pp. 1–300.)

Luther, D. D.—Report on the Geology of the Livonia Salt Shaft. (13th Ann. Rep't N. Y. State Geol., 1893, pp. 21–130, 1894.)

Luther, D. D.—The Stratigraphic Position of the Portage Sandstones in the Naples Valley and the Adjoining Region. (15th Ann. Rep't N. Y. State Geol. for 1895, 1897, pp. 223–236.)

Pohlmann, Julius.—The Life History of Niagara. (Transact. Am. Inst. Min. Eng., Buffalo meeting, pp. 6–17.)

Prosser, C. S.—The Upper Hamilton of Chenango and Otsego counties, N.Y. (Proc. Amer. Ass. Adv. Sci., Vol. XXXVI., p. 210, 1888.)

Prosser, C. S.—The Thickness of the Devonian and Silurian Rocks in Western Central New York. (Amer. Geologist, Vol. VI., pp. 199–211, 1890.)

Prosser, C. S.—Thickness of Devonian and Silurian Rocks of Western New York. (Proc. Rochester Acad. Sci., Vol. II., pp. 49–104, 1892.)

Prosser, C. S.—The Thickness of the Devonian and Silurian Rocks of Central New York. (Bull. Geol. Soc. Amer., Vol. IV., pp. 91-118, 1893.)

Prosser, C. S.—The Devonian System of Eastern Pennsylvania. (Am. Journ. Sci., 3d Ser., Vol. XLIV., pp. 210–221, 1893.)

Prosser, C. S.—The Upper Hamilton and Portage Stages of Central and Eastern New York. (Am. Journ. Sci., 3d Ser., Vol. XLVI., pp. 217–230, 1893.)

Prosser, C. S.—The Classification and Distribution of the Hamilton and Chemung Series of Central and Eastern New York. Part I. (15th Ann. Rep't N. Y. State Geol. for 1895, 1897, pp. 83–222, Pls. I.–XIII.)

Randall, F. A.—Report on the Geology of Cattaraugus and Chautauqua counties. (13th Ann. Rep't N. Y. State Geol., 1893, pp. 517–528, 1894.)

Ries, Heinrich.—Physical Tests of the Devonian Shales of New York State to Determine Their Value for the Manufacture of Clay Products. (15th Ann. Rep't N. Y. State Geol. for 1895, 1897, pp. 673–698.)

Ringueberg, E. N. S.—A New Dinicthys from the Portage Group of Western New York. (Amer. Journ. Sci., Vol. XXVII., pp. 476–479, 1884.)

Simpson, G. B.—Discussion of the Genera of Fenestellidæ. (13th Ann. Rep't N. Y. State Geol., 1893, pp. 685–727, 1894.)

Simpson, G. B.—A Handbook of the Genera of North American Palæozoic Bryozoa. (14th Ann. Rep't N. Y. State Geol., 1894, pp. 403–608, Pls. A–E, I.–XXV.)

Spencer, J. W.—Discovery of the Pre-glacial Outlet of the Basin of Lake Erie into that of Lake Ontario, with Notes on the Origin of our Lower Great Lakes. (Proc. Amer. Philos. Soc., Vol. XIX., pp. 300–337, 1882.)

Spencer, J. W.—Notes on the Origin of the Great Lakes of North America. (Proc. A. A. A. S., Vol. XXXVII., pp. 197, 198, 1889.)

Spencer, J. W.—High Level Shores in the Region of the Great Lakes and Their Deformation. (Amer. Journ. Sci., Vol. XLI., pp. 201-212, 1891.)

Spencer, J. W.—Origin of the Basins of the Great Lakes of America. (Amer. Geol., Vol. VII., pp. 86–97.)

Spencer, J. W.—Deformation of the Lundy Beach, and Birth of Lake Erie. (Amer. Journ. Sci., 3d Ser., Vol. XLVII., pp. 207–212, 1894.)

Ulrich, E. O.—New and Little Known American Palæozoic Ostracoda. (Journ. Cinn. Soc. Nat. Hist., Vol. XIII., pp. 104–137, 173–211, Pls. VII.–XVIII.)

Whiteaves, J. F.—On Some Additional or Imperfectly Understood Fossils from the Hamilton Formation of Ontario, with a Revised List of the Species Therefrom. (Cont. Can. Pal., Vol. I., Pt. V., 1898.)

Williams, H. S.—The Recurrence of Faunas in the Devonian Rocks of New York. (Proc. Amer. Ass. Adv. Sci., Vol. XXX., pp. 186–190, 1882.)

Williams, H. S.—The Undulations of the Rock Masses Across Central New York State. (Proc. Amer. Ass. Adv. Sci., Vol. XXXI., p. 412.)

Williams, H. S.—On the Classification of the Upper Devonian. (Proc. Amer. Ass. Adv. Sci., Vol. XXXIV., pp. 222–234, 1886.)

Williams, H. S.—On the Different Types of the Devonian of North America. (Proc. Amer. Ass. Adv. Sci., Vol. XXXVI., p. 207, 1888.)

Williams, H. S.—Report of the Sub-committee on the Upper Palæozoic (Devonic). (Amer. Geol., Vol. II., pp. 225–248, 1888.)

Williams, H. S.—Different Types of the Devonian System in North America. (Amer. Journ. Sci., Vol. XXXV., pp. 51–60, 1888.)

Williams, H. S.—On the Relation of the Devonian Fauna of Iowa. (Amer. Geol., Vol. III., pp. 230–233, 1889.)

Williams, H. S.—The Cuboides Zone and its Fauna: a Discussion of Methods of Correlation. (Bull. Geol. Soc. Amer., Vol. I., pp. 481-501, Pls. XI.–XIII., 1890.)

Williams, H. S.—Palæontological Researches, Genesee Slate. (Science, Vol. I., pp. 190, 191, 1880.)

Williams, H. S.—Comparative Palæontology of the Devonian Formation. (Science, Vol. II., pp. 836, 837, 1883.)

Williams, H. S.—On a Remarkable Fauna at the Base of the Chemung Group in New York. (Amer. Journ. Sci., 3d Ser., Vol. XXV., pp. 97–104, 1883.)

Williams, H. S.—A Revision of the Cayuga Lake (New York) Section of the Devonian. (Amer. Journ. Sci., 3d Ser., Vol. XXXII., p. 321, 1886. Abstract.)

Williams, H. S.—The Making of the Geological Time Scale. (Journ. of Geol., Vol. I., pp. 180–197.)

Williams, H. S.—The Elements of the Geological Time Scale. (Journ. of Geol., Vol. I., pp. 283–295.)

Williams, H. S.—Dual Nomenclature in Geological Classification. (Journ. of Geol., Vol. II., pp. 145–160, 1894.)

Williams, H. S.—Southern Devonian Formations. (Amer. Journ. Sci., 4th Ser., Vol. III., pp. 393–403.)

Williams, H. U.—Notes on the Fossil Fishes of the Genesee and Portage Black Shales. (Bull. Buffalo Soc. Nat. Sci., Vol. V., No. I, pp. 81–84.)

Williams, Samuel G.—The Tully Limestone; Its Distribution and Its Known Fossils. (6th Ann. Rep't N. Y. State Geol., 1886, pp. 13–29, map, 1887.)

Williams, Samuel G.—The Tully Limestone; Its Distribution, Its Irregularities, Its Character, and Its Life. (Proc. A. A. A. S., Vol. XXXV., pp. 213, 214, 1887.)

GENERAL INDEX.

INDEX TO SPECIES.

Note.— Reference to page where species is described is given in heavy numbers.